Stop
Where the Parking Lot's Full

A Collection of *Sandlapper's*
Favorite Restaurants

Enjoy, Explore,
and always
get dessert!

Aida

Sally & Jonas,
Thanks for being such
great friends. Always
try the pickled pigs fut
at Gasthaus Zur Elli.

D1531085

Stop
Where the Parking Lot's Full

A Collection of *Sandlapper's*
Favorite Restaurants

Library of Congress: 2008907566
ISBN: 978-0-9666288-1-4

Sandlapper is a registered trademark of
Sandlapper Society, Inc.
Manufactured in the United States of America
First Printing, October 2008 - 3,000 copies

The proceeds from the sale of this book will be used by Sandlapper Society, Inc. to further its mission of promoting the positive aspects of South Carolina.

Stop
Where the Parking Lot's Full

A Collection of *Sandlapper's*
Favorite Restaurants

Aïda Rogers • Tim Driggers

Photography by Becky Hyatt Rickenbaker

Sandlapper
Society, Inc.

Post Office Box 1108 • Lexington, SC 29071 • (803)359-9954 • www.sandlapper.org

Note to Readers

The authors and publisher of "Stop Where the Parking Lot's Full" have made every effort to ensure the accuracy of the information contained in this book. All content is based on information available at time of publication and is subject to change. Many of these reports were condensed for space or edited to reflect changes discovered while updating information, so they won't read exactly as they did when they appeared in *Sandlapper Magazine*. It's a good idea to always call ahead and confirm hours, address, prices, forms of payment, and menu when making restaurant plans. Also remember that restaurants open and close. It took a long time to research, write, and publish this book, so some restaurants may no longer be in business. Keep in mind that restaurant features, ownership and management, policies, and cuisine may change over time.

Prices

Prices are determined by the cost of one entrée,
not including tax, tip or drinks.

Inexpensive • $10 and less
Moderate • $10 - $20
Expensive • $20 - $35
Very Expensive • $35 and more

Dedicated to Bob Wilkins,
founder of *Sandlapper Magazine*,
who came up with the name
"Stop Where the Parking Lot's Full,"

and to Rose Wilkins,
who always kept him so well fed at home.

For the countless hours and miles given to "Stop Where the Parking Lot's Full" since 1989,
Sandlapper Society is deeply grateful to columnists Tim Driggers and Aïda Rogers.

For Starters ...

An immediate laugh is a good sign. That's what happened in 1989, when Bob Wilkins named the restaurant column I was ordered to write for *Sandlapper Magazine*. "Maybe we'll call it 'Stop Where the Parking Lot's Full,' " he said, and our tiny staff knew instantly we had a great name for a fledgling column. What we didn't know was how popular it would become.

Soon recommendations were coming from everywhere. Everyone, it seemed, had a favorite restaurant to suggest. And so we were off, learning first-hand that South Carolina is rich in food. Besides homey meat-and-threes, old-style barbecue huts and nostalgic drive-ins, we've got exquisite gourmet palaces and surprising ethnic choices. We were never short of places to write about for our readers.

"Stop Where the Parking Lot's Full" brought us a bit of international acclaim. We've been covered in newspapers and magazines, and got our 15 minutes when Anthony Bourdain consulted us for his *No Reservations* television show. For a couple of hours, we gorged on fried chicken and red rice, Coca-Cola cake and banana pudding, for his Travel Channel program. We figured we'd arrived, having made the international air waves.

But then I realized, we hadn't arrived. We've been here all along. And so have the people who own these special restaurants. They're in their kitchens before dawn and after midnight, making sure their guests are happy. They're scouring their local markets for the freshest fish and prettiest produce. They're the reason South Carolina has such a fine reputation for food.

This book, then, is a tribute to them—those hardworking artists and entrepreneurs who've invited us into their lives for a taste of their frustrations and worries, victories and daily specials. We think they're terrific.

So get in your car and check them out. Let us know if you find something we haven't. You want flavor? We got flavor.

- Aïda Rogers, August 2008

Contents

Historic Charleston

Lowcountry & Resort Islands

Upcountry

Anderson, Cherokee, Greenville, Pickens, Oconee & Spartanburg Counties

Anita's Mexican Restaurant, Simpsonville
Greenville County

Anita's Mexican Restaurant, 101 Alice Avenue, Simpsonville; (864) 963-3855. Open Tuesday-Friday for lunch from 11 a.m.-2 p.m. and for dinner Tuesday-Saturday, 5 p.m.-10 p.m. Closed on Sunday and Monday. No reservations. Credit card and checks accepted. No smoking. Inexpensive to moderate.

Sangria, Salsa and a Big Happy Family

I first heard about Anita's Mexican Restaurant in 1990 while doing a story on a now-closed restaurant in Laurens. But Anita Navarro Baldwin is still in high salsa in Simpsonville. In fact, her bright, bustling restaurant is doing better than ever.

Anita's is a family restaurant in every way. Husband John is the jolly host, often wearing funny hats customers have been bringing him since 1985. That's when he and his Mexican bride opened their restaurant to send their three boys to college. Today, those boys are still here—by choice. Oldest son Kenny has inherited his mother and grandmother's love for cooking. He experiments in the kitchen and talks about the diversity of Hispanic food. He makes it plain that the family didn't know what they were doing when they bought an old home and fixed it up for business, that they didn't follow any rules, that all they had was their mother's ability to whip up great salsa, enchiladas, and guacamole. But 23 years later, with their sons out of college, Anita's has taken off. Its success is based on interesting, good Mexican food, a friendly atmosphere, and reasonable prices. Some people come every week—for the same table, on the same night.

"It's a labor of love," Kenny says. "A lot of these folks have known me since I was 17 years old."

Anita's sangria (with orange, lemon, and apple juices) is famous. Kenny brought me a glass and the Jalapeno bean dip for our trio to try. Fresh cilantro is the key here, along with cheese sauce. Two baskets of chips and salsa are complimentary. They go fast, too: Ten gallons of salsa are made each day, and chips are fried in the kitchen. Other Antojitos (appetizers) are nachos, homemade guacamole, stuffed jalapenos, and quesadillas filled with shrimp, cheese, mushrooms, chicken, or sirloin tips.

"Authentic" has been the most popular word for Anita's in the dozen years I've been hearing about it. Tamarindo Chicken proves the point. Served with rice, black beans, and sour cream, this dinner is mainstayed by a chicken breast sautéed with onions in a tamarindo sauce and topped with toasted sesame seeds and fresh cilantro. The most popular item is the Pollo or Carne Fundido, a tortilla pocket stuffed with shredded sirloin tips or chicken breast, with cheese sauce, rice, beans, guacamole, or sour cream. Other "Especialidades de Anita" include Fajitas with grilled gulf shrimp, flank steak, or chicken and the Pescado or Camarones Morelia—a half-pound of grilled cod fillet or gulf shrimp on Spanish rice and vegetables.

Chile rellenos, chimichangas, chalupas, enchiladas, burritos, and tacos are available, along with several vegetarian entrees and a children's menu. Kevin Baldwin, the second son and co-manager, points out that Anita's food is healthfully prepared.

"My mom is real health-conscious about all the food we serve," he says. "The way most people cook Hispanic food is with lard and they deep-fry the pork for Carnitas. But we cook ours in a Dutch oven. It has the same taste, but it's not as greasy. Ours is just as good."

Desserts ("Postres") are as intriguing as the entrees. We took Kenny's advice and ordered the Mexican Coffee. Served hot in a mug, this cinnamon-chocolate drink drew sounds of happy amazement. We also plowed into the rice pudding, another cinnamon finale, and the Spanish flan.

The Postres menu is bigger than you'll find in most Mexican restaurants: Nine items include Choco Tacos, the Bunuelo (pastry with honey and cinnamon and sugar) and Xangos (cheesecake wrapped in pastry tortilla, fried with cinnamon and sugar).

With three sons and long-time employees running the restaurant, Anita and John, a Florence County native, have been able to semi-retire. No longer does Anita get up at 6 and work past midnight. But she still frequents her second home, where many customers have become her best friends. She admits she gave up a lot when she started her business, but says the rewards made the sacrifices worthwhile.

"I have very good relationships with my people that help me here and it's just like a big family. I would say we have the best customers in the whole world. We really do."

- Aïda Rogers

Anita's Mexican Restaurant has the distinction of being the oldest restaurant in Simpsonville and the third-oldest Mexican restaurant in Greenville, Spartanburg, and Anderson counties. "We're South Carolina's Mexican meat-and-three restaurant," Kenny Baldwin said. "Everything we cook is made from scratch." He and brother Kevin took over the day-to-day operation of their mother and father's restaurant in 2004. When asked their titles at Anita's, Kevin said, "I guess we're the managers, but we're really more like indentured servants." Pollo Fundido continues to be their signature dish. "It accounts for about 70 percent of our total sales," Kenny said. "I personally think our Carnitas are the best item on the menu. It's mesquite barbecue pork with cilantro, onion, and a splash of lime juice." Count on good service at Anita's: three of the waitresses have been with the Baldwin family for 22 years.

- *Tim Driggers*

Aunt Sue's Country Corner, Pickens
Pickens County

Aunt Sue's Country Corner, 2 miles east of Table Rock State Park on Scenic SC Highway 11, Pickens County; (864) 878-4366. Open Tuesday-Thursday, 11 a.m.-7 p.m. and Friday-Sunday, 7:30 a.m.-8:30 p.m. Breakfast is served Friday-Sunday, 7-10:30 a.m. Operating hours are seasonal. Reservations requested for groups of 10 or more. Credit cards and checks accepted. No smoking. www.auntsues.com. Lunch and breakfast: inexpensive. Dinner: inexpensive to moderate.

Oh Fudge!

Over the years, I've enjoyed meandering the 115 miles of Scenic Highway 11 in the Cherokee foothills of South Carolina. Whether camping on the banks of the Chattooga at Burrels Ford, climbing the escarpment at Whitewater Falls, exploring Stumphouse Tunnel, or hiking the trails at Lake Jocassee, I've always been captivated by the history of the Up Country and its natural beauty. At times during these excursions, when hunger overcame my wanderlust, I would scoot my car back onto the main road and head to Aunt Sue's Country Corner.

Depending on which way you're heading on Highway 11, if you pass Pumpkintown, you've either just missed Aunt Sue's or are about to run right into the parking lot. It's part of a village of shops selling candles, stuffed animals, handmade woodcrafts, and religious items to "flatlanders" and locals. Aunt Sue's, named after the wife of the original owner, opened in 1984 beneath the shadow of Table Rock.

You're welcomed by an organist on the restaurant porch. Don't expect the latest hits; Phyllis is strictly into old standards, although she might take a request. Open the door and you'll see a well-stocked candy counter to the right, the ice cream and fudge counter directly ahead, and an easy chair and checkerboard on the left. The dining room is spacious with plenty of windows, allowing Mother Nature to sit at your table. An adjacent deck is perfect for warm weather dining.

Easley resident Jimmy Bikas bought the restaurant in 2001. "I had eaten at Aunt Sue's and liked the family atmosphere," he said. "I thought, 'Hey, I can do something with this place.'"

And do something he did. Jimmy started by enlarging the kitchen, allowing full dinner meals in addition to the staple sandwiches.

The changes are working. Aunt Sue's Country Corner was one of 10 South Carolina destinations named to Travelocity's "Local Secrets, Big Finds 2005" listing.

High cotton indeed—but let's talk about the food. Heather and Reggie Corley of Lexington have been eating at Aunt Sue's since their days at Furman University. "We absolutely love it," Reggie said. "They have a wonderful peppered breast of turkey sandwich with ranch dressing. It's served with potato salad, and we always have a big bowl of ice cream topped with mountain apples."

Reggie and Heather aren't quite finished. They grab some fudge on the way out; during the holidays, seasonal peppermint fudge is a favorite. Heather has one other recommendation. "Get a table where you can see the top of Table Rock."

Like the Corleys, I couldn't make the door at Aunt Sue's without a takeout of four tons of fudge. Jimmy Bikas calls Marsha Barkus his chief of staff. She's also in charge of the fudge department. Besides the usual flavors, Marsha offers exotic pineapple upside-down fudge and peanut butter-and-jelly fudge. "We make it twice a week, 120 pounds at a time," she said. "It's a big seller; we ship it all over the country."

The recipe is something Marsha will never tell. Not a secret is the taste. "It's just good," she said. I ordered Marsha's favorite, maple fudge, and Jimmy's choice, vanilla. The maple fudge did not survive the drive home; the vanilla fudge was decimated at the office. "I have a lot of fun with our customers," Marsha said. "I love people; I guess when I quit liking them, I'll just go home."

- Tim Driggers

Since we last visited Aunt Sue's Country Corner, Phyllis the organist had retired and Joe the banjo picker added to pick and grin on the porch. The dinner menu is a big hit, with shrimp and grits, hamburger steak, and rack of ribs being the favorites.

- T. D.

The Beacon Drive-In, Spartanburg
Spartanburg County

Beacon Drive-In, 255 John B. White Sr. Boulevard, Spartanburg; (864) 585-9387. Open (summer hours) Monday-Saturday 6:30 a.m.-10 p.m. No reservations, first-come first-serve to "talk" and "walk." American Express accepted with ATM machine available, checks accepted with identification. Smoking in one room. www.beacondrivein.com. Inexpensive.

We Can't Leave This One Out

Big, loud, cheap and good. That's The Beacon in Spartanburg, all right. Nothing subtle about it. The food is basic. The setting is plain. And if you leave with an empty stomach and a grimace about grease, then you can't appreciate The Beacon and the blue collar way.

"I want to serve the masses and the masses eat just what I sell," declares owner John White, who built the restaurant in 1946. White says he never dreamed his unpretentious drive-in would become famous worldwide. But it did, drawing Charles Kuralt and John Connally, Elizabeth Dole and George Will. Former Gov. Donald Russell hired The Beacon to cater his inaugural luncheon in 1963. Jimmy Carter feasted on Beacon barbecue in 1980; Strom Thurmond ate here for years.

While politicians and other luminaries are well and good, it's everybody else White most appreciates. "My biggest celebrity is the customer who comes here every day and helps me pay the light bill, the water bill and all that. The average person is my biggest celebrity."

At The Beacon, you see all kinds. Young, old, black, white. Throngs of men, solitary workers, elderly couples, Mormons in ties. School children come by the bus load; sometimes 10 buses pull up at one time. There are customers who come two or three times a day and a businessmen's group that meets twice a month for Bible teaching and breakfast. So popular is The Beacon that security guards direct traffic inside at lunch and supper.

No doubt people come for the food, which is as All-American as the free apple pies White gives customers who spend more than $20. But they also come for the atmosphere. As employee Troy Edwards puts it, "it's wild."

"It's an experience," says Kerry Norman, who comes every Friday with coworkers. Norman has learned how to maneuver in the organized bedlam that marks the lunch hour. But for the timid or uninitiated, The Beacon can be harrowing. The trick is to know what you want before you order, and stay alert until you've paid John White at the end of the line.

"He who hesitates is lost," says White. "It's just like an auction. Open your mouth and you've bought something."

At the front of the line is J.C. Stroble, who is almost as famous as White. He or Charles Wiggleton, Jr. will take your order. Actually, they command it.

"Talk!" they boom in foggy baritones. That's your cue to order. "Walk!" is the next command, which means you need to get a tray and move in line beside the long stainless steel counter until you reach the cash register. In the meantime you'll see Stroble or Wiggleton lift their heads and open their throats, bellowing orders to the cooks beyond. You can watch burgers sizzling and smell the onion rings, but mainly your hearing will be affected. At The Beacon, everybody yells.

Think of it as a little music with your meal.

Now in its third building, The Beacon is located on a three-acre lot on Reidville Road. It has five large dining rooms, glassed–in sun rooms, a deck and a helicopter pad across the street for those flying overhead who want to drop down for a quick bite. The Beacon seats 400 and is believed to be the biggest drive-in in South Carolina.

White says his success is based on quality, quantity, and the golden rule. "We treat people like they're supposed to be treated. People spend $20,000 to go to college to learn how to do business. All they got to do is open the door, treat people right, and give 'em a quality product and service. It's so simple."

The Beacon stands for old-fashioned things. God. Country. A decent meal at a fair price. Tales of White's kindness are legion.

"He'll roll up a hundred-dollar bill and put it in the church plate," says one admiring customer. "When my child had a wisdom tooth pulled, he came through the line and gave him a milkshake," says Janice Calvert, a teacher at D.R. Middle School in Duncan.

White has paid rent for people who couldn't and donated food to workers picking up litter. He's sent hot chocolate to band students selling fruit in cold weather and ice cream in dry ice to someone in a hospital in Columbia. He took Stroble, his chief order taker, to New York and St. Louis to find treatment for his glaucoma. "He's just such a good person," Calvert says.

But naturally, White won't brag. Only his family merits that. His family and Spartanburg where, aside from a Navy stint in WW2, he's lived since he was 6. "We love Spartanburg. It's been so good to me."

That's obvious by the décor. Signs about Spartanburg County high school athletic and band victories cover the walls. A photo of White's granddaughter, a tennis champion, hangs from the ceiling. New menus are printed every six weeks, the better to showcase a different person, business or school in Spartanburg on the cover.

Beacon recipes are all White's, who started his restaurant career as an 11-year-old carhop. Besides the famous burgers, onion rings, and iced tea, the restaurant serves seafood, chicken, hash sandwiches, and ice cream. More unusual items include banana sandwiches and chicken gizzards. Beef comes from New Zealand and Australia; onions by tractor-trailer. The Beacon is Tetley Tea's number one user, and more than a ton of meat is served daily. Once it was calculated that if the bread bought by The Beacon each week was placed end to end from its front door, it would reach downtown Charleston.

The restaurant got its name when White tried to put a giant light on top of the building to attract people. He scrapped that idea when he learned it would have to be marked on air charts.

Today, carhops work only at night, which means you can still get that old-time drive-in experience. Chances are you'll be served by an old-timer with plenty of experience – 84-year-old Ezell Jackson or 74-year-old James Thomas. They're all familiar with those old Beacon standbys: the banana split so big five people can't finish it, the unique iced tea available by the gallon, the onion rings piled high on the Chili-Cheese Aplenty.

Order that Chili-Cheese Aplenty next time you go. Stop and admire it before you plunder. In a way, it's a work of art. Spartanburg-style.

- Aïda Rogers

This story about the legendary Beacon Drive-In first appeared in Sandlapper *in 1996. We've visited several times since then, usually ordering the Chili Cheeseburger A-Plenty, onion rings, and a large Beacon iced tea. Now celebrating its 62nd year, The Beacon still presents an amazing scene. J. C. Stroble is still barking "talk to me" at the front of line. Taking orders for 54 years, he's as much an institution as the nationally known A-Plenty menu. If he's not there, Jerry Wiggleton, a veteran of 22 years, takes his place. On one late-night stop, we spotted Garrison Keillor of* A Prairie Home Companion *face-down in a plate of burgers and fries. That's typical of all Beacon diners, a tradition that's made it the second largest drive-in in America, serving more than a million customers a year.*

Founder John White retired in 1998, turning over The Beacon to brother-in-laws Sam Maw and Steve McManus. The new owners, along with General Manager Kenny Church, haven't changed too many things. The street outside is now John B. White Sr. Boulevard and in 1999 The Beacon Dairy Bar was added. Sam (a Wofford alum) and Steve (a Citadel grad) stage The Beacon Iced Tea Bowl during the week of the annual Terrier/Bulldog football clash with Beacon-sponsored commemorative events on the Wofford campus. Quick facts: The Beacon serves three tons of onions, three tons of potatoes, four tons of beef, chicken and seafood, and orders 3,000 pounds of sugar each week. It once was considerably more, but Paul McCravy, our Assistant Culinary Expert, eventually graduated from Wofford and now hardens his arteries in Columbia.

- Tim Driggers

Betty's Hungry House, Seneca
Oconee County

Betty's Hungry House, 400 South Fairplay Street, Seneca; (864) 882-7665. Open Monday-Saturday, 5 a.m. -2 p.m. Closed Sunday. No reservations. No credit cards; checks and cash only. Smoking allowed in back dining room. Inexpensive.

Just How Big *Are* Those Biscuits?

Throughout history, mankind has embarked on quests seeking the unknown, the lost, and the seemingly impossible. King Arthur charged the knights of Camelot with finding the Holy Grail, Magellan circled the globe to discover the Pacific, and Indiana Jones traipsed the globe pursuing the lost Ark of the Covenant. Thanks to Marcia Cook Purday of Leesville, I set out to find the ultimate treasure of the Golden Corner of South Carolina—big biscuits! Were the biscuits of Betty's Hungry House in Seneca merely legend or were they in fact real? Some said they were gigantic, others said they were merely huge. One ole timer from Walhalla said he was driving past Betty's Hungry House one morning and a big biscuit rolled out the front door, smashed into his Olds 88, and totaled the vehicle. Naw. No biscuit could be that big. Or could they? "Yes they are," Marcia said. "No way," I said. She was right.

Marcia first discovered Betty's Hungry House while traveling the state for BellSouth. "I had heard they had big biscuits and that fatback biscuits were their specialty," she said. "Being a southern girl, I had grown up eating fried fatback, so I just had to try these biscuits. They were massive; as big as the Hungry House itself." Well Marcia, maybe not quite that large, but the biscuits are a good 4 to 5 inches long and 3 inches wide. Besides being big, the biscuits meet another Purday requirement. "There is a rule in the South that if you're going to serve a biscuit, then it must be a real, live biscuit," she said. "I know the biscuits at Betty's Hungry House are real. The cooks have flour all over their faces."

Each day more than 500 biscuits are served to the 300 to 500 diners making Betty's Hungry House their breakfast and lunch destination. Located in a rustic wood building in a residential neighborhood near Seneca's business district, Betty's Hungry House has the comfort and feel of eating in your own kitchen. Leon Wheeler, an auto body technician at Auto Works Unlimited, eats breakfast and lunch here almost every day. "I like their runnin' chicken," he said. To the uninitiated, that's an over-easy egg with the yolk running all through the egg whites. For lunch he favors the macaroni and cheese and chicken. Leon likes the cooks to add extra milk to the macaroni and cheese. "I like to make it runnin' too."

Betty Outz first opened Betty's Hungry House in 1981 and over the years it has become a Seneca institution. Ownership passed down the family line to son Harold and on to niece Michelle Rankin in 1999.

To serve hundreds of diners and make all those biscuits is quite a job. Michelle rises at 3 a.m. and is at the restaurant an hour later. By 5 a.m., the crowds start arriving. "My aunt believed in giving people plenty of food at a reasonable price and making sure no one left hungry," Michelle said. "She made all of the biscuits by hand and now so do my dad, stepmother, and I."

What's the secret? "They are made the old-fashioned way, from scratch and rolled by hand," she explained, describing a method that includes butter chips and self-rising flour. Michelle has served as many as a thousand biscuits in a day and it's not unusual for local companies to place orders for a hundred or so. Ham and sausage are the most popular, with fatback close behind. Also available are city ham, bacon, bologna, steak, country ham, tenderloin, and chicken biscuits. You can add an egg (runnin' or not) for half a dollar. Plain, butter, and jelly biscuits are available too.

"Unbelievable," is how Mayor Dan Alexander describes them. "They just melt in your mouth." He makes it a regular stop and not just for breakfast. "I really like their hamburger steaks at lunch," he said. "There is plenty of it. I didn't get to be 275 pounds eating small portions." Oconee County Sheriff James Singleton eats breakfast here two or three times a week. "If you order the country ham, then you get a whole slab of ham, not just a small slice," he noted. He has his own special biscuit order. "I like them inside and out," he said. "That's where they take out the dough in the center and fill it with either ham or sausage."

There's more to Betty's Hungry House than biscuits and breakfast. "We try to run a friendly restaurant that serves home cooking the old-fashioned way," Michelle said. "Our goal is to serve a meal like you'd get at your mother's on Sunday."

- Tim Driggers

Michelle tells us she's tossing around the idea of building a new Betty's Hungry House adjacent to the present location. She promises she'll still be baking those big, big biscuits. That's sure to cause a collective sigh of relief throughout the Upstate because Betty's Hungry House is one of the best breakfast spots around.

- T. D.

Calhoun Corners, Clemson
Pickens County

Calhoun Corners, 103 Clemson Street, Clemson; (864) 654-7490. Open Monday-Saturday, 5-9:30 p.m. Closed on Sunday. Credit cards accepted. Reservations recommended. No smoking. www.tigergourmet. com. Moderate to expensive.

With an Eye to Preservation and Good Food ...

Christmas in Clemson means dinner at Calhoun Corners, where a 30-foot Christmas tree is hauled in from the mountains and the place is aglow with yuletide lights and spirit. You can really celebrate by ordering Beef Wellington with Bordelaise, an item you don't see too often. With its puff pastry made with goose pâté, spring onions and fresh mushrooms, the Beef Wellington is special occasion fare.

"We worked on it a long time before we dared put it on the menu," says George Corontzes, owner/chef. "We've got it down pat now; I sell about 10 or 12 a week."

Corontzes is equipped to run a restaurant. His grandparents owned the Capitol Café in Columbia, and he grew up working there with his brothers. When he came to Clemson in 1979, he worked at Calhoun Corners as a waiter. He was just about through with graduate school when he had a chance to buy it. It was a good decision.

"I love cooking; I just love the business," Corontzes says. And he loves Clemson, which he now considers home. Because he and his brothers Ted, Nick, and Zach also own Pixie & Bill's, Clemson's other fine dining restaurant, the Corontzeses have entrenched themselves here.

They couldn't have picked a more appropriate spot. Calhoun Corners is in old Calhoun, the railroad town renamed Clemson in 1943. Today the restaurant is in a distinctive 1893 building that once was a civic center, general store, and Presbyterian church. Located next to the railroad tracks, Calhoun Corners is immediately recognizable for its handmade brick. The combination of old brick, wood floors, fireplaces, and Christmas tree makes Calhoun Corners popular for the holidays. "It has a real Christmas feeling," Corontzes says.

The dinner menu offers prime rib, lobster, seafood, pasta, chicken, and fresh fish, along with cappuccino, latte and café au lait. Fresh desserts are prepared by a local baker. The owners have heeded their Greek heritage: Spanakopeta and Tiropeta enliven their menu. Not surprisingly, Calhoun Corners is busy during graduation. Many couples have gotten engaged here, and business meetings happen in the more private "Fireplace Room" upstairs.

Calhoun Corners respects its roots. Local artist Ginger Sebeck's watercolors depict upstate scenes: Lake Keowee, Campbell's Covered Bridge, Ashtabula. Cold weather sportsgear–snowshoes, skis, an ice pick–are on one wall. An engraving of John C. Calhoun is in the pub upstairs, near a moosehead.

What could be more suitable?

- Aïda Rogers

It's been the best of times and worst of times since we visited Calhoun Corners in the winter of 1995. In 1997, a fire ravaged the restaurant. The Corontzes family preserved as much of the original structure as feasible and reopened in December 1998. The dining area continues to feature hardwood floors, old brick, and fireplaces. The Beef Wellington Bordelaise remains a signature dish, and the menu is replete with prime rib and beef selections, fresh fish and seafood, as well as duck, lamb, chicken, pork, trout, and vegetarian entrees.

- Tim Driggers

The Clock Drive-In, Greenville
Greenville County

The Clock Drive-In, 1844 Wade Hampton Boulevard, Greenville; (864) 244-5122. Open Monday-Thursday, 9 a.m.-11 p.m.; Friday-Saturday, 9 a.m.-midnight; Sunday, 9 a.m.-10:30 p.m. No reservations. Cash and checks accepted. Smoking outside only. Inexpensive.

Everything Under the Drive-In Sun

The Clock Drive-In in Greenville is an upstate tradition where the past is time-warped into the present. You can envision Richie Cunningham and The Fonz driving in a souped-up dragster for a cheeseburger and fries, or Little Richard biting down on a chili dog and shouting "wop bop a loo bop a lop bam boom" in glee. To say a visit to The Clock Drive-In is fun is like saying Elvis could sing a little.

Dwight Eisenhower was serving his first term as president when The Clock Drive-In #3 opened in 1953. The post-war years were when America's love affair with the car began in earnest. It was a time of the drive-in movie theater and drive-in restaurant, and The Clock Drive-In established itself as the place where any self-respecting high-schooler wanted to be seen. Legend has it that The Clock Drive-In got its name from the song "Rock Around the Clock," written in 1952. "Back then, The Clock was strictly a drive-through," said John Banias, who owns the restaurant with cousin George Medeckas. "In those days, The Clock was a teenage hang-out. Each high school in Greenville had its own place to congregate, and The Clock became the home of Eastside and Wade Hampton High Schools."

Norma Manchester of Taylors remembers those days. "We'd park and sit around talking, waving, and smooching. If the owners saw us smooching out in front they'd run us off. We'd just drive around to the back and start smooching again." Norma Greene has been dining here since it opened. "Back in those days, we really didn't have a lot of places to go," she explained. "Before classes, we'd make plans to meet at The Clock after school." She and husband David loved the place so much that on their wedding day, they stopped at The Clock on their way to the church.

Mike and Cindy Chibbaro of Greenville eat here at least once a week with their three teenage sons. Mike attended Wade Hampton High School in the late '70s; Cindy finished at nearby Riverside High. "The Clock is a lot like it was in those days," Mike said. "They still have those boxes stacked in the window for take-out orders. The food and the people are pretty much the same." Mike still loves the jumbo cheeseburger and a Clock favorite, the half-and-half—a mix of onion rings and French fries.

"Our best sellers are the hotdogs and burgers," John noted. I tried the chili cheeseburger with onion rings. Both were mouth-watering, with none of the greasy taste often associated with fast food. Norma Manchester vouches for the hot dogs; in fact, she was making her second visit of the day to grab one. "The chili is extra fine, with no gristle," she said. The menu features about everything under the drive-in sun.

The Clock is like a valued family heirloom. It's as if some Wellesian time machine has traveled 50 years back and returned with the city's most cherished teenage memories. It's definitely one place where living in the past isn't such a bad idea at all.

- Tim Driggers

The Deli Korner, Spartanburg
Spartanburg County

The Deli Korner, 1445-A Fernwood-Glendale Road, Spartanburg; (864) 583-9518. Open Monday-Thursday, 10 a.m.-5:30 p.m.; Friday 10 a.m.-6 p.m.; Saturday 10 a.m.-4 p.m. Closed Sunday. Reservations unnecessary. Credit cards and checks accepted. No smoking. Inexpensive.

Eating German With Cousin Dan

One of my favorite stories about my editor-cousin Dan is that during his years at USC, he ate at the IHOP regularly for an ethnic dining experience. Always the explorer of music and food, Dan had been listening to a CD of German hunting songs the day he discovered The Deli Korner in Spartanburg. What karma.

"It's real plain," he told me over the phone, as if I care about fancy. Dan had just regaled me with talk of Bitburger beer, the sound of German chatter in the kitchen, and the European gourmet products available on shelves and in glass refrigerator cases. I had to go.

Two days later we were there, sitting at a table and looking at posters of Bern and the Matterhorn. Dan grew up in Lexington County, where Germans settled two centuries ago. To him, lunch at The Deli Korner has past-life undertones. "This is my kind of fare," he said over German potato salad, Landjaeger, and Mike's Special. "See that guy? He looks like he's from Lexington. So many people look familiar here. I wonder if that's one of those ancestral flashbacks you were talking about."

The clientele did have a WASPish look about them, and seemed very comfortable that meatloaf here doesn't have ketchup on it. German meatloaf is more like ham. You can try it on Gerd's Special, which comes fried with melted Cambozola cheese, or Mike's Special, an open-face sandwich with tomatoes, spring onions, and melted Swiss. Because Dan and I don't know the meaning of restraint, we ordered two entrees, two kinds of salad, two kinds of beer, and one dessert. That was the apple strudel, served thick and cold, full of cinnamon and filo. We asked our waitress, "Lisa as in

Mona Lisa," which dessert to try. "Catfish strudel," we were sure she said, although we realized later we got tangled up in her accent.

Open since 1988, The Deli Korner has "imports and delicatessen" written on its business card. New Yorker Bill Barnes, in Spartanburg studying at the Sherman College of Straight Chiropractic, labels it the best deli in town. "This is good and fresh and friendly," he said, enjoying Swedish ginger snaps with his friend Margaret Claypool, a Massachusetts native and student at the Southeastern School of Neuromuscular and Massage Therapy.

Bill and Margaret were planning to buy European chocolates for their friend Gretel. Too bad they couldn't take the iced tea: Light and lemony, it's a house specialty. Dan and I, with our Spaten and Dinkel Acker beer, noticed everyone drinking it so we ordered some, too.

I was curious about the difference in American and German chef salads. At The Deli Korner, similar ingredients are used: turkey, ham, lettuce, tomatoes, cheeses, and boiled eggs. The difference is the dressing, a creamy dill.

We filled up fast between that and the potato salad (creamy and a little sweet, with bits of ham and spring onions), Mike's Special and Landjaeger. Something like summer sausage, Landjaeger is two smoked meatsticks served with bread and mustard. Other items include Morf's Special (Black Forest ham, Raclette cheese), Smoked Bratwurst (with potato salad, bread, and mustard) and Swiss veal. Cheese and meat platters, smoked Scottish salmon, knackwurst and Krainer Wurst are on the menu.

For the less adventurous, there are sandwiches of various salamis, turkey, corned beef, and bologna—including tongue bologna.

It shouldn't surprise anyone that the Deli Korner would be operating in Spartanburg, because European companies have been here for decades. Owners Vreni Dreher and Rosmarie Schwendeler, Swiss nationals, have been here almost 40 years.

"It's like a big family here, a big international family," said David White, a lawyer and regular customer. "These people do a wonderful job." Maybe White can appreciate the work more than most; he's the youngest son of John White, founder of the famous Beacon Drive-In.

Serving only lunch, The Deli Korner has eight tables and a heavy take-out business. While you wait at the register, check out the cheeses and pâtés, cookies, and candies. I left with meringue cookies from Scotland and pâté from Atlanta. Dan was inspired in a different way. "I'm going home to read about Martin Luther."

- Aïda Rogers

Vreni Dreher and Rosmarie Schwendeler tell us The Deli Korner remains just as it was when Sandlapper *made a visit in 1999. 'They don't need to change anything,"said "Cousin Dan" Harmon, who eats at the Deli Korner at least once a month. Mike's Special and Gerd's Special are still "big" on the menu, Dan reports. "I get two sandwiches at a time when I'm coming off a fast," he says. Our advice, get two then start a fast.*

- *Tim Driggers*

Grits and Groceries, Belton
Anderson County

Grits and Groceries, 2440 Due West Highway, Saylors Crossroads, Belton (or as Heidi and Joe say, "that's Highway 185 for you city folk"); (864) 296-3316. Open Tuesday-Saturday, 6 a.m.-2 p.m. for breakfast and lunch only. Closed Sunday. Call for once-a-month evening dinner time. No reservations. No smoking. Credit cards accepted. wwwgritsandgroceries.com. Inexpensive.

"Toto, This Sure Isn't Waffle House!"

The rumors are true. I didn't think they could be, but I discovered the reality was even better than the reports reaching Lexington. Shane Bradley had raved and Bill Rogers was positively giddy. Shane has some credibility; he's been Teacher of the Year at Dixie High School and is a member of the Due West town council. Bill, that's another story. As executive director of the South Carolina Press Association, you'd assume he'd be a beacon of verisimilitude (look that one up in your Funk & Wagnalls). But can you honestly believe a man who really thinks the University of North Carolina is *the* Carolina?

I set out early on a Wednesday morning to see what Grits and Groceries was all about. Rode through Laurens, passed by Ware Shoals and Donalds, made my way through Honea Path, and then at the intersection of SC highways 284 and 185 near Belton—there it was. I was actually at Saylors Crossroads. Beautiful countryside, but that old white frame building couldn't be Grits and Groceries. No way.

"I thought we were going in to get a can of Vienna sausages and a coke," reports Bill, explaining that Butch Hughes, publisher of *The Anderson Independent*, introduced him to the place. A taste of Heidi and Joe Trull's chicken livers converted him. "They had paired chicken livers together with pepper jelly," he said. "I would never have put that combination together, but it was great. I've been looking for an excuse to go back."

Bill's reaction is typical. When I walked through the door, I felt transported back to when country groceries were the focal point of community life. On the shelves were assorted breads, signs, photos, even a pair of scales. The floor and ceiling were remnants from its 1901 beginnings. It had remained a grocery and post office until abandoned in the mid-1980s. Then Heidi and Joe Trull happened along in 2005.

The restaurant they created has become legendary. Who would have imagined upscale dining in a rustic country store in tiny Saylors Crossroads? That's part of the magic of Grits and Groceries and its in-house wizards.

Sumter-born Heidi graduated from culinary school at Johnson and Wales in Charleston and for the next five years apprenticed at restaurants in St. Louis, Nova Scotia, Japan and Greece. Meanwhile, in Winston-Salem, North Carolina, Joe Trull was honing his credentials at the family bread bakery. He found himself drawn to pastries and eventually to New Orleans' French Quarter, where he became executive pastry chef at Emeril Lagasse's Nola restaurant for the next 10 years.

By this time Heidi and Joe had been hitched and Heidi was also working at Nola. Soon after Heidi opened her own restaurant, Elizabeth's, in New Orleans' Bywater district. Elizabeth's quickly earned a reputation for excellence, with *New Yorker Magazine* labeling Heidi's cooking style as "eclectic soul food."

Then came Tom Trull, the couple's first child, and that's how the executive pastry chef for Emeril Lagasse and the New Orleans restaurant diva eventually landed in Saylors Crossroads, South Carolina. "Joe and I decided we wanted to raise our child nearer our families," Heidi said.

Consider the denizens here some of the luckiest diners on the planet. "It's definitely out of the ordinary for this area," Shane said. "It's certainly not your standard menu or restaurant space. Grits and Groceries serves a high quality meal at reasonable prices in a great atmosphere."

He's right. I had just sat down when I noticed that Tephanie Ashley, my personable waitress, kept leaving, running to the door, and hugging most everyone who entered. She grew up here and knows almost everybody. "If I don't know somebody's name, I will by the next time they come in," she promised. "I want my customers to feel like they're eating at my home."

It was breakfast and Tephanie said she would bring me a sampling of dishes. The menu changes weekly and seasonally. Foolish me, I thought Tephanie would soon reappear with a standard plate of grits, eggs, sausage, and a 30-year-old biscuit. I was stunned. There was praline bacon, a delicious thick-sliced portion of bacon with candied, syrupy pecan. Then came the tomato pie, an incredible blend of fresh, local tomato and onion, with mayonnaise, pepper, and salt in a flaky 3x3-inch pie crust. It was accompanied by Joe's homemade corn relish with dill cream. Then Tephanie added Smoked Salmon Shirred Eggs. Toto, this sure wasn't the Waffle House. I was flabbergasted, or so I thought, until there appeared French toast stuffed with cream cheese and fresh strawberries. Is this heaven or what?

Shane loves the catfish, with grits and eggs. "They've taken breakfast to the next level," he understated. Three ladies sitting near me agreed. Vickie Davis and Billie Barton of Honea Path and Reba Cameron of Donalds eat here every day and twice on

Saturday. "They have such a variety each day," Vickie observed. "It's not the same old, same old." Vickie loves the tomato pie, Billie the occasional seafood broil of shrimp, crab legs, crawfish, corn, and potatoes, and Reba swears by the fried chicken.

It was almost lunch time when I finally mustered the strength to leave. I had eaten so much, I felt a wheel barrow was needed to take me to the car. Then here comes Tephanie with a to-go plate of New Orleans Jambalaya chocked with pork, chicken, and beef and served with Joe's cornbread. What a place!

- Tim Driggers

The Hare & Hound Pub, Landrum
Spartanburg County

The Hare & Hound Pub, 101 East Rutherford Street in Landrum; (864) 457-3232. Open Monday-Saturday, 11 a.m-10 p.m. and Sunday, 11 a.m.-4 p.m. Credit cards accepted. Reservations not required. No smoking. www.thehareandhound.com. Lunch: inexpensive to moderate. Dinner: moderate to expensive.

Pub Grub in Ralph Lauren Country

Every now and then—usually when I'm off—I succumb to one of life's small but glorious pleasures: I have a drink at lunch. In Landrum at The Hare & Hound, I settled into a booth with some good friends and a Black & Tan. What could be more appropriate at a British-style pub?

"Oh, boy, that is exactly the kind of place I'd want to set up and do my thing," raves Dan Harmon, my infamous editor-cousin. Dan is a lover of all things British, Irish and Scottish. The Hare & Hound, with its dark wood, darts, and imported beer, is ideal for his alter-ego, Dan the Wandering Folk Musician Who Sings Sad Songs of the Sea When Not Fighting Word for Windows Ten Thousand. Dan, like numerous others in our Lexington County clan, likes music and food. Oh, the rapture of taking a break from the bagpipes and bouzouki for a supper of shepherd's pie!

"It's absolutely out of this world," Dan remembers of an earlier visit to the pub. "Rustic atmosphere – it was my kind of place."

He's not alone. Hear these words from Lyn Owen, a horse trainer and riding teacher from Inman. "You can come in here with sweaty jods on and smell like a horse, and nobody looks at you funny. We can't go anywhere but here."

Where would she go if it disappeared? "Into depression," she says, seriously.

Lyn was lunching with two of her students, Sara and Zach Chappell, who were out of school this fine Friday. She decided to forgo her usual chicken salad—"the best anywhere in this world" – for the Hare & Hound salad (two lettuces, two cheeses, boiled egg, almonds, chopped ham and bacon). Her pupils chose another favorite, the chicken strips basket.

"It's real simple pub food," says owner Harry Grymes, a boyish 30-year old who came to Landrum with wife Sheila, an avid horsewoman. His partner is his mother-in-law Evelyn Garrick. Together they chose to open a pub to suit that area's diverse population. "There are a lot of people who've grown up here and others who've come from elsewhere," Harry explains. "Anyone should feel comfortable in a pub."

And comfortable it is. No dainty doilies or rich velvets; here are hunt prints, beer posters and the Irish flag on the ceiling. On tap are Guinness, Bass Ale, Harp Lager, and Michelob Light. On the chalkboard are today's soups: chicken noodle, black bean and rice. Also listed are another specialty: the pies. Today's are strawberry, apple, and rhubarb, but it's blueberry cobbler that inspires most reverence. "It tastes like your grandmother would make," says Bobbie Levin, a horsewoman from Columbus. "It's to die for," agrees Lyn. "You have to pick the seeds out of your teeth, but oh my God!"

Open since 1994, The Hare & Hound serves a variety of American food with a few "pub fare" standards. The Shepherd's Pie is a stew of ground beef, peas, and carrots topped with a sturdy crust of mashed potatoes and cheese. A fish and chips basket contains strips of fried flounder and fries. Burgers, salads, sandwiches, wings, fried mushrooms, and potato skins are other offerings. In the evenings, steak, flounder, salmon, and mahi-mahi are available.

"We're not a bar," Harry emphasizes, adding that only wine and beer are sold. "There are kids lined up at the counter as much as adults. We're like England and Ireland, where business people—everybody—comes to the pub for lunch."

Our crowd ordered desserts and few of us tried the rhubarb—a true oddity in South Carolina. Harry's father-in-law, a pharmacist and gardener, grows it in Easley. Many elderly customers like its refreshing tartness, he observes.

But if you're not into food, you can always soak up that outdoorsy, horsey feeling Landrum has come to embody. "We call it 'The Ralph Lauren Look,' " jokes Bobbie, remembering a friend's description of the town. "Old money," adds her lunchmate Suzanne Wiseman. They laugh—loudly and a lot. At The Hare & Hound, loud laughing is right in line.

- Aïda Rogers

December 2, 2002 was not just another day for Patty Otto. Besides being her birthday, it was the day she bought The Hare & Hound from Sheila and Harry Grymes. But not to worry, The Hare and Hound Pub still has that British pub atmosphere, the beer taps continue to flow, and the pub fare remains a popular lunch and dinner choice. Favorite dishes are the Guinness Beef Pie, braised sirloin tips and vegetables served with Guinness beer and topped with whipped potatoes; the Honey Child, chicken salad served in a toasted croissant with almonds and honey sauce on the side; and the Baby Back Ribs, accompanied by sweet potato fries and homemade blue cheese Cole slaw. Also on the menu are a variety of steak, seafood, and fish selections. There's also live music on occasion.

- Tim Driggers

Ike's Corner Grill, Spartanburg
Spartanburg County

Ike's Corner Grill, 104 Archer Road, Spartanburg; (864) 542-0911. Open Monday 10 a.m.-3 p.m.; Tuesday-Wednesday-Friday 10 a.m.-9 p.m., Thursday 10 a.m.-11 p.m. (karaoke night with grill shutting at 9 p.m.). Saturday, 6:30 a.m.-3 p.m. (Saturday is the only day Ike's serves breakfast). Closed Sunday. Reservations not necessary. Credit cards accepted. No personal checks. Smoking allowed. Inexpensive to moderate.

"Boy, Do The Cheeseburgers Taste Right"

Where is South Carolina's best cheeseburger? Ike's Corner Grill in Spartanburg, says Bill Rogers, executive director of the South Carolina Press Association. Located in the Beaumont community, a mill village a few minutes from downtown, Ike's has been the center of the Upstate's cheeseburger universe for almost 50 years. It has the feel of a neighborhood hangout, with a long bar dominating the interior, but it's much more than a place to grab a beer and burger on the way home from work. Under the ownership of three generations of the Isom "Ike" Rodgers family, Ike's has evolved into a multi-faceted restaurant open for breakfast, lunch and dinner.

Its 8-ounce cheeseburger is its calling card. "We hand-patty between 250-300 a day," said present owner Neil Rodgers. The patty was developed by Neil's father Lewis. "He liked a good cheeseburger and felt the patty needed just the right fat content to make it good," said cook Monty Rodgers, Neil's brother. "We use the best and freshest hamburger available. If you use the cheap stuff, then there's no way it can be good."

Ike's cheeseburgers all come with chili. "It's my grandmother's recipe," Neil said. "She'd come by the restaurant each day just to make sure the chili tasted right." And boy, do the cheeseburgers taste right. Juicy, fresh, plump, and incredibly scrumptious. "They're always consistently good," said Jocko McGaha, a regular customer.

Don't overlook the fries. They're cut straight from the potato using a slicing machine from 1979. Ike's goes through about 1,600 potatoes a week.

"Like many towns in the Piedmont, folks once identified with their local cotton mill communities," reflected Paul McCravy, my trusty culinary assistant. "Ike's is no exception, as a Beaumont Mill banner is proudly displayed over the busy grill. Ike's started selling food to the mill workers and their menu still appeals to those hardy types who require more than a soup and salad. The nearest thing to a fancy salad is the Lettuce and Tomato Sandwich stacked high on an inch-thick fried bologna sandwich."

All ages and professions can be found here. "It's a place where good food and a family atmosphere bring people together," Monty notes.

It doesn't hurt that Ike's has those famous cheeseburgers and fries.

- Tim Driggers

Kelly's Steakhouse, Blacksburg
Cherokee County

Kelly's Steakhouse, 101 Little Hope Road, Blacksburg; (864) 839-4494. Open Tuesday-Thursday 5:30-9 p.m. and on Friday and Saturday 5:30-9:30 p.m. Reservations accepted. Credit cards and business checks accepted. Smoking at bar only. Moderate to very expensive.

It's a Family Tradition

Like the best jazz musicians, hair stylists and shaggers, good cooks are instinctive and hands-on. They're comfortable in a kitchen and unafraid to improvise. I think it's genetic, and if so, the family at Kelly's Steakhouse in Blacksburg proves the point.

"They're all good cooks," says Isabel London, a long-time family friend who helps at the front counter. "His daughter's a chip off the block." That's Ann Kelly Tadlock, the masterful woman who cuts and cooks meat in the back. Her father, Charles Kelly, started the restaurant in a small farmhouse in 1960. An Army mess sergeant in WWII, "Kelly" was unhappy in his father-in-law's dry-cleaning business. His fingers itched to cook and feed.

"He would cook steaks at the house and everybody would say, 'Kelly, this is wonderful. We can't get stuff like this anywhere,' " Ann relays. "He just decided he couldn't stand it any longer. He fixed up the old farmhouse and worked at the dry-cleaning business at the same time, and he'd cook after he got off work. It took a little while but it finally took off."

In a big way. Kelly's has regulars from Shelby and Charlotte, and Spartanburg, Greenville, and Columbia. No longer a humble farmhouse, Kelly's is a sprawling dinner club-style place with a long awning-covered entrance, white tablecloths, large bar, and menu of old, fine favorites. Look for steak and lobster here, flounder stuffed with crabmeat, and marinated herring in sour cream sauce.

Kelly died in 1997 and was mourned by many from miles around. In his last years, as his daughter Ann began taking over in the kitchen, he moved out front where he became a fixture at the TV, especially during basketball games. Some customers can't bear to come around since his death. But they're missing out. Ann's been experimenting and the results are good.

Our threesome started with two appetizers: the traditional oyster pie and a special, the roasted boneless duck quesadilla with black beans, spinach, and jalapeno peppers. The quesadillas are one of Ann's creations: Crispy and fried, they're served with sour cream and salsa. Other special appetizers this evening include baked Brie with almond slices and currant preserves and spring rolls stuffed with Chinese vegetables.

"I'm always trying something," Ann says. "I'll go to Charleston and try something and say, 'Well, I can do that.' I come back and do my version of different things."

Still, steak and seafood are the main draws. The steaks range from ground sirloin to a large filet mignon. Rib steak, strip sirloin and T-bones are available. They're brought to your table on a cart, sizzling. Sautéed onions and mushrooms are available on the side.

A variety of fish are available too: salmon, swordfish, rainbow trout, grouper, and red snapper. Catfish and flounder come in two sizes, and there's a fried seafood platter. A children's menu features chicken strips, chopped steak, and fried shrimp.

One popular seafood item is the shrimp and scallops, which can be grilled or fried. I tried them grilled, and though there were only four shrimp, they were huge and juicy—same for the scallops. Served on skewers, it was a plentiful meal that included salad and potato. All dinners include a choice of soup or salad, baked potato or fries. If you want your steak or fish blackened, that's available also.

Centrally located between Greenville and Charlotte, just off I-85, Kelly's can attribute some of its success to its ability to serve alcohol. Customers from the dry counties in North Carolina patronized it regularly in years past. These days, you can order a cocktail at your table or have a seat in the bar.

Because Kelly's has several dining rooms of various sizes, private parties are easy and often. Ann likes to talk about how a local gentleman, who grew up in the house before it was converted into a restaurant, was born in the Tiger Room. (There's a Cockpit for USC fans.)

The Kelly family spirit pervades the 220-seat restaurant. Ann's mother Marie greets guests in the front; Ann's husband Michael sautés in the back. Charles Kelly's special catfish stew recipe lives on to remind people of his culinary talents, and the house dessert—pie filled with strawberries, blackberries, raspberries, and rhubarb—remains a favorite.

- Aïda Rogers

Lake Lanier Tea House, Landrum
Spartanburg County

Lake Lanier Tea House, 351 Lakeshore Drive between Landrum and Tryon on Lake Lanier; (864) 457-5423. Open Thursday-Saturday, 5-10 p.m. and for Sunday brunch, 11 a.m.-2 p.m. Closed Monday-Wednesday. Reservations available. Credit cards and checks accepted. Smoking in designated areas. www.lakelanierteahouse.com. Expensive to very expensive.

Patty Otto raises a glass with her staff at the romantic Lake Lanier Tea House.

A Place for Fred and Ginger

I wasn't around in the 1940s and '50s, when couples dressed up and went out for dinner and dancing. There was always a band, a hat check and sparkling conversation. I know this from black-and-white movies and some chat from my parents. I'm pretty sure this kind of place doesn't exist anymore, but somehow, you get the impression those classier times remain at the Lake Lanier Tea House.

Established in 1925, the Tea House is relaxed, romantic and rustic. Manager Ted Kerhulas says it averages at least one engagement a week, and sometimes there are two or three. Weddings occur in front of the large stone fireplace in one dining room, with receptions following in other parts of the restaurant. Meanwhile, the terrace looks over the clear waters of Lake Lanier, a five-mile lake named for the poet Sidney Lanier. How could it not be romantic?

"This is a one-of-a-kind spot," Ted says. "We try to serve a reasonable dinner that people will enjoy, but the view is really the selling point."

It is gorgeous. Located in the northeast corner of Greenville County, one mile from Tryon, North Carolina, Lake Lanier is surrounded by mountains that make you sigh. You can sit on the terrace and watch the boats, take in the air, and be twinkled upon by the tiny lights in the trees that emerge from the boards in the floor. You can have a cocktail and dinner outside in the warmer months, or inside by the fireplace when it's cold. "I love it in the winter," says Helen Gillespie, proprietor of Lakeshore Bed & Breakfast nearby. "It's so cozy to sit by the roaring fire."

Since it was July, we sat by the window. I could have remained bemused by the view had not the regal Ted King appeared. "Anyone care for a hard drink?" he inquired. At 84, with beautiful enunciation and exacting memory, Mr. King "called the menu"– there is no printed menu–as he has for 20 years. Our party of seven was large enough to try every entrée: chicken cordon bleu, prime rib, rainbow trout, roast lamb, grilled salmon, and filet of beef. Entrees were served with squash casserole, crispy green beans, fried mushrooms and crescent rolls. The food is very good, but not show-offy. Tribute that to Clarence Morrison, cook here for 35 years. "Clarence is a southern-style cook, but he doesn't cook things to death," Ted observes. "He does do casseroles and soufflés. We're not real fancy by any means."

But that's not a bad wine list they have, and the desserts are like the menu–classic. Available this evening: vanilla ice cream, a chocolate sundae (vanilla ice cream with chocolate syrup) and Peach Alaska–frozen angel food cake with peach frosting and fresh peaches. "That's one of our summertime desserts," Ted reports. "We do strawberries and sometimes we do raspberries." (Shall we moan?)

Ted is the third-generation Kerhulas at the Tea House. His grandfather, Ernest Kerhulas, came up from Union and bought the place in 1941. Ernest and his son Theo ran it for years, before Theo took over. Today, the handsome Theo, 80, is still around, taking care of many of the same families he's served for decades. Sons Ted and Mark– even Mark's fiancée Sherry Wilson–work here.

Lake Lanier was built for recreation and homes in the mid-1920s. The logs from the lake were used to build the Tea House. Today, its distinguishing feature is the logs– intact after 75 years. Its rough-hewn walls and white tablecloths create an atmosphere of comfort and specialness–not easy to achieve.

Nor is it easy to achieve a perfectly fried chicken. But somehow, Clarence has. It's available only at the Sunday buffet. When they're out, Sherry says, "there's a huge echo from everyone."

- Aïda Rogers

There's an old saying that all things must someday end. It should be noted that sometimes when things end, they start back up again. That's the case with the 83-year-old Lake Lanier Tea House. With the passing of Theo Kerhulas and son Ted, the restaurant ended its 64-year-run under the ownership of the Kerhulas family in September 2005. Fast forward two years and Lake Lanier Tea House has been reborn. Patty Otto, who also owns the Hare and Hound in Landrum, fell in love with the Tea House soon after moving to the upstate. It was only natural for that fondness to translate into ownership. After extensive renovations, Patty reopened the restaurant on August 8, 2007, with a revised menu and plans to rebuild the old boat house, perhaps add a deck. There's a new dock and private dining room and she's converted the former bathhouse into a stylish bar. Appetizers on the new menu include Crab Cakes, Fried Green Tomato Napoleon, Pork Confit, and House Cured Salmon. Entrees featured are Filet Mignon with fois gras butter and truffle-scented demi-glace, pan-seared free range chicken with prosciutto ham, halibut, crispy salmon filet, pecan crusted trout, petit rack of lamb, smoked pork chop, and Tea House New York Strip. The glorious view of Lake Lanier is free.

- Tim Driggers

Larkin's on the River, Greenville
Greenville County

Larkin's On the River, 318 South Main Street, Greenville; (864) 467-9777. Open for lunch Monday-Friday, 11:30 a.m.-2 p.m. and for dinner Monday-Saturday, 5-10 p.m. Open Sunday after Peace Center performances. Reservations recommended. Credit cards accepted. No smoking. www.larkinsontheriver.com. Lunch: inexpensive to moderate. Dinner: moderate to expensive.

Fine Steaks and Volcano Cakes

Greenville's trendy West End Historic District is a perfect place to relax and dine after viewing the works of Andrew Wyeth at the Greenville County Museum of Art or attending a performance at the Peace Center. Larkin's on the River opened in 2005, part of the Peace Center complex. Located in the 1847 Gower Coach Factory, Larkin's retains the exposed beams of the stagecoach plant and original brick walls pressed from river mud. Add white linen tablecloths over hardwood tables, an extensive wine rack, a prominent bar, and Larkin's becomes your quintessential steak house.

"Our meat is all aged and cut specifically for us in Atlanta," said general manager Bob Munnich. Trained as a chef at the Culinary Institute of New York, Munnich made restaurant stops in Philadelphia, San Francisco, and the New Jersey shore before joining owners Larkin and Mark Hammond in 2005. "Our signature dish is the bone-in filet mignon," Munnich said. Cut from the heart of the porterhouse, this specialty outsells everything on the menu. "It's the leanest cut of beef you can get," Munnich said. "It's the one dish we really focus on and is really unique."

Larkin's also serves an aged filet mignon. Other steaks are the 28-ounce aged bone-in ribeye, 18-ounce aged bone-in New York strip and beef tenderloin with cognac cream sauce au poivre.

Steaks aren't the only thing on the menu. "Our chef, Alex Castro, is really inventive with seafood," Munnich said. "He really knows how to serve a piece of fish. Our seafood specials sold so well that we decided to add them as a permanent part of our menu." Among others, you can try the Chilean sea bass with shrimp sorito sauce, peppered Norwegian salmon filet with ginger wild mushroom sauce, and the obligatory shrimp and grits.

I ordered the bacon-wrapped sea scallop maltese appetizer and a citrus salad special with bay scallops recommended by my server. The salad was delicious, as was my appetizer. "Everything we make is from scratch," Munnich said, "including our desserts. Our specialty is the Chocolate Volcano Cake. We cook it to order with a liquid center and it's served with vanilla bean ice cream, raspberry sauce, and vanilla custard." The lunch menu is basically a smaller version of the dinner fare. Featured is Larkin's Gourmet Surf and Turf Burger, two jumbo shrimp and a half-pound hamburger made from beef imported from Kobe, Japan.

- Tim Driggers

The Lazy Islander, Pendleton
Anderson County

The Lazy Islander, 134 Exchange Street, Pendleton; (864) 646-6337. Open Monday-Saturday 11 a.m. until (sometimes as late as 2 a.m.). Closed Sunday. Reservations accepted. Credit cards and checks accepted. Smoking and non-smoking sections. Inexpensive to moderate.

Tropical Impudence In a Revered Old Town (Or, "Hurling With Pat")

One of the great joys of this job is working with photographers. They're fun, they're funny, and they're always ready to eat. So when I found myself in Clemson, I called Pat Wright to join me for dinner. We met at The Lazy Islander in Pendleton, which overlooks the town square. I'd heard about it many times, and Pat, who works for Clemson University, has been here often. He couldn't wait to tell me about his first episode there.

"I had six or seven double screwdrivers, and I went home and screw-drivered the yard," he recalled. "I hurled!" That's what I like about Pat–he celebrates his misery.

The Lazy Islander is joyful, too, impudently playing Jimmy Buffet and serving calamari among palm trees and bamboo. This is unusual in quaint Pendleton, a town famous for history and antiques. We ordered the calamari, which appeared with salsa for dipping. "Fork or fingers?" I asked Pat.

"You're asking me? I'm a farm boy from Honea Path; culture and I do not go hand-in-hand." I can't remember what we used but we ate it and declared it very good.

Pat got the blackened mahi-mahi and I got one of the popular stir fry dishes—they come in steak, shrimp, and chicken. It's a colorful combination of meat, onions, mushrooms, cabbage, and ginger sauce in a taco shell. It reminded me of a piñata that burst on my plate.

The Lazy Islander serves a variety of seafood dishes along with salads, soups, and sandwiches. It offers a daily "hungry hour"—raw oysters and boiled shrimp on this night-and serves tiny muffins with cinnamon butter in place of hush puppies.

When it was time for dessert, the choice was easy. I ordered Key Lime Pie; Pat got Kentucky Derby Pie. Mine was light and cool; his was thick and rich, full of walnuts, whipped cream, and fudge. Pat is a chocoholic. "I have no problem admitting that," he said. "I eat chocolate 'til I hurl."

- Aïda Rogers

Sandlapper first visited The Lazy Islander in 1992. Since then, owners Matthew and Molly Crenshaw have moved to their present Exchange Street location. The calamari appetizer remains a popular selection. Other favorites include seafood fettuccine, potato encrusted grouper, prime rib and rib eye steak. Matthew says the Lazy Islander is famous for its hamburgers and offers a wide variety of sandwiches and salads. All soups are homemade.

- *Tim Driggers*

The Liberty Hall Inn, Pendleton
Anderson County

Liberty Hall Inn, 621 South Mechanic Street, Pendleton; (864) 646-7500. Open for lunch Tuesday-Friday, 11 a.m.-2 p.m. and for dinner Thursday-Saturday, 5:30-8:30 p.m. Closed Sunday and Monday. No smoking. Credit cards accepted. Reservations accepted. Lunch: inexpensive. Dinner: moderate to expensive.

Stop "Inn" Here For An Elegant Feast

The Liberty Hall Inn in Pendleton is the definition of elegant dining in the upstate of South Carolina. The restaurant itself is a small part of this rambling bed and breakfast—

just two small rooms downstairs, divided by a hallway. But the feeling is cozy, not cramped, and the food is top-notch.

Do like I did and get the beef tenderloin. Cooked in port wine, soy sauce, herbs and spices, it's the pride of the menu. I have no adjectives for this one, but trust me; it's good. "I don't eat beef," said waitress Timmi Wrinn, "but I'll eat this." The tenderloin is always available, as is the Veal Lombardi. Chicken and fish dishes vary nightly.

Dinner at Liberty Hall is a four-course affair, and the menu is always spoken. It begins with a soup (French onion, the night I was there in 1990) and moves on to a salad. Let me stop here and share my salad notes: "wonderful, generous, crisp and fresh." I also recall it was topped with homemade poppy seed dressing and crumbled bleu cheese.

But it's wise not to fill up on the first two courses, because after the third one, there's still dessert to follow. Chocolate Sin is the ultimate finale, a square of chocolate goo with chocolate syrup, whipped cream, walnuts and "butter, lots of butter," according to Tom Jonas, who was proprietor at the time.

The fireplace, hunting motif and dark green/light peach colors give the restaurant a classy warmth. It seats about 60 and, when I visited, it was only open during the evenings, although bridal luncheons and special occasions for midday are available upon request. These days, Liberty Hall is open for both lunch and dinner.

A mile and a half from the quaint Pendleton town square, Liberty Hall Inn attracts diners from Greenville, Keowee Key and Anderson. But people across the state should know about it, too.

- Aïda Rogers

Built in 1850, Liberty Hall Inn was an antebellum home that was renovated in 1985 into a 7-room bed and breakfast and restaurant. Present owners Janet and Kevin Martin obtained the property in September 2004. Known for its eclectic menu, Liberty Hall Inn favorites are now shrimp and grits, the pork dishes, crab cakes, blue crab bisque, and lobster with macaroni and cheese.

- *Tim Driggers*

Mac's Drive-In, Clemson
Pickens County

Mac's Drive-In, 404 Pendleton Road, Clemson; (864) 645-2845. Open Monday-Saturday, 11 a.m.-11 p.m. or until the last student straggles out. Closed Sunday. Reservations: not even for CU President James Barker (well, maybe for Danny Ford). No smoking. Inexpensive.

A Tiger Den With Burgers and Fries

There's just no doubt where you are when you walk in Mac's Drive-In in Clemson. The color scheme is orange. The cooks wear Clemson T-shirts. The menu says "Go Tigers." Gosh, is this what they mean when they say "sense of place?"

"I was raised on this place," said Lee Thompson, who grew up nearby. Now that he's in seminary in Charlotte, Lee makes sure he stops in when he comes back. "I probably first came here when I was 10. I've eaten a steady stream of cheeseburgers ever since."

Lee was sitting at the counter—there's nowhere else to sit—when I wandered in. I'd heard about Mac's Drive-In for years—10 years, to be exact. That's when my sister married Jiggs Tompkins, a devoted Clemson graduate who might be even more devoted to Mac's. I swore I would stop in when I got the chance.

"I always got the cheeseburger and I would top it off with a little Thousand Island dressing," Jiggs said. "That was my thing and it was great."

But what was really great was getting away from campus. "It was not downtown Clemson, so it was a break from the students," he pointed out. "You could go there, sit at the counter, talk with Mac and find out about real life. I like the neighborhood, only-locals-know-about-it kind of places."

But word about Mac's and its proprietor has spread, Lee told me. "He's famous. He's been in *Sports Illustrated*."

"Didn't start out to be famous," said Harold "Mac" McKeown, a stocky, clean-cut man who opened for business in 1956. If Mac's is famous for anything, he believes, it's "for being here 40 years."

On the menu is typical grill fare. Besides hot dogs and hamburgers, there are fish and steak sandwiches, chicken plates and shrimp baskets. You also can get milkshakes, ice cream, and a cup of gravy. A filling lunch easily will leave change in your pocket.

Located in a small brick building, Mac's does a big take-out business. Or you can eat at the counter and study the many photos of Clemson athletes on the wall—unless you want to check out the soap opera playing on the TV.

Elaine and Ted Hunter bought the restaurant from Mac about 10 years ago, but didn't change a thing. That includes Mac, who's still behind the counter. "You can't run him out – and then he fusses because he's there," Elaine jokes. She remembers when the original restaurant was in a trolley car. "It had six stools in it," she said. Today, there are 15. "We thought when we moved in this building, we'd have all the room in the world!"

The fact is, you might have to wait for a spot at the counter. But when you get one, you could find yourself beside Gov. David Beasley or Bob and Bill Peeler. Danny Ford ate lunch here every day when he coached Clemson football and still drops in.

I found myself with Lee Thompson on my left and brothers George and Jimmy Martin on my right. George and Jimmy always get hot dogs. "We've been coming since the '50s," George said. George lives in Georgia, Jimmy in North Carolina. They were in town for a wedding, but seemed much more excited to be at Mac's. "Every time we come back to town, we got to come here."

- Aïda Rogers

Mac's Drive-In continues to be one of the great Clemson University hangouts. Just when you think there's not another inch of space to tack another Tiger athletic moment on the wall, Elaine and Ted Hunter will miraculously find room for that photo of Dwight Clark, Tree Rollins, or Khalil Greene. There are 15 stools in the place and seating is still a game of musical chairs. Don't ask for a menu, there isn't one. Think short order grill and ask for a burger, fries, and a shake; they're Mac's favorites and the most popular choices of Tiger students and alums.

- *Tim Driggers*

McGee's Irish Pub and Restaurant, Anderson
Anderson County

McGee's Irish Pub and Restaurant (formerly Corbett McGee's Irish Pub), 116 West Orr Street, Anderson; (864) 261-6401; Lunch 11:30 a.m.-2:30 p.m. Monday-Friday. Dinner 4-10 p.m. Monday-Saturday. Late night menu until 11:30 p.m. The bar is open Monday and Tuesday from 11:30 a.m. to closing time; Wednesday-Friday 11:30 a.m.-2 a.m.; Saturday 4 p.m. to midnight. Closed Sunday. Credit cards accepted; no checks. ATM cash machine available. Reservations appreciated for parties of 15 or more. Smoking and non-smoking sections. www.mcgeesirishpub.com. Lunch: inexpensive. Dinner: inexpensive to moderate.

Pub Grub in the Upstate

A step into McGee's Irish Pub puts you on the Emerald Isle. But that's not such a big leap when you consider the influence the Scots-Irish had on South Carolina and its religion, music, and food.

"It's just like coming home," owner Dixie McGee Benca says of her three trips to Ireland. "A lot of things are similar. The home cooking that my mother and grandmother cooked is very similar to what they would eat there."

Soups, stews, lots of vegetables, and a little meat is how Dixie describes Irish meals. "That's the way we ate growing up. The biggest meal of the day would be noon instead of supper. And you see a lot of root vegetables, like turnips."

Dixie and her husband John have recreated those cooking philosophies at their Anderson enterprise, a rambling, rustic building they restored from a former car dealership and warehouse. The flags of the United States, South Carolina, Scotland, and Ireland fly outside the front door; inside you're greeted by autographed photos of the many Celtic musicians who've played here. Live music, "pub grub," an Irish trivia night, and Irish and English beer let you know the Bencas are serious about providing an authentic experience for their customers. The musicians are the real thing, and recipes come from Irish cookbooks.

"You can't get good shepherd's pie in Iowa," deadpans Steve Pradarelli, a former newspaper reporter in Spartanburg and Sumter who's left for colder climes. His wife Melinda, an Iowan he met in Spartanburg, eyed the shrimp po boy on the menu. "We don't have that in Iowa either," she adds.

While the Pradarellis ordered thusly, the rest of us followed suit. Among our choices: the Blarney Burger (1/3-pound grilled ground beef), the Irish Stew (braised New Zealand lamb with vegetables and mashed potatoes), and the Corned Beef and Cabbage. Fish & Chips (fried Newfoundland Cod filets and fries) and Chicken & Chips (fried chicken tenderloins and fries) also are available on the lunch menu. These items are slightly higher on the evening menu, which includes more formal fare. For instance, there's Cornish game hen, basted with raspberry butter and served with mashed potatoes and a Waldorf salad, and Irish Whiskey Steak, a 12-ounce marinated, grilled strip. Bangers & Mash is the famous Scot's sausage with apple-onion chutney, chives, tomatoes and mashed potatoes. Even shrimp and grits are on this menu, which includes a range of salads, sandwiches, pastas, appetizers, and desserts.

"We never thought the menu thing would be a big deal," Dixie recalls. "We started off with a little menu with mostly sandwiches and shepherd's pie, the typical Celtic stuff. Everybody liked it so well, we figured out early on that we needed to expand on that."

By education, Dixie is a landscape architect and John an engineer. When they graduated from UGA, a slow economy kept them in the restaurant and bar business, which is how they earned money as students. Combining their love for Irish pubs with their desire to be self-employed, they opened McGee's in 1997, on St. Patrick's Day. Anderson, Dixie's hometown, was receptive from the start. Pretty soon, people began coming from North Georgia and other parts of upstate South Carolina.

Maybe they've got a subconscious yen for Irish soda bread and Guinness Stout, something they've inherited from their long-ago forebears. As the menu states, the Scots-Irish "made up almost 50% of the ethnic population of the SC 'Back Country' by the early 1700s." How fun to salute them with drink and song, two centuries later.

- Aïda Rogers

Owners Dixie and John Benca say their pub has the best draught beer in Anderson. They also say they have the only legitimate craic (pronounced krak) house in town. Lest you be alarmed, that's Irish for "the combined sensation of good conversation, good times, good atmosphere, etc; good fun." Follow me on this one: There's Pub Grub including Bumbershoots (breaded and fried mushrooms in horsy-ranch dressing), Mini Mutton Bridies (seasoned ground lamb stuffed in puff pastry), Cheezy Welsh Rarebit, and the Celtic Classics – Bangers and Mash, Cottage Pie, Shepherd's Pie, Irish Stew, Dublin Style Corned Beef and Cabbage. Signature entrées include Fried Chicken Liver, Roasted Cornish Hen, Chicken Bog, Drunken Chicken Breast (marinated in whisky and spices), Honey Mead Chicken (tenderloin soaked in honey and wine and topped with Black Forest Ham), Galway Bay Crab Cakes, Irish Whiskey Stew and Leg of Lamb. Also try the Norwegian Grilled Soda Bread Cheese Sandwich Supper Platter. I'll stop here. I think you get the picture.

Dixie and John recently opened Jax New Orleans Bistro on North Main Street in Anderson, for, as they say on their website, "an elegant evening out."

- Tim Driggers

Never On Sunday, Greenville
Greenville County

Never on Sunday, 210 East Coffee Street, Greenville; (864) 232-2252. Open for lunch on Thursday and Friday, 11:30 a.m.-2 p.m. and for dinner Tuesday-Saturday, 5:30 -9:30 p.m. Credit cards and checks accepted. Reservations accepted but not necessary. No smoking. Inexpensive to moderate.

Hello Hugs and Goodbye Kisses

At Never on Sunday in Greenville, Iris Tassiopoulos is the great dispenser of wisdom, food, and hugs. My brother Clifton and I had barely looked at the menu when a group of women came in, met Iris at the counter and a burst of hugging, laughing, and exclaiming ensued. Two glasses of homemade Greek wine and a combination plate later, I was ready to do the same. Iris and her husband Nick make sure you don't leave a stranger.

"Nick and Iris are our family," said Eleanor Wynn, who lives on Hilton Head Island but doesn't come to Greenville without suppering at Never on Sunday.

The Wynn family was so regular that their son David started taking his plate back to the kitchen when he was 8. Now David and his sister Lauren are grown, but they still love Never on Sunday. When Lauren visits from Atlanta, she stops by for a meal; and if she doesn't have time to eat there, she'll order a takeout of Greek potatoes.

Now Lauren is a mother, and a photo of her 4-year-old son is in the restaurant. So are the photos of 199 other children in Never on Sunday, and Iris knows them all. "I love every one and I leave a dollar to every one in my will," she said.

Never on Sunday has been serving inexpensive, well-seasoned Greek food since 1967. Nick is as well-loved as Iris. As ritualistic as a hello hug from Iris is the goodbye kiss from Nick. We watched a blonde woman head back to the kitchen after her meal, ready for her farewell smacker. "Close the door!" Iris called after her.

With all this action, it might seem the food gets forgotten, but it doesn't. It's more likely the food, family and friendship become intertwined and enmeshed, so that one is part of the other. Dining at Never on Sunday is more experience than meal.

At our table, Clifton and I started with the tiropetes, an appetizer of crispy filo stuffed with a feta cheese and egg mixture. I could have eaten a whole plate of those, no matter how grounded in the real world my brother is. "This has got some fat grams in it," he announced. "I can feel it on my lips."

I submit there's a place in the world for fat grams (they've got to go somewhere), and what better place than Never on Sunday, where the wine keeps magically appearing? I had just moved over to talk to Eleanor and company when Iris brought me a second glass. "That's your wine. You can talk better."

Eleanor's sister Carolyn Stevenson told me that at Never on Sunday, they never got menus. "It's kind of like Mom's Diner. She knows what we want." Tonight, the ladies were served broiled chicken pelafee, seasoned with Greek spices and served with rice. Carolyn's daughter Elizabeth, 13, has been eating here since her high-chair days and remembers getting the menu only once.

Clifton and I were allowed menus. Clifton ordered the keftedes, which are Greek meatballs, and I ordered the combination plate which, along with the lamb stew, is the most expensive entrée on the menu. Iris and Nick can keep prices low because they have no help and because they do everything themselves—right down to growing their own grape leaves.

The combination plate is a filling sampler of Greek specialties. My favorites were the dolmades, or stuffed grape leaves, and pastichio which, to the southern eye, looks like a square of macaroni but translates into a melt-in-your-mouth, custardy something else. The platter also includes the keftedes and beef shish kebob. Clifton and I were quiet, except for those satisfied noises we make when we're eating food we like.

Never on Sunday serves lunch and supper at its inconspicuous location on Coffee Street. Beef, lamb, veal, and chicken dishes are available, as are gyros, souvlaki, baklava and Greek salads.

Nick is famous for his Greek dressing, which is for sale. Iris is famous for remembering everything a customer orders. At Never on Sunday, bills are never given. Generosity is.

It's not unusual for someone to order a glass of wine and get two. If that happens, don't think Iris is scatterbrained. She isn't. She's the one who's been cooking for years and has yet to write down a recipe.

"If I start to forget things," she vows," that's when I retire."

- Aïda Rogers

When we checked in with Nick and Iris Tassiopoulos to find out what was new at Never on Sunday, the answer was quite simple. "We haven't changed anything in 41 years." Never on Sunday remains a restaurant where you're welcomed as an extended member of the Tassiopoulos family and invited to share their dinner table. That's the way Iris and Nick always want it to be.
- *Tim Driggers*

Nu-Way Lounge and Restaurant, Spartanburg
Spartanburg County

Nu-Way Lounge, 373 East Kennedy Street, Spartanburg; (864) 582-9685. Open Monday-Friday, 11 a.m.-2 a.m., Saturday, 11 a.m.-midnight. Closed Sunday. Reservations recommended for parties of 10 or more. MasterCard, Visa, and personal checks accepted. Smoking allowed; non-smoking area available during lunch. www.myspace.com/nuwayrestaurantlounge. Inexpensive to moderate.

Applause for the Redneck Cheeseburger

Paul McCravy and I love cheeseburgers, so the Nu-Way Lounge and Restaurant in Spartanburg is our type of place. The building is solid black with a Pabst Blue Ribbon beer sign hanging prominently over the bright red door. The bar runs the length of the dining room, providing plenty of space to eat and guzzle. A beer sign touts "Bud 'n' Burgers" among a bevy of other neon-lit beer advertisements. A juke box along the wall was playing "Third Rate Romance," and the requisite pinball machines live here too. Most importantly, a refrigerator adjoins the bar, holding mass quantities of hamburger meat and hot dogs.

As we sat at the bar, Paul and I were informed by bartender/cook/"whatever-needs-to-be done" Stephen Parris that the Nu-Way dates to 1938. "We're the oldest juke joint left around," he said. "We cater to good ole boys and girls."

Paul, a good ole boy from Easley, was already sipping on a can of PBR. "This is the coldest beer I have ever had," he said. "It's so cold, I can hardly hold it." Still, he managed to get it down, and we ordered the Redneck Cheeseburger. While we waited for Stephen to cook the Nu-Way masterpiece, I moseyed to the far end of the bar where Ryan Poag and Christine Gowan were eating a late lunch. Ryan, a Spartanburg native and real estate agent, has been coming here "since I was old enough to stay after hours." Christine, a market designer, has been a customer since middle school.

"The food is great and you always meet a friend, even a friend you don't know yet," Ryan said. "The folks who come to the Nu-Way are reflective of Hub City. It doesn't make a difference if you're the richest or poorest person in town." Christine agrees. "It's like the Cheers of Spartanburg," she observed. "The service is as good when the place is empty as it is when it's full."

While we chatted, Paul kept interrupting, motioning me to come taste my Redneck Cheeseburger, which was waiting on the bar. "Be there in a minute" didn't seem to placate him a bit. "You have to come down here and taste this," he insisted.

Let me try to describe the Redneck Cheeseburger. It's a fresh patty, with mustard, lettuce, tomato, pimento cheese and chili, and a dash of seasoning. Paul and I unanimously agreed that no finer cheeseburger had ever passed our lips on the way to our tummies. To say it was delicious is like saying the Beatles were just another band from Liverpool. We were stunned.

But Ryan wasn't surprised. "The chili on the cheeseburger is awesome."

Becky Hammond owns the Nu-Way, and her mother makes the pimento cheese. The chili is made fresh daily. The patties are handmade from fresh ground beef and nothing is frozen. "A Redneck Burger would induce gluttony in the most devout," Paul reflected later. "Am I glad we found our way to the Nu-Way. Not once did we miss the brass and ferns of those expensive watering holes."

We left determined to round up a passel of friends and return one weekend to down those burgers again, tipple ice-cold PBRs, and dosey-do to the live music on stage. That's just what good ole boys do in South Carolina

- Tim Driggers

O.J.'s Diner, Greenville
Greenville County

O.J.'s Diner, 907 Pendleton Street, Greenville; (864) 235-2539. Open Monday-Friday, 7 a.m. to 5 p.m. Closed Saturday and Sunday. Reservations not required. Credit cards accepted. No smoking. Inexpensive.

"We Cook the Old-Fashioned Way"

Flipping through the pages of old photo albums and seeing your life unfold through the years recalls so many special times. Those snapshots reveal something interesting: Many of our favorite family memories are tied to food.

O.J.' s Diner in Greenville recalls those special family meals. First, just about everybody who works here is a member of the Johnson family–owner Olin, son Doug, daughter Quiwanna, assorted sisters, a brother, and nephew. Second, a trip down the buffet line is like savoring the down-home meals at a Johnson family reunion. Though you might not be a member of the Johnson family when you walk through the doors, you will be by the time you leave.

For 27 years McBee Diner was a signature restaurant in downtown Greenville. During much of that time, Olin Johnson worked as a machine operator in the area's textile mills, earning a reputation on the side as a cook of considerable skill. Then Olin and his sister Lonita bought the place and O.J's Diner was born.

Located on the northern side of Greenville in a modern red brick building, the restaurant can seat up to 100 diners and is dominated appropriately by the buffet and kitchen areas. Folks scurry in for lunch; folks scurry back to work. If you're a regular, you know the specials and just what you will select from the buffet. Fried chicken, fried fish, and beef stew are daily staples. On Monday, add pork chops; Tuesday turkey and meatloaf; Wednesday fried beef liver; Thursday country-style steak and chicken pot pie; Friday, barbecue pork ribs. That's just the meats. Most days, the buffet also features macaroni and cheese, rice and gravy, beans of every variety, turnip greens, fried okra, okra and tomatoes, stewed cabbage, and corn. For dessert, try the homemade peach, apple and sweet potato cobblers, and banana pudding.

Breakfast also brings in a crowd. "We cook the old-fashioned way–the way people want to eat," Olin said. "There were times when people couldn't get bacon, so we cook the sort of food they could get–fried bologna, sausage and salmon patties, fatback bacon, corn beef hash, and potatoes smothered in onions. I also serve the best buttermilk biscuits you will ever eat. It's not unusual for people to order three or four at a time." O.J.'s has a daily breakfast special of rice, grits, hashbrowns, eggs, toast or biscuits, along with a choice of the aforementioned. "We have such a crowd in the morning that it makes you wish we had a red light at the buffet."

I chose the grilled chicken and yellow rice. It was seasoned with garlic herbs and had a teriyaki taste that was pleasantly different. It's the creation of Olin's son and chief cook Doug. He has a simple explanation for keeping the good graces of his father: "I don't cook anything unless he's satisfied with it."

Moot Dirtwan, a delivery man for Kirkland Metals, eats here two or three times a week. He loves Wednesday's beef liver. "You can't find it anywhere else," he noted, "and the peach cobbler ...oh, man, it reminds me of what my mother and grandmother cooked." Sonya Campbell of Greer craves the desserts. "Oh, oh, the sweet potato cobbler is simply awesome," she said. "It is absolutely perfect. Not too sweet and not mushy at all."

Paraphrasing a campaign slogan of 1992, at O.J's Diner, "it's about the food, stupid." Food and family–powerful forces that forge memorable dining experiences.

- Tim Driggers

When we called to check in with Olin Johnson, he wanted one thing made perfectly clear: Everything is made from scratch at O. J.'s Diner. "We're a throwback to yesterday," he said. We're OK with that, O.J., and so are the hundreds who ravenously attack your buffet each day.

- T. D.

The Palms, Greenville
Greenville County

The Palms, 246 North Pleasantburg Drive, Greenville; (864) 370-9181. Open Tuesday-Saturday, 6-9 p.m. Closed Sunday and Monday. No smoking. Credit cards and checks accepted. Reservations not required. Moderate to expensive.

"Picasso On a Plate"

Food, like any art, cannot be described in words. You have to be there. So I won't do the dance of the adjectives for The Palms restaurant in The Phoenix Inn in Greenville. I'll just let owner Steve Moore describe what happened when he and Peter Oaks first came across the cooking of Donald Hiers, the chef they enticed from Atlanta to their dream hotel in the upstate. All it took was one bite of the confit of duck.

"That is it," they announced simultaneously and immediately. And almost two years of weekend travel ended for Steve and Peter, hot on the chase for just the right chef. What they found was what they wanted: someone who could create food that was different, unexpected, and out of this world. "It was just instant, you know?" Steve recalls. "You know when something is right. It was just so"–he pauses for the right word–"good."

Good might be an understatement for the confit of duck, or anything on The Palms menu. Read it out loud and pretend you're Julia Child. Let "duxelle of fresh mushrooms" and "potato and chive garlette" warble from your lips. "Brandade of cod" was my favorite; I said it over and over, to the irritation of those nearby, and even ordered it so I could say it again.

But it was the confit of duck that made Steve and Peter believe in love at first bite.

"I thought it was going to be a piece of duck," Steve recalls. "Well, it's a duck leg with green bean salad and these wonderful crispy potatoes, all in an *au jus* sauce. It was just fabulous–the presentation, the flavor. It was an instant 'this is what I want. If I can't get him, I want to find somebody who can cook like this.' "

Back in Greenville, Steve and Peter began the campaign to bring Donald to The Palms. "We sent out a love letter and said, "We're trying to create something in Greenville and we fell in love with your food in Atlanta and would you consider helping us in our endeavor to find your clone?" After a phone call and a visit, Donald decided to take the challenge. He turned down offers in Charlotte and Atlanta, helped transform the restaurant from a country buffet to something much more elegant, and brought fine dining at its finest to Greenville. "The reception has been overwhelming," Steve says. "He's brought something that people always had to go out of town to find."

I myself had never heard of pasta nests, particularly when served with Macadamia nut-crusted swordfish with zucchini and gin grapefruit sauce. Halibut sautéed in couscous with soft, herbed polenta and lemon basil butter also sounded exotic. But my entree, the fish special with smoked trout in smoked tomato coulis and Opah in ginger cream sauce, was Picasso on a plate.

"Don really, really loves to create, and that's the artist in him," says Sharon Van Vechten, a publicist for the restaurant and inn. "He's like an adventurer on a quest. He's an explorer. He's on the holy grail!"

Sounds of ecstasy arose from the table, where some diners ordered the steamed mussels with fresh pasta (made in the kitchen) in white wine, garlic and shallot broth. Others ordered the game plate of veal in mushroom cream sauce, lamb in honey vinegar sauce and duck in red wine sauce. Sauces and seafood are Donald's hallmark– he trained with French chefs in California and Atlanta–but as Steve will say, even his typical entrees are extraordinary. "Things you've had before, like rack of lamb, veal chops–his are the best rack of lamb, the best veal chops. And his sauces really bring it alive." Not one for waste, Steve sops the crusty multigrain rolls in the sauces, and admits he's gained 20 pounds since The Palms opened in January 1995.

Besides Donald, the executive chef, The Palms has an executive sous chef, Tim Sprague, and executive pastry chef, Karyn O'Connor. Desserts dazzle as much as entrees. How to choose between mango-lime crème brulee, millfeuille of chocolate and coffee mousse with mint ice cream or lemon poppyseed cake with a chocolate center on a bed of blueberries? The apple tart with cinnamon ice cream tops the list; because it's made to order, it takes 15 minutes.

Dinner is served in a cranberry, white and dark green dining room with red roses at every table and chocolate truffles after each meal. You can order cocktails and hors d'oeuvres in the piano bar before your meal or espresso and cordials after.

It'd be easy to find a meal as exquisite as one at The Palms—if you were in New York or Paris, Sharon and Steve say. "Unexpected" is Steve's favorite description; "oasis" is Sharon's. To me, it's a great place to pamper and tantalize your taste buds. Gather your favorite foodaholics and go.

- Aïda Rogers

Sandlapper visited The Palms in the autumn of 1997, and it was with great relief that we discovered Don Hiers remains as executive chef. Let's all let out a collective "whew." Current favorites are the New York Strip steak, salmon, chicken, and duck.

- *Tim Driggers*

The Pauline Café, Pauline
Spartanburg County

The Pauline Café, (formerly Rachel's Pauline Cafe') 2960 SC Highway 56, Pauline; (864) 582-2990. Breakfast and lunch served Monday-Saturday, 5 a.m.-2 p.m. Supper served Tuesday and Thursday, 4-8 p.m. During deer season, the café opens at 4:30 a.m. Closed Sunday. No smoking. Visa, MasterCard, Discover, and checks accepted. Reservations not necessary. Inexpensive.

"This Restaurant Cooks Food Like Your Grandma Cooked Food"

The Pauline Café is named for its hometown, which was named for the postmaster's daughter in 1895. Established in 1776 on the banks of Dutchman Creek in Spartanburg County, Pauline shares an elementary school with Glenn Springs. Word is teachers cross the highway to The Pauline Cafe for one of the daily home-cooked specials or short-order sandwiches. But teachers are just one small segment of the fan club here. Retirees come en masse (the inexpensive seniors menu might be one reason why). So do hunters. They're catered to here. During the season, The Pauline Café opens earlier than usual for breakfast—4:30 a.m.—the better to feed the camouflaged.

"I'm here at 3:30," said Maynard Miller, a retired deputy and father of former owner Rachel Hughes. "I make the fatback gravy, grits and sausage and bacon and country ham. That's what I was raised on."

It's a repertoire that keeps the hunters coming. Hash browns, tomatoes, and cheese or gravy for your grits are extras for plates that include eggs, omelets, biscuits, toast, and other breakfast meats including bologna. But cereal, oatmeal–even French toast and pancakes–are on the menu too.

Breakfast was over by the time I pulled in at 11:25 a.m. It was Election Day: rainy, cold and, outside on Highway 56, silent. Not so inside. The grill was sizzling, the phone was ringing and the patrons and help were not speaking in murmured tones. People here will ask you to pass your salt and sugar if there isn't any at their table. And they will say thank you.

"Best local feel" is the description three Wofford students gave the café in their book *Exit Ramps and Cheese Grits: Hole in the Wall Adventures in the Carolinas*. Two of the students met me there. While I passed the bowl of chicken stew (brothy, with milk and corn, with a whole long package of saltines), author Jeremy Bishop passed me stickers for Republican candidates. A government major, Jeremy is thinking about law school. Co-author Richard Webb is heading toward medicine. In January 2002, they and their buddy Jeff Goree spent their Wofford interim session researching, writing and printing their book. The result is a paperback covering 28 restaurants between Columbia and Asheville–always off the interstate, never a chain. The Pauline Café, in business since 1974, clearly qualifies.

"This is one of the better models," Richard said, looking around at the customers at the counter, many in overalls. Jeremy knocked on the cinderblock walls and discussed his appreciation for one-of-a-kind places. "You can go to a regular restaurant, like Outback, but this restaurant cooks food like your grandma cooked food. It's the homestyle deal."

The special of the day was cubed steak, green butterbeans, corn on the cob, rice and gravy and a choice of chocolate cake or carrot cake. The hash plate–pork and beef hash, slaw, fries and onion rings–is Maynard Miller's creation, as well as the popular vegetable soup and chicken stew. "That man's been making homemade sausage and good country ham and he does more for the community," said Jim Hamrick, a Pauline resident and twice-a-day customer. "He delivers Meals on Wheels and his wife sits with elderly people. I couldn't keep up with him."

Hamrick remembers when Miller, still working as a deputy, only had to pick up the phone to call in people he had a warrant for. He knew residents so well there was no need to go after them. Hamrick appreciates what Miller and his family have done for Pauline through their place of business. "This is where you find out who's sick, who's in the hospital, who needs help."

A little local information with your meal can't be discounted.

- Aïda Rogers

Former waitress Stacey Doremus bought Rachel's Pauline Café in November 2007 and altered its name, but not much else. Teachers, hunters and retirees still clamor for the daily special and Maynard Miller's famous hash plate. One big change Ms. Doremus made is to open the café on Tuesday and Thursday evenings. Now that's good news for people who like a hot filling meal.

- A. R.

Pixie and Bill's, Clemson
Pickens County

Pixie and Bill's, U.S. 123 Bypass, Clemson; (864) 645-1210. Open for lunch Monday-Friday, 11:30 a.m. -1:30 p.m. and for dinner Monday-Saturday, 5:30-9:30 p.m. Closed on Sunday. Credit cards accepted. Reservations recommended on weekends. No smoking. www.tigergourmet.com. Lunch: inexpensive to moderate. Dinner: moderate to very expensive.

Prime Rib and Plaid Carpet

Pixie and Bill's in Clemson is a friendly restaurant. It was started by friends, it was run by friends, and you can be darn proud to take your friends there. That's why the best way to appreciate it is with friends–preferably old ones.

This reporter found herself in just that situation one rainy July evening. Her dining companions were Oconee County's finest: Walhalla Mayor Julian Stoudemire and his wife Roddey, his law partner Lowell Ross of Seneca, and pharmacist Ken Johns and his wife Juanita, a Walhalla town councilwoman. It was Friday night, and Roddey and Juanita don't cook on Friday night.

"It's a philosphy," Roddey explained, adding she'd like to have her usual: Pixie and Bill's beef kabobs. "They're glorious," she said. "Nectar of the gods."

Eating out on Friday night is this group's special tradition. But Pixie and Bill's is a tradition, too, as famous for its plaid carpet and pineapple motif as it is for its prime rib. "I never eat prime rib anywhere else. There's just no point," said Lowell, himself an esteemed cook known for his talents with prime rib.

"It's so good, it kinda melted in my mouth," noted Cort Flint, a Greenville lawyer who was dining with his wife and a friend. Lowell had sent me to their table to get a few good quotes, and a good idea it was, because here's what they supplied:

"I thought I'd died and gone to heaven," Suzanne Flint said, raving about the seafood platter she'd had the last time they were here. Because she's from Georgetown, her husband respects her opinion on such matters. "I tasted her seafood" (on the previous visit), "and I had a tough time deciding whether to get that or the prime rib," he said. As is often the case at Pixie and Bill's, the prime rib won out.

So busy was this reporter talking to the Flints that her spinach salad arrived at the other table and sat there untouched for many minutes. At the waiter's strong suggestion, another salad was brought out; the warm vinaigrette dressing had cooled, he explained. It's this picky attention to detail and open attitude to customers–Suzanne Flint later sent her fudge crepe dessert over to be sampled–that makes Pixie and Bill's an upstate institution.

"It was the first tricounty restaurant specializing in fine dining," says Bob Lusk, an Anderson lawyer who remembers when it opened in 1971. "People come from Anderson, Pickens, and Oconee counties, and Toccoa, Athens, and Greenville."

Drink in one hand, gesturing with the other, Lusk looked quite at home conducting an impromptu tour. But it *was* home years ago, when he washed dishes, waited tables, cooked and became a maître d' while going to Clemson University.

With the campus nearby, Clemson University memorabilia is evident, but not overwhelming. An IPTAY plaque and a framed orange tiger greet you as you wait to be seated. Otherwise, Pixie and Bill's is tasteful and subtle, a big city restaurant in a small town.

"I've had somebody call and say, 'Can you buy me an anniversary card and have it on the table?' In a big city, you can't do that," said Elaine Grogan, who with Bob and her husband Dan has worked here since the restaurant opened. They know better than anyone else how flooded it gets during football and basketball seasons. "We've had so many regulars coming for so long we don't even have to put their reservations down."

Our table was 100 percent Gamecock, but everyone was comfortable in this Tiger den. No doubt the celebrities Pixie and Bill's has served felt equally at home.

"We had Burt Reynolds and Ned Beatty when they filmed *Deliverance*, and Bob Hope, Bruce Jenner, and Susan Clark," Bob and Elaine were saying.

"Anyone else?" I wondered.

"Danny Ford," Bob said. "What other legend could you want?"

- Aïda Rogers

Owned by the Corontzes family since the fall of 1991, Pixie and Bill's is a magnet for Clemson townsfolk, students, and Tiger alumni. There is now lake access to the restaurant via the Larry Abernathy Waterfront Park on Lake Hartwell. You can even call the restaurant for boatside delivery (be sure to call for availability of this service). The Corontzes also now own the Calhoun Corners Restaurant at 103 Clemson Street.

- *Tim Driggers*

Renato Ristorante, Spartanburg
Spartanburg County

Renato Ristorante, 221 East Kennedy Street, Spartanburg; (864) 585-7027. Open for lunch Monday-Friday 11:30 a.m.-2 p.m. Dinner Monday-Saturday 5:30-11 p.m. Reservations recommended for dinner. Credit cards and checks accepted. Smoking section available. Lunch: inexpensive. Dinner: moderate to very expensive.

Yes, This is Definitely "Good in Your Mouth"

Everything comes together at Renato Ristorante in Spartanburg. Music, atmosphere, and food have been choreographed for an experience, not a feed. So when trusty photographer Pat Wright and I came together for a late Tuesday lunch, our conversation was every bit as sophisticated.

"We are really sinning," I told Pat as we dipped our crusty Ciabatta in a bowl of olive oil. "Sinning is good," he responded. "It builds character."

We built a lot of character during our two-hour sojourn at Renato. This is not a place where you scamper in and out. You want to dawdle, and revel in the voices of Dean Martin and Frank Sinatra while you're sipping and dipping. Renato's olive oil is 100 percent pure—imported from Italy, flavored with sage, rosemary, and garlic. As my friend Martha Stewart would say, "It's a good thing." I would say it's a very good thing, and I would be there now if a little thing like work didn't get in the way.

We started with the Fritto Misto del Golfo. This appetizer of shrimp, scallops, and calamari is lightly fried and served with marinara sauce. There are six appetizers, and on this day, the special was Oysters From Heaven—steamed on the half shell, with spinach and roasted red peppers.

Entrees were a bit more difficult to choose. The menu is lengthy, with pastas, salads, soups, and veal, beef, chicken, and fish. Popular items include the Vitello (veal) Salto in Bocca, veal medallions sautéed with sage leaves, garlic, and white wine and finished with fresh mozzarella and Italian prosciutto ham. Our waiter told us "Salto in Bocca" means "Good in your mouth." The menu is good about translating basic Italian words.

Linguine con Gamberi Positano was Pat's pick. Jumbo shrimp sautéed in olive oil, garlic, and white wine, tossed with al dente linguine noodles, this entrée made our Boy Photographer a Happy Boy Photographer. I was burrowing into Renato's all-time most popular dish: Grouper alla Francescana. Black grouper, battered with egg and Parmesan, then sautéed in olive oil, garlic, Mediterranean capers, natural lemon juice, and white wine, this entrée—as all others—is served with a choice of pasta or vegetables. As the southern phrase goes, it was "a gracious plenty."

The genius behind Renato is Renato Marmolini. He left the family shoe business in Florence, Italy, for a culinary career in the U.S. He retains partnership in Ciao Bella, a restaurant in Chicago, but has settled happily in Spartanburg. It wasn't easy; he was brought to the Hub City as chef for another Italian restaurant. When it folded shortly after, he was left with $20 in his pocket. Thanks to a loan from some good friends and his cooking skills, he launched his namesake restaurant. That was 1989.

Because Renato has one parent from southern Italy and another from northern Italy, he figures he can serve the best of both regions at his restaurant. Leaving the shoe business was the right thing to do. "Too many headaches in that. But to see people eating and happy, that makes me happy. This is wonderful."

- Aïda Rogers

Besides serving their classic Italian cuisine, Renato and wife Stephanie host live musical events featuring special menu pricing, nostalgic reminiscing and trivia. They've celebrated the music of Frank Sinatra with "Mangia in Italiano" and "Devine Divas", recreating the stylings of world famous operatic divas. Extremely popular are the Pesce (fish) entrees, which include Jumbo Shrimp, Norwegian King Salmon (grilled and then sautéed), Bluefin Tuna, Atlantic Swordfish, and a Tuscan plate of fresh cut fish and shellfish served over linguine pasta.

- Tim Driggers

Rick Erwin's West End Grill, Greenville
Greenville County

Rick Erwin's West End Grill, 648 South Main Street in Greenville; (864) 232-8999. Open Monday-Thursday, 5-10:30 p.m. and Friday-Saturday, 5-11 p.m. Closed Sunday. Reservations required. Credit cards accepted. Smoking only at bar. www.rickerwins.com. Moderate to very expensive.

"An Extraordinary Dining Experience"

A modern, stylish restaurant with classic steakhouse hardwood décor, Rick Erwin's West End Grill offers quality steaks and seafood with a decidedly masculine appeal. Don't expect to find sushi or quiche anywhere near the place. This is where the John Wayne crowd eats and the other crowd runs for cover.

I had been seated only a short time when I discovered this was a serious steakhouse —a really serious steak house. How serious? Well, when my server brought me the same knife Jim Bowie used to defend the Alamo, I knew there were two distinct dining possibilities awaiting: One, the steak was going to be so thick it would take a Bowie knife to cut, or secondly, a herd of Angus cattle would stampede through the restaurant and I'd need the knife to claim my dinner. I didn't relish the thought of wrestling a half-ton steer into submission, but after devouring a mouth-watering, 20-ounce certified Angus bone-in ribeye, I think the risk would have been worth taking. Not that I needed the Bowie knife to cut the steak; it was tender, moist, flavorful and all meat, no gristle or fat. It filled the plate and had a wonderful aroma reminiscent of campfire grilling on the back 40 of a Montana cattle spread. This was one good cut of meat.

My experience was just what Rick Erwin wanted when he opened his restaurant in May 2005 a few blocks from The Peace Center. A 28-year veteran of the restaurant wars, Erwin instilled his outgoing personality into the eatery. "People want to see Rick when they come to the restaurant," said general manager Colin McDonald. "He makes his guests feel welcome and comfortable."

Colin takes pride providing an enjoyable dining adventure. "I want our positive energy to be transferred to the guests," he said. "If somebody walks out the door unhappy, then we've all failed. We strive to provide the full package to our clientele; always making sure that all requests are met." Colin is up to the task, roaming the restaurant like a ringmaster, orchestrating everyone's enjoyment, intent on creating just the right mood.

Most entrees are served a la carte. Not satisfied with merely hardening my arteries, I decided to firmly cement them shut. I chose the three-cheese macaroni and cheese and cheesy mashed potatoes to accompany my ribeye. Okay, my side dishes were not too good for the ol' cholesterol, but they were a big hit with my taste buds.

Other carnivorous delights are the 14-ounce certified Angus bone-in New York strip, certified Angus filet mignon, rack of lamb, veal porterhouse, prime sirloin, and Niman Ranch bone-in pork loin chop. Fresh seafood abounds. On the menu are sashimi-grade tuna, Chilean sea bass, Parmesan-crusted grouper, salmon stacks, crabcakes, and lobster tail. Rick Erwin's also has an extensive wine list. "A great steak and good wine go hand in hand," Colin said. "It doesn't have to be a special occasion to enjoy a nice bottle of wine." For dessert try the Carnegie Deli cheesecake—yes, *the* Carnegie Deli cheesecake, flown in from New York City daily.

An attentive staff, unbeatable ambience, and succulent dining selections make Rick Erwin's a must on the Greenville dining scene. "We go to extraordinary lengths to serve and prepare the finest steak possible for an extraordinary dining experience," Rick said. Mission accomplished.

- Tim Driggers

Saskatoon, Greenville
Greenville County

Saskatoon, 477 Haywood Road in the Regency Square Shopping Center, Greenville; (864) 297-7244. Open Monday-Thursday, 5-10 p.m., Friday-Saturday, 5-11 p.m. and Sunday, 5-9 p.m. Reservations suggested, especially for Friday and Saturday evenings. Credit cards and checks accepted. No smoking. www.saskatoonrestaurant.com. Moderate to expensive.

The Northwest Comes to Greenville

There was a moment of shock when the three desserts arrived. Three pairs of eyes bugged out, and three mouths dropped open. Silence, until then absent from this giggly table, swooped upon us like some great prehistoric bird. Then came the noise. Shrieking, forking, squealing, pure disbelief. "It's, like, six inches tall," exclaimed Erin, staring at the chocolate mousse pie. Courtney and I were equally dumbfounded by the whiskey sauced-bread pudding and Bailey's white chocolate cheesecake. "You didn't tell me it was so tall," Erin told our server, almost accusingly.

Looking back, I don't know why we were surprised. Everything about Saskatoon, a "Northwoods Hunting Lodge" in Greenville, is a surprise. Even though you park in a typical shopping center, this restaurant is far from that. With its antlered light fixtures and hanging canoe, Saskatoon takes you far from the American South. If not for the comfort, you'd think you were on a rugged camping trip on the banks of a cold rushing river, schools of salmon just a spear tip away.

"We're not just serving run-of-the-mill fare," understates Edmund Woo, owner-manager. "Trail Guide" is the title on his business card–appropriate for a place that serves antelope and elk, emu and kangaroo. Wild game, fish, and steaks are the fare; quiche lovers best go elsewhere. "Lodge Specialties" include appetizers of mustard-fried alligator tail and wild game sausage of smoked buffalo, duck and elk sausages. Hickory-grilled antelope is farm-raised in Texas, then marinated and grilled in Cabernet wine ginger sauce. Tonight's mixed grill is quail, llama, and beef skirt steak, grilled over hickory. Little wonder Saskatoon jumps on Father's Day.

"I personally like kangaroo, which is one of our features this evening," our waiter told us. Accustomed to describing the unusual, he helped us choose an appetizer special: elk filet with red wine ginger sauce and portabella mushrooms. Ostrich and antelope taste like filet or venison, he explained, mentioning their low fat content. Maybe that's why each of us ordered thusly. "Oh, how tender," Courtney moaned about her emu, slicing it with her fork. Erin, *Sandlapper's* summer intern, ordered caribou, declaring it akin to beef jerky. She smiled the whole time. I ordered ostrich, which was topped by a "beggar's purse"–a pastry filled with carrots and mushrooms. I think we felt like explorers, in our naïve, white-girl way.

Saskatoon is popular with businessmen during the week, and for social gatherings on weekends. The woodsy atmosphere, with snowshoes on the wall and a big fireplace, evokes Jack London and dog sleds in a world of business suits and barbecue. Salmon is prepared Northwest Native American-style, oven-roasted on cedar slats. Buffalo is from Minnesota, rainbow trout from Idaho. Beef is Midwestern, corn-fed and aged. Wines are from Washington State and Oregon.

Don't come if you're not hungry. Entrées include a choice of Caesar or mixed green salads, a loaf of wheat bread with blueberry, cinnamon and plain butters and a variety of potatoes: "golden roasted," baked or roasted garlic mashed. The last is Saskatoon's trademark.

"What we're serving has a certain level of integrity to it," Edmund said. And, as our girly group would say, "it tastes good too."

- Aïda Rogers

Edmund Woo continues to bring the unique tastes of the Northwestern United States outdoors to the dinner plates of upstate South Carolinians. The menu is revised every 4-6 weeks, rotating Elk Tenderloin, Ostrich Filet, Buffalo Flank Steak, Pecan Encrusted Salmon, Sizzlin' Rainbow Trout, and the Mixed Grill trio. For those less adventurous, there's Campfire Chicken, pork tenderloin, ribeye, filet mignon, and sirloin steaks, a blackened prime rib, and citrus shrimp and scallop skewers. Each comes with a suggestion for an accompanying wine. The casual, fine dining atmosphere is augmented by a full service bar.

- *Tim Driggers*

Skin Thrasher's, Anderson
Anderson County

Skin Thrasher's, 203 Hudgens Street, Anderson; (864) 225-9229. Open Tuesday-Saturday, 10:30 a.m.-6:50 p.m. Closed Sunday-Monday. Credit cards and checks accepted. No smoking. No reservations. www.skinshotdogs.com. Inexpensive.

"This is the *Only* Restaurant in South Carolina"

She was so careful, that quiet old lady, as she walked down the steps of the shabby building in the decaying neighborhood. She was careful not to miss a step in her heels, and careful not to drop the small brown bag she was holding. Not only did it contain her lunch; it contained one of the treasures of Anderson County: a hot dog from Skin

Thrasher's. "Nobody cooks a hot dog like they do" is what the locals say.

At "Skin's," people come for one thing: hot dogs. "Just say how many and how you want 'em," says Bob Chapman, who's come from Williamston with his brother-in-law Bonnard Roache. "Food's good, place is clean. This is the only restaurant in South Carolina."

Bob and Bonnard got a craving for a Skin's hot dog when they were across town on business. They love the hot dogs—they each get three—and they love the bottled drinks. Bonnard held up his bottled Diet Coke. "Do you know any place where you can still get that? Everything is cans and plastic and Styrofoam."

Not here. Skin's is like an old country store that went into the hot dog business and decided to keep a few extra items just in case. A big jar of pickles and Moon Pies sit on the counter. Crackers, chips and soft drinks are available; so are milk and beer. Dessert comes in the form of cold candy bars. But food wise, hot dogs are it. Your only decision is whether you want onions, mustard, mayo, hot sauce or the famous homemade chili.

"No plans to diversify," says Matt Thrasher, youngest son of Lloyd "Skin" Thrasher and his wife, Peggy. "We can't keep up with what we got now." That includes adding the fancier fixings—cheese, sauerkraut, slaw—which may be why Skin Thrasher's is so successful. "We give a good quality product at a reasonable price," Matt says. "And we treat everybody like family when they come in the door."

Skin's opened in Anderson's Toxaway mill village in 1946, when three mills were in operation. It wasn't unusual for Skin's to sell 300-400 hot dogs at a time to mill workers on shift. Skin Thrasher—named after an unfortunate teen-age haircut—started selling them five for a quarter when mill league baseball was popular.

The mills are closed now, but Skin's thrives at multiple locations. Some people believe the hot dogs are cooked in beer, which Matt will neither deny nor confirm. He will say they're a blend of pork and beef, made especially for Thrasher's by Greenwood Packaging. Matt eats four a day ("usually the mistakes") and is quick to say his cholesterol and blood pressure are fine.

At the Hudgens Street location, Skin's seats 35. Aside from a few tables, people sit at a large horseshoe-shaped counter. Here you can see the kind of people who love Skin Thrasher's: "construction workers, street bums, lawyers, doctors, judges, Secret Service agents," Matt says. Jimmy Carter has sampled the hot dogs, though he was hiding in the back of the Presidential sedan while Secret Servicemen fetched him wieners to go. "Now this is a folk tale," Matt will tell you. "I'm not sure it's true."

Why not lie for the sake of a good story?

He shakes his head. "That's one thing about Thrashers. We're honest and decent-living. My daddy would say this is a decent living, and I thought that meant a good living, as in money. But he meant being decent."

- Aïda Rogers

When Sandlapper *visited Skin Thrasher's in 1995, it included three restaurants in Anderson. Now there are 11 locations in the Upstate. The recipe for the chili—made fresh daily at each location—remains a closely guarded secret. What owners Matt Thrasher, brother Mike, and brother-in-law Wayne Harbin will reveal is that 10,000 hot dogs are served a week; that's about 20 hot dogs downed each minute of the business day. Add the 6,000 pounds of chili consumed per month and it's apparent Skin Thrasher's sells a whole bunch of hot dogs to a whole bunch of people. "We're a family owned business operating much the same as when we first opened in 1946," Matt said. Chances are Skin's will never change. For hot dog lovers, that's just fine.*

- *Tim Driggers*

Stax's Omega Diner, Greenville
Greenville County

Stax's Omega Diner, 72 Orchard Park Drive, Greenville; (864) 297-6639. Open Sunday-Thursday, 6:30 a.m. until midnight; Friday-Saturday, 6:30-3 a.m. Reservations accepted for large parties. Credit cards and checks accepted. Smoking allowed only at bar. www.staxs.com/omega. Inexpensive to moderate.

You Name It, They Got It

If you can't find something you like at Stax's Omega Diner, you've got a serious problem. Here are the numbers: 16 salads, 51 sandwiches, 20 omelettes, seven kinds of Eggs Benedict, 12 meat-and-threes, 10 varieties of waffles and French toast. Then there are entrées that range from the rugged (liver and onions) to the refined (chicken cordon bleu). Stir-Fry comes four ways (shrimp, chicken, steak, vegetable), and the 41 side items include such diversities as sauerkraut and Italian sausage. The 5,000-square-foot bakery next door turns out fresh bread every day—and 30 different desserts.

"Any place that's got Sudden Death by Chocolate on the menu, that's for me," says Joy Simpson, a Charlestonian who always stops at Stax's Omega when in Greenville on business. Though tonight she'll order the Chocolate Chip Waffle, she frequently tries

An omelette with "American Fried Potatoes" at Stax's Omega Diner.

their omelettes. Like many, Joy is amazed by the variety and volume. "You're reading along and you see country cooking and all of a sudden there's Crab Benedict, Eggs Florentine and Greek stuff. I mean look at this: You can get a lox omelette. Now tell me where else in Greenville can you get a lox omelette?"

Joy is preaching to the choir with our third companion, Chris Worthy. A Simpsonville resident and writer, Chris is an Omega fan. So is her family. Their two children rush to the two aquariums, and find much happiness in the cheese fries and chicken strips. "Lots of ketchup" is how Chris describes it. "You order something one time and you order it the next time you come, it's exactly the same. It's wonderful."

A vegetarian, Chris orders the mushroom and cheese omelette. Like the other omelettes (Denver, Greek, Farmers, Spanish, Italian, Three Cheese, shrimp and more), they're served with "American Fried Potatoes" or grits and a choice of rye, wheat, white, and Greek toast.

I'm the one who's torn. Stuffed French Toast, filled with cottage cheese, sour cream, and cream cheese, topped with strawberries, apples or blueberries) draws my eye. So does one of the "Greek Specialties"—Beef Tips and Shrimp Santorini (sautéed tips and shrimp with onion, tomato, Kalamata Olives and Feta Cheese). When our friendly waitress tells us the Santorini is "The Bomb," I order it. It's a big order, accompanied by Greek potatoes, Greek salad and sautéed vegetables.

Appetizers are exotic (Dolmades, or rice-stuffed grape leaves), and everyday (fried mushrooms, mozzarella cheese sticks). We aim for the one we've never heard of: Saganaki. "Flaming Greek Cheese," Saganaki is prepared table-side, with chefs lighting a skillet of goat cheese. Spread it on crackers or bread. Say *ummmm*.

Billing itself as "Greenville's Big City Diner," Stax's Omega is one of six Stax enterprises. There's the upscale Peppermill, Grill and Piano Bar, the bakery and a catering company. The Omega opened in 1988, seats 350 and keeps late hours. All derived from Stax's Original, opened by George Stathakis in 1975. Serving Greek food was "just automatic," he reflects.

George grew up in Greenwood, a second-generation Greek working in his parents' restaurant, The Grill Café. His grandfather, from Sparta, and his grandmother, from Kalymnos, came to America in 1914.

With the help of partner Stanley Koumoustiotis, a native of Greece who'd cooked in some of Chicago's finest restaurants, the Stax empire grew. "We stuck our necks out back in the mid-'70s and did things people in Greenville didn't do," George says now. Stanley's tableside cooking, flambé desserts, and European entrées were novel.

Not anymore. Greenville in the 21st century is sophisticated and international. George concedes Greenville's not the place he moved to in 1969. At that point, he'd just left the Navy and didn't know where else to go. His parents had moved to Greenville, so here he came. "God bless 'em, it's one of the best things that ever happened to me."

- Aïda Rogers

I don't have nearly enough fingers and toes to count all the items Stax's Omega Diner serves on its breakfast, lunch, and dinner menus. I guess that's why breakfast is available all day. Very possibly, it'll take you that long just to decide. Some of the dishes mentioned when Sandlapper *first visited in autumn 2003 are no longer served, but a ton of others have taken their place. George and Stanley now have 15 salads, 43 sandwiches, 17 omelettes, 3 kind of eggs, 17 meat-and-threes, and 8 different "Stax Stacks." At lunch and dinner, you can also order the multi-dished "Greek Faves" and "Italian Faves." I think you get the idea. If you want to eat it, Stax's Omega Diner probably has it, and if they don't, then it's most likely in some alien super galactic food service transport orbiting I-385 over the Upstate this very moment.*

- *Tim Driggers*

The Steak House Cafeteria, Walhalla
Oconee County

The Steak House Cafeteria, 316 East Main Street in Walhalla; (864) 638-3311. Open Tuesday-Saturday, 11 a.m.-8 p.m. and Sunday, 10:45 a.m.-3 p.m. Closed Monday. No reservations. VISA, MasterCard and checks accepted. No smoking. www.thesteakhousecafeteria.com. Inexpensive.

Now *This* is Fried Chicken!

Despite its name, The Steak House Cafeteria in Walhalla isn't famous for its steak. It's the chicken that brings the crowds–some from as far away as Atlanta. Those would be travelers on their way to the mountains, who know a trip up winding roads is best done on a settled stomach. You can get a very satisfied stomach here, especially after a plate of Abduulltef "Abed" Yassen's famous "Arabian Rooster Fried Chicken." Somehow, that chicken has come to symbolize this Palestinian's tasty merger of Middle East and American South.

"He calls this place 'The M & M,' for 'The Methodist and the Muslim,' " says his niece Tonja Lee Almajjar, the manager. Like her aunt Gloria, Tonja grew up in Westminster and married a man from Jerusalem. Tonja's husband, Ammar Almajjar, works at the family-owned, family-style restaurant, too. "Everybody just helps everybody; nobody's a boss," Tonja says.

Walk in the door and you're immediately faced with Abed's Coca-Cola collection. Move through the cafeteria line and notice the olive wood camels on a windowsill. Pay at the register and realize you've gotten a big lunch for a reasonable price. Besides the faithful fried chicken, you'll find other southern favorites, including baked ham, stew beef, chicken livers, pork chops, barbecue pork, chicken pot pie, hamburger steak, and roast beef. Tonja says Gloria's influence on Abed is reflected in the cooking. "He was willing to try things, like turkey and dressing on Sunday. I mean, every Sunday. If we don't have it, people tell us 'you gotta have it!' "

The offerings don't come without imagination. Abed's spinach has Alfredo sauce, and his squash is coated with melted cheese. His baked potatoes are popular (stuffed with beef tips) and his rice-stuffed Cornish hens were a recent big seller. But those more comfortable with traditional home cooking find plenty to plunder in the sweet potato soufflé, candied carrots, and macaroni and cheese. It's clear that while Gloria Cleveland didn't convert her husband by faith (she met Abed on a mission trip to Jerusalem), she did by food.

Gloria and Abed bought The Steak House Cafeteria in 1973. Back then, it was known simply as The Steak House. But the rise in steakhouse chains propelled them to offer a varied menu with a wide range of vegetables, starches, salads, and desserts. The fried chicken, seasoned with a secret recipe, has prompted many locals to call it

The Chicken House.

"If you don't like that chicken, you don't like chicken," insists Don Blackwell, a correctional officer who's eaten here for years. "I was raised in the country, and it's hard to beat this."

At Easter, more than 600 orders of chicken were sold, Tonja reports. Football Saturdays are just as busy. Steaks do exist, but not as T-bones or filets. Here, they're hamburger, Salisbury and country-fried.

The seat of Oconee County, Walhalla attracts a diverse group of citizens. Ditto for The Steak House Cafeteria. Besides city and county employees, there are retirees who've adopted this mountain-lake area, Clemson students hungry for a home-cooked meal, and folks who love antique shopping (Walhalla's refurbished Main Street is bumper-to-bumper). When court's in session, judges, lawyers, jurors, and plaintiffs arrive. Many customers come every day. "We know what to put on their plates before they come through the line," Tonja says.

While they come for the food, they also come to see Abed. "The thing I'm most proud of is I'm a member of the community," Abed says. "I came from a foreign background to the land of The American Dream. It was always my dream to have a business of my own. They adopted me, and I never felt segregation or racism."

Our chatty threesome got quiet over plates of ham, lima and green beans, collards, rice and gravy, beef stew, and fried chicken. Our coconut cream pie and cheesecake disappeared fast. "I almost licked the bowl but I couldn't in front of all these people," said Rian Tompkins, 11, my energetic dining partner and niece.

Imagine the difficulty we would've had if the apple dumplings had been available. Wrapped in pastry and topped with caramel sauce, they appear alongside chocolate cream pie, strawberry shortcake, and red velvet and carrot cakes. All desserts but one are made here, and many of them are from old recipes.

For Abed, who worked in a hotel in Jerusalem, owning a Walhalla restaurant is heavenly. "If you live in Walhalla, you're closer to God," he declares. "The love of the people keeps me here."

- Aïda Rogers

The Steak House Cafeteria is your quintessential American family restaurant. It's just that here, the family is half-Palestinian and half-American by origin. The restaurant has always served cafeteria-style, with each food item priced individually. Abed and Gloria recently remodeled and expanded the dining room to accommodate upwards of 65 customers. Abed calls Walhalla "The Great Blue Hills of God." We'll shorten that a bit to describe The Steak House Cafeteria: It's simply "great."

- Tim Driggers

Sugar-n-Spice, Spartanburg
Spartanburg County

Sugar-n-Spice, 212 South Pine Street, Spartanburg; (864) 585-3991. Open 10 a.m.-10 p.m. Monday-Saturday. Closed Sunday. No reservations. No smoking. MasterCard and Visa accepted. Inexpensive.

"This is the Best Place in Spartanburg to Eat"

Harry and John Stathakis grew up as friends in the same village in their native Greece. Immigrating to America, the pair opened Sugar-n-Spice in 1961 as a place for students at local high schools and Wofford and Converse colleges. "They wanted a drive-in serving hot dogs, hamburgers, and fried chicken," explained present owner Pete Copses. Over the years, business grew and the menu expanded, resulting in the remodeling of the restaurant into its present state in 1976. Curb service continued until the early 1980s. All that remains of the original drive-in are the curb awnings and its short-order favorites.

Danny Waldrep of Spartanburg has been coming here for almost 40 years. "Back then it was a hangout for hot cars and motorcycles," he said. "There was always a debate in the parking lot as to whose car was the fastest. We'd leave the drive-in and go to the back roads to find out." Although he fondly remembers the car hops and intercoms, Danny prefers "seeing the food cooking." His favorite? The cheeseburger.

I ordered the requisite cheeseburger and Paul McCravy, my brother in Cheeseburgerdom, chose the small souvlaki plate. He also ordered the crinkle-cut fries, while I selected onion rings. Both of us ordered Cole slaw, which was good, not too mayonnaise-heavy. The cheeseburger was tender, tasty, and flavorful. "These are great grilled onions," Paul said as he sliced a healthy portion of it from my plate. I didn't mind; it was huge.

Paul then spotted an old Wofford College classmate. Skipper Lancaster has been a regular since it opened. "All the high schools in Spartanburg had different drive-ins they'd go to," he said. "The kids from Boiling Springs and Chesnee all came to Sugar-n-Spice. We'd back our cars into the parking spaces and sit on the hoods."

Skipper ate lunch here every day after he graduated from Wofford. "I ate everything on the menu, but the cheeseburger a-plenty" (with onion rings and fries) "and steak a-plenty were my favorite sandwiches. In fact, when I walked through the door they'd throw a cheeseburger on the grill. They knew what I wanted."

For a hometown guy, this is the place for sustenance both social and culinary. "I always meet people I know," Skipper said. "The owners are here all the time and they treat me like a member of the family. This is the best place in Spartanburg to eat."

Paul has his own description. "In the 1960s, when cruising was king, Sugar-n-Spice was where you wanted to be and be seen," he said. "If you had a hot car, nothing attracted attention like 'chirping' your tires when leaving the parking lot. For some, it was the automotive burp after a great cheeseburger and fries at the curb. Today, fine cheeseburgers and Greek specialties are main meals inside. As a reminder of the past, the car hop awnings still stand as a remembrance of the time when it was cool to eat in your car with the A/C running."

- Tim Driggers

T-60 Grill, Fair Play
Oconee County

T-60 GRILL, 340 Port Bass Drive, Fair Play; (864) 972-2860. Open April-October, Tuesday-Thursday, 11 a.m.-9 p.m. and Friday-Saturday, 11 a.m.-10 p.m. Closed on Monday and Sunday. Reservations accepted. Credit cards and checks accepted. Smoking allowed on deck. www.t-60grill.com. Moderate to expensive.

This Coach Can Cook!

When Joe Crosby retired from football in 2001, owning a restaurant was probably the last thing on his mind. After nine successful seasons as head coach at Savannah State College and Morris Brown College in Atlanta, Coach Joe decided that instead of teaching kids to block and tackle, he and the Mrs. would move to Lake Hartwell near the town of Fair Play and start a new career selling real estate. Selling property had to be a lot less hectic than the pressures of college athletics.

Then came the fateful summer day. "I was taking a lady by boat to look at a house on Lake Hartwell," Coach recalled. "It was nearing noon and she wanted lunch. There was no place to eat and she was really disappointed. When I got home that evening, I told my wife that I had almost lost a sale because there wasn't a restaurant on the lake." That's when the light bulb in Coach's noggin popped on.

"I decided I would do it," he said. "People thought I was crazy when I told them I was going to open a restaurant alongside my house. I heard a lot of 'you're going to do what?', but I prayed on it and came to the conclusion that a lot of people who lived on the lake would like to stay on the lake to eat out."

Joe was right and now they come in droves from on and off the lake to eat at the T-60 Grill on Lake Hartwell off Scenic South Carolina Highway 11. And just how did Coach decide on a name for his restaurant? "We decided to name it after the buoy floating out on the water in front of my house," he said. "A buoy is really a guide and the name T-60 hopefully lets a boater know they're getting close to our restaurant." Diners apparently have no trouble finding the restaurants, especially on the nights Coach's famous low country boil is on the menu.

I discovered that the low country boil is indeed a thing of beauty; a heaping mound of Dungeness crab legs, kielbasa sausage, red potatoes, and corn cob marinated in Coach's world-famous special seasoning. "I've tasted the seasonings in Texas and Louisiana and this is the best," declared Chet Reynolds of Independence, Missouri. "It's spicy, but not too hot. It won't make you break out in a sweat." My food was sprinkled with the muddy red coating of the seasoning and the taste was excellent.

The low country boil is served on Tuesday, Thursday, and Saturday. "I cook about 150 pots a night," Coach said. "People come from everywhere and you definitely need a reservation those nights."

Other favorites are Coach's gumbo, the crab corn chowder, and the main course meals of the Buckhead Steak Sandwich, Buoy Burger, the Blackened Salmon BLT, the 12-ounce rib eye, and the crab cake and shrimp dinner. There are nightly specials, including prime rib ("to die for" say Ben Sibert) and the traditional surf and turf.

"When people come to the T-60 Grill, we want them to relax and enjoy the casual atmosphere and view," Coach Joe said.

Coach, you don't have anything to worry about. The T-60 Grill is definitely an enjoyable stop on Lake Hartwell for the terminally hungry.

- Tim Driggers

Coach Joe still serves his famous low country boil at the Lake Hartwell location, although he closed his other T-60 Grill in McCormick County. He has a popular catering service, too. When you order the crab boil at Hudson's Smokehouse in Lexington, that's Coach's secret seasoning on the plate.

- T. D.

Twigs, Landrum
Spartanburg County

Twigs, 130 North Trade Avenue, Landrum; (864) 457-5155. Open Monday-Saturday, 11 a.m.-9 p.m. Closed Sunday. Credit cards and local checks accepted. Reservations highly recommended. Limousine service available. No smoking. Lunch: inexpensive to moderate. Dinner: moderate to expensive.

A Break From the Holiday Madness

You might ask, why in the name of Ebenezer Whatchamacallum would anyone drive 100 miles to the foothills of the Blue Ridge to purchase Christmas presents? Well, I was told to go there. Of course, I'm glad I followed this prime directive, for Landrum has a wealth of gift shops, antique stores, and restaurants in its pedestrian-friendly downtown. This is where Twigs enters the picture.

Mosey up the main drag of East Rutherford and take a right on North Trade Street and you'll soon happen upon Twigs. Can't miss it. Wouldn't want to. Located in a renovated circa 1911 bank building, Twigs opened in 1997 and, for the past several Decembers, that's where I've spent a pleasant lunch hour between perusing the aisles of the always-fascinating Landrum Hardware, investigating the used book inventory at the many antique stores in town, and taking a look-see in the myriad gift shops.

"Casually elegant" is how local real estate developer John Grambling describes Twigs. In a town jealous of preserving its historic landscape, Twigs is a pleasant accompaniment to Landrum's quaint nature. With its attractive wood motif, accented by scattered plants and–yes, plenty of twig adornments–the restaurant embodies the quiet beauty of the surrounding mountain backdrop. At Christmastime, that peacefulness pervades the restaurant. There are no eat-and-dash shoppers, no maddening clatter, just diners enjoying a finely crafted meal against a background of ambient seasonal melodies.

Helmut Zeigler was brought on board as executive chef by owner Barbara Britt in 2007. A native of Munich, Germany, Helmut has worked in restaurants throughout the world.

Although he learned to cook as a child "on the chair next to grandma," Helmut's culinary style blends several distinctive influences. "I have eclectic tastes," he said. "My roots are in traditional German fare, but stops between Charleston and New Orleans have brought about an appreciation for low country cooking." Not surprisingly, Helmut's signature dish is wiener schnitzel, served on Twigs' Tuesday evening German menu. As for low country favorites, he recommends his bourbon fried shrimp, andouille sausage, and spicy tasso ham served over Carolina stone-ground creamy cheese grits. Another specialty comes from nearby mountain streams. "My rainbow trout is unique," he said. "I serve it with shrimp, capers, and artichokes in a tomato based sauce. For the serious steak eater, there's the filet served at the occasional Twigs' wine dinner. "It's awesome," Helmut said. "I prepare it with a garlic balsamic reduction and sides of mashed potatoes and squash."

Joe Erwin moved from New York City to the Hunting Country between Tryon and Columbus, North Carolina in 1976. Joe, a retired professor of piano and keyboards at The Juilliard School, and wife Kathleen make a habit of eating at Twigs several times a month. "It's the closest thing to a gourmet restaurant you can get here," he said. Kathleen likes the crab cakes ("they're all crab") on the lunch menu, while Joe usually opts for the tenderloin steak sandwich. "It's very tender, just right," he said. "The tenderloin is not just choice steak, it's prime quality." Kathleen values the atmosphere. "What they've done with the twigs is so creative and natural. Joe adds another superlative. "Twigs always has excellent food and the prices are quite reasonable. And the wait staff is gracious, attentive, and pleasant."

My lunch at Twigs was highlighted by a bowl of smoked herb tomato bisque. On a blustery winter's day, it was the perfect means to chase away the cold. The soup was creamy, thick, and absolutely delicious, with tasty bits of roasted tomato throughout. I paid the bisque my highest compliment, scraping the bowl until my spoon found every morsel. I added a sandwich of grilled chicken on an English muffin and was sufficiently fortified to complete my rounds about town.

"During the holidays, I traditionally bring my out-of-town friends to dine at Twigs," John Grambling said. "It's a restaurant I'm proud to take my guests. Twigs serves excellent food and never disappoints." What more can be said?

- Tim Driggers

Two Chefs Delicatessen and Market, Greenville
Greenville County

Two Chefs Delicatessen and Market, 1204 South Main Street, (Carolina First Plaza) Greenville; (864) 370-9336. Open Monday-Friday, 8:30 a.m.-7:30 p.m. Closed Saturday and Sunday. Two Chefs to Go, 8590 Pelham Road #29 in Greenville; (864) 284-9970. Monday-Friday 10 a.m.-8 p.m. and Saturday from 10 a.m.-5 p.m. Closed Sunday. No reservations. Credit cards and checks accepted. No smoking. www.twochefsdeli.com. Inexpensive.

Fast Gourmet in Contemporary Surroundings

If you're looking for an ordinary lunch, you won't get it here. Nuh-uh. Walk in and look at the menu. You can get a tuna melt, but it comes with capers, scallions, dill, and Havarti. There's nothing average about the chicken salad, either. You can get it Asian-style with mandarin oranges, cashews, lo-mien noodles, and sesame ginger vinaigrette. Or get it grilled with fresh pears. Chef Judy Balsizer isn't afraid to challenge the taste buds. And judging by the line of customers snaking outside the door, it's evident she's making taste buds very happy. "Everybody loves her wild rice and dried cranberry salad," manager Lisa Kilby reports.

You can try the wild rice salad as part of the Half & Half Combo, which provides a choice of two items: soup, "simple single" half-sandwich, or a variety of salads. Steve Marlow, a Greenville photographer whose works adorn the walls of Two Chefs, is one wild rice salad fan. He shared some with me: Besides dried cranberries, it has almonds and mandarin oranges.

Like many who work downtown, Steve and his wife Janie are regulars at Two Chefs.

It's a convenient stroll from their business, The Map Shop, on Coffee Street. Located just off the lobby in the Carolina First building, Two Chefs draws business people and shoppers who want a gourmet lunch fast. With its vibrant colors – purple, yellow, and red – and in such a modern structure, Steve feels he's in Atlanta, not Greenville. "This looks uptown, big-city," he notes. "Greenville is a little more traditional. But you look in here and the ambiance is very contemporary."

Steve and Janie have learned to order their favorites, the half sandwiches of pepper-crusted turkey and rosemary ham, with fruit salad and the wild rice salad. I was so flustered by the choices I gave up and ordered the special, tomato Florentine soup and a grilled cheese on rye. But it was smoked cheddar and Havarti on rye, and a lot of it: cheese oozed from the front and back of the sandwich. It was perfect for this cold, windy day.

Two Chefs is a two-part enterprise. While Judy, a Culinary Institute of America grad, runs Two Chefs Deli and Market downtown, her husband Bill runs Two Chefs To Go on Greenville's east side. Both from Ohio, the pair worked for Hyatt before landing here. Much of their appeal lies in their catering and take-out businesses. Box lunches and "Crafted Carryout" meals are available from both locations. On this menu are different lasagnas, chicken entrees, crab cakes, dilled salmon, barbecued ribs, individual pizzas, and numerous vegetable dishes. "We simplify things for people who are busy and want a nice meal for home," Kilby says. "You can come in for lunch and pick up your dinner at the same time."

Gourmet grocery items are available, along with coffees, teas, nuts, olives, and spices. Desserts are likewise exquisite, although simple brownies are a favorite, says pastry chef Janet Archer. Our trio took Judy's advice and sampled the tiramisu– individually made in a round, stacked form, with a coffee bean on top. We also had the peanut butter pie and a Meltaway Bar. This last goody should satisfy any craving for sweets with its combination of caramel, coconut and chocolate chips. Also in the dessert case: croissants, cookies, muffins, cheesecakes, and tarts.

The very fact that tarts are available clues you in to the Balsizers' expertise. But don't think Two Chefs is intimidating. Meals come on plastic and you order from a counter. But your choices are sublime, if you're the least bit adventurous.

- Aïda Rogers

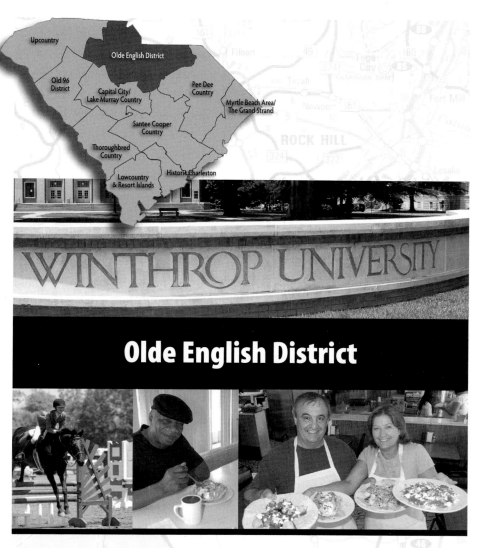

Olde English District

Chester, Chesterfield, Fairfield, Kershaw, Lancaster, Union & York Counties

Beth's Country Cooking, Pageland
Chesterfield County

Beth's Country Cooking, 1209 South Pearl Street, Pageland; (843) 672-2650. Open for breakfast Monday-Friday, 6-10 a.m. and lunch, 11 a.m.-2 p.m. Sunday's lunch buffet is 11 a.m.-2 p.m. Closed Saturday. Reservations not required. Credit cards and checks accepted. Inexpensive.

What Small Towns Are All About

I grew up in Lexington when Hite's Restaurant was *the* place to eat–before they tore it down in 1997. And even though a ton of chain restaurants have opened here since, Hite's never has been replaced. Sure, the barbecue was great and the cheeseburger deluxe out of this world, but food was just an excuse for folks to stampede there each day for lunch. They really went to meet friends and laugh, joke, and swap gossip.

It's a shame that sort of place doesn't exist anymore. Or so I thought until I discovered Beth's Country Cooking in Pageland. The parking lot was jammed–always a good sign–and inside, it was packed with people downing buffet fare and gabbing up a storm. It's a modest building, really a dining hall of sorts, with a single waitress running frantically between tables pouring tea and asking, "Everything all right, honey?"

After piling my plate about a foot high with fried chicken, a dab of meatloaf, a bite of lasagna and every vegetable grown in Chesterfield County, I grabbed a seat with a group at a large table in the middle of the dining room. We were strangers for all of about 10 seconds. After that, it seemed I was dining with old friends.

It's the atmosphere Beth Carroll envisioned when she opened in 1996. "I wanted a restaurant reasonably priced with a warm feeling," she said. "Pageland had mostly fast-food places and I thought the town needed a restaurant where you could sit down to a healthy, balanced meal." It doesn't hurt that Beth loves people and seeing them enjoy themselves. "I've been blessed with customers who eat here every day. They look forward to seeing each other, and I've become attached to them."

Peggy Strickland of nearby Monroe, North Carolina, concurs. "It's like eating with family here," she said. Her favorite: pork chops, Friday's lunch buffet feature. Co-worker Paulette Wilson, also of Monroe, agrees. "You go in some restaurants and the food tastes like it just came from some can," she said. "Beth home cooks everything."

Don Poole of Pageland comes every day. "Nothing is greasy," he said. "I was having a problem with high cholesterol and my doctor asked where I was eating my meals. I told him I ate at Beth's and he said, 'That's a good place to go.' If your doctor recommends a restaurant, then you know that's the place to eat." Don's favorites are country-style steak ("not too soft or crusty; it's perfect") and shrimp ("it's delicious; you can't get in the parking lot when Beth serves shrimp").

Michael Barrows and Harold Little, employees of First Health of the Carolinas, are regulars too. They love the fried chicken. "You can't beat Beth's chicken," Harold said. "I've tried for a long time to find something better, but I haven't found it."

What makes it so special? "It's nice and crunchy on the outside and always moist and tender on the inside," Michael observed. Like Peggy, both Harold and Michael were digging into the pineapple cake.

A different entrée is featured each day. On Monday, Beth brings out the meat loaf; on Tuesday, stew beef; on Wednesday, people line up for the Calabash shrimp. Thursdays there's flounder; Friday's specialty is pork chops–served fried, baked, or barbecued. Beth's is also open for breakfast.

"The restaurant business is in my blood," Beth said. "I don't care anything about becoming wealthy. I need to be around people and this restaurant provides the perfect opportunity." Beth, on behalf of your legion of diners, I'm glad you feel that way.

- Tim Driggers

Camden House of Pizza, Camden
Kershaw County

Camden House of Pizza, 545 DeKalb Street, Camden; (803) 432-1446. Open Monday-Thursday, 11 a.m.-2:30 p.m. for lunch and 5-10 p.m. for dinner. Open Friday and Saturday, 11 a.m.-11 p.m. Closed on Sunday. Visa and Mastercard accepted. No reservations necessary. Smoking allowed. Inexpensive to moderate.

Pizza, Stromboli, Manicotti ....

I really, truly was not hungry–nor was my fellow ED (explorer/diner)–when we happened across the Camden House of Pizza. I stood outside the door, staring at the menu, while something echoed in my head: "I've heard of this place, and I've heard it's good." I must have said it out loud, because a lady in a blue car leaned out from the window and confirmed it. "But be careful," she called out. "They give generous portions." She said she and her husband have to divide the strombolis.

Oh, those generous Greeks. Oh, my lack of willpower. "Just something to drink," I said to ED, as we settled into a cozy booth. A waitress brought menus, but we said maybe not. It was 3 p.m., and we just had eaten pizza for lunch. The next thing I knew, I was outside scouting my notebook, and ED was ordering the House Special Pizza. Well, at least he got a small one.

"It's good pizza," confirmed waitress Lee Martin, quickly bringing a doozy with black olives, green peppers, onions, pepperoni, sausage, and mushrooms. The crust on this pizza is wonderful–sweet and soft, easy to eat. No gnawing here.

Owned and operated by the Megadrosos family, Camden House of Pizza serves a variety of Greek and Italian dishes, as well as sub sandwiches, salads, and the basic American BLT. With its ceiling fans and posters of Greece, it's not particularly unusual, but it's affordable and comfortable, and the food is good. Families come here for supper, workers for lunch, and high school crowds before basketball games. On a Saturday afternoon at 3, a couple of young women are finishing a pizza and lingering over beer (Aegean, a Greek import, is available).

When Arthur and Soula Megadrosos bought the restaurant in 1990, they left the name alone but remodeled inside and added a few things to the menu. Daughter Elaine is a junior at Camden High; she works here after school and weekends. "At school, kids say, 'Oh, your parents have that little Greek place.' " To Elaine, everything at the restaurant is good. She laughed. "Today I'm craving chicken parmesan."

- Aïda Rogers

Soula and Arthur Megadrosos have retired and the restaurant is now operated by their daughter Georgia. Everything is pretty much the same including their delicious pizza. "Personal pita pizza" comes with all the standard ingredients. Also available are Greek dinners–souvlaki chicken, souvlaki pork and home-style spaghetti–and Italian dishes, including baked manicotti, baked lasagna, veal parmigiana, and stromboli. Best sellers are the Greek and Italian Stromboli.

- *Tim Driggers*

Carolina Restaurant and Steak House, Chesterfield
Chesterfield County

Carolina Restaurant and Steak House, 13882 SC Highway 9, three miles west of Chesterfield; (843) 623-2601. Open for lunch buffet Sunday-Friday, 11 a.m.-2 p.m.; dinner Thursday through Saturday, 6-10 p.m. Reservations accepted. Credit cards and checks accepted. Smoking allowed. Inexpensive to expensive.

Fine Fare in the State's Smallest County Seat

If you've never been to Carolina Restaurant in Chesterfield before, chances are you'll be struck by the portrait of the exotic brunette on the wall. Dressed in dark pink, with a comb in her hair, she's a Spanish-style Mona Lisa in this southern town of white houses and front porches.

"Everybody thinks it's her," manager Mitchell Davis says about his wife Cynthia.

She looked like that when she was young."

Mitchell and Cynthia have been working here since Cynthia's parents, Eleanor and Tommie Gulledge, opened it in 1972. They modeled it after the Meadowview Steak House in Matthews, North Carolina, where they frequently went for supper. Mitchell trained with the staff at that restaurant, then brought his learning here. What Meadowview didn't share with him was its steak seasoning. Mitchell created his own. "And actually, I like it better."

Steaks are the big sellers here. People from this border area of the two Carolinas keep it hopping on Friday and Saturday nights. North Carolinians from Albemarle and Wadesboro are regular, bringing their dollars and appetites to this town of 1,374. Mayor John Douglas says Chesterfield is South Carolina's smallest county seat. How fortunate that steak and lobster is available in a town this size.

"They have the best baked potatoes," John said during the lunchtime buffet. Like many of his generation, John's been coming here all his life. His parents brought him as a child; today he attends the monthly Lions Club lunch meeting here. Because Carolina Restaurant can seat 150, it's the logical place for civic gatherings. "For a small town, we've done well," Mitchell says.

Today's lunch buffet has the requisite fried chicken (crispy) and chicken and dumplings, smoked sausage and sauerkraut, greens, fried squash, rice and gravy, slaw, potato salad, tossed salad, pickled beets, peaches, and cottage cheese. Guests serve themselves and can go back for more. It's a filling, affordable lunch. Many items are the recipes of Eleanor Gulledge, who maintained ownership after her husband died in 2000. Mrs. Gulledge still comes in to make sure things are running smoothly.

"The first Sunday we serve turkey and dressing; people are waiting in line to get that," Cynthia says, adding that the pork barbecue on the third Sunday is equally popular. But it was the banana pudding and sauerkraut that kept drawing Kerry Collins, former quarterback with the Carolina Panthers in Charlotte.

Like the lunch buffet, evening entrees are reasonable. Steaks are served with slaw or salad, rolls and butter, and baked potato or French fries. The garlic cream topping is why the baked potatoes are famous, and Mitchell's homemade blue cheese and Thousand Island dressings are often requested.

How did Carolina Restaurant get its name? "Because we're in South Carolina and I thought it would be an easy name to remember," Cynthia says.

Three generations of the Gulledge family have kept Carolina Restaurant going–cooking, washing dishes, waiting tables. "Over the years, you learn to do it all," Cynthia says. Her sisters DeLores Brigman and Lynn Beaver and their offspring–Gregg and Kent Demby and Stacy Lynn Beaver–have all lent a hand. So have Cynthia and Mitchell's sons Tommie and Austin. "Stacy Lynn just turned 13 and she's helping wait tables. She's the last grandchild so she's getting in the business, too."

Soon, one of Cynthia's sons will be back home from Charleston to help out.

"We're just kind of going around in a circle," Cynthia observes. And the lady in the pink dress on the wall is still watching. Who could she be? The Gulledges don't know. They got her from a local furniture store.

- Aïda Rogers

The specialty steak at Carolina Restaurant and Steak House is the Rib Eye, but you can also order a Delmonico, Filet Mignon, T-Bone, New York Strip, chopped Sirloin, Beef Kabob and a steak and lobster combination. The seafood menu features gilled shrimp, grilled Mahi Mahi, fried oysters, flounder, scallops and shrimp, deviled crab, rock lobster tails, and something you don't find often–frog legs. The Davises also have a variety of chicken and pork dishes, as well as a barbecue plate.

- *Tim Driggers*

Catawba Fish Camp, Fort Lawn
Chester County

Catawba Fish Camp, 6131 Lancaster Highway, Fort Lawn, telephone: (803) 872-4477. Open Wednesday and Thursday, 4-9:30 p.m.; Friday and Saturday, 11 a.m.-10 p.m. Closed on Monday, Tuesday, and Sunday. Credit cards accepted. Reservations accepted. No smoking. www.catawbafishcamp.com. Inexpensive.

Big Fish

You know a place is good when it seats 555 people and you still might have to wait outside. That's the story in Fort Lawn, where the Catabwa Fish Camp has been drawing the masses for a half-century. So badly was it missed when it burned in 1975 that 50 people were waiting outside when it reopened in 1976.

"I bet they had smiles on their faces," I say to owner Robert "Bob" Edwards. He laughs. "Smile on *my* face."

A mess sergeant during the Korean War, Bob entered the world of civilian kitchens in 1953. A textile colorist at a printing and finishing company, he spent weekends cooking with his uncle Pleasant Baker, who opened the fish camp in 1952. They served simple fried fare: perch, catfish, chicken, flounder, and fantail shrimp. Today, you can get those items and a lot more: tilapia, crab leg clusters, catfish filets, deviled crab, Calabash shrimp, and scallops. Landlubbers can choose broiled and fried chicken, breaded chicken strips, and chicken livers. Prices are exceptionally reasonable.

Its good prices, good food, and casual atmosphere attract people from Columbia, Charlotte, Camden, Spartanburg, and Greenville. Many eat here once a week. "It's such a large place that people see people they know and they see them every week, so it becomes a social gathering," says Tom White of the Lancaster County Chamber of Commerce. Though it's located in Chester County across the Catawba River from Lancaster, people in Lancaster feel like it's theirs, Tom explains. It's popular for church groups and bus tours; indeed, many people discovered it on the way to PTL and came back with friends. Though PTL is no more and many new restaurants have opened recently, The Catawba Fish Camp goes on. "My business has held up through all of this," Bob says. "I'm holding on to my customers."

And his employees. One cook has been in the kitchen since 1952, others from 10 to 40 years. The manager has worked here since before 1968, when Bob bought the place from his uncle. Some of the waitresses like the food so much they "sit down and eat right after they punch the clock," Bob says.

Catawba Fish Camp is family-style. Food is served in paper trays, customers eat on Styrofoam plates, and no alcohol is served. Neither is dessert, but a huge table of candy at the register is bound to attract the sweet of tooth. "Desserts didn't sell well, but everybody loves candy and chewing gum when they leave. Very few people go out the door that don't buy candy."

Open four days a week, the fish camp serves more than many restaurants do in a month. Bob estimates 1,200–1,400 pounds of flounder and two tons of potatoes are served in a week. French fries are a point of pride here; only fresh potatoes–cut and peeled in the kitchen–are used.

With its immense river mural and three lanes for drive-through service, The Catawba Fish Camp sure is different from that "little old wooden shack" that sold all-you-can-eat perch and chicken for a dollar. Why do people love it? "I don't really know," the modest Bob replies. "This is just fish country."

- Aïda Rogers

President George W. Bush visited the Catawba Fish Camp on the campaign trail in 2000 and the camp has seen the likes of most every candidate to stump South Carolina. Even more important for die-hard Carolina football fans, USC head coach Steve Spurrier has been a guest at Gamecock Club functions.

- Tim Driggers

The Company Store and Restaurant, McBee
Chesterfield County

The Company Store and Restaurant, U.S. 1 North, McBee; (803) 335-8834. Lunch buffet served Sunday-Friday, 11 a.m.-2 p.m.; Thursday and Friday, 5-9 p.m. Inexpensive to moderate.

Recipes from "Big Mama"

Lou Ellen Clark was combing out her granddaughter's hair when we strolled into The Company Store and Restaurant in McBee. She ran a beauty shop for 33 years before taking over the kitchen at this Chesterfield County meeting place, so hair combing is as natural to her as biscuit making. She figures she makes between 800 and 1,000 for the Sunday buffet, a mere 250 on a weekday. Laurie Drafts and I arrived on a Wednesday, roast beef day. Biscuits–small, flat and delicious–were waiting right between the roast beef and fried chicken. Laurie and I had found Paradise.

"This is a comfort food buffet," Laurie observed, making note of the creamed corn, macaroni and cheese, baked chicken, hushpuppies, string beans, roasted squash, greens and rutabagas. A salad bar and two desserts–chocolate cake and pineapple upside-down cake–finished off the spread. While The Company Store is famous for its buffet (Tuesday is mashed potatoes and meatloaf, Thursday is pork chops, and fried and baked chicken are every day), its salads are well-respected too. The specialty salads all involve chicken: Jamaican, Cajun, blackened, lemon-peppered and pecan. Sandwiches–turkey, steak, ham, chicken, oyster–also are available. Sandwiches are served with French fries, soup or chips.

The menu's diversity may account for the clientele. Men in ties and men in caps take their lunch here, and so do women of all ages and professions, and families. Many locals gather in the front room, where Lou Ellen and her family converge after cooking and waiting tables. Because of its size–The Company Store seats about 170–it can accommodate the local Lions Club, and county and school district functions.

It wasn't always so big. Lou Ellen's son Rod gutted the building, a former Laundromat, for a grocery store. He stocked meats, cheeses and fresh produce, and asked his mother if she might contribute her famous chicken salad. It didn't take long for this simple operation to take off, and within 10 years, The Company Store was serving people from Camden, Columbia, and North Carolina. Its Thursday night seafood buffet is famous, and its rib eyes and sirloins aren't cut until they're ordered.

While Rod cuts steaks, Lou Ellen manages the rest. She is a true cook–one who started as a child and improvises with ease. Her pineapple upside-down cake, a marvel of moistness, included mandarin oranges on this day. "I didn't have enough pineapple so I went to the storage room and got a can of mandarin oranges and put it in the filling," she explains. "I do that a lot. I do all kinds of things."

Lou Ellen cooked her first Thanksgiving dinner at 12. Her grandmother–"Big Mama"–helped. Today, many of Big Mama's recipes live on at The Company Store, where the entire Clark family is involved. Daughters Stephanie and Shauna, both teachers, help when they can; and Lou Ellen's husband Jiggs often runs the register. Grandson Rod Jr. buses tables. Like many operations, The Company Store caters.

"People ask me, 'Don't you get tired of this?' And I say, 'I get tired but not tired of cooking,'" Lou Ellen says. She honors her late father, who had a heart condition, by not using animal fat, only canola oil.

The Company Store manages to be elegant *and* countrified. Ceiling fans whir above farm-style tables, and prints and paintings of rural scenes cover the walls. The Clarks are good citizens; Lou Ellen recently helped McBee's depot get listed on the National Register of Historic Places.

"That Sunday meal is real good," notes Glenn Odom, mayor of McBee and owner of the local Huddle House. He comes two or three times a week, but Sunday's his favorite. "The only problem is getting in the door."

- Aïda Rogers

McBee Town Clerk Karen Threatt says The Company Store's famous buffet is as fabulous as ever. While the cut-to-order rib eye and sirloin steaks are her favorites, she confessed true love for Lou Ellen's fried chicken. "Oh my gosh, it is so, so good," she gushed. "It's just right crispy, not too over and not too under." That's McBee talk for finger-lickin' good. Lou Ellen says she named her restaurant The Company Store because "we treat our guests as company every day." Everything is still homemade, including the popular barbecue, made on premises. Two types of homemade barbecue sauce are featured: "The Sandhill," which is catsup-based, and "The Tarheel," which is vinegar-based. The Company Store still serves some mighty fine seafood, and Karen Threatt suggests to do yourself a favor and have Lou Ellen cut you a slice of homemade chocolate cake.

- Tim Driggers

Cromer's Cafeteria, Kershaw
Lancaster County

Cromer's Cafeteria, 322 North Hampton Street, Kershaw; (803) 475-6912. Open Monday-Friday and Saturday 11 a.m.-2 p.m. Closed on Sunday. Credit cards not accepted. No reservations required. Smoking is allowed in one dining room. Inexpensive.

"This is Hospitality Food"

There should be a sign somewhere at Cromer's Cafeteria, and it should say one thing: "You just can't beat it." It's a battle cry, an echo, a fact of life in Kershaw, where the Clyburns are prevalent and the feeling is Mayberry.

"We've eaten all over the beach, and we come back home and find better food here than anywhere else," says a satisfied Tommy Clyburn, Kershaw native and Cromer's regular. Clyburn, 75, and his wife Nell have been eating at Cromer's since the '50s, and they still get what they came for back then: good food at a good price. Like plenty of other folks in town, they say you just can't beat it.

The Clyburns offer almost as strong a testimony as Sketter (pronounced "SKEE-ter") Watts. From where he sits behind a mountain of pinto beans, macaroni and cheese, cornbread, rice and gravy, country-style steak, and coconut cake, Sketter is a one-man Kershaw welcome wagon and expert on what makes good food good. Cromer's, he says firmly, has good food.

"This is southern food right here, hospitality food," says Sketter, who eats here every day or doesn't eat at all. "Yankees put milk and sugar on their grits. Whoever came up with that?"

With his tattoos and long black ponytail, Sketter fits in with the businessmen in ties, ladies from the office, and older folks passing through town. They don't come to lunch; they come to eat. Or as Sketter puts it, "I don't like sandwiches. I like a meal. This is as close to Mama's cooking as you can get."

And it's going to stay that way, says Kerry Snipes, who owns and runs the place with endless energy and a constant smile. "If there's one thing I've learned, it's not to change anything." That's why Cromer's famous fried chicken and country-style steak are offered each day at lunch - the only meal Cromer's serves. A third meat varies between salmon croquettes, fried flounder, meat loaf, ham, smoked sausage, and chicken livers. The vegetables are wonderful and plentiful, and customers are invited to take as much as they like. For bread, there are crispy cornbread muffins and soft southern biscuits; luckily, Cromer's lets you have one of each.

Officially called Chris Cromer's Cafeteria and Catering, Cromer's has been owned and run by women since it opened almost 50 years ago. Mrs. Snipes worked here five years before purchasing the restaurant in 1985. No special recipes or tricks to its popularity, she says, only quality food and cooks who prepared it like your grandmother did.

A Wisconsin transplant, Snipes says she's still unaccustomed to the fatback factor, although she makes sure it's included in the vegetables. But customers know she fries everything in low-cholesterol oil. "She's got a lot of old folks here like us to take care of," Tommy Clyburn says.

A word about the décor: plain. No paintings, no carpet, no music. The round, pale green plates are reminiscent of public school lunchrooms. Plastic pitchers of iced tea are on each table, also plain and without pretension.

Sketter hopes they don't change a thing. Where else can you get all this food, plus tea, at a price that won't make you wince? Even now, with his buddy talking about the wife who left him after five days, the feeling is jovial. After a hot meal at Cromer's, it'd be hard not to feel better than when you came in.

- Aïda Rogers

Since this article first appeared in Sandlapper's *January/February 1990 issue, Cromer's moved to a larger location. Tommy Clyburn sadly is no longer with us, but wife Nell remains a regular and Sketter...well, he's still what Kerry Snipes calls a "character." Chicken Liver Day has become a big deal on Wednesdays and Cromer's catering business is going strong as ever.*

- *Tim Driggers*

The Cyclone Restaurant, Chester
Chester County

The Cyclone Restaurant, 249 Columbia Street, Chester; (803) 377-1500. Open Monday-Saturday, 7:30 a.m.-8:30 p.m. Closed Sundays. Credit cards accepted. Reservations not required. No smoking. Inexpensive to moderate.

How Could Anything Taste That Good?

Usually, after I come back from what we call "the town photo essay" assignment, people ask me what I learned. For this issue, I could talk about Chester's restored downtown, wealth of history and friendly people. But what really made me marvel was the baked potato at the Cyclone restaurant, a favorite with locals for years.

"Get you a baked potato," said Nancy Anderson, who was giving me a tour of the town. "They make their own sour cream and they put garlic in it. People come here

Volcanic with flavor – that's The Cyclone's famous baked potato.

and buy just that."

Who was I to say no? Still, I wasn't prepared for that potato, big and hot and running over with sour cream. I felt my eyes pop. How could anything taste that good?

"We don't use small potatoes," said George Vastis, who's been serving the delicacies since 1970. That's when he and his brother Andrew designed and built The Cyclone and opened for business. People have tried to wrangle the sour cream recipe from them, but so far, no good. "They say, 'Why don't you put it on the market,' but you need a good promoter for that," George said, adding that maybe he'll call Paul Newman to get his advice.

In the meantime, the Vastis brothers sell their sour cream and extra large potatoes at their restaurant. "Some people buy it by the gallon," George said, explaining that he's sold from 40 to 200 potatoes at a time to people having parties. The sour cream, topped with a little bacon, makes a good dip.

Others prefer to come into the restaurant just for the potato. There's the regular and The Cyclone Potato, the latter loaded with ham, cheese, and bacon. They're so big that one alone makes a decent lunch.

- Aïda Rogers

George Vastis sold The Cyclone Drive-In Restaurant to Mary Petrou some years back, but his famous Cyclone Potato remains the specialty of the house. The Chicken Alfredo, a boneless breast of chicken swimming in a creamy Parmesan cheese sauce over fettuccini is the signature dish of Mary's husband-chef, Milton. Also popular are the Chicken New Orleans and Chicken Athens, a chicken entrée sautéed with green peppers and tomatoes, served over rice topped with feta cheese. The Cyclone now features daily homemade specials and during the winter months, a soup du jour. Breakfast includes omelets and grits with homemade sausage gravy. Mary's daughter bakes the desserts and her chocolate and New York-style cheesecake are always in demand. The potatoes, and the Vastis' special sour cream and hamburger steak sauce, remain take-out favorites. The old-fashioned wood paneled décor of the Cyclone is exactly the same.

- Tim Driggers

The Front Porch, Richburg
Chester County

Front Porch, 3072 Lancaster Highway, Richburg; (803) 789-5029. Open daily from 11 a.m.-9 p.m. (some months have shorter hours; call first). Credit cards not accepted, but there's an ATM machine inside. Personal checks are accepted. No reservations required. No smoking. Inexpensive.

"But the Biggest Favorite Seems to be Libby"

In celebration of fresh summer vegetables and because I'm running out of friends, I took my mother on my latest South Carolina eating spree. We decided to go to a country-cooking restaurant, one of those meat-three-and-tea places that tell me the South is not about to disappear. My mother made a fine co-eater, which wouldn't surprise anyone who knows our food-oriented family.

We zoomed up I-77 toward Charlotte, headed for the Front Porch restaurant, a place I'd heard about months ago. It's in Richburg, 12 miles east of Chester. Not too far away are exotic sounding places we'd never heard of - Lando, for instance, and Edgemoor. People from those communities come to eat at the Front Porch, which is probably the most popular spot off Exit 65, where SC 9 crosses I-77.

Customer Steve Turney teaches at Oak Dale Elementary School, but since it was spring break, he could eat with his children and father-in-law. He'd just sold $4,000 worth of cows at Chester Livestock, where cows are auctioned every Tuesday, so lunch was on him - even dessert. Daughter Stephanie got the house favorite, apple cobbler; son Drew chose the Boston Crème pie. Their grandfather, Miles Lineberger, passed on dessert because the candied yams were sweet enough for him.

Blueberry, apple, or peach pies and cobblers with or without ice cream are other options. The Front Porch is located halfway between Cleveland and Miami, and people

The ever—welcoming Libby Gaston at the Front Porch.

have been stopping here for years on their way north or south. Loyal customers send Christmas cards to owner Libby Gaston, who flutters graciously between kitchen and guests. "I can't keep up with their names, but I know their faces," she said.

Customers love the way Libby makes them feel at home. "We felt we had known her all our lives," said Emma Gupton of Charlotte. "I'm telling you, not only is the food wonderful, but I've never seen such hospitality. You walk in the doors and you never meet a stranger."

Emma and her old friend and nursing school roommate, Ruth Spoon, were both having the baked chicken and squash casserole. They eat lunch here every two months on their way back from the pharmacy at Fort Jackson. Before they discovered the Front Porch (Ruth heard about it from her sister-in-law in Florida), they used to leave early in the morning to have breakfast in Rock Hill. But this is the routine they prefer.

At the Front Porch, travelers make friends with the locals. Snowbirds, bikers, families, old people, business people and children can all be found here. The parking lot, full of pick-ups and Mercedes, reflects the diverse clientele. One of the reasons Chester County Councilman Buddy Martin comes so often is because he likes to talk to the assortment of people from other places. Another is because he likes to call the waitresses "Fatty," he jokes, "regardless of size."

When Buddy comes in for coffee, he sits at the round community table near the kitchen. That's where you can find Donna Lisenby, Trudy Taylor, and Joe D'Alessandro, a businessman who lives in Chester and Rock Hill. Joe likes being able to order fresh rutabaga and having a place to bring clients from Charlotte. Donna likes the down-home atmosphere. "If you don't come in for a while, they ask you where you been; and if you have muddy boots on, they tell you to come back."

What she doesn't like so much is how crowded this little stretch of country road has become. The Front Porch, which looks like an old farmhouse, was a family homeplace until I-77 came through. Then it became a firecracker store. Now it's sandwiched between a McDonald's and Kentucky Fried Chicken. Convenience stores and motels have sprung up near the exit, and brochures of area attractions have been designed for people stopping through. But Donna's not one to stay glum long, especially when waitress Barbara Jackson says it's time to wrap silver. Members of the community table roll knives, forks, and spoons into napkins. They grumble, but they don't mind. They're practically family.

Libby said she had no place to start a restaurant, but friends kept asking her to because she was such a good entertainer. The result is a 23-year-old, seven-day-a-week success. Because it's a travel stop, customers come at all hours, but it's been a plus for the community, too. Artwork by local students covers the walls. A new banquet room is used for business lunches, receptions, and parties.

The Front Porch is your grandmother's house, or what it would be if you grew up Mayberry-style. Here you will find flowery wallpaper, ruffled curtains, and a piano with a copy of *A Goodly Heritage-History of Chester County, South Carolina* on it.

Four meats and several vegetables are prepared fresh each day. Favorites are the baked and fried chicken, pork chops, squash casserole, and all the desserts; but the biggest favorite seems to be Libby. Donna and Trudy will never forget how she got in her car and led some friends of theirs to a party they were having. Three times they got lost; three times they came back to the Front Porch to get directions.

"Where else would a restaurant owner lead strangers to a party?" Donna wondered, but Trudy countered with the truth: "Well, she didn't look at them as strangers."

- Aïda Rogers

It was in 1993 when Sandlapper *trekked to the Front Porch. Libby Gaston still owns the restaurant and the daily specials now include chicken and dumplings, roast beef, fried chicken, ham, and a collection of 14 side dishes, including the popular fried green tomatoes. They've added their own barbecue, slow-cooked over wood for 18-20 hours. The Front Porch has also added another large dining room. Since this story first appeared, Buddy Martin and Joe Dalesandro have died, but legions of Chester-area citizens still make the Front Porch their foremost dining destination.*

- Tim Driggers

The Garden Café, York
York County

The Garden Cafe, 307 Liberty Street, York; (803) 684-7109. Open Tuesday-Saturday for lunch, 11 a.m.-2:30 p.m. and for dinner, 6-10 p.m. Credit cards accepted. Reservation recommended. Smoking at the bar only. www.thegardencafeyork.com. Inexpensive to expensive.

"It's Delightful, It's Delicious ..."

I tend to stay away from the word "delightful." But that's my adjective for The Garden Café in York. Like a Viennese waltz, it's always pleasant and fun.

"We come every chance we get," says Vernon Moss, a Gastonia resident who lunches here on Saturdays with wife Carolyn. "There are a lot of places we could go in Gastonia, but we love this."

Who wouldn't? The décor is country French, with flowers painted on the walls and umbrellas above tables. Outside is a patio for dining among the blooms. On Friday and Saturday nights, live music beckons.

"It's real laid-back," says owner Teresa James. "We don't push them out. One couple came from Charlotte and was here four hours."

Teresa has a successful catering business in Lake Wylie, which prompted her to open The Garden Café. Business is great. "Everybody wants me to come to Chester or Dilworth or Rock Hill," she reports. "If I knew I'd be this popular, I would have gone somewhere bigger."

Soups, salads, sandwiches, and combinations of all three are available for lunch, along with quiche and pasta. One favorite is the 3-Cheese Grilled Sandwich, which combines provolone, Swiss, and cheddar on sourdough. Other popular items are The Fresh Tuna Salad Pita, made with Tongol light tuna, and the Chunked Chicken Salad Croissant, prepared with a sour cream base. Accompaniments are fruit and a side; choose between pasta or potato salad or soup.

"There's always a gentleman who wants red meat," Teresa observes. That's why prime rib has always been a featured dinner selection. (Notes Mr. Moss from Gastonia: "We hear you can eat the prime rib with a spoon. And a pastor said that, so you know he's telling the truth.")

Other longtime dinner favorites include the grilled salmon and asparagus salad and pecan-encrusted chicken salad.

In keeping with its décor, The Garden Café serves French Onion Soup and a French dip sandwich. Children can order grilled cheese or peanut butter and jelly sandwiches, with fruit, chips and cookies. Cappuccino, espresso, and café latte are available. "Everything we do is fresh from scratch," Teresa says. "I do all the desserts. That's why I look so bad."

She did look tired above her shiny case of cakes, pies, and cookies. Key Lime pie and bread pudding are favorites - better reserve a portion early. Our threesome, lunching late on a Saturday, tried the walnut pie, peanut butter cheesecake, and five-flavor pound cake.

The desserts are just another artistic element at The Garden Café. The peanut butter cheesecake, three-and-a-half inches high with chocolate icing, is pure inspiration. Be careful; it could bring out the Monet in us all.

- Aïda Rogers

Although The Garden Café has switched locations a few times and the interior touches have changed, the Country French atmosphere and décor continue to provide guests with the same "delightful" dining experience we first reported. There is now a set menu of 30 entrees and appetizers. Signature dishes are the filet mignon baked in bacon and the buttermilk pie. Pizza has been added to the menu. The restaurant has a full-service bar and live entertainment on Friday and Saturday nights. Local musician Susan Vinson Sherlock has paid homage to her hometown with the composition "Garden Café Waltz" played on hammered dulcimer.

- *Tim Driggers*

Gus' House of Pizza, Kershaw
Lancaster County

Gus' House of Pizza, 101 South Hampton Street, Kershaw; (803) 475-9937. Open Monday-Saturday 11 a.m.-10 p.m. Closed Sunday. No reservations. Credit cards and checks accepted. Smoking and non-smoking sections. www.pizzabygus.com. Inexpensive to moderate.

You Like - a Greek Pizza? Come Here...

You may not know this - I certainly didn't - but Kershaw is a regular hotbed of international dining. At the corner of Marion and Hampton Streets, there's Gus' House of Pizza, which has served Mediterranean cuisine since 1988.

At first it was known as Bobby's House of Pizza, but soon afterward changed names to reflect new ownership. Gus' House of Pizza is one of two restaurants run by the same family.

Gus and Effie Deligiannidis ("a real Greek name," Effie says in her heavy accent) bought the restaurant in Kershaw from their cousin Bobby Ouzounidis, who lives in

Camden. Born in Greece, Gus came to America to get a master's degree in business. Obviously the education is paying off. "In a small town like Kershaw, I'm selling a lot of pizzas."

The menu is Greek and American, and one of the specialties is Grecian beef tips, which are served with either rice and gravy, fried okra, or salad.

"It sounds American," Gus says, "but the meat and ingredients, the touch - it's all Greek.

- Aïda Rogers

Sandlapper *first visited Gus' House of Pizza in 1990. Gus and Effie hadn't changed the name of the restaurant yet, but their native recipes were already attracting hordes of converts to home-style Greek dishes. The building had once been a jewelry store and another time housed a pawnshop. Its finest hour came when the Deligiannidis clan renovated the location into a family-oriented downtown restaurant with a decided Greek twist. Gus and Effie say their gyros and pizzas are the most popular selections. Pizzas include the Meat Lovers (hamburger, Italian sausage, pepperoni, ham, bacon, and cheese), Greek (Gyro meat, tomatoes, black olives, and Greek and mozzarella cheeses), Hawaiian (ham, pineapple, and mozzarella cheese), Vegetable (with onions, bell peppers, mushrooms, black and green olives, tomatoes, and cheese) and the House Special (resplendent with seven toppings). You can get the pizzas in small, medium, large, or personal sizes, with a choice of 13 different toppings.*

The menu also contains hot subs, "the best salads in town," strombolis, burgers, and Greek sandwiches. Bigger dinners are lasagna, manicotti, veal parmesan, eggplant parmesan, cheese ravioli, beef ravioli, meatball casserole, stuffed shells combination platter and six different spaghetti selections. Greek dinners include Greek marinated beef tips, beef Souvlaki, chicken Souvlaki and Greek spaghetti. Top it all off with an order of Baklava and you're one happy Greek for-a-meal

Gus and Effie also own Gus' Family Pizza in Lancaster, voted Best Italian Restaurant in the Lancaster Daily News *2006 Reader's Choice survey.*

- *Tim Driggers*

Midway BBQ, Buffalo
Union County

Midway BBQ, 811 Main Street (SC 215), Buffalo; (864) 427-4047. Open Monday-Saturday, 9 a.m.-6 p.m. Closed on Sunday. Credit cards and checks accepted. No reservations. No smoking. Inexpensive.

The Hash & Chicken Stew Capital of the World

On this cold, wet Saturday, I would much rather be sipping the hot chicken stew at Midway BBQ than writing about it. When the sky is cloudy and your eyelids are falling, there's nothing much better than an order of that, followed by a nap.

"It's what you want when you're sick or cold," says Amy O'Dell Allen from behind the counter of this wonderfully authentic barbecue and country-cooking restaurant. Sawdust is on the floor, red and white cloths cover the tables, and salt and pepper come in little Mason jars. The low ceiling ensures a cozy atmosphere. Midway BBQ can afford to be unpretentious in décor, because the food is so good. It is, after all, "The Hash & Chicken Stew Capital of the World."

Hash and chicken stew are serious business here. Eight cast-iron pots—six 30-gallon pots and two 100-gallon pots—keep those specialties in ready supply. On rainy days, the cooks know to make more stew. "I always add Texas Pete to mine," Amy says. Amy is the daughter of Jack O'Dell, who started Midway BBQ in 1941 from a 10 x 12-foot shack. The chicken stew is his creation. Unlike the thick, rice-based chicken stew served elsewhere, Midway's chicken stew is brothy. Served with saltines, it's the pinnacle of comfort food. As for the hash, another Jack O'Dell recipe, it's the best beef variety around.

"A lot of customers are old cattle buyers and farmers and they say, 'We know when Jack puts his hand up it's the best one in the barn.' I have been told that 50 times." That's Jay Allen talking, Amy's husband, who gave up his white-collar career in Greenville to run the family business in Union. He's a world away from his Atlanta upbringing and Georgia Tech industrial management degree, but he loves it. Serving people—at the restaurant, through catering, and their meat market business—is fulfilling. In that way, he's much like his father-in-law.

"My dad's joy is to see people eat," Amy says.

Though Jack's health keeps him from being here full-time, he still buys the meat and makes sure things are on track. Besides his daughter and son-in-law, his two brothers help. Fred O'Dell, an 81-year-old veteran and Silver Star recipient, works 32 hours a week, cooking barbecue and handling the meat counter. When he retired from a textile company at 62, he lasted six months before coming in. "I couldn't stand it," he says. "I think this has prolonged my life." Jack and Fred's brother Bill comes in every afternoon and works all day on Saturday. A former grocery store owner and city councilman, Bill is 72.

It takes a hard-working family, with help from long-time employees, to keep this barbecue haven (it's 100 percent hickory-smoked) going. But Midway serves so much more than barbecue. The menu has all the regional favorites: fried and baked chicken, pork chops (fried, smoked or with gravy), roast beef, meat loaf, country-style steak, liver and onions, baked ham. There's plenty for vegetarians: rice and gravy, macaroni and cheese, candied yams, fried okra, squash casserole, cabbage, baked and green beans, baby limas, turnips. Fatback is used in the green beans, a fact the staff relays to vegetarians. This love-or-hate southern staple is sold from the refrigerated cases, burgeoning with steaks, chops, liver pudding, and other meats.

Desserts include the top choice, banana pudding, along with strawberry cake and cobbler, pineapple and honey bun cakes, peach cobbler, and chocolate chip pie.

Midway customers come from all over, and most come frequently. Monte Lancaster, vice president and cashier of Arthur State Bank, knows the daily specials so well she can build her weekly calendar around it. "On Wednesday I can get my fried okra and Mondays I can get fried pork chops," she says, adding that she always gets the marinated vegetables, which are available every day. "Everything here is good."

Not the least of which are the owners. Mrs. Lancaster points out that Midway BBQ supplies the Buffalo Meals on Wheels program and donates holiday meals for charitable fundraisers. "They are always giving, always helping. They are very community-minded." Amy concurs. "My dad would have been a very wealthy man if he hadn't been so generous."

Midway BBQ got its name because it's "midway" between Union and Buffalo. Smart people know to get here before noon. Chances are they heard Jay talking about that day's menu on WBCU, which he does Monday through Friday.

It's enough to make you jump in your car and go straight there - just hoping you don't have to stop and get gas.

- Aïda Rogers

Amy and Jay Allen want you to know that they've added two new barbecue sauces to complement their Midway BBQ original: One's a vinegar-pepper and the other a mustard base. Watch for the license plates in the parking lot on Saturdays. Folks come from as far away as California and New York to savor Midway BBQ. After all Buffalo, South Carolina, is just a short jaunt down the Jersey Turnpike or Slauson Cutoff.

- *Tim Driggers*

Oskars Restaurant and Bar, Cheraw
Chesterfield County

Oskars Restaurant and Bar, 130 Second Avenue, Cheraw; (843) 320-0303. Lunch Monday-Friday, 11 a.m.-2 p.m. Dinner Monday-Saturday, 5:30-10 p.m. Bar opens at 5:30 p.m. Smoking is allowed. Reservations are preferred. Cash, checks, and credit cards accepted. Moderate.

A Little *Gemutlichkeith* in Old Cheraw

I visited Oskars Restaurant and Bar in Cheraw one cold, wet winter night. It didn't take me long to discover this was going to be a memorable experience. In fact, I knew it the moment I stepped out of the freezing rain into the cozy foyer and was greeted by a woman with a smile wider than the Great Pee Dee River. Legend has it Sherman's army spared Cheraw because they just liked the town. If Uli Mossig had been around in those days, no doubt Sherman would have gone a step further and enlisted in the Confederacy. That's the power of Uli's personality. To the undying gratitude of devoted diners, the menu matches Uli's wit and charm.

Second Avenue hasn't always been the home of Oskars. Cheraw hasn't always been the home of Uli and Helmut. Born in Wolfsburg, Germany, home of the Volkswagen Beetle, the couple moved here 1973. Helmut worked at INA, a German bearings manufacturer. Uli found a job as secretary for local chiropractor Prue Owens.

"We have about 20 German couples living in Cheraw," said Helmi Helmtraud, who with husband Bernd were already living in town when Uli and Helmut arrived. "There is a German word to describe how we socialize - gemutlichkeit - which means a comfortable togetherness. That's how we feel when we get together and dine. In Germany, you don't just eat and leave. You stay around and enjoy each other's company." Uli and Helmut decided in 1999 to bring gemutlichkeit to Cheraw's restaurant scene.

"Helmut and I had dreamed about opening a restaurant for 20 years," Uli said, "but were scared of going in debt." Finally, with the help of Oskar Wetternek, a friend from INA, they acquired a small place on Second Avenue and started to renovate. Soon afterward, the adjoining space became available. On March 31, 2000, Oskars was born. Wetternick, the namesake of the restaurant, retired last year, bequeathing many of his recipes and cooking styles to present chef John Linton.

The main dining room is attractively decorated with art on the walls and seating for 75 at tables adorned with green tablecloths topped with white lattice. On the night I visited, the room was packed and the mood decidedly upbeat. Uli suggested I start with an "appe teaser" of frog legs, crab meat muffin bites, and stuffed mushrooms. The combination was fabulous. The frog legs were lightly fried and so tasty I momentarily considered grabbing a gig, heading to the river, and bringing Linton more croakers for his kitchen. The muffin bites were beyond delicious, premium lump crab bound with a creamy cheese mixture, and the mushrooms, stuffed similarly, were pure heaven.

I could have paid my bill and left then a happy man but the meal had just begun. Uli was at my table with a plate of jaegerschnitzel, a cutlet of pork splashed with mushroom gravy and accompanied by potato dumplings and red cabbage. What a feast.

Beside other German favorites including wienerschnitzel and zigeunerschnitzel, Oskars features a full American menu of shrimp and scallops in wine sauce, shrimp and grits, cornish hen, stuffed orange roughy or tilapia, marjoram noodles with pork tenderloin, and chicken cordon bleu. There are salads and soups, desserts, "oskarettes" (the children's menu), wines, and imported and domestic beers. The bar, leading from the restaurant's entrance, is where friends linger long into the evening.

Dr. Owens eats at Oskars at least twice a week. "I think of it as home," he said. "Helmut and Uli always join me for my meal. It's not like other restaurants where I feel like I'm dining alone." His favorite meal is the shrimp and grits. "The grits are not cooked like plain grits. They are cooked with real cream and are much better."

Helmtraud is a fan of the rouladen, beef thinly cut in a roll with onions, pickle, mustard, spices, and gravy. Dr. Owens gives his own guarantee. "If you come here and don't like the food, I'll pay for it." No takers have been found.

- Tim Driggers

The River Rat, Lake Wylie
York County

The River Rat, 5301 S.C. 557, Lake Wylie; (803) 831-1901. Open Monday-Thursday, 4-10 p.m. and Friday-Saturday, 4-11 p.m. Closed Sunday. Smoking and nonsmoking sections. Credit cards accepted, but no checks. www.theriverrat.com. Inexpensive to expensive.

Blackened Oysters, Barbecued Shrimp

The River Rat has been on my list of restaurants to visit for some time. But with this one, I committed that most odious of Sins Against Journalism: I assumed. Yes, I assumed a place with the word "River" in its name would have a river outside its door. Surely there would be a moat to cross, a bridge, a something.

But the closest bridge was the quaint Buster Boyd, which crosses Lake Wylie three miles away. On one side is the ever-encroaching Charlotte. On the other, prosperous—but still pastoral—Lake Wylie.

Our party halted in front, unsure of the next step. We drove around the parking lot, went inside, got back in the car, studied the menu, conferred, then decided: The River Rat has the *spirit* of water. That *is* a respectable puddle in the parking lot. The guy in the patio bar *is* playing Buffet. And lo—those lobsters in that tank are swimming in something, and it doesn't look like Kool-Aid. Yes, we are here.

"We were never on the water," waitress Karen Glenn told us as she brought our drinks and recommended appetizers. " 'River Rat' is what people who live here year-round are called."

Though Lake Wylie was created from the Catawba River in 1904 and enlarged in 1925 when an existing dam was replaced, old-timers still call it "The River." Karen herself is a river rat; she remembers spending summer days on the lake as a teenager and then coming to The River Rat for the River Dunk, a roast beef hoagie *au jus*.

Back to those appetizers. Karen bragged about owner Al Powell's Blackened Oysters, so good they win the "Best of Charlotte" award. "I never liked oysters, but they talked me into having a blackened oyster; it's the only reason I work here," confessed Karen. "They are going to send me to Betty Ford to get me off them."

Equally tasty are the jumbo shrimp, which you can get grilled, fried, or barbecued. We chose barbecued, which pleased everyone including the reluctant young Sims Patton who, upon sampling, immediately licked her lips.

Prime rib and seafood are the River Rat's specialties. I ordered the seafood trio, which includes two kinds of fish, and jumbo shrimp, each cooked however you want—blackened, grilled, or broiled. This evening, the fish was swordfish and salmon. Other times it's grouper, tuna, mahi, redfish, red snapper and mako shark. Choices for side orders are baked potato, french fries or vegetable medley.

The menu also includes South American lobster tail, salads, steaks, crab cakes, beef ribs, sandwiches and pasta. Aside from the market-price lobster tails, the most expensive entree is the 10-ounce filet mignon.

While the food draws people from Charlotte, York, Rock Hill, Clover, and Gastonia, it was a different story when the River Rat opened in 1979. Back then, Gaston County was dry, but customers could cross the state line for drinks at The River Rat. The bar is still a big part of the restaurant and a pleasant place to wait for a table. In the summer, live music on the patio is available on weekends.

Started by Gastonia residents Red Powell and his wife Peggy, The River Rat is now owned by son Al and daughter Gina Bolin. Red died a few years ago; a room at The River Rat is named in his honor. Al's love for the Charlotte Hornets/Bobcats and Panthers is evidenced by posters and photos on the walls.

Dim lighting, booths and Tiffany-style lamps give the restaurant a comfortable feel. For many customers and employees, it's a second home. "We have so many regular customers that when you come to work, it's like being with friends and family," Karen says. A recent barbecue fundraiser to help a waitress' daughter with medical bills drew plenty of customers and lots of donations.

For dessert, there are cheesecakes and pies. The peanut butter pie, rich and delicious, inspired a chorus of "*Ummmms.*" Fellow diners Gerry Lynn Hall and Dolly Patton echoed each other. "Isn't that just heaven?"

- Aïda Rogers

Sandlapper *visited The River Rat in the fall of 2000 and when we checked in again, we were pleased to find Al and Gina still at the controls. John Currence, Al's son, tells us that Al's Blackened Oysters are still on the menu (when available) and that prime rib remains their specialty. Thursday nights feature lobster, Wednesday is all-you-can-eat BBQ beef ribs, and on Monday evening, The River Rat has buy-one-get-one-free Dijon clams. The restaurant will celebrate its 30th anniversary in 2009.*

- *Tim Driggers*

The Seafood Hut, Camden
Kershaw County

The Seafood Hut, 2538 North Broad Street, Camden; (803) 432-1762. Open Thursday, 4-9 p.m. and Friday-Saturday, 4-10 p.m. Closed Sunday through Wednesday. Senior citizen discounts available. Credit cards accepted. No reservations. Smoking in designated area. Inexpensive to moderate.

Camden's Old Faithful

Walking into The Seafood Hut is like walking into a comfort zone. Here, the booths are vinyl, the service is friendly, and the hushpuppies are hot and fast. Owner/hostess Audrey Issac brings them to your table in a plastic bowl with a tub of honey butter.

The buffets are what The Seafood Hut is known for, along with its catering business, 3 Chefs Catering. It has prepared food for weddings, parties, companies, and the occasional movie crew. Recently it fed the people working on *Other Voices, Other Rooms* at Edisto Beach. Audrey's stepdaughter runs the catering company; her son is the restaurant manager. Husband Morgan is co-owner and originator of many of the recipes. It's a family business and a family restaurant that's been a Camden success story since 1977.

Here comes Lois Gandy, followed by four generations of her family. They're here to celebrate her 96th birthday. Audrey stops to give her a hug. "Celebrating all weekend," Mrs. Gandy says, moving on to a table big enough to seat 14 people 14 months and older. The Seafood Hut is perfect for the Gandy clan, centrally located for family members in Charlotte, Raleigh, Columbia, and Lexington. Mrs. Gandy, a Camden resident, comes to the Seafood Hut twice a week, usually for shrimp cocktail and a baked potato. Son Harry says the Seafood Hut is a favorite. "It's one of the few restaurants that's not too candlelightish and formal. It's come as you are. I like that."

Indeed, The Seafood Hut is simply an old-style seafood restaurant two hours inland. Fishnets, shells, and starfish hang on the walls; an aquarium and tropical fish art are here, too. What the Issac family has created in Camden is becoming harder to find at the beach. Many customers say they'd rather eat seafood here than there.

Oyster stew and clam chowder are popular; they're served hot and thick in coffee mugs. The menu has basic seafood items: jumbo and calabash shrimp, crab, fish, oysters, clams and seafood platters. It also has shrimp creole, stuffed flounder, and a mixed grill of snowcrab, halibut, salmon and swordfish. The Issacs try to keep prices reasonable for senior citizens.

Open daily for evening meals only, The Seafood Hut has a buffet every night - sometimes more than one. Wednesday's first buffet is prime rib and snowcrab legs, steamed shrimp and fried shrimp. The second Wednesday buffet is a country buffet of fried chicken and vegetables. The buffet Thursday night is all-you-can-eat seafood (whiting, fried and boiled shrimp, oysters, deviled crab, clam strips).

Friday and Saturday buffets are an all-you-can-eat oyster bar—which includes steamed and fried oysters and boiled and fried shrimp. You can get crab legs with that. A half pound of jumbo shrimp, fried or grilled, is available Friday and Saturday.

The oysters have their fan club, Audrey says. "One doctor comes every Friday night with his wife and they bring gloves. They don't get salad or anything, just oysters."

After oyster season, a "steam pot for two," which includes shrimp, oysters in the shell, snowcrab, sausage, corn, and new potatoes, is available Friday nights.

Mary Stokes and Jennie Moseley are having a seafood supper together, something they do once a week. They worked 25 years together at Sears. At The Seafood Hut, they can catch up on each other and their families. They brag about the fish, the shrimp salad, the kindness of Audrey Issac, and the care the staff take. "They'll watch and if they think you're not pleased, they won't let you pay," Mary says. "Where do you go to get that kind of relationship?"

- Aïda Rogers

When we wrote about The Seafood Hut in 1995, we told the story of the doctor and his Mrs. who visit every Friday with their gloves to attack the oysters. They're still regulars, only now, they also bring a bag of ice to keep the oysters fresh while shucking. Since The Seafood Hut has been open for 30 years, owner Audrey Issac has probably seen it all. Audrey's son, Doyle Lewis, manages the restaurant nowadays, as well as the catering division, 3 Chefs Catering.

- Tim Driggers

Shiloh Fish House, near Chesterfield
Chesterfield County

Shiloh Fish House, 3382 S.C. 102 near Chesterfield; (843) 623-7204. Open Thursday-Saturday, 5-9:30 p.m. Closed Sunday-Wednesday. No smoking. Credit cards accepted. No reservations needed. Inexpensive to moderate.

Seafood in Shiloh

One straight-talking woman is Johnnie Watson McCright. Johnnie and her husband Mike run Shiloh Fish House in the Shiloh community, four miles from Chesterfield. Known simply as Shiloh's by those who frequent it, the restaurant is decidedly unfancy and so is the food. Johnnie is down-to-earth, and she said the most endearing thing I think I've ever heard: "Never did I realize I'd grow up to wear a hair net."

Johnnie took a quick break and shook off that hair net at our table one busy Thursday night. She harbors no romanticism for the restaurant business; she and her two sisters grew up helping in the kitchen, the youngest standing on milk crates to roll fish in batter. Johnnie said when the restaurant's not open it's "nothing more than cleaning a house behind thousands of people."

Johnnie has a degree in art education from USC, where she met Mike, who was on his way to becoming an optometrist. But when she brought him home to meet the family and eat at Shiloh's, those plans changed. Now they're parents and, because of that, glad to live in a small town. Johnnie didn't give up art; her work is on the walls downstairs and Mike's photography is upstairs.

But nothing's more famous than the food. People say they'd rather get their seafood fix at Shiloh's than anywhere else. "When I go to my mom's in Myrtle Beach, she'll say, 'Wanna go get seafood?' I'll say, 'No, we'll wait 'til we get home and go to Shiloh's,'" said Temple Thomas of Cheraw.

What I like about Shiloh's is that management has gone ahead and made a decision for us: Everything, except the boiled shrimp, is fried. "Let me tell you, there's a good thing in that," Johnnie said. "My father said, 'Keep the menu simple and make sure everything on it's good. It's easier on you.' Daddy said it and I believe it, too."

I ordered the incredibly huge seafood platter. It comes with shrimp, deviled crab, oysters, fish, fries and six hushpuppies (I counted. I'm used to places that give you two.) I don't know what's more amazing, that it was so reasonably priced or that I couldn't finish all the shrimp. I'm still telling all my friends.

The seafood platter is much different from Shiloh's first offerings. When it opened in 1966, the restaurant served nothing but platters of fried flounder, buckets of slaw, and tea. Shrimp and oysters were introduced slowly by Ralph Watson, Johnnie's father. Now Shiloh Fish House serves more shrimp than flounder.

Today's menu includes those items and catfish, spot, black bass, fried chicken and a T-bone steak. The buttermilk hushpuppies are popular.

Shiloh Fish House is located in an old grocery store on S.C. 102. Because of its success, it's been expanded to include downstairs meeting rooms and a dumbwaiter for faster service. But some things haven't changed: The seafood is still cooked in salt-and-pepper batter and the kitchen is run by women—all in hair nets. It draws customers from Camden, Pamplico, Hartsville and Cheraw. Some come all three nights.

"It's like a family reunion," Mike said. "People visit from table to table."

Mike knows Shiloh's is special. His favorite story involves a friend who was a hunting guide in Alaska. The guide was leading a group from all over the country, and they exchanged information about where they were from. "They were sitting under the stars, and one guy said, 'Chesterfield.' Another guy said, 'That's where Shiloh Fish House is.' He had visited an aunt in Charleston who had relatives in the area and they had come here to eat."

The Watsons are a restaurant dynasty. Johnnie's sister runs Shiloh Family Restaurant, which serves steak and barbecue. Her mother, Ernestine, runs Shiloh to Go, a take-out place selling seafood, barbecue, pizza and her famous hot fudge cake.

Authenticity is the secret at Shiloh Fish House. The McCrights don't overimpress or overcharge you. They just give you good food at a good price fast.

- Aïda Rogers

Sandlapper *first visited the Shiloh Fish House in Spring 1994 and the McCrights tell us that the huge, fried seafood platter remains the house favorite. They've added some grilled items, including grilled shrimp and Cajun and Key West grilled tilapia, to the menu. Johnnie still has her art work on display. Son Damon, a graduate of Florence-Darlington Technical College, is waiting in the wings to become the next of the Watson-McCright clan to run the Shiloh Fish House.*
- *Tim Driggers*

Old 96 District

Abbeville, Edgefield, Greenwood, Laurens & McCormick Counties

The Dixie Drive-In, Greenwood
Greenwood County

The Dixie Drive-In, 600 Montague Avenue, Greenwood; (864) 229-2312. Open Monday-Saturday, 10 a.m. to 10 p.m. Inexpensive.

A Cheeseburger with Substance

There are a million reasons to write about the Dixie Drive-In in Greenwood. There's that nostalgic, *Happy Days* feeling it exudes. There's the American Dream story behind it: A Greek family opened it years ago and from it carved successful lives. There's the staff, together so long they've become family. And then there's Robert Adams, who's worked here from the very beginning and still hasn't been interviewed.

"All my life I never had an interview on anything," he said, pausing between various kitchen tasks. "If I don't find my name in that book, I'm not going to buy one."

And because we at *Sandlapper* want to sell as many magazines as the Dixie Drive-In sells burgers, we don't think it will hurt us to include Robert in our story. But Robert, like anyone else who works here, will tell you there's only one star at the Dixie Drive-In, and it's nobody behind the counter. The real hero is the Dixie Cheese.

"Welcome to the Dixie, home of the Dixie Cheese," declares the menu, but nobody reads it. They already know what they want and can recite it in a sort of rhythmic patter. Listen to Presbyterian College student Whit Bishop, home on holiday, tell waitress Barbara Herron what he wants: "Dixie Cheese, no tomato, half-and-half and tea."

You can hear that same order everywhere you turn—behind you in the to-go line, next to you at the counter, outside in the parking lot. The Dixie Cheese has been a pleaser since The Dixie opened in 1959, and it hasn't disappointed anybody yet. "I've been back from school three days and this is my third trip here," Whit said. "This is the best restaurant in town."

But The Dixie is not so much a restaurant as a local institution. High schoolers cut lunch to come here, where they see their coaches and teachers doing the same thing. Blue collar workers mix with businessmen, shoppers and police officers at the long horseshoe counters. At The Dixie, you can wear your cap, your football uniform or your prom night finery.

And while the fried chicken and roast pork sandwich are also popular, the Dixie Cheese has all but assumed mythic status in Greenwood. It is not a dainty, ladies luncheon kind of cheeseburger. Nuh-uh. It is a mighty, sprawling, swaggering, John Wayne kind of cheeseburger. The pickles are thick. The tomatoes are ripe. When you eat it—and you need both hands—juice and mayonnaise are likely to dribble into wondrous tasty glops on your chin or plate.

Now this is a cheeseburger.

And it ain't gonna change, says Perry Kerhoulas, who runs The Dixie with a pencil behind his ear and an apron around his waist. Greek immigrants, Perry and his brother Pete owned the Dixie until Pete died. Now Perry, his wife Pepitsa and a gang of loyal workers are making sure things continue as always.

"Put 'God Bless America' in there," Kerhoulas said. "Thank God we came east and not west. You can't find this life anywhere you go, I don't care what you say."

Nor can you find a cheeseburger like the Dixie Cheese. Even though he's all grown up and selling insurance now, David Hill still remembers when he cruised town in a '57 turquoise-and-ivory Chevy, always stopping at the Dixie Drive-In.

"When you're down and out, you go to The Dixie and get a Dixie Cheese and your rejuvenation is back," he said. "I guess it's the best thing since sliced bread to come to Greenwood."

The Dixie Cheese. It's the pride of the Emerald City.

- Aïda Rogers

Changes are afoot at this Greenwood institution. Perry Kerhoulas sold the Dixie Drive-In to Gus Koutsoukos in early 2008, and Scott McCravy, Perry's son-in-law, and Gary Culbertson, who's been with the Dixie Drive-In for 38 years, are now managers. Gary and Scott tell us the Dixie Cheese and companion Half and Half remain the big sellers on the menu. The Chicken Tender Platter, Fried Chicken, and Chef's Salad are popular as well. A couple from Florida recently stopped by craving a Dixie roast pork sandwich. What keeps folks coming to the Dixie Drive-In after almost 50 years? Gary has a simple explanation. "We have great food and great atmosphere," he said. "It's a family deal here. We know everyone in town." No orders are written down at the Dixie Drive-In. You just tell the cashier what you've had on the way out the door.

- *Tim Driggers*

La Cantina, Clark's Hill
McCormick County

La Cantina, 1750 Garrett Road. (864) 333-5315. You'll need directions: Take I-20 toward Augusta and turn at Exit Number 1 (SC Road 230), merge onto SC 230 toward Edgefield, go 9 miles and turn left on Garrett Road (SC Road 143). Continue for about 7 miles. Look for a sign and restaurant on the right. Open Wednesday-Saturday, 6-10 p.m. Reservations required. Cash and checks accepted, but not credit cards. Smoking allowed on veranda. Moderate to expensive.

A Twinkling Surprise

Marvelous and magical—that's La Cantina, a romantic little getaway in the depths of the Sumter National Forest. Its official address is Clarks Hill, a McCormick County town not far from the water that divides South Carolina and Georgia. But La Cantina is such a twinkling surprise, full of music and art and good smells, that state borders and all things worldly seem to dissolve. Here's a restaurant— and that's clearly the wrong word—that truly transports.

"We eat at Applebee's a lot and this isn't like that at all," said Philip West in a mighty understatement. Philip and his wife Sabrina have driven here from South Augusta, 25 miles away. That's not unusual for customers here; word has gotten as far as Savannah and Atlanta that something wonderful is waiting on 400 acres of wooded property where an artist and a musician have set up shack. With La Cantina, Laura Buchanan and Rusty Lindberg have put South America in the American South.

"North America and South America— it's the same culture," Laura said, pointing to an African mask that looks South American. "All people all over the world did the same thing; it's universal."

Laura should know; she's a double-degreed horticulturist who's been everywhere but Russia and Hawaii (you can even catch her in the Woodstock video). She's also a potter and painter, and like Rusty, a divine cook. Laura manages the kitchen while Rusty, a civil engineer, master woodworker and classical guitarist, takes care of the outdoor cooking. All this talent is on abundant display at La Cantina, the product of their love relationship.

"We're like Ricky and Lucy. People tease us all the time," said Laura, a fair-skinned redhead of Scots-Irish descent. Rusty is from Cleveland, son of a Norwegian father and Puerto Rican mother, and wearer of a long black ponytail and handlebar moustache. "Welcome, amigos" is how he greets customers; if they're lucky, he'll pull out his guitar. "Even the loudest people celebrating will quiet down and listen," waiter John Swafford said.

But usually Rusty is busy cooking, and guests are treated to recordings of music of all kinds— Spanish guitar, Hawaiian folk, calypso, Celtic, and American popular songs from the '20s, '30s, and '40s. Bing Crosby was singing "I Don't Stand a Ghost of a Chance with You" when Tom Gray and Laura Talbert obeyed the instinct to dance. "This is the kind of place you can do that," Tom said.

It's also the kind of place that serves extraordinary food. Tom and Laura have ordered tonight's specials: the Pico de Gallo-seared steak and the Cornish game hen stuffed with Grand Marnier mango chutney. Lobster-stuffed pheasant is another.

Like everything at La Cantina, the specials are cooked outside in the horno (pronounced OR-no), an adobe oven that looks something like an elongated igloo. Rusty built it himself, using a postcard of one from South America as a model. He and Laura are proud that everything at La Cantina was built from scratch, using material on the property. Rusty even made the bricks to build the horno, using clay, sand and straw; Laura uses the horno as a kiln for pots and ashtrays.

"And now, for the magic," Rusty said, shoving a long-handled pan in the horno. "It's the only horno east of the Mississippi, and one of the biggest in the country."

Hornos are ancient; the oldest was found in France, where it was used 26,000 years ago. The Spanish used them, and the American Indians, after the Spanish came to North America.

At La Cantina, the horno is part of the entertainment. Guests follow Rusty to the open air porch—here called a "veranda"— and watch as he sends it into the glowing embers 2,000 degrees hot. Such intense heat changes the flavor of the food, giving it a smoky taste. Then, almost ritual-like, Rusty walks back to the table, sizzling pan six feet in front of him, a trail of customers behind him single file. "It's like the Pied Piper and the aroma comes in after him," says John, the waiter.

La Cantina can serve an item from each of the 30-some Latino countries; the Cornish hen is from southern Mexico and Central America, the seared steak from Brazil. The food is mildly spicy, and as John says, "exciting but not overwhelming." It's a description for everything about La Cantina.

In operation since 1992, La Cantina has become a favorite pilgrimage for Atlantans who rent limos and travel 250 miles for the evening. Because Clarks Hill has little in the way of lodging, Rusty is thinking of putting teepees— equipped with Jacuzzis—near the restaurant. He has other plans, one of which is to bring Brazilian guitarist Raphael Rabello here to perform. Flamenco dancers from Panama have already performed impromptu; Rusty wants to schedule the national flamenco dancers from Spain.

Pretty exotic stuff this is for a stretch of land given 10 generations ago to Laura's family by King George III of England. Buchanans have been in McCormick and Edgefield ever since; Laura is a great-great granddaughter of "Pitchfork Ben" Tillman. Her roots and wings can be seen at La Cantina; a mask from the Philippines is on the wall across from her great-grandmother's wood-burning stove.

Not surprisingly, "authenticity and antiquity" are important to her. When a snowstorm caused the electricity to go out, Laura and Rusty were unruffled. Candles created enough light, and the horno works, regardless of weather. Using a 150-year-old axe, Rusty chopped a tree to let 21 stranded guests in for supper. "It was just like 100 years ago," Laura said. "We served steak fajitas and had the best time."

For people who like a dash of adventure with their dining, it's a must. Rusty remembers when a group of people drove up, looked out the car window, shook their heads and left. "They saw our tinted windows, and here we were in the woods, and you know what kind of reputation those places have," he said. "One of our customers said, 'Not Cantina material.' "

– Aïda Rogers

We guess we ought to just come right out and admit it, La Cantina is one of our favorite restaurants in South Carolina. Over the years Rusty has continued his passion for woodwork with new hand-carved furnishings throughout the restaurant and Laura still regales customers with tales of the historical family tract upon which La Cantina is located. The grill is still blazing, spawning Salmon Del Rio, Lamb Istanbul, Portuguese Pork, Seafood Macarhena, Shrimp Cuervo, Calypso Chicken, Horno Steak, Steak Fortant, and their signature Stuffed Horno Steak (a New York strip cooked like a Horno Steak, but topped with shrimp). Try the appetizers; they're equally exciting, as is the mixed bread Laura brings to the table. The veranda now has a roof, which makes it La Cantina's most popular dining room. At the end of the evening, after his cooking chores are completed, Rusty still delights customers with classical and flamenco guitar pieces. He also might turn ventriloquist and perform with Harvey the Janitor or Bernice, the ex-Waffle House waitress, two of his seven handmade characters.

– Tim Driggers

Little Mexico, Johnston
Edgefield County

Little Mexico, 502 Calhoun Street in Johnston; (803) 275-5011. Open Monday-Friday, 11 a.m.-10 p.m.; Saturday, noon-10 p.m. and Sunday, noon-9 p.m. Reservations not required. No smoking. Inexpensive.

And the Cops Eat Here Too

Unless you drop straight down from a spaceship, you're going to pass fields and fields of peach trees on the way to Johnston. This is Edgefield County, famous for fruit and fiery leaders.

So it's fun for an outsider to wander down Calhoun Street, lined with local businesses, and come upon Little Mexico. Bright and bustling, Little Mexico teems with the smells and sounds of that country.

"I like the tacos, I like the margaritas, I like the hours," says Lou Lewis, having a late supper with her husband Jack, who runs the pharmacy next door. It's a Monday night about 9. Families, seniors, blacks, whites, and—best of all—law enforcement officers are here. It's that latter category of human that recognizes a good restaurant. "Try the fried ice cream," advises Sgt. Robert Carroll with the Johnston Police Department. "It's goooood."

At 6'6", Sgt. Carroll needs a big meal. He looks satisfied after his Mexican steak supper, and says he'd have to drive to Augusta for Mexican food if Little Mexico hadn't opened. Lou and Jack, enjoying a Corona and a margarita, also are glad. "It was such an oddity for us to have a Mexican restaurant," Lou says. "This is the only place on Calhoun Street in the town of Johnston to serve a mixed drink. We nearly fainted."

Little Mexico plans to expand the restaurant and bar, and the church set is coming on Sundays. Business definitely is booming for sisters Ofelia and Isidra Cardenas, their brothers Luciano, Ricardo, and Agapito, and brother-in-law Pedro Cervantes.

"You wouldn't have seen this 10 years ago," Jack says. But since then, the influx of Mexican migrant workers has resulted in a permanent Latino population. The Cardenas family lived in Florida before coming to South Carolina. Now they live in North Augusta. From Ofelia and Isidra, we learned something about Mexico:

- Mexican soap operas have limited life spans. Playing this evening at Little Mexico, "La Mentira," or "The Lie."
- Field work is worse than kitchen work.
- Tortillas are made with corn and flour. Ofelia gets up at 4 a.m. to make them for her husband.

I don't think Bonnie and Dianne from my yoga class are going to do that anytime soon. But Bonnie, of German lineage, and Dianne, of Scots-Irish-English-German heritage, are Mexican at heart. And appetite. "I love Mexican food," Dianne announces, ordering chicken fajitas. "I could eat it every day," Bonnie seconds, launching into the chips and salsa. "Oh, it's hot," she says. "That's a good sign."

Little Mexico serves a variety of Mexican standards and more unusual items. Camaron Fajitas are shrimp with bell peppers, onions, and guacamole. Carne Azada is ribeye steak with onions, guacamole, and pico de gallo. Quesadilla Verde is a stuffed cheese quesadilla with a choice of beef tips, ground beef, chicken, or refried beans.

The fried ice cream was rightly recommended. Served in a peanut tortilla crust, it brought lots of cinnamony pleasure to Dianne, Bonnie and me.

Maybe Bonnie paid Little Mexico the ultimate compliment. She said she'd move from Columbia, knowing Little Mexico was here.

- Aïda Rogers

Ricardo Cardenas has assumed the ownership of the restaurant from the rest of the members of the family, but the menu and atmosphere of Little Mexico continues.

- *Tim Driggers*

Old Edgefield Grill, Edgefield
Edgefield County

Old Edgefield Grill, 202 Penn Street, Edgefield; (803) 637-3222. Open for lunch Tuesday-Saturday, 11 a.m.-2 p.m. and for dinner Wednesday-Saturday, 6-9 p.m. The bar is open Wednesday-Saturday, 5 p.m. until. Reservations required at lunch for parties of 6 or more and strongly suggested for dinner (you're gambling if you don't, the chef warns). Visa and Master Card accepted. Smoking on porch only. www.oldedgefieldgrill.com. Moderate.

"Stylish Interpretations of Southern Cuisine"

When the house is 1906 and there are two grand magnolias on either side of it, and lacy curtains hang from windows of wavy glass, can there be any doubt that pecan pie is waiting inside? Could there be any doubt that I would order it? There was crème brûlée, of course, and white chocolate cheesecake, but when you're in Edgefield, with Strom Thurmond memorabilia decorating one room and prints of early American game hanging in another, it would be unseemly to order anything that's not distinctly southern. And that's what the Old Edgefield Grill is, a "Fine Southern Restaurant," according to its menu.

There's no fried chicken (it's grilled with roasted garlic and shallot sauce), but there are fried green tomatoes, mashed potatoes, and macaroni and cheese so imaginative and delectable it silenced our gabby group of four. After a few swallows, Fred Robertson spoke up. "Oh my," he got out. "This is not macaroni and cheese. It's celestial macaroni and cheese."

The menu describes it as a "pasta tower." Its attributes include Parmesan, smoked cheddar, and smoked Gouda. "It's very Gouda," Fred punned.

The Old Edgefield Grill is just off the town square. Customers come from Augusta and Aiken, and many locals are regular. "We were members of the Pinnacle Club in Augusta and every time my husband would say

Delectable dining in a quaint county seat.

'Let's go to the Pinnacle Club,' I'd say, 'No, let's go to the Old Edgefield Grill,' " said Jean Quarles Jones, enjoying an appetizer. "Sean is a magnificent, magnificent chef, and I've never had anything that just wasn't absolutely the best."

Sean Alexander Wight is the co-owner. With a degree in culinary arts from the Art Institute of Fort Lauderdale, he worked at four- and five-star restaurants in Florida and Atlanta. He's put his special touch on the fish, fowl, beef, and game he serves in Edgefield, where he lived as a teen. Occasionally braised rabbit is on the menu (served over white cheddar grits with fried sweet potatoes) and venison tenderloins (with a sage demi-glace). We ordered the salmon (grilled with herbed mashed potatoes, sautéed greens, and a tomato/onion and caper salsa), and the pork loin chop (grilled with cranberry compote and the celestial mac-and-cheese). Gerry Lynn Hall, our self-avowed "carnivore," tried the medallions of Angus beef tenderloin (with Andouille sausage and crawfish tail cream sauce, served with mashed potatoes and veggies). Debbie Price ordered the tuna (with a veal reduction, grilled asparagus, and mashed potatoes with oven-dried tomatoes).

Until all that arrived, we sampled both soup de jours (sweet potato and crab bisque, roasted tomato garlic). We also enjoyed the fried green tomatoes (over grits with cucumber relish), Cajun fried popcorn (crawfish tails with remoulade sauce), and rustic baguettes with chive butter.

Anchovies accompany the Caesar salad; the coffee is Kona. The bar room shows off Wight's expertise in wines: *Wine Spectator* called him "a young knowledgeable chef" with "stylish interpretations of Southern cuisine." Look for a list that's lengthy and affordable.

Like any Old South home, this one has a good-sized porch. Lights wrapped around the columns add festivity to the evenings. This night, a birthday club of laughing women cocktailed al fresco before adjourning inside for dinner.

Our quartet journeyed from Lexington in a heavy rain, passing through the homey towns of Leesville, Batesburg, Ridge Spring, and Johnston en route to our destination. What a sweet conclusion.

- Aïda Rogers

Open less than a decade, the Old Edgefield Grill has won a loyal following. The menu changes seasonally, but that doesn't stop diners from asking for favorite meals. "We have many regular customers who come and order the same thing each meal," Chef Sean Wight said. Current best sellers are the Shrimp and Grits, Grill's Salad (with choice of Fried Crawfish Tails, Grilled Breast of Chicken, or Southern Fried Chicken), and Carolina Fried Shrimp. At lunch, look for the Blue Crab and Brie Cheese Fondue and the Mesquite Grilled Burger and for dinner, the Braised Carolina Rabbit, Edgefield Egg Rolls (with Smoked Pork, Collard Greens, and Local Peach Mustard), and Slow Braised Lamb "Osso Bucco" over Creamy Goat Cheese Grits. Because this is Peach Country, you can revisit the orchard with Peach Mustard Glazed Salmon over Fingerling Potatoes with Garlic Baby Spinach. It's so good, I'd bet Ole Strom might even come back from the Great Beyond for just one last meal.

- Tim Driggers

Pascal's Café and Grill, Greenwood
Greenwood County

Pascal's Café and Grill, 307 West Cambridge Avenue, Greenwood; (864) 223-2329. Open Monday-Saturday, 5:30-10 p.m. Closed Sunday. Wi-Fi available. Reservations strongly recommended. Credit cards and checks accepted. Smoking at bar only. www.pascalscafe.com. Moderate.

Where the Food is Art

Monet, Rubens, Van Gogh, da Vinci, Raphael...Hurtebize? The first five names are recognizable as some of the most famous artists to ever apply oil to canvas. This

Hurtebize guy may be more obscure. Not that he should be; it's just that his work isn't seen at the Musee d'Orsay or Louvre. Hurtebize, however, belongs with the Pollacks, de Koonings, Gorkys, and Rauschenbergs of the mid-20th Century American expressionist movement. Pollack was noted for his splash-and-drip technique, Hurtebize for his dappling of sustenance on porcelain.

Pascal Hurtebize's medium is the plate—more specifically, the plates at Pascal's Café and Grill in Greenwood. I've always thought of chefs as artists. Instead of creating with easel and brush, they forge culinary masterpieces in the kitchen. Pascal takes it a little further. Not only are his dishes edible treasures; they are presented with the eye of an artist.

I ordered an appetizer of Maryland blue crab cakes with Beurre Blanc sauce, thinly sliced Granny Smith apples, and Pascal's signature tomato preserve. The plate was absolutely gorgeous and the taste equally good. Complementing my meal was the ambience: French prints, local art, abounding bottles of wine. There was even a "flural," a mural on the entryway floor; as artist Judson Arce put it. It depicted a French fish pond and led to a doorway painted with a cascading waterfall.

My entrée was even more spectacular. Keenan, my attentive waiter, served roasted veal and sage ravioli in a creamy sweet basil pesto sauce bespeckled with small tomato cubes surrounded by a spinach leaf border. "When I present a plate, I want my customers to eat with their eyes first," Pascal said. "That's French cooking. Not only must the food taste good, but it should look good. Both must work together." It isn't surprising that Pascal aspired to be a cartoonist early in life. "My father asked if I wanted to be a starving artist or make a living, so I followed his advice and enrolled in cooking school."

Pascal spent two-plus years at the Culinary Institute of Paris, where he was born. He was an apprentice to famed chef Gilbert Drouelle, the maitre cuisineiere de France, at La Dariole de Viry Chantillon, a Michelin restaurant guide restaurant. "He took me under his wing. To learn beside a chef renowned throughout France was unbelievable." It was while employed at the Palace Hotel Scribe restaurant that he met the French consul of South Carolina, Jackie Dietrich, who invited him to move to America and become chef at her restaurant in Spartanburg, Le Bistro.

In 1988, Pascal moved to Greenwood to run the Inn on the Square. After 10 years, Pascal and wife Lisa decided to open their own restaurant. They bought the site of Pascal's Café and Grill in 2000. The 1930s home had been the Sigma Nu fraternity house at Lander College before becoming a restaurant.

They change the menu a couple of times each week. "Nothing drastic," Pascal explained. "I would have been shot if we had taken our shrimp and grits, crab cakes, and salads off the menu."

He and Lisa aim to provide an enjoyable evening away from home. "We want to transport you somewhere else," Pascal said. "My background is French, so I've created a fusion of French cuisine combined with southern flavors."

It's a successful formula. Harriett Kinard of Greenwood has been dining with her bridge club here for years. "We always start at the bar—it's warm and cozy—and after drinks, head to the dining area. In the summer, we prefer to eat on the porch. Pascal is invariably accommodating and the food is always consistent." Harriett prefers the small plates and often chooses the romaine salad with tossed nuts, Gorgonzola, and sweet Vidalia onion vinaigrette.

Randy Davis, who has appeared in this column numerous times as my culinary assistant, used his friendship with Harriett to again get a word in. "Pascal's is not only classy, but it's comfortable," he opined. His favorite is the grilled wild Alaskan salmon. "It's cooked slightly blackened, which is perfect for my taste."

Pascal's Café and Grill offers a dining experience unique on many levels. Great food with great service presented in a pleasing atmosphere. That's a combination difficult to beat.

- Tim Driggers

The Red Barn, Gray Court
Laurens County

The Red Barn, 1955 Trinity Church Road, Gray Court; (864) 682-2771. Open for dinner Friday and Saturday, 5:30-9:30 p.m. and for brunch Sunday, 10:30 a.m.-2 p.m. Closed Monday-Thursday. Credit cards (no Discovery Card) and checks accepted. Reservations suggested for parties of 6 or more. No smoking, except on patio. www.redbarnsc.com. Moderate.

Customer to Chef After Dessert: "Marry Me"

Many of us have, or have had, access to a farm. And a pond, where catfish could be caught and fried that night. But chances are that catfish wasn't served with a Cajun rémoulade, and the mashed potatoes didn't come with a sauce of smoked Gouda.

Wonderfully for those who appreciate the unexpected, there's The Red Barn Restaurant near Gray Court. Here, in the upper reaches of Laurens County, where the hills are rolling and the pastures are plenty, you can have a supper of lamb and prawns followed by a dessert of chocolate and fruit fondue. Watching goats circle the fishing ponds and boys reel in their catch is not a bad thing, if you like a fresh-air view with your first-class meal.

"We're a cross between your grandmother's table and a fine French restaurant," said Chef Michael Burnham, who worked at various restaurants in Greenville before coming one county south. Witness his southern egg roll appetizer. It's stuffed with

Gourmet pleasures await guests at The Red Barn.

collard greens, black-eyed peas, and country ham, with a honey Tabasco sauce for dipping. Then there are the fried green tomatoes, another appetizer, served with sweet smoked tomatoes. Even the "Texas Toast Burgers" are special, available with mushrooms or a variety of cheeses.

It wasn't always that way. With Michael's help, owners Jim and Alvina Meeks transformed a bait-and-tackle shop selling hotdogs and hamburgers into something much different. "We wanted something we could be proud of," Jim said.

That they have. The Red Barn Restaurant manages to be elegant and rustic, with a main café-style dining room (red booths, white tablecloths), two private dining rooms and patios for pretty weather. Sunday brunch happens here; so do wine tastings. About two dozen wines are served; you can see the bottles stacked in the rack built from BiLo produce boxes.

Michael learned to cook from his mother, Jane Flanagan of Travelers Rest. "She'd take a cast-iron skillet and invent stuff, and it'd always come out really, really good." He inherited that talent for cooking recipe-free, and honed it in different kitchens. His last stint was at the Commerce Club in Greenville.

The menu he's created for the Red Barn includes the familiar—grilled New York Strip (12-ounce Angus with herb butter) and fried or blackened catfish. For the more adventurous, there's Hazelnut Crusted Salmon (with creamy orange Dijon sauce) and Grilled Pork Tenderloin (with bourbon apricot and cherry chutney).

Our foursome ordered two specials and two menu items. The specials were scallops and prawns in saffron broth with sun-dried tomato orzo and julienned vegetables, and lamb with apple bacon chutney, grilled potatoes and asparagus. From the menu came crab-stuffed chicken with smoked Gouda sauce and shrimp and grits (fried cheddar grit cakes with shrimp, prosciutto, green onions and a garlic cream sauce). The entrées were colorful, beautiful, and topped with fresh herbs.

Maybe it was those fresh herbs, maybe it was the full moon, or maybe it was because we girls don't get out much, but a rollicking supper ensued. Two of us, "Malibu Barbie" and her sidekick "Skipper" enjoyed frosted pilsners of Heineken and Bud Light while the other two went for iced tea. Upon learning our chef is single, we began some serious discussion that can't be repeated here. But when a sampler plate of desserts arrived, including the chocolate and fruit fondue (bananas, mangos, raspberries, peaches, for two), all restraint departed.

"Oh my God, do you want to get married?" That was Malibu Barbie calling out to Michael after a bite of the cheesecake du jour, a banana nut confection with pecans, rum, butter, and brown sugar. Michael makes a different cheesecake every weekend, from plain with fruit to Chocolate Cappuccino, Orange Ginger, and Maple Sweet Potato. We also had the key lime pie and crème brûlée, which inspired more unfit-to-print conversation.

Finally our Barbie took a deep breath and leaned back. "That's the most sinful thing I've done in a very long time," she said. She never looked more content.

- Aïda Rogers

A great sadness has fallen upon the female population of the Upstate, bachelor chef Michael Burnham no longer cooks at The Red Barn. But guys, you have your chance now. Two years ago, Jennifer McNeil took charge of Jim and Alvina Meeks' kitchen and now creates crowd-pleasing delicacies including crab-stuffed chicken, pecan encrusted grouper with saffron sauce, and Italian chicken pasta. The Red Barn's signature appetizers, southern egg rolls and fried green tomatoes, are as popular as ever and great to try while dining on the patio. Alvina and Jim recently added a lounge that's become a favorite place to hobnob, relax, and enjoy a glass of wine or spirits.

- Tim Driggers

The Village Grill, Abbeville
Abbeville County

The Village Grill, 110 Trinity Street (near the Town Square), Abbeville; (864) 366-2500. Open for lunch Tuesday-Saturday, 11:30 a.m.-2 p.m. and for dinner Friday-Saturday, 5:30-10 p.m. Closed on Sunday and Monday. Credit cards accepted. Reservations recommended for parties of 8 or more. Smoking at bar only. Moderate.

The Abbeville Special

Only a true malcontent could not find something to like at The Village Grill in Abbeville. With its friendly atmosphere and expansive menu, it's a favorite with locals and visitors coming to tour this historic town and take in a show at the Abbeville Opera House. On this breezy spring Saturday, it's prom night for Abbeville High. As is the custom, prommers gather in the Court Square to mingle, check one another out, and suffer their parents taking photos. Could there really be anything better than watching the glittery jittery hubbub, and then strolling two minutes away to a great restaurant in blue jeans?

Our quartet slid happily into a booth, where we eyeballed the specials first thing. Written on a chalkboard on the wall of each booth, the specials are the raison d'être for owner Bill Savitz and his wife Molly. "The specials are what make us so popular," Bill said. "We put a lot of time in them and research."

They indeed looked special. The appetizer tonight is grilled Asian sesame-apricot barbecue ribs over fried onions. For entrées, the specials include grilled Portobello topped with blackened beef tenderloin, sautéed spinach, sun-dried tomatoes, bleu cheese with Chipotle aioli, and fried potato cakes. Another is grilled cherry Chipotle barbecued fresh salmon over cheese grits with Cole slaw and Jalapeño glaze. It doesn't take long to realize that despite the casual atmosphere—there are posters of B horror movies on the wall—the Savitzes are serious about food.

"We're closed on Sunday and Monday and that's when Molly does most of her desserts and that's when I'm working on the specials," Bill explained. "We just throw ideas back and forth at each other. Sometimes, you just need somebody to help you focus and we're good at helping each other."

At our table, we helped each other choose what to order. It's not easy, because there are soups, salads, sandwiches, pasta, steak, and seafood in the lineup. Danish baby back ribs are popular; so is Steak Dianne (beef tenderloin pan-fried in fresh garlic, sherry and shallots). Finally, we decided on the Bacon-Brie Cheeseburger, the quarter rotisserie chicken, and two specials: seared fresh sea scallops with mushrooms and tomatoes over angel hair pasta and lobster cream sauce, and bowtie pasta with grilled chicken, prosciutto, mushrooms, spinach, and red onions in roasted garlic cream. Salads are inventive, with almonds, eggs, and red peppers atop mixed greens.

Desserts are just as creative. Molly's custard-based ice creams have become her calling card. Tonight's is a tropical mango and pineapple, served on coconut pound cake. Bill brags about her peach rum flavor, available in summer. Cheesecakes change too. Tonight's are Turtle with Oreo crust and plain with raspberry drizzle.

Bill, an Abbeville native, always wanted his own restaurant. He opened The Village Grill in 1992, in an old Belk-Simpson cloth shop. Like many of the buildings around the square, it's on the National Register of Historic Places. At the time, Abbeville didn't have any restaurants serving upscale food, and he was successful from the start. When you love to cook, and people appreciate your culinary experiments, life is pretty good, he said. "There's a lot of satisfaction when you feel like people are enjoying what they're eating. I get a lot of pleasure doing what I think is a job well done."

- Aïda Rogers

If it's not broke, don't fix it. Somewhere it seems I've heard that admonition before. Might have been in Abbeville, where everything about the Village Grill stays the same. And that's good. Bill still agonizes over his chalkboard specials and Molly continues to slave over her desserts, much as they always have during their 15 year run in downtown Abbeville. It's hard work, but Bill and Molly wouldn't have it any other way. They love their restaurant and fawn over their diners. It doesn't hurt that they also serve an upscale cuisine that invariably delights town folk and visitors to their quaint burg. Specials dominate the menu, but best sellers also include the Baby Back Ribs, Steak Diane, and Rotisserie Chicken.

- Tim Driggers

Capital City / Lake Murray Country

Lexington, Newberry, Richland & Saluda Counties

Al-Amir, Columbia
Richland County

Al-Amir, Murraywood Shopping Center, 7001 St. Andrews Road, Irmo; (803) 732-0522. Open for lunch Monday-Friday, 11:30 a.m. to 3 p.m., and dinner 5:30-10 p.m. Saturday hours are 11:30 a.m. to 10 p.m. Sunday hours are 11:30 a.m. to 9 p.m. Reservations accepted. Credit cards and checks accepted. No smoking or alcohol. Moderate.

A Taste of the Middle East In the Midlands

This story tells all you really need to know about Al-Amir and its owner, Mohammed Saadeddin. Shortly after midnight, the telephone rings at Saadeddin's home and there's a lady on the line with an insatiable craving for Al-Amir's Damascus bread and hummus. Instead of slamming down the receiver or informing the caller of the restaurant's business hours, Saadeddin simply says, "No trouble," scrambles out of bed and heads to Al-Amir. He stokes the charcoal of his brick oven and begins blending ingredients and baking bread. About 1:30 a.m., a sheepish husband pecks on the front door for the carry-out plate, and off he drives into the night with his prized entree.

Saadeddin didn't charge a penny. "I loved to do it," he said. "This country has been great to me and I'm always looking for ways to give back to the community."

Located in an Irmo shopping center, Al-Amir is a visit to the bazaars and byways of the Middle East. Seated amid Mediterranean tapestries are sophisticated Muslim and non-Muslim veterans of Middle Eastern cuisine and uninitiated first-timers, regular patrons, and those simply curious about the food and Arab culture.

Accompanying me were Columbia's premier ballroom dancing duo, Breedlove and Richard Durlach. Not only can they dance; they know everything about everything. As we seated ourselves, I anticipated an evening of great food and conversation.

Our guide to the menu was the aforesaid Mr. Saadeddin. A native of Damascus, Syria, Saadeddin came to America in 1983, aspiring to earn a computer engineering degree on the West Coast. After eight years in Los Angeles, he moved east and eventually landed in Columbia as owner of a handmade rug business. Later he opened Al-Amir, which is Arabic for "Prince."

We began with appetizers of sesame and blessed seed laden Damascus bread, hummus, labneh (creamed yogurt spread topped with dry mint and olive oil), and baba ghanouj (oven-roasted eggplant with tahini sauce, garlic, and lemon juice). "I sampled so many things from everyone else I'm not sure which one was mine," Breedlove said of our communal feast. Next came the salad selections of traditional tabouli and fettoush, and the Al-Amir, a combination of diced tomatoes, cucumbers, onions and mint, marinated in lemon juice and olive oil.

Richard and Breedlove both ordered the lamb kabob. "Delicious," Richard said.

"I imagined myself living in the beautiful countryside of Lebanon preparing lamb over a fire under a starry sky." Breedlove noted the fresh taste that was "complemented by a special spice from Mohammed's native land that he grows in his own garden. That impressed me." I opted for the Damascus bread topped with kufta, which is ground sirloin with spices, onions, and parsley. I could readily taste why it's a favorite dish. A neighboring diner was raving about the Shawarma, tender thin slices of lamb or chicken marinated in traditional Arabic spices.

Richard liked the aesthetics. "The atmosphere was quiet enough to have a conversation," he noted. "The presence of the expatriate Lebanese there to enjoy their own culture indicated the food must be good. It was like stopping at a diner with 18-wheelers parked outside. It was the ultimate compliment."

A great menu, an owner who delights in mingling with his guests and relating the history and culture of the Middle East, and a wide diversity of patrons make Al-Amir a most pleasant dining experience. If hopping a jet to Lebanon for kibbeh, mujadara, or Damascus hummus isn't practical, then a drive to Irmo and Al-Amir will do just fine.

- Tim Driggers

Devine Foods, Columbia
Richland County

Devine Foods, 2702 Devine Street, Columbia; (803) 252-0356. Open Monday-Saturday for lunch, 11 a.m.-2:30 p.m. and for dinner, 5-9 p.m. Closed Sunday. No reservations. Smoking only on patio. Accepts checks and credit cards except American Express. Inexpensive.

It's Greek and It's Goooooood

"This wine tastes like Greece," proclaims Aphrodite Kondurous, a full-blooded Greek-American from Sumter. Daughter of Greeks, wife of a Greek...the Greek spills out of her mouth as easily as South Carolina-style English. At home this morning, she made an omelet of fresh tomatoes, onions, and feta cheese. Today for lunch, she treats us to Macedonia white wine, served in clear plastic cups, and tells us how wonderful it tastes with feta cheese.

It's obvious Aphrodite is at home at Devine Foods. "If they were busy I'd get up and work. It's part of the deal."

Our foursome languishes over Greek-style burgers with feta and today's special sandwiches, a tuna steak sandwich and chicken wrap. We sip our wine, listen to the enthusiastic Greek conversation in the kitchen and learn a little about a culture exotic to us. Aphrodite, a lawyer and writer (she covered the Catawba nation and its famous pottery in a previous issue of *Sandlapper*), is also a patient teacher. We learned:

- "Never on Sunday" comes from the Greek rule that prostitutes don't work on that day.
- Greeks never start anything on Tuesday, because that was the day Constantinople fell to the Turks.
- Many Greeks, including Devine Foods co-owner Georgia Trifos, come to this country by way of Nova Scotia.
- Greeks celebrate Easter a week after Protestants.

For Easter, a leg of lamb from Devine Foods is a tradition for many Midlands families. You can order that and other Greek entrees by the pan, including spanekopita, and tiropita, a cheese pastry. Also available on a catering basis are dessert cheesecakes, a bleu cheese cheesecake and a smoked salmon cheesecake.

"Are those Greek?" I wonder. Aphrodite shrugs. "Georgia's a merchant. She'll make whatever you want." Georgia Trifos, a former nurse, and her husband Angelo have been serving Columbians almost 11 years. Named for its location on fashionable Devine Street, Devine Foods offers a range of fresh Greek fare: salads full of olives and feta, moussaka, the eggplant/potato/ground beef casserole, and pastichio, a macaroni and ground beef casserole. Every Friday's lunch special is the lightly breaded ocean trout, served over rice with dill butter and salad.

"We usually get the usual," jokes Mike Bryant, who comes for lunch almost every day with his colleague Andrew Summerell. Their usual is the 6-ounce grilled chicken, served over rice with tossed salad and garlic bread. Not only is it low-fat and low-price; it tastes good, they say. "It's like eating Greek food at your house," Andrew observes. "Georgia and Angelo are like your mom and dad. Of course, Angelo yells at me, so I know he likes me."

Angelo's strong personality is belied by his deftness with desserts. His Bananas Foster Cheesecake—a confluence of lady fingers, Graham crackers and banana liqueur—is particularly famous. "If you don't taste that, you're going to hate yourself," Aphrodite promises. But one dessert can't satisfy four women, so a round of baklava appears. "Is that made by an artist?" Aphrodite challenges, holding up the perfect diamond-shaped pastry for us to admire.

Georgia's chocolate chip-pecan-oatmeal cookies are another house specialty. Many customers buy one or two for the way back to work.

Devine Foods does such a big take-out business at lunch that it can be hard to get inside the dining room. But sidewalk dining is available, and a porch has been closed in and brightly decorated. In keeping with the unpretentious décor, utensils are plastic and plates are Styrofoam. Aphrodite looks up at the walls and chuckles. "Only Greeks will have open bottles of wine on a shelf."

The meaning of that is lost on me. I can't worry about it right now. Food awaits. As any good Greek would say, "Kali Orexi!"

- Aïda Rogers

Since we last visited Devine Foods in the Summer of 1999, nothing really has changed and...we like that! Owner Angelo Trifos retains his charismatic, animated personality, entertaining all who venture into his popular Devine Street restaurant. You never know who is going to drop by. The members of Hootie and the Blowfish are regulars, as are the Carolina football coaches. Angelo can often be seen these days wearing a Steve Spurrier/USC visor while "coaching" his staff at Devine Foods.

- Tim Driggers

Edna's #1, Columbia
Richland County

Edna's #1, 3609 River Drive, Columbia; (803) 252-6696. Open Monday-Saturday, 10:30 a.m.-7 p.m. Closed Sunday. No smoking. No credit cards, cash only. Inexpensive.

Fries with a Wiggle, Dogs That Don't "Snap"

Edna's #1 (there's no Edna's #2) is in a small, white building distinguished only by a "Hot Dogs and Hamburgers" sign on the siding. Meals can be consumed on five ancient picnic tables outside. Orders are taken at the window and customers patiently await their meal outside. We found the wait more than worth the effort.

Open for about 50 years, Edna's #1 is a Columbia institution. When discussing the midlands' best cheeseburgers, it's often mentioned, even though some folks don't remember the name, only its address at the corner of Broad River Road and River Drive, and that it's been there for a long, long time. Customers arrive in suits and overalls, a cross-section of Columbia looking for a good, quick meal and vying for a seat at one of the picnic tables.

"I've been coming to Edna's since I was a kid," said Paul McCravy, an expert on all things burger and dog. "It's withstood time. You eat al fresco in a sort of garden retreat under shade trees, with cars flying by and whiffs of cat food in the air."

If that sounds a bit too outdoorsy, it's really not. It's all part of the experience. "It reminds me of eating in a small town during the 1940s, a place you stopped when you and your family were on the road," Paul continued.

The food is the real draw. John Derrick, director of Alumni and Church Relations at Newberry College, and I ordered cheeseburgers. John chose the bacon cheeseburger while I opted for the plain cheeseburger. Emily Bogdan, my godchild, tried the chicken filet sandwich and Paul tackled a couple of hot dogs. Each of us added fries and the famous Edna's tea.

"Edna's tea is the definition of southern sweettea," Paul said. "That's one word in South Carolina. It's got plenty of sugar, which makes the taste very sweet and syrupy." John noted one important extra: "The refills are free." As for the fries, Paul said they meet his standard for quality. "They've got to have a little wiggle. You don't want a stiff fry." Emily agreed. "Very flavorful," she pronounced. "They were crispy on the outside and soft in the middle—much better than fast food chain fries."

The cheeseburgers are large and taste great. "Edna's definitely does not serve a pre-fab burger," John said, admiring the thick, crispy bacon, perfectly melted cheese, and hand-pattied meat.

Paul raved about the hot dogs. "Edna serves a less expensive wiener, not like those expensive types that are tough to eat. Edna's hot dogs are southern hot dogs—they don't have that snap sound when you bite into them."

- Tim Driggers

The Flight Deck, Lexington
Lexington County

Flight Deck, 109-A Old Chapin Road, Lexington; (803) 957-5990. Open Monday-Thursday, 11 a.m.- 9 p.m. and Thursday-Friday, 11 a.m.-10 p.m. Closed Sunday. No reservations required. Credit cards and checks accepted. No smoking. Inexpensive to moderate.

Lift Off for Lunch! (And Supper, Too)

As you walk to your table at the Flight Deck restaurant, don't be surprised if you run into King Kong. Not to worry, it's not the 50-foot-tall ape from the jungles of Skull Island; it's a 6-foot display of the famous 1933 movie scene depicting Kong swatting Navy biplanes atop the Empire State Building. Odd? Not hardly. At the Flight Deck, owner Ted Stambolitis has combined his lifelong passion for flying in a fun, casual restaurant that's become a local favorite.

Look at the menu and you'll see the aviation influence. Sandwiches include the Avenger, strips of grilled marinated chicken in pita bread, named for the famous torpedo bomber of World War II. The Marauder, sliced roast beef and mozzarella on a hoagie bun, honors the B-23 bomber that fought in Europe and the South Pacific. The

Memphis Belle, a homemade chicken salad sandwich, is named for the renowned B-17 Flying Fortress of movie fame. The Flying Tiger, a baked cheese sandwich, remembers the P-40 Warhawk that battled Japanese Zeroes in the Pacific theatre. If you don't see a particular airplane, check the walls. The Flight Deck is filled with models and photographs of vintage airplanes.

"I've loved aviation since I was a little boy," Ted explains. "I wanted the Flight Deck to reflect my enthusiasm for flying and vintage aircraft. I searched antique shops and classified ads to build my collection and customers started donating different items. Every picture has a story of how it landed in the restaurant."

At the Flight Deck, you'll see your friends, sample some mighty good food, and meet Ted Stambolitis. He wanders the dining hall greeting guests and making sure the service and food is satisfactory. He might also discuss a little town politics: Ted's a member of Lexington Town Council. Children can play video games in the arcade. On the way out, grab a bag of homemade baked cookies. And don't be surprised if Ted's at the door thanking you for your visit and inviting a return.

A Florence native, Ted was reared in a restaurant family. His dad John operated restaurants for 48 years, including the Market Restaurant, an institution in Columbia. Ted started his own place, Plato's, in Columbia in 1984. Then he decided booming Lexington, where he'd lived since 1988, was ripe for a new restaurant.

The original Flight Deck opened in 1992; it was so popular Ted closed it and built a bigger one six years later. Now the restaurant operates in a bustling complex he created that reflects the World War II era. "I envisioned 1942 America during the war years where visitors would feel like they were walking into another time and place," he says. Business still booms, and Ted expanded the facility in 2007 for group meetings and special events.

Besides sandwiches, The Flight Deck offers dinners. Try homemade lasagna, spanokopita, spaghetti and meat sauce, chicken parmesan, chicken cordon bleu, Stromboli, grilled pork chops, hamburger steak, and country fried steak. There's also a lunchtime Blue Plate Special, where $5.95 provides a choice of homemade spaghetti, pot roast, roast chicken, country fried steak, meat loaf, fried pork chops, chicken tenders, Salisbury steak, barbecued pork, or fried chicken breast. Two vegetables and iced tea are included.

Pete and Diane Oliver of Lexington come once or twice a week. Pete loves the meatloaf and the sweet southern tea. "Ted's father served meatloaf in Florence," he said. "It's a traditional family recipe that's slightly spicy and very good."

Diane likes the gyros and hospitality. "Ted doesn't take any diner for granted," she said. "He visits each table and makes every guest feel special."

- Tim Driggers

Garibaldi Café, Columbia
Richland County

Garibaldi Café, 2013 Greene Street, Columbia; (803) 771-8888. Open Monday-Thursday, 5:30-10:30 p.m., Friday-Saturday, 5:30-11 p.m., Sunday, 5:30-10 p.m. Reservations recommended. Credit cards accepted. No smoking. Valet parking available. Moderate to expensive.

Sous Chef Derek Poole adds whipped cream to tiramisu.

Out of this World on Christmas Eve

Garibaldi's is one of the few restaurants in Columbia to open for dinner on Christmas Eve, but rather than being an imposition upon the Yule, it's a celebration of all that's wonderful about the season. Amidst the art deco stylings and strings of miniature white lights are familiar faces I see each December 24th. For them, like me, dining at Garibaldi's on Christmas Eve is a tradition. Husbands/wives/boyfriends/girlfriends dressed to the hilt enjoying each other's company, celebrating family and friendship. Teenagers with their families and dates, making their initial foray into the adult world, trying to impress while nervously tugging at best suits and dresses, making sure hair is perfectly styled. Plenty of smiles, plenty of laughing, and lots of great food.

"Our number one priority is consistency," said general manager John Glasgow. "We strive to serve the freshest food available prepared with a quality distinctively good." Garibaldi's more than succeeds. "At most restaurants, there is usually one thing on the menu that's a specialty," noted West Columbia decorator Ellen White.

"At Garibaldi's, everything is good. The service is impeccable. The moment you walk through the door, you're treated like royalty."

Beside the regular menu items, Garibaldi's features nightly specials usually consisting of three salads, a soup, six entrees, and a variety of desserts. Beegie Truesdale of Camden, now a theatrical producer in Los Angeles, dines at Garibaldi's on her visits home. "They have a very inventive cuisine," she said. "I'm impressed that Garibaldi's creates a variety of flavors in a variety of cuisines within the context of Italian foods."

The signature dish is the crispy scored flounder with apricot shallot sauce. "It's simply wonderful and always perfect," Ellen said. Bill Carrick of Aiken, a political consultant in Los Angeles, agrees. "It's a classic; fresh, meaty, and decidedly high-end." Other menu favorites include these appetizers: Cornmeal Encrusted Fried Green Tomatoes and Oysters, Pan Seared Scallops with Polenta Fries, Buttermilk Battered Calamari, and Black Mussels in a Basil Pesto Cream Sauce. Entrees include Pan Seared Jump Lump Crab Cakes, Beef Tenderloin and Sautéed Shrimp Linguine, Almond Encrusted Tilapia, Veal Scaloppine Piccata, and Chicken Pagmigiana and Chicken Milanese. My personal favorites are the seafood dishes, especially the oysters and scallops. Even if they're not on the menu, ask for them anyway and you may be rewarded with perhaps the best seafood in the midlands.

No trip to Garibaldi's would be complete without dessert and their what-we're-known-for almond basket, a combination of fresh fruit and ice cream in an almond flavored waffled cone. "It's to die for," Ellen said. "Simply out of this world."

- Tim Driggers

Gasthaus Zur Elli, Prosperity
Newberry County

Gasthaus Zur Elli, 205 Main Street, Prosperity; (803) 364-9008. Open Monday, 5:30-9 p.m.; Thursday, 5:30-9 p.m. and Friday-Saturday, 5:30-11 p.m. Closed Tuesday, Wednesday, and Sunday. Credit cards and checks accepted. Reservations recommended (call the restaurant and Wendy will return the call). No smoking. Moderate to expensive.

He's a Gasthaus Groupie

Gasthaus Zur Elli is located in an unassuming brick building near the square in downtown Prosperity. It's small, seating only 50 or so, but correspondingly huge in personality and charm. Step through the door and enter an unexpected world that magically transports diners from everyday humdrum to Old World Bavaria. Atmospheric, rustic ... yes, Gasthaus Zur Elli is all of that, but—surprise—in a restaurant world of faux ethnicity, it's flat-out German every which and way.

Cuisine is but one component of eating at a German restaurant. Along the Rhine, there's a certain buoyant spirit that makes dining an exhilarating experience. Try as you might to stay seated at your table, chances are that before the evening is over, you'll be swaying arm-in-arm with new friends, singing beer hall favorites, and dancing in the aisles. You might be Elmer Fuddy Duddy, but you *will* sing and you *will* dance; that's the German way.

That same conviviality is found at Gasthaus Zur Elli. It's not eat and run; it's a memorable night of dipping a fork, hoisting a stein, and raising the roof. Wendy Steiner makes sure of that. Owner, chef, and hostess, she was born in Birnfeld, Germany, and learned her way around the kitchen from mother and mentor Elli, a master chef in Wurzburg. "She made everything from scratch," Wendy said. "It was authentic old-time German country cooking."

Wendy came to America in 1978 and settled in Columbia where she managed convenience stores until the restaurant bug bit in 1999. "I took every penny I had and opened a coffee shop in Prosperity," she said. "Mama told me I was too old to do such a thing, but I had faith I could be successful." Following her mother's death in 2001, Wendy renamed the restaurant in Elli's memory, expanded the seating, and inaugurated a dinner menu.

Wendy cooks everything on two regular home stoves in the restaurant's small kitchen. "I don't go by recipes. I create. I take a dash of this and a pinch of that and blend it all together. Sometimes when I arrive at the restaurant, I haven't a notion of what I'm going to cook." But cook she does, offering six to eight different dinners each evening. "All my meals are honest-to-goodness German," she said, "each pan-fried with genuine German seasonings and ingredients."

The signature dish is the veal Wiener Schnitzel. Served with red cabbage and German potato salad, it's simply delicious. And if somehow you're still hungry after downing your meal, Wendy will come to the rescue. "Honey," she said to me, "I'll be glad to fix you an extra plate if you didn't eat enough." That was tempting for sure, but being completely stuffed to the size of a Gamecock left tackle, I declined—only to regain my senses and ask, "Wendy, you wouldn't mind if I took that plate to go?" That's what being a Gasthaus groupie does to you.

Gasthaus Zur Elli features Sauerbraten, sweet and sour roast beef with gravy and dumplings, the first week of each month; Hungarian Goulash, beef and pork tips in a spicy gravy with noodles on week two; Roladen, thin sliced beef with gravy and stuffed with bacon, onions, pickles, and mushrooms over noodles or dumplings on week three; and Schweinebraten, pork roast with gravy over mashed potatoes or spatzle, the fourth week. The regular menu includes a variety of schnitzels (pork, veal, and chicken), as well as Geschnetzeld (beef strips), Rindfleisch (beef roast), Rinderbraten (beef), and Cordon Bleu. Wendy also serves traditional German favorites Wild Boar and Rabbit. "People love rabbit in Germany," she said. "I pan-fry the rabbit with carrots and leeks in a German butter and serve it with spinach and noodles." Gasthaus Zur Elli has a variety of German beers and wines available. And you won't want to leave without sampling either the Apfel Strudel or Italian Creme Cake.

I've taken many a guest to Gasthaus Zur Elli and never had anyone who couldn't wait to return for another helping of great food and Wendy's effervescent personality. All the reasons that Gasthaus Zur Elli is my favorite restaurant in South Carolina.

- Tim Driggers

Hampton Street Vineyard, Columbia
Richland County

Hampton Street Vineyard, 1201 Hampton Street, Columbia; (803) 252-0850. Open Monday-Friday for lunch, 11:30 a.m.-2 p.m. and for dinner Monday-Saturday, 6-10 p.m. Bar opens at 5 p.m. Reservations recommended. Credit cards accepted. No smoking. www.hamptonvineyard.com. Moderate to expensive.

French Cellar Ambience in the Capital City

Across the street and down Hampton from the Columbia Museum of Art is Hampton Street Vineyard. With French prints complementing the subterranean décor of stucco, brick and wood, and decorative vases and plants prominent throughout, Hampton Street Vineyard has a decided European bent. From outdoor tables on the Hampton Street sidewalk, diners can indulge in another French passion: people watching.

The cuisine is varied and imaginative. "Our menu changes every three months, but the one thing that never changes is our consistency," said Leigh Talmadge, who along with Bill Murphy owns the restaurant. It certainly impressed me and Randy Davis, my dining companion. We started with a hearty, spicy black bean soup. Randy, who usually vacuums food like a Hoover Steam Vac, slowly savored his first course in rapt joy. He then ordered the Grilled Beef Filet, accompanied by roasted fingerling potatoes, cauliflower puree and Bourdelaise. I chose the Balsamic and Dijon marinated pork tenderloin with sweet potato puree, grilled asparagus and apple jelly drizzle. The marinade was a perfect accompaniment to the succulent pork.

Hampton Street Vineyard has two signature dishes: Sautéed Lump Crabcakes over honey-glazed fingerling potatoes and sautéed spinach with a cucumber and yogurt sauce, and Seared Hudson Valley Fois Gras, served on butternut squash and apple salad with honey balsamic drizzle and toast points. "Not many people do Fois Gras in Columbia," Talmadge said. "Ours has been extremely popular."

The menu at Hampton Street Vineyard recommends various selections of wine to accompany each entrée. If that doesn't suit, a 26-page wine menu features more than 650 vintages. The restaurant has received *Wine Spectator's* "Best Award of Excellence" each year since 1998, an honor given only three restaurants in South Carolina.

"It's an impressive restaurant," Randy noted. "It has a French cellar atmosphere and the menu is top-notch. It's a small place with a bit of a clamor, but has a cosmopolitan feel." Indeed, the cuisine is extraordinary. Randy proved it when he almost etched the enamel off his plate trying to consume every morsel.

- Tim Driggers

Hudson's Smokehouse, Lexington
Lexington County

Hudson's Smokehouse, 4952 Sunset Boulevard, Lexington; (803) 356-1070. Open Monday-Saturday, 10:30 a.m.-9 p.m. and Sunday, 10:30 a.m.-3:30 p.m. Smoking allowed in bar; ventilation fans carry away the smoke. Reservations unnecessary. Credit cards and checks accepted. www.hudsonssmokehouse.com. Inexpensive to moderate.

Barbecue and So Much More ....

Most every Friday, Hugh Rogers and I will grab some friends and head out on the barbecue trail. That lunchtime path usually leads down U.S. Highway 378 from Lexington to Hudson's Smokehouse.

Usually the parking lot is already full when we arrive, and a line has formed outside. Not that anyone minds. It's what's inside that matters. What in the name of John C. Calhoun is a few minutes' wait when some of South Carolina's best barbecue is only a few feet away?

The line moves fast and the moment of decision is at hand. Reaching the front, you're confronted with the obligatory, "what'll you have?" and then the panic starts. You think you know, but doubt creeps in. You think you've come for the Barbecue Pork Plate and three sides, but wait, what about the other choices on the menu board?

There's the Barbecue Beef Brisket Plate, the Barbecue Rib Plate, the Barbecue Chicken Plate, the Smokehouse Catfish, or the Surf and Turf Combination Plate of pork, brisket, catfish, ribs, and wings. Then further doubt sets in: Maybe I shouldn't eat so much, maybe a sandwich will do. So you consider the huge Barbecue Pork, Beef Brisket, or Catfish sandwiches with fries. Then there's the 2-piece chicken dinner. Dinners come with three sides and who can figure that out? Besides sweet potato casserole, hash and rice and fried okra, there are the French fries, sweet potato fries, macaroni and cheese, corn, and beans, beans, beans (baked, string, and lima). It's too much. Your brain is about to explode and you blurt out an order.

Hugh orders the 2-piece chicken dinner and I, dripping with perspiration from my anxiety attack at the counter, order the catfish sandwich. The paradox then hits. What are two lifelong barbecue lovers doing at Hudson's Smokehouse, named by Turner Broadcasting System as one of the four best barbecue restaurants in the Southeast, and not ordering an ounce of barbecue between us?

The answer is quite simple: Everything is delicious. The barbecue will be there tomorrow, but today might be the day you hanker for chicken, catfish, or even a hot dog or cheeseburger basket. While a barbecue restaurant is sacred ground, as a person of faith, I firmly believe that the sin of a non-barbecue order can be forgiven.

Robin Hudson grew up around barbecue, spending summers in Samson County, North Carolina, with his grandfathers. "My grandfathers could smoke some really good pork. I learned quite a bit about barbecue just being around them." They also made a vinegar-and-pepper barbecue sauce that Robin still uses today.

A combination of oak and gas are used to cook the barbecue, and pork is constantly basted in a three-tiered rotisserie. Open seven days a week, Hudson's serves barbecue that was cooked that day. "Any leftovers are turned into hash," Robin says.

Unlike many Palmetto State barbecue places, Hudson's offers brisket. "Lexington residents have relocated from all over the United States and people who've lived west of the Mississippi are accustomed to brisket," Robin explains. "When we started, we might serve 30 pounds of brisket a week, now it's up to 400 pounds of shredded and sliced brisket a week."

The restaurant includes a bar, patio, and dining room. With its bright hardwood interior, Hudson's Smokehouse has brought the stereotypical barbecue restaurant design from its traditional cement block style into the 21st Century.

Lexington radio legend Redd Reynolds likes the barbecue chicken, mashed potatoes, baked beans, and slaw. He and gamecockcentral.com's Scott Hood are regulars Monday night for the radio broadcast of the "Carolina Crow Line and Clemson Hotline." Says Redd: "Everything on Robin's menu is good. It's amazing how many people in Lexington eat out. You can hardly get in this place most evenings." Scott orders the pork barbecue with macaroni and cheese, sometimes a double order.

Hudson's features live music on Friday nights and trivia contests on Thursday evening. Once a month, banjo wizard Randy Lucas and Duane Davis, Dave Holder, and Ronnie Gregory perform their own brand of Carolina bluegrass on the patio.

Hudson's Smokehouse has won a reputation for quality in a relatively short span.

It's a reputation well earned. By the time Hugh Rogers says "wanna go to Hudson's," I'm already in the car.

- Tim Driggers

The Hunter-Gatherer Brewery and Ale House, Columbia
Richland County

The Hunter-Gatherer Brewery and Ale House, 900 South Main Street, Columbia; (803) 748-0540. Open Tuesday-Saturday, 4 p.m. to "whenever." Reservations not required. Credit cards and checks accepted. Smoking allowed. Inexpensive to moderate.

Black Bean Dip, Hummus, and Really Great Beer

The Hunter-Gatherer brew pub on South Main has always been one of my favorite spots in Columbia. Located near the University of South Carolina and only blocks from the state capital, Koger Center for the Arts, Carolina Music School, Nickelodeon Theater, Colonial Center, and Carolina Coliseum, it attracts a diverse clientele with its rustic decor, distinctive musical offerings, excellent homemade beers and time-tested menu ranging from fresh salads and tempting appetizers to pub sandwiches and savory entrees. When the inevitable question "Where do you want to eat?" is asked before or after a show in Columbia, The Hunter-Gatherer is a likely destination. It's a comfortable venue for friends to gather while eating great food, sipping arguably the best beer in town and, on Thursdays and Fridays, listening to some of the best jazz in the midlands.

On a recent visit, I was accompanied by my godchild Emily Bogdan, an honor roll student at Brookland-Cayce High School. We spotted our friends Judy and John Fisher of Cayce and their precocious 4-year-old daughter Callie upstairs and invited ourselves to pull up a couple of chairs. Our second-floor vantage point gave us a wonderful view of the brew pub's open-beam ceilings, worn brick walls, gothic lighting, and decor of African murals, spears, shields, masks, totems, and original art. The tavern-style tables, each with chairs of differing styles, adds a bohemian touch, while owner Kevin Varner's 10-barrel brew station dominates the main floor and indeed the entire building.

Not just a restaurant/brewery, The Hunter-Gatherer is a living organism where the inanimate is given life by the vibrancy of customers and ambience. At the bar, women and men are laughing, talking, meeting, and mixing. As evening progresses, especially on Thursday when jazz legend Skipp Pearson takes the stage, the search for an empty table can be exhausting.

I chose the evening's special appetizer of pan-seared duck breast with yellow cherry-sherry vinegar reduction, Ginny's Blue Cheese Salad, and the what we're-known-for Hunter-Gatherer Burger with white horseradish cheddar. Yes, I made an unashamed P-I-G of myself. The duck was tender, succulent, and absolutely delicious. So was the salad of mixed spring greens with bacon, gorgonzola, red onions, almond slivers, and vinaigrette dressing—so tasty the flavors seemed to leap from my plate. My cheeseburger, perfectly scrumptious, was served with the unconventional side of nongreasy hashbrowns. Emily, who freely delved into my duck appetizer, ordered the hummus plate. "The dish was arranged beautifully," she said. "The grapes added sweetness to the flavor."

Judy was equally satisfied. "I find The Hunter-Gatherer so unpretentious," she said. "It's the closest thing we have here to Asheville. You can dress up or dress down and still feel at home."

Kevin, a Greenville native, worked for three years at Hale's Ales in Seattle, perfecting his skills as a master brewer. In 1994, when the state legalized brew pubs, Kevin knew it was time to come home and open his own place. "I wanted a brew pub that specialized in fully brewed English ales," he said. "They are good ales in the traditional English style."

While Kevin says his beer is "good," local beer expert Gerald Jowers has another adjective. "Kevin's beers are outstanding....He doesn't serve many varieties of beers, maybe four at best, and his facility is small, but his beers are exceptionally well-brewed. Kevin has an English-style technique, crafting English ales with American hops for a spicier favor. His beers are also fresh and that is everything when talking about beer."

On this night, The Hunter-Gatherer was serving a wheat beer, a pale ale, its signature ESB (extra special bitter), and an organic stout. "The ESB is their best beer without question," Gerald said. "Bitters come in ordinary, special and extra special. The extra special is the most robust and stronger in favor."

Though not ready to sample beer, Callie Fisher still has her own opinion. "It's my favorite place," she trilled, clapping her hands. A lot of folks in Columbia feel the same way.

- Tim Driggers

Jackie Hite's Bar-B-Q, Batesburg-Leesville
Lexington County

Jackie Hite's Bar-B-Q, 476 West Church Street (between S.C. 23 and U.S. 1), Batesburg-Leesville; (803) 532-3354. Open Wednesday-Thursday, 9 a.m.-2 p.m. Friday, 11 a.m.-8 p.m. Saturday from 9 a.m.-8 p.m. and Sunday, 11 a.m.-2 p.m. Closed Monday and Tuesday. Checks and cash accepted. No reservation required, except for large groups. Smoking discouraged. Inexpensive to moderate.

Feel Like a Little Barbecue?

It's noon on Friday. Do you know where your father is?

I know where mine is. He's moving down the line at Jackie Hite's Bar-B-Q buffet in Batesburg-Leesville. His buddy Frank Gulley is with him. Together they've traveled the slow road from Lexington to Leesville for something well worth the half-hour ride. At Jackie Hite's, it's called "fresh pull."

"You really oughta come out there, Alley Oop," he told me months before I finally traveled that slow road myself. "It is really something to see."

He was right. A long line of pickups are parked out front. Tables full of men are parked inside. And on the buffet is the guest of honor, a pig cooked last night and ready for picking now. For people who love barbecue, it doesn't get much better.

"It's a whole lot easier to come in here and enjoy it instead of doing it yourself," says a satisfied Craig Lybrand of Summit. "You don't have to buy the hog, cut the wood, invite the people, and spend 12 hours cooking it. Jackie takes all the hard work out of it. All you got to do is give him ten bucks."

To be exact, it's $9.95 for Friday's pig-picking, a great price for an all-you-can-eat choice of fresh barbecue, mustard-based barbecue, fried chicken, rice and hash, green beans, baked beans, cooked cabbage, mashed potatoes, beets and hot curried fruit. (The curried fruit is great with the barbecue.) A salad bar and dessert bar of various puddings are available, too. So is iced tea—sweet and un. But the attractions are the pig...and Jackie Hite.

"I'm tired but not RE-tired," says Hite, friendly and flashy in a bright blue satin jacket from a recent fishing tournament. Jackie's love is fishing, and you can tell that by the stories he tells and the art on the walls. Known as the Santee Cooper "Crappie King," Hite has fished with Roland Martin and appeared on *Sports South*. One favorite story involves a very thirsty Jackie Hite doing without water for the camera's sake until he finally cupped his hands in the minnow bucket and drank from there.

In short, barbecue with Jackie Hite is a double pleasure: good food and funny conversation. But he'll stop that conversation if he thinks there's something not quite right with your meal. "That's not crunchy enough," he tells my father when he examines his pork skins. "Let me get you another piece."

Jackie Hite started barbecuing hogs when he was 8 years old. Today, he's 67 and doing it the same way. "I came up in the old school where your father showed you how," he says, recalling how he and his sisters and brothers helped their dad with his weekend barbecue business. "Time and patience have a lot to do with it. It takes 24 to 30 hours straight to do barbecue right."

During the Fourth of July, Jackie cooks about 40 hogs, 400 chickens and a thousand quarts of hash. Some customers say the chicken is the big draw. "It falls right off the bone," notes Fowler Cary, a regular at the Sunday buffet.

Today, Jackie's wife Mickey and four daughters work with the business. When his children were younger, they delivered barbecue to customers, just as he delivered his father's barbecue when he was a teenager.

Somewhere in between, Jackie found a way to become one of Leesville's first citizens. Besides being a water commissioner, town councilman, fire chief, and head of the rescue squad, he was mayor of Leesville three times. "I won't say I won't run again," he says.

His ambitions don't stop with public service. Country music might have been an option if he'd started sooner. "Three or four years ago I went to Nashville alone to try to get on a star show, but I found out it'd take six months to get in the door." Undeterred, he went to a recording studio and sang "Lovesick Blues" and "Your Cheatin' Heart." In Monetta, he recorded "Waltz Across Texas" and "Walking the Floor Over You." Both got air time on WBLR radio.

"I'm just trying to sing like Ernest Tubb," he says.

As you can see, this man is irrepressible. And his barbecue is great.

- Aïda Rogers

I was watching The History Channel the other night and almost fell out of my chair when I saw Jackie Hite on the screen stoking the coals under his massive barbecue pit in Batesburg-Leesville. I shouldn't have been surprised. Jackie's quite a celebrity these days. He recently appeared in the documentary "Barbecue Is A Noun" about barbecue culture in the Carolinas and was featured on WIS-TV's "Back Roads Bar-B-Q" series. WIS personality Joe Pinner gave this assessment of Jackie's famous pork skins and pulled pork on wistv.com, "I would give it a four (3 being the highest), if there were a four." Pretty heavy stuff. Hugh Rogers, his son Clifton, and I make Jackie's a regular stop and we've never been disappointed. Whether it's eating barbecue or downing catfish, I've learned from Hugh to tuck my tie inside my shirt, load my Styrofoam plate to the ceiling, and dig in like this is going to be my last meal on earth. If that did happen, I would probably beg St. Peter for just one more chance at the Jackie Hite buffet.

- *Tim Driggers*

Juniper, Ridge Spring
Saluda County

Juniper, 640 East Main Street, Ridge Spring; (803) 685-7547. Open for lunch Monday-Saturday, 11 a.m. until 2:30 p.m. and for dinner Thursday-Saturday, 6-9 p.m. Open for Sunday brunch, 11 a.m.-2 p.m. Closed Wednesday. Reservations requested for parties of 8 or more for dinner. Credit cards and checks accepted. No smoking. restaurantjuniper@hotmail.com. Moderate.

A Dining Surprise in Peach Country

Juniper is in a renovated 1880s store that has been home to a hardware store, florist, hair salon, auto parts business and delicatessen. In Juniper, the old building may be experiencing its crowning success.

Somehow, I don't believe while growing up in Poughkeepsie, New York, Brandon Velie ever envisioned himself someday taking root in Ridge Spring, South Carolina. Someday owning a restaurant, maybe; someday owning a restaurant in Ridge Spring, hardly. But it's here where he and wife Jeanne have landed and they could not be happier. "We have fallen in love with the town," Brandon said. The same can be said of how the townsfolk have taken to Juniper. It's a restaurant that is many things: a laid-back midday lunch spot, an upscale restaurant Thursday, Friday and Saturday nights, and an after-church meeting/dining stop on Sunday. "When we first opened we asked ourselves, 'What are people going to say,' " Brandon recalled. "We were quite certain Ridge Spring had never seen a menu like ours. Our first week, we had so many people come by and their common response was, 'I love this place!' "

Three of us began with corn chowder and salad. We could have stopped there and been quite happy. The house salad (mixed greens, smoked bacon, red onion, tomatoes, croutons) was topped with a tangy blue cheese vinaigrette that was fantastic.

Before ordering entrees, our very knowledgeable waitress, Tammy Dyson, brought four dishes of creamy grits topped with salmon. "Amusez la bouche," Aïda exclaimed, a French expression meaning "a small gift from the chef to please the mouth." Brandon more than succeeded, because our "gift" was extraordinary. Later we learned Brandon had mixed coconut milk and vindaloo, a curry, into his grits (Adluh, for him). "I like to prepare meals that are creative," he said. "I'm inspired by a wide variety of influences."

Juniper offers little plates, which Aïda, Mary Fletcher, and Randy selected; and big plates, from which I chose (only because Aïda had preempted my order). Both sizes were substantial and more than we could eat, particularly after the chowder and salad.

The ever-adventurous Mary Fletcher ordered a main dish of pan-fried frog legs with cheddar and bacon grits and barbecue sauce, while Randy chose the pimiento cheese-stuffed crispy chicken breast with mashed potatoes. Aïda selected the pan-seared tuna with avocado smash and blueberry vinaigrette. I ordered the pan-seared flat-iron steak with a Juniper crab cake, mashed potatoes, asparagus, and sauce hollandaise.

Juniper is a dining surprise. Simultaneously unpretentious and upscale, the Velies' vision is matched by Ridge Spring's small town charm. "For those planning a day trip through South Carolina, Ridge Spring and its surrounding communities are a must," Randy said, "and Juniper would be the perfect place for lunch or dinner."

- Tim Driggers

Juniper's menu changes both weekly and seasonally, as does the local artwork adorning its walls. For lunch; the crab cakes and French dip are favorites while the pimiento cheese-stuffed chicken breast wows the dinner crowd.

- T. D.

Kathy's County Line Store, Lake Murray
Saluda County

Kathy's County Line Store, (formerly The County Line Store), 3881 Columbia Highway (on U.S.1 at the Lexington and Saluda County line); (843) 532-3533. Open Monday, Tuesday, Thursday, and Friday, 7 a.m.-8 p.m.; Wednesday, 7 a.m.-1 p.m., Saturday, 8 a.m.-8 p.m., and Sunday, 8 a.m.-1 p.m. You might check with the fish in Lake Murray for their schedule. No reservations needed. Credit cards accepted; no checks. Smoking allowed on front porch rockers. Inexpensive.

Simple Heaven in a Bait-and-Tackle Store

My editor-cousin Dan has many talents. He's a writer and musician, foremost. But the attribute I admire most is his knack for finding great cheeseburgers in small places. Not everybody can do that.

"I think I was driving by after one of our editorial meetings," he relayed over quarter-pound cheeseburgers at The County Line Store, just over the line from Lexington to Saluda County. "I just stopped by and found out they had a grill. I had a quarter-pound cheeseburger and it was the closest thing I can remember to the way my mom used to make them."

That was two years ago. Dan has been stopping by The County Line Store ever since, either to or from Spartanburg, where he lives now with his wife, daughters, two dogs, and Quaker parrot. With all the cacophony in his life, a homemade cheeseburger in a dimly lit bait-and-tackle store begins to take on great meaning.

"I like the atmosphere," he explained. "It's an old, old country place. It relaxes me, and it reminds me of being a kid in the country." Those barefoot days are long gone, at least in our hometown of Lexington. But just over the line (the address is Leesville but the county is Saluda) you can still find those unassuming pleasures. At The County Line Store, the sign says "Bait, Tackle and Cold Beer." You can get a cheap country breakfast, a blue-plate lunch, and whatever you need for a fishing excursion on Lake Murray. There's even a jukebox and an ATM topped by a little white Christmas tree.

"We thought we'd take it slow and retire, but it fooled us," says Claudia Hall, who took over the place with her husband James in 1996. It was just bait, tackle, and beer then, but Claudia, whose father ran a small restaurant in York in her childhood, wanted to add a grill. She and James had spent their careers trucking, and ate a lot of bad food. When they retired to fish on Lake Murray, they decided to give people what they would have wanted. "We slow-cook everything. That makes the food a lot better."

Today's lunch special is fried chicken, green beans, potato salad, a slice of tomato, and two rolls. You can serve your own tea or grab a soda from the refrigerated cases on the wall. While you're wandering, check out the minnows in the tank in the rear, and observe those great staples of any self-respecting country store: Vienna sausages, Mount Olive dill chips, canned beef stew, and of course, pork skins.

The County Line Store has six tables. One is a green, 1950s Formica dinette Claudia bought at a garage sale. Antique merchants want to buy it, but she refuses. "That's the Lying Table," she says, explaining that about eight old-timers sit there every morning to solve the world's problems. Its comfy chairs, sturdier than more modern ones, are easy for them to get in and out of.

Breakfast here is appropriate for the surroundings. The Country Breakfast is a full plate with two eggs, grits or hash browns, toast and jelly, and a choice of bacon, sausage, or ham. The Pancake Breakfast includes two eggs with bacon or sausage. If you need breakfast to go, a variety of sandwiches and biscuits are available, including gravy biscuits and a liver pudding and egg sandwich. One little girl has her birthday breakfast here every year with grandparents and friends; her birthday cake is a candlelit Moon Pie.

I suspect Dan wanted The County Line Store to be his little secret, and he thought I, a female, would never appreciate it. Ha. Anyplace that sells tater wedges and Cokes in glass bottles gets the authenticity award from me.

- Aïda Rogers

There's a new owner at The County Line Store. Former owners Claudia and James Hall passed away and Kathy Kimes reopened the store April 1, 2007. "We've changed just about everything," Kathy said. "It's a diner, convenience store, bait and tackle shop for fishermen—but basically we're a country store." Business is booming at the new County Line Store and Kathy's added two additional tables and revamped the old menu to accommodate her customers. The Breakfast Special has two eggs, toast, and a choice of bacon, bologna, sausage patty, onion sausage, or country ham. Kathy also serves a variety of biscuits: country ham, sausage patty, onion sausage, bacon, egg, sausage gravy, and bologna. Sides and extras include pancakes, hashbrowns, grits, lettuce and tomato, and toast. The lunch and dinner menu features 1/3 pound hamburgers and cheeseburgers, patty melts, hot dogs, slaw dogs, corn dogs, sausage dogs, BLTs, and grilled cheese, flounder, chicken, fried bologna, ham, turkey, club, chicken salad, and pimento cheese sandwiches. For dinner you can get all the lunch items in a basket with fries and slaw and a hamburger steak served with salad. The best seller is the cheeseburger Dan raved about. Prices are reasonable, very reasonable. When I visited Kathy's County Line Store, the rockers lining the entranceway were filled with customers trying to create a breeze on a hot August afternoon. They were adept at shooting the breeze as well. Something you'd expect to find up Saluda way.

- Tim Driggers

The Lexington Arms, Lexington
Lexington County

Lexington Arms Restaurant and Lounge, 314-A West Main Street, Lexington; (803) 359-2700. Open for dinner Monday-Thursday, 5:30-9 p.m. and on Friday and Saturday, 5:30-10 p.m. Lounge opens at 4 p.m. Closed on Sunday. Credit cards accepted; checks only with prior approval. Reservations requested and required for five or more people. Smoking allowed only in lounge. Moderate to expensive.

Whether It's German, French or American, It's Gooooood!

Feeling the need to break away from family members and family restaurants, I escaped to The Lexington Arms, two minutes away from this office. I went with Sarah Wilkins Weiss, old family friend, daughter of my boss, public school kindergarten teacher and the person who makes sure you get your *Sandlapper.* "Oh, I looooove The Arms," Sarah said.

Sarah and her husband Wayne visit Lexington Arms frequently —sometimes when Sarah's working at *Sandlapper* late at night, or for Valentine's Day and birthdays. I love the way she whispers when she's serious. "Wayne and I come on German night," she said, and leaned across the table. "I looooove it," she whispered. "Wayne loves the

Jaeger Schnitzel. It's delicious. Wayne gets the Spatzel, and I get the German potato salad." She leaned forward again, and whispered. "It's goooood!"

But Sarah and I were there on French night, which meant no German potato salad for us. Normally on French night (Tuesday and Wednesday), Sarah would get the Veal Oscar. But she stuck to her diet and ordered the marinated chicken breast from the everyday menu. I ordered Steak Diane from the French menu. That way we could get Duncan Crowe to ourselves.

Duncan Crowe is the brave Brit who came to Lexington in 1979 and made fine food sell. His wife Elisabeth is from Germany, and she's the cook. Duncan, however, will prepare Steak Diane at your table – flames leaping – and if you're lucky, he'll laugh his famous laugh. Cherries Jubilee and Bananas Foster are other Duncan Crowe tableside performances.

People have been coming to Lexington Arms for years; even people from Columbia. McLeod Bellune, publisher of *The Lexington County Chronicle*, figures there's no need to go to Columbia when the best is right here. Lexington Arms is comfortable, relaxed, and the food is great, she upholds. "I've grown up all over the world and eaten in five-star restaurants, and I love this," she said, and complimented the Arms' hard-to-describe, fancy-but-not-fancy atmosphere. "People who eat hog jowls and grits will be comfortable in Lexington Arms."

McLeod was sitting with her husband Jerry, editor of *The Chronicle*, and two other couples. Printer Norb Simpson, consultant Perrin Love and Jerry have been celebrating birthdays together for years.

"Once we made the mistake of going some other place, but we came back here," Jerry said, and compared it to *Cheers*. "Everybody knows your name."

Though they tease Duncan and say they like to watch him "fawn over us," they also say they can count on him to impress their guests. "I can have people come in from out of town and I'll call Duncan and we'll be taken care of any day of the week," Perrin said. Norb just calls it the "classiest restaurant in this four-county area."

Pat and Tony Callander are so regular the waitresses know to bring a Bass Ale to the table immediately. A CPA from Australia, Tony likes to spar with Duncan about beer and eat the German food. (German nights are Monday, Thursday and Saturday.) They both remember when Lexington didn't have that much variety when it came to eating out. The Crowes changed that.

They brought prime rib and lamb chops, Lobster Francaise and frog legs. They brought Tournedos Henry IV, sauerbraten and rumpsteak. Seafood in puff pastry and pasta of all kinds are other Lexington Arms offerings. So is the apple strudel, Elisabeth's cinnamony native dessert. You can't help but think because Germans settled here so long ago that the Lexington Arms was always supposed to be here. This town wouldn't be the same without it.

- Aïda Rogers

Duncan Crowe still makes sure that everything is house-made at his Lexington Arms. Steak Diane continues to be his most popular entrée on the French Nights of Tuesday and Wednesday and Veal Oscar on the German Nights of Monday, Thursday, and Saturday. Orders from the regular menu can be made each evening. Other top meals now include Prime Rib, Beef Claudia, and Shrimp and Crab dinner.

- Tim Driggers

Mediterranean Café, Lexington
Lexington County

Mediterranean Café, 327 East Main Street, Lexington; (803) 356-6294. Open Monday through Saturday for lunch, 11:30 a.m.-2:30 p.m. and Monday-Thursday for dinner, 5:30-9 p.m. and for dinner Friday-Saturday, 5:30-9:30 p.m. Closed Sunday. Reservations not required. Credit cards and checks accepted. No smoking. Inexpensive to moderate.

Lexington's "Cheers" Comes with Hummus and Tabbouleh

Azmi Jebali was born to own a restaurant. His friends enjoyed his home-cooked Eastern Mediterranean dishes and showed up in droves when he prepared meals at church functions. Whenever he cooked, he was perpetually peppered with "when are you opening a restaurant?" That question was answered in 2003, when Azmi launched the Mediterranean Café in Lexington.

In the small town of Tybey, 30 miles northeast of the Israeli capital of Tel Aviv, the large Jebali family rarely left home to eat. They didn't need to; Azmi's mother was a great cook. So it wasn't surprising that Azmi brought her influence to America when he came to USC. He delighted in sharing the robust flavors of his native land, using the requisite basics of garlic, onions, tomato, and eggplant, with heavy emphasis on olive oil, to provide a welcome alternative to standard dorm fare. His kitchen expertise also helped him land a wife. "When we were dating, he would cook me dinner at least twice a week," Beth Hendrix Jebali said. "He is such a wonderful guy and it didn't hurt that he is also a wonderful cook."

After graduating, Azmi opened a landscaping company in Lexington, but felt the lure of opening a restaurant. It helped that his father-in-law, Charlie Hendrix, was quite a cook himself. Charlie, once-owner of Charlie's Quic-Pic near Lexington, was known for great hot dogs and chili. Also, Azmi's brother Ahmad had opened the Mediterranean Tea Room in Columbia and was enjoying terrific success. After 20 years of planting trees and cutting grass, Azmi traded his lawn mower for a kitchen stove.

Grilled Cowboy Steak with mixed vegetables at Mediterranean Cafe.

"People supported me from the very beginning," Azmi said. "My family and friends all seemed to want a quality neighborhood restaurant." He's answered the challenge. "Azmi makes everyone very welcome," observed Susan Shumpert. "It's like everyone is going to Azmi and Beth's home for dinner."

Some of those people are my sisters. Listen to Dale: "My friends and I meet at Azmi's often and we each have our own favorites. I stick to the Greek chicken salad and Jan makes a meal of the hummus appetizer and warm pita bread. Linda loves the chicken kabobs, while Carol prefers the pork chops and sucks them to the bone."

My other sister, Donna, is right there with Carol on those pork chops. "They are so juicy and tender they almost melt in your mouth."

"Azmi learned everything from his mother," Beth Jebali said. "Nothing at the restaurant is pre-fab. Everything is completely fresh."

The menu features the foodstuffs Azmi grew up with, some new creations, and a few modified versions of old favorites. "Most of our food—the hummus, baba ghannouj, falafel, tabbouleh, gyros, and mijadarah, are all strictly authentic," Azmi said. "We change around some things, like our shrimp dinners, but not too much.

"The secret to Mediterranean cooking is using the right ingredients, making sure they're fresh, and keeping quality consistent," he added. "I use lots of olive oil and garlic, but not too many spices." Azmi frequently shops at the State Farmers Market and local farms.

Signature dishes include the hummus and filet mignon steak, which is marinated in a special sauce and grilled. Also popular are gyro sandwiches, lamb and beef kofta burger, salmon and tuna over yellow rice, and a vegetarian plate of tabbouleh, hummus, falafel, olives, and feta cheese. Extensive wine selections and wine tastings add to the café's sophistication.

- Tim Driggers

Mediterranean Tea Room, Columbia
Richland County

The Mediterranean Tea Room, 2601 Devine St., Columbia; (803) 799-3118. Lunch Monday-Saturday, 11:30 a.m.-2:30 p.m., dinner Monday-Tuesday, 5:30-8:30 p.m., Wednesday-Saturday, 5:30-9:45 p.m. Closed Sunday. No reservations. Credit cards and checks accepted. Smoking only on outside deck. Inexpensive to barely moderate.

Of Olives, Dates, and a Bedouin Breeze

Lunch for me is frequently a nondescript sandwich at my desk. But oh, the anticipation of supper with good friends at The Mediterranean Tea Room in Columbia. I can wallow in all the olive oil I want.

"I like the lemon," confides Leyla Mason, a Persian now living in Columbia. When the MTR opened, she found a place—outside her kitchen—to satisfy her need for tabbouleh, hummus, and baba ghannouj. These Middle Eastern standards generally aren't found at other Mediterranean restaurants, the Greek and Italian ones. You can get a gyro and Greek salad at the MTR, but check out all the eggplant, lamb, and tahini. Say the word "tahini" and feel that Bedouin breeze.

"I do very traditional cooking," says owner Ahmad Jabali, a Palestinian who grew up near Jerusalem. "Traditional" for him means garlic, fresh lemon juice, and olive oil. Don't look for butter and cream sauces here, unless you order the salmon special. You can expect the reddest tomatoes and the crispiest parsley and cucumbers. Try the Falaheen salad and you'll get the idea.

"It's the freshness of the food and the style of cooking," Ahmad explains about the MTR's success. "I go to the Farmers Market to pick up my produce every day."

Because Mediterranean cooking is low on salt, sugar, preservatives, fat, and other enhancers, people with health problems have become regular customers. So be warned. "Some people, their taste buds are used to lots of salt and sugar, and when they taste something fresh, it isn't normal," Ahmad says. "Even if you don't like the taste sometimes, it's good for you."

I have yet to meet someone who doesn't like the tastes available at the Mediterranean Tea Room. "I think their tabbouleh is some of the best I've ever had," says Dolly

Brothers Azmi and Ahmad at the Mediterranean Tea Room in Columbia.

Patton, a Florence native with an adventurous palate. Tabbouleh is a refreshing salad of parsley, bulgar wheat, tomatoes, and scallions prepared with lemon juice and olive oil. At the MTR, it's served as a salad appetizer.

I met Dolly for the proverbial Girls Night Out. We were going to "do it right," which meant two kinds of wine, an appetizer, two entrees to share—and because we're girls—dessert and coffee.

When you love Middle Eastern food, choosing your meal can be an excruciating delight. Will it be the Shepherd Meza, a plate of feta cheese, olives, sliced tomato, cucumber, pickles, and pita bread? Or the eggplant appetizer, fried eggplant topped with jalapeno, garlic, and lemon sauce with tomatoes and parsley? The hummus is the most popular; it's a dip of garbanzo beans, fresh garlic, lemon juice, and tahini, which is a sesame seed paste. Finally, over a glass of Louis Latour Chardonnay, we selected the baba ghannouj, a blend of roasted eggplant, tahini, fresh garlic, lemon juice, jalapenos, and olive oil. "It's very heavy on garlic," our server told us, which only made that decision easier.

The MTR appeals to meat eaters and vegetarians, and Dolly and I sampled both. We shared two entrees, the wonderful Mijadarah, which Leyla had recommended one winter evening. Middle Eastern comfort food, the Mijadarah is rice and lentils cooked together with caramelized onions and cumin. It's served in a big bowl with the crunchy Falaheen salad and pita bread. For our meat dish, we chose the Kofta steak—ground lamb and beef over yellow rice served with a Greek salad.

Other popular entrees are eggplant pita pizza and marinated chicken, served as kabobs or more intact, with rice and salad. Ahmad, who has become an American citizen, says "99.9 percent" of his customers are not Middle Eastern. They prefer to eat heavier meals at home, while Americans like his fast service and combination of meat and salads. No doubt Americans also like his exotic teas (he has 10 kinds), desserts and coffee. Dolly and I had switched to Montevina Fume Blanc, and had no trouble deciding we'd want the Turkish coffee to finish things off. But what about this plate of sweets our waitress is showing us? Could we take the whole tray, get on a flying carpet and leave the capital city, eating them all? The MTR has five to choose from. Besides pistachio baklava, there's the Kataifi, walnut-and-almond-filled phyllo, and Mamuul, a date-filled pastry. We chose the cashew-filled lady's finger and the Harissa, a dense cake with a coconut flavor. It's made of cornmeal, honey, and sugar.

The Turkish coffee is served in a pot. Ahmad describes it as a lighter espresso, bittersweet with cardamom flavor.

Although customers come from Augusta and Charleston, Ahmad's biggest concern is keeping his many regulars happy. Some come twice a day. "My staff has been here for years and they know most of my customers by name," he said. Two are Leyla Mason and her husband Pat. Though Leyla wishes Ahmad had time to make vegetable lasagna more often (it has eggplant, spinach, and feta), she appreciates the efficient service, quality of food, and that it's right around the corner from home.

- Aïda Rogers

The Pine Cupboard, Leesville
Lexington County

The Pine Cupboard in The Attic Gift Shop, 114 Main Street, Leesville; (803) 532-3016. Open Monday, Tuesday, Thursday and Friday, 11:30 a.m. – 2 p.m. Closed Wednesday. No smoking. No credit cards. Reservations accepted but not required. Inexpensive.

Old-Timey Eats in Western Lexington County

There is good news and bad news about the Pine Cupboard in Leesville. The good news is that it's the perfect lunch spot: cute, relaxed, cheap and good. The bad news is that it's in Leesville, too far from Lexington when I have just an hour for lunch.

But when duty calls, exceptions are made, so our robust staff of three took the 19-mile drive to the home of the South Carolina Poultry Festival. I ordered a chicken salad sandwich in its honor.

"That seems to be a hit, if you can call it that," said proprietor Larry Lorick, who doesn't like to make chicken salad or even really eat it. The trendiness of chicken salad is something he admitted he doesn't understand.

Still, it's one of the most popular items on the menu, and after one bite, I found out why. It's the combination of fresh creamy chicken salad between slices of homemade sourdough bread. When I go back, it will be hard not to order it again.

The Pine Cupboard is like your grandmother's kitchen, if your grandmother had gone gourmet. Nice touches are everywhere. Iced tea is served in wine carafes; tiny corn muffins accompany the vegetable soup; fruit salad comes with cheese crackers. Plates are mix-and-match, usually with a doily; sandwiches come in baskets with chips and a pickle.

Dan, my lovable but sometimes hard-to-figure editor/cousin, wanted a hot lunch because it was a hot day. He ordered the Reuben sandwich, vegetable soup and peach cobbler. The soup looked just like my grandmother's, full of corn, ground beef, potatoes and string beans. Dan had had the soup before and knew it was so good it didn't need salt. He's been here several times; it's one of his haunts when he's out roaming country roads.

"I love the music more than anything," he said, as harp and hammered dulcimer played. "These people are Celtic-type folkies just like me."

Joey, our coworker, wanted a cold lunch because it was a hot day. He ordered the ham/pineapple and Swiss on croissant and a slice of cheesecake, the only thing the Loricks don't make.

Located in the back of The Attic gift shop, The Pine Cupboard has been open since 1987. "Country-classy" is the description we agreed upon.

Larry and wife Elwanda like old things, and that's reflected in their store and lunch spot. They rescued an old pine pew from a church in the country; now people sit there while waiting for takeout orders. Their business is in a hardware store built in 1903; ceiling fans whir from high, pine, tongue-in-groove ceilings.

Not surprisingly, the Loricks like a quiet, slower-paced life. Running a small-town business beats banking, which is what Elwanda did for years. Larry sold cars and was a deputy warden with the Department of Corrections. They have no interest in opening the restaurant in the evenings or on weekends, although the gift shop is open on Saturdays. They like the fact that much of Leesville shuts down on Wednesday afternoons; on those days, the Pine Cupboard isn't open at all.

Sometimes Larry is amazed by how popular the place has become. "I wish you could have been here yesterday," he said. "This place was packed. People are patient. They're not ugly; they'll wait. I told one person I wouldn't wait this long for food."

But in circumstances so pleasing, and with the result so satisfying, waiting wouldn't be a problem at all.

- Aïda Rogers

The biggest thing to happen at the Pine Cupboard since Sandlapper *stopped here in 1993 is the consolidation of Batesburg and Leesville. Though "The Twin Cities" now officially are one, travelers may want to note that the Pine Cupboard is in Leesville proper, which is 2 miles east of Batesburg. Larry Lorick tells us he and Elwanda are operating their lunch nook as they always did, and that the strawberry shortcake has surpassed the peach cobbler in popularity. The Pine Cupboard still maintains its old-fashioned "Wednesdays-off" schedule.*

- Tim Driggers

Rising High Natural Bread Company, Columbia
Richland County

Rising High Natural Bread Company, 1508 Main Street, Columbia; (803) 252-6111. Open Monday-Friday, 7 a.m.-5 p.m. and Saturday, 9 a.m.-3 p.m. Closed Sunday. Reservations not required. Credit cards and checks accepted. No smoking. Inexpensive.

A City Lunch Downtown

One of my favorite childhood memories was when my grandparents would drive me in their 1953 Chevrolet BelAir to Hook's Store in West Columbia to catch the SCE&G bus into Columbia for the Saturday morning movie at the Ritz Theatre. After watching Hopalong Cassidy save Sweet Sue from Snidely Whiplash, I'd amble up Main Street to Silver's 5&10 and the Kress Dime Store to spend any money left over. I marveled at the grown-ups sitting at the luncheonette, hoping someday I'd be tall enough to perch on a stool and order one of those 15-cent hamburgers.

The Kress 5-10-25 Cent Store was built in Columbia in 1935, designed by famed architect Edward F. Sibbert. The building is listed on the National Register of Historic Places and is widely recognized as the best example of art deco in the midlands. Kress closed in Columbia in 1988.

The Rising High Natural Bread Company began operations in 1994 and moved into the old Kress Store six years later, says general manager Tim Sullivan. It retains its art deco feel with original columns, interior clock, doors, ceiling, and exterior Kress sign. Adorning the walls are paintings by local artist Clifton Batten of the landmark Hiller Hardware, Adluh Flour, Bassett Warehouse, Sylvan, and Moe Levy buildings.

At breakfast and lunch, the dining room is busy with locals buzzing in and out. Orders are taken quickly, meals served pronto. This is downtown and most people are in a hurry. "Everything we serve is made from scratch," Sullivan said. "We don't use any preservatives. All our foods are natural and healthy. We take pride in serving only the freshest items."

I ordered the signature chicken salad sandwich with a side order of pasta salad. While many chicken salads drown in mayonnaise, the Rising High sandwich was to the point: all white meat with ripe tomato and lettuce, clearly homemade. It was served on a black sweet roll that was fresh and delicious. Same formula with the pasta salad: no oily dressing, just pasta, carrots, and tomatoes; decidedly bare bones and healthy.

Reba Campbell, director of advocacy and communications for the nearby Municipal Association of South Carolina, comes frequently. "It's a great downtown lunch spot," she said, alternating bites of her grilled cheese sandwich ('it has a lot of cheese") with reading the newspaper and people watching from her streetside table. "This is a good place to go whether by yourself or with friends. It's easy to get in and out of and I enjoy sitting outside on a warm day looking at the business types and museum crowd on Main Street."

Besides the egg salad sandwich, which she describes as "not too gooey," Reba recommends the cookies, which are "real big and gooey, which is good for a cookie."

- Tim Driggers

Rockaway Athletic Club, Columbia
Richland County

Rockaway Athletic Club, 2719 Rosewood Drive, Columbia; (803) 256-1075. Open daily, 11 a.m.-11 p.m. Bar closes at 2 a.m. Credit cards accepted. Reservations not required. Smoking allowed. Inexpensive to moderate.

These Burgers Require Both Hands

Fat Tuesday. What a great day to be at Rockaway Athletic Club, that bastion of cold beer, good food, and loud music in Columbia. What am I giving up for Lent? Guilt. That's why I had no qualms about ordering the famous Pimento Cheese Fries with jalapeños and dominating them at our table of four. My suppermates had ditched their guilt, too; but by the time we were through, our pants were tight and we were happy.

Rockaway's has that effect. "Rockaway's has the best of everything in Columbia," upholds regular customer Bob Medlock. "I'm crazy about it and I'm more crazy about it the more I come."

Besides the food, Bob likes its Everyman appeal. "The last time I was here, the boys from Pope-Davis Tire Company were here. You could tell they'd been doing hard labor and were taking a break for the South's Greatest Hamburger. At the next table was Hugh McColl and the state officers of NationsBank. To be in a room with this mix is incredible."

David Beasley went to Rockaway to celebrate winning the governorship in 1994. USC students who once came for beer and socializing now bring their children and parents. During the years he lived in the Rosewood community, Gary Stanfield often walked to Rockaway for a beer and sandwich. This evening, he's seated in a booth eating a heaping plate of jambalaya. "This place has evolved," he said, noting that the side dining room was a storage area not long ago.

Rockaway is the very successful project of brothers Forrest and Paul Whitlark and their friend David Melson. Once more of a bar, it's clearly a restaurant now. While the burgers are best known—*Southern Living* called them some of the best in the South— it's the cheese options that impress me. Gouda on a burger? I'll try that next time. For now, I'm excited to find a place that puts anchovies on a Greek salad. "The owners wanted the real thing," Comptroller Maureen Helms said. "There are certain things they individually like and they want it done to their liking."

The chef salad is almost as popular as the burgers. Radio/television personality Gary Pozsik orders one just about every time he comes in. Occasionally he breaks down for his other favorite, the bacon double cheeseburger. A few words about the burgers: They're massive and messy and require both hands.

Seafood and Cajun fare is popular. Check "the board" for specials: soft-shell crab and oyster po boys or dinners, shrimp, blackened fish, and prime rib. Tonight's special is chicken and sausage jambalaya, with French bread and fried green tomatoes. "I'm sweating profusely," Gary joked.

Melson's Louisiana roots are responsible for Rockaway's red beans and rice special, various étouffées and yearly crawfish festival. Former USC basketball star Jack Thompson, who spent 19 years in New Orleans, is one of many who appreciate the effort. "There's a certain eclecticism that reminds me of the French Quarter," he says, admiring the dark wood and roughhewn tables. "This is what we'd call a neighborhood bar." It's hard to beat that.

- Aïda Rogers

Rockaway Athletic Club burned to the ground in March 2002, and reopened for business in early January 2004. Established in 1983, Rockaway's continues to be famous for pimiento cheeseburgers, seafood, and Cajun "board" meals, cold beer, and its neighborhood bar scene.

- *Tim Driggers*

Sesame Inn, Columbia
Richland County

Sesame Inn, 280 Harbison Boulevard, Suite A, Columbia; (803) 732-7867. Open Monday-Friday, 11 a.m.-10 p.m.; Saturday 11 a.m.-11 p.m..; Sunday 11:30 a.m.-9 p.m. No smoking. Credit cards accepted. Reservations not required. Inexpensive to moderate.

A Mandarin Paradise on Harbison Boulevard

Dan—who is called Daniel by our boss, and Daniel the Spaniel by me—was my lunch partner at Sesame Inn, a spiffy Chinese restaurant in Harbison Court. We were smart and went for a late lunch; people line up on the sidewalk outside on Friday and Saturday nights. But it's worth the wait. There is something immediately superb about the service, the food, the atmosphere.

Waiters in tuxedo shirts bring ice water, crispy Chinese noodles, duck sauce and a pot of hot tea as soon as you sit down. They will also help you decide what to get. We went with our waiter's choices; the spicy Hunan chicken and General Tso's Chicken, which was more on the sweet-and-sour side. And we splurged—Spaniel got a bottle of Tsing-Tao and a bowl of the hot-and-sour soup. Dan is a sucker for spicy soup, and the waiter said it was good in the winter. The Span Man ruminated on why he likes spicier food the older he gets. "Are my taste buds dying," he wondered.

We liked the menu. We like any menu that has something on it called "Buddhist Delight." And we liked the food. It's Mandarin, not Cantonese, which is what most of us are used to, owner King Long Lee explained.

A native of China who came here from Pittsburgh, Lee explained that the spicier Mandarin food is more common in the northern U.S. That's why so many of the newcomers in the St. Andrews/Harbison area immediately took to Sesame Inn.

Obviously, the old-timers have found it too. After only a few months in business, *The State* newspaper voted it best Chinese in Columbia.

Lee says his restaurant is gourmet, not family-style, and just right for a developing area. And though the New York chef is introducing things like Mongolian Hot Pie, he's not above chop suey, which Lee calls American-Chinese. General Tso's Chicken, he added, is the most popular Chinese dish in America, but it's hard to find in Columbia.

What amazes me about Sesame Inn is that somehow you can forget the huge discount store next door and the crazy parking lot outside. Maybe it's the spare, bare, cityish feeling it exudes or the New Age piano music. No plastic Chinese lanterns here. You could be anywhere in the world, but you're in that infamous strip of Richland County that used to be Lexington County, somewhere near Irmo.

- Aïda Rogers

Sesame Inn has established itself as one of Columbia's favorite Chinese restaurants. Favorites are the Tangerine Beef, General Tso's chicken, Three's Company (a combination of Lemon Chicken, General Tso's Chicken, and Moo Goo Gai Pan), Spicy Shrimp and Scallops, Double Happiness (shrimp and chicken breast sautéed with vegetables in a white sauce), Vegetarian Paradise (bamboo shoots, mushrooms, baby corn, snow pea pods, broccoli, and tomatoes sautéed in a mild spiced sauce), and Mongolian Triplet (chicken, pork, and beef sautéed with green and white onions in the chef's special sauce).

- Tim Driggers

Shealy's Bar-B-Que House, Batesburg-Leesville
Lexington County

Shealy's Bar-B-Que House, 340 East Columbia Avenue, Batesburg-Leesville; (803) 532-8135. Open daily (except Wednesday and Sunday), 11 a.m.-9 p.m. Visa and Mastercard accepted. No reservations. No smoking. www.shealysbbq.com. Inexpensive.

The Motherlode of Barbecue

Shealy's Bar-B-Que House has been on my list of restaurants to cover for years. Anytime I tell people about this column, Shealy's invariably comes up. The reason? It's the buffet of buffets.

"We love it; we think it's good," said Teresa Bass Miller, who was voted "Best Looking" in our high school class of '79. Teresa and her family were sitting at the table where we sat down; they were celebrating the last day of work at their peach stand. As for us, we were lucky to find two empty places on a Saturday night around 8. At Shealy's people sit where they can at any of several long picnic tables.

Here, the emphasis is on family and food. Prices are reasonable, and the generosity is palpable. "You never have to worry about not having enough," Teresa said. "The string beans are the best I've ever tasted and I like the barbecue—it's spicy. And it's quick. Even if we wait in line, we don't wait long."

And then Teresa uttered the four words most common to Shealy's customers: "I eat too much." That's not hard to do. Walk down the line and smell the steaming rice and hash, mustard-based barbecue and fried chicken. Check out the famous creamed corn, the barbecue beans, the crisp streak-o-lean, and fried livers and gizzards.

Although it's known worldwide for its barbecue, everything else is just as good. And that's the surprising truth about Shealy's. Betty Smith of Newberry said it's the fried chicken that brings her from 35 miles away. She took the seat Teresa had vacated minutes earlier and said this was her second trip today. At Shealy's it's hard to be disciplined. "You can't beat it," she said, explaining that she'd brought her mother and a friend here for lunch, and then her husband wanted to come for supper. Betty didn't put up a fight. "It's a home-cooked meal."

Shealy's started in 1969 with a two-eyed stove, says Ola Bell Perry, who's worked here for years. Ola Bell is one of many long-time employees at Shealy's; her daughter and granddaughter work here, too.

Shealy's was started by Victor and Sara Shealy, and their portrait is on the wall close to the buffet. Victor died in 1986 and Sara retired not long ago, although she's still a fixture at the register.

Today, their son Tommy owns the business and Todd Shealy (no close kin) manages it. They cook about 75 hogs a week, serve about 7,500 plates a week and use about five tractor trailers of beans year. The business has expanded to include a separate take-out counter, a catering company and a gift shop. Buses of people come from all over the state and beyond; one church group comes monthly from Charleston.

In Leesville, Shealy's is a good citizen. Besides employing 65 people, the restaurant sponsors a Dixie Youth baseball team and supports the March of Dimes, the U.S. Air Force and the local schools. Management throw the staff a Christmas party each year and takes them on a day trip in the summer—Six Flags, Dollywood, or Lake Murray. Employees are loyal, and they like the food, too, says employee W.C. Miller. If the buffet is overwhelming, they can resort to Shealy's lesser-known offerings: its salad bar, soup and sandwiches.

The majority of vegetables at Shealy's are fresh frozen; some are canned. Family recipes are used, and rarely are there any leftovers.

Proof of how well Shealy's is loved is the number of people who come for lunch an hour before it's served. Black and white families eat together, all agreed on one thing: The food is good.

The day of its 25th anniversary, the 25th person who came through the line ate at 1969 prices- $1.75 for supper. Today, Shealy's is still a good deal.

- Aïda Rogers

Steven W's Downtown Bistro, Newberry
Newberry County

Steven W's Downtown Bistro, 1100 Main Street, Newberry; 803-276-7700. Open Tuesday-Saturday, 5 p.m. until the last reservation is served (or as Steven Foulis says "when everybody's fat and happy"). Closed on Monday and Sunday. Credit cards and checks accepted. Reservations recommended. No smoking. Moderate to expensive.

Potato-encrusted salmon is served with glazed baby carrots and baby limas at Steven W's.

What An Opera House Spawns

It takes a village of optimists—indeed, a whole town—to raise an opera house, and Steve Foulis is one. In Newberry, where citizens have rejuvenated downtown by restoring an 1882 French Gothic music hall, Steve has created a restaurant for before and after the show. His curtain's been up since November 1997.

No doubt the people of Newberry are excited to have this restaurant, particularly one so elegant. But don't be intimidated. The atmosphere is relaxed. "I would love for everybody to come in here and eat," Steve says, explaining he dislikes the words "upscale" and "fine dining" because they imply an elitist attitude. "I want to share what I do with everybody. I don't try to hide things. When somebody comes to me and asks for a recipe, I give it to 'em. One of the things I learned a long time ago is there are no new recipes out there. Everything's been done and been done again, gone away and come back. So I don't claim anything as original ideas."

Still, his menu is far from lackluster. Eddie Anderson, a downtown merchant and civic leader, is still licking his lips over the New Zealand greenlip mussels with red curry sauce. Deborah Smith, executive director of the Newberry Opera House Foundation, calls the lamb "exquisite." And Dr. Jim Wiseman Jr., the retired dentist who led the campaign to restore the opera house, chuckles about the restaurant's opening gala. "People couldn't believe there were people standing out on Main Street drinking wine! Oh, heresy!"

The premier was a showcase of what Steve and his brother Mark can do. Mark specializes in cold food, ice sculpture, and other forms of *garde manger*– the banquet art of making flowers and birds from vegetables and other foods. Steve does the hot food, and both brothers do desserts. Combine their talents with the restaurant's location in a spacious, beautifully restored 1909-10 drugstore, and there's no wonder Newberry is thrilled. What small town wouldn't be?

On the appetizer list are crab wontons with apricot sauce and smoked salmon with horseradish parfait. Entrees include pecan-crusted chicken with blackberry sauce. Customers are traveling from Greenville and Columbia; receptions, reunions, and dinners have been held in the banquet room upstairs. Steve, a woodworker at heart, is particularly enthralled by his restaurant's wide heart-of-pine staircase. A bride is scheduled to come down these stairs soon, and Steve hopes many will follow.

A longtime chef with Garibaldi's in Charleston, Savannah, and Columbia, Steve also spent many years working in Atlanta, his hometown. After almost 30 years in the business, he's glad to have his own place, where he can offer "a hodgepodge of ideas" culled from his experiences. And he's happy to be doing it where the people are so supportive, so he in turn can support the opera house. For him, that means keeping plenty of variety on the menu.

"I don't want to limit my market to just being an Italian restaurant or a French restaurant or Greek or Thai or Southern American cuisine. I like to do them all. It keeps me interested, it keeps the folks who come in here and try different things interested, and it just keeps it mixed up so nobody can get bored coming into Steven W's Downtown Bistro. Nobody."

- Aïda Rogers

The beautifully restored Newberry Opera House is going great guns and Steven W's has earned a well-deserved reputation as one of the better restaurants in our state. The Newberry Opera House fetches world-class actors and musicians to town and Steven W's continues to wow diners with their classic but understated menu. The restaurant is the place to go before a show or to simply enjoy a great meal in a distinctive setting. If you're going to the Opera House, it's best to make reservations at Steven W's in advance; otherwise, they could be booked solid. Apricot flounder remains "what they're famous for."

- *Tim Driggers*

Sunset Grill and Restaurant, West Columbia
Lexington County

Sunset Grill and Restaurant, 1213 Sunset Boulevard, West Columbia; (803) 475-6912. Open Monday through Friday, 6 a.m.-2:30 p.m. and Saturdays, 6 a.m.-11 a.m. Closed on Sunday. Credit card and checks accepted. No reservations required. Smoking allowed in designated areas. Inexpensive.

Even the President Eats Here

Richard Jackson is *Sandlapper's* chief sugar daddy, and sometimes he likes to take Dolly Patton, the society's former executive director, and me out in his truck (for research). We never know where we'll end up, but we know we'll get fed. Not long ago we found ourselves at the Sunset Grill and Restaurant in West Columbia, a place Richard likes for its "meat and potatoes" menu and unpretentious atmosphere. As a reporter, I like the gems that fall out of Richard's mouth, especially this one: "These biscuits are so fluffy they'll float off your plate."

You can get biscuits at the Sunset, and cornbread—which "isn't Jiffy," as Dolly noted. You can also get great fried chicken, an array of vegetables and peach, apple, or cherry cobbler. Dolly and Richard tried the meatloaf and I had the rightly recommended fried chicken.

The Sunset is big, with lots of tables, lots of people and lots of country music. The late Frank Argoe opened it in 1973 and sold it two years later to Betty Jackson, his niece, who runs it now (she formerly opened the Stadium Restaurant in Columbia). The Sunset serves breakfast and lunch and closes at 2:30 p.m. It's hard not to wish Richard would clone it in Lexington, particularly now that Hite's is gone.

People always know they'll get a generous helping of home cooking and Betty's cheery "hello and how are you" when they arrive. You'll see more than locals here. Look around and you might spy a Republican candidate for president. George W. Bush ate here while running in 2000 and 2004, as have most every candidate seeking the party nomination for the White House. "They better come here," Betty Jackson says, "if they want to get elected."

- Aïda Rogers and Tim Driggers

The Tomahawk (a.k.a. "Dopey's"), Newberry
Newberry County

The Tomahawk (Dopey's), Luther Street across from Cromer Hall on the Newberry College campus, Newberry. Call Newberry College at 1-800-845-4955, ask to be connected to the Cromer Hall dorm, and ask if the red light is on at Dopey's. Inexpensive.

College Days, Happy Days

Anyone who has ever lived in a dorm knows there is no such thing as a bad time to head out for something to eat. During my years at Newberry College, "dinner" often occurred after 2 a.m., when a group of us walked down the street to Dopey's for the finest cheeseburger known to mankind.

Buzz Edwards, son of the late John L. "Dopey" Edwards, owns the place now. Brightly painted in Newberry College scarlet and gray, Dopey's is quite small, with a few stools along the counter and even fewer booths. The old jukebox is just a memory, and so is the Andy Taylor and Barney Fife team of Dopey and Dunc. Dopey ran the place and played ringmaster to the Animal House scene unfolding each evening. Paul "Dunc" Duncan, a plumber by day, dispensed doses of questionable wit and wisdom as he delivered cheeseburgers and egg sandwiches. I can't say I ever agreed with anything Dunc ever said, but I always marveled at the words that flew out of his mouth. "He had an opinion on everything," said Vince Bouronich, class of 1970.

Dopey's never had a set time to open or close. A red light atop the door would signal the place was open and legions of students would stream across the street. In those days, Dopey's was purely a male enclave and no self-respecting co-ed would ever think of trying to set foot in the place. That changed in the late 1970s.

"We would sit outside our dorm waiting for the girls to walk by on the way to Dopey's," recalled Nelson Rickenbaker, who attended Newberry from 1979 to 1983. "That's when we would go, even if we weren't hungry." Nelson, who played on the baseball team, roomed in the Cromer Hall athletic dorm, across the street. "I'd just look out my window until the red light came on," he said. "Many nights, that wasn't until 11 p.m. or midnight."

Dopey allowed students to run tabs. "More times than not, he didn't know our names or when he'd be paid," Nelson continued. "That didn't keep him from tracking us down." Stories abound about Dopey's collection methods. "If you owed him money, he wouldn't forget," said Mandy Caughman Derrick, class of 1981. "He would chase you at graduation exercises or alumni reunions if you owed him money."

Mandy and classmate Althea Hendrix remember late-night trips to Dopey's. "If we ate really late, there was always a paper wrapper soaked in grease on my dorm dresser the next morning," Althea remembered. Added Mandy: "We never went before 10 p.m. and a lot of evenings, didn't go until 2 or 3 in the morning."

A few words about the food: "The Dopey Burger was very good, very juicy, and very messy," Mandy said. Nelson and Althea preferred the egg sandwiches. "It was fried and came with cheese," Althea said, "and it had a ton of mayonnaise."

After a trip to the Newberry Opera House, I drive by Dopey's. Sometimes it's open; more often, it's not. That doesn't stop me from looking for the red light, and reliving memories of the greatest cheeseburger a college student ever ordered.

- Tim Driggers

Touch of India, Columbia
Richland County

Touch of India, 1321 Garner Lane, Columbia; (803) 731-5960. Open for lunch Tuesday-Saturday, 11:30 a.m.-2:30 p.m.; for dinner Tuesday-Thursday, 6-9 p.m. and Friday-Saturday, 6-10 p.m. Open Sunday, 11 a.m.-2 p.m. and 6-9 p.m. Closed Monday. No smoking. Credit cards accepted. Reservations not required. Inexpensive to moderate.

Mango Pickle, Mango Milkshake – Mighty Good

When Devi Raju opened Touch of India—her tiny, plain Indian restaurant and grocery store in the St. Andrews suburb of Columbia—she introduced locals to mango milkshakes and Madras soup.

Sandlapper first visited in 1992, and that's when we spotted Bernhard Mayerhofer, an Austrian architect who lives between Camden and Bethune, dining in his own distinctive style. He comes here five days a week for the vegetarian dishes and the chance to eat with his fingers. That's devotion.

Although we're not half as regular, Touch of India has become a favorite place for me, my friends, and Dan, my long-suffering associate editor/cousin. (We go on pay day.) We've tried just about every dinner platter, or thali, on the menu: chicken, lamb, shrimp and vegetarian. Dan loves the Mulligatawny, a spicy, head-clearing soup, and I like the Vegetable Pakora, the Indian version of fried veggies. Served with a sweet Indian salsa, Vegetable Pakora is carrots, potatoes, onions, cauliflower, eggplant, and "anything we find to dump in," Mrs. Raju says.

Mrs. Raju and her husband opened the restaurant and its adjoining grocery store almost 20 years ago. They did it on the strong urging of their American friends, although the many Indians who live in Irmo patronize it. "They forced me to do it," she said, laughing in her wonderful melodic accent. To me, that's another reason to try Touch of India—to hear the soft sounds of that whispery language.

Mrs. Raju says she's the owner, cook, manager, waitress and cleaner. Add teacher to that. She helps customers decide what to order, describing the traditional dishes she's brought from Bangalore, her home in South India. "The first thing I say is, 'Do you like spicy food?' This is an Indian restaurant; expect hot food."

I asked her about this wicked pickle thing that nearly did me in once. She laughed. "That's a mango pickle. Children in India practice on that." Luckily, a thick mango milkshake is available to cool you off.

Go to Touch of India with an open mind and an adventurous spirit. When Dan and I go, we just point to the menu and deal with the many clinking platters and compartments of stainless steel later. We don't talk much, we just eat; and maybe that's necessary, because eating Indian food can be tricky. I had taken to mixing everything together, smearing the different soups and sauces on the rice, or pulao, with a fork. But then I met Mayerhofer, who gave me a lesson on how to eat Masala Dosa his way. Masala Dosa is a large crepe (dosa) filled with a spicy mix of vegetables (masala), served with separate cups of lentil soup and coconut chutney.

I won't get into the specifics of Mayerhofer's hands-on style, but I will say I made a mess trying to imitate it. Then I watched Mrs. Raju eat the same thing. Her thin brown fingers were so quick and neat, I felt like a dumb American, klutzy in comparison. The more she talked, the more she made sense, and the more I realized a week in the jungle would make me a smarter person.

"Your fingers are your fork," she said. Why didn't I realize that before?

My friend Marcia has taught me to finish each meal with the hot tea, which is like a frothy, spicy coffee. I take mine with sugar, and am always hard-pressed to figure how the world can be so bad with something like this in it.

- Aïda Rogers

Touch of India features the lunch buffet, although menu orders are available. The Masala Dosa remains the what-we're-known-for selection.

- *Tim Driggers*

Villa Tronco, Columbia
Richland County

Villa Tronco, 1213 Blanding Street in Columbia; (803) 256-7677. Open for lunch Monday-Friday, 11 a.m.-3 p.m. and for dinner Monday-Saturday, 5-10 p.m. Closed on Sunday. Reservations accepted. Credit cards accepted. No smoking. Inexpensive to moderate for lunch. Moderate to expensive.

The Capital City's Italian Bastion

Villa Tronco is Columbia's dining institution, the city's oldest and arguably finest Italian restaurant. The traditions begun by the Carnaggio and Tronco families a century ago remain very much alive at the converted 19th Century fire station on Blanding Street. A meal at Villa Tronco is a trip back in time to when the Farmers Market bustled on Assembly Street, troops training at Fort Jackson for service in Europe flooded downtown, and bobbysoxers at USC danced to the music of Benny Goodman and Tommy Dorsey. If I had an Italian grandmother back in the old country, then Villa Tronco serves the cuisine I imagine cooking on her stove.

It all started with Sadie Carnaggio Tronco. Born in 1901, Sadie married Philadelphia native James Tronco during World War I and the couple eventually took root in Columbia. "They opened a fruit store at 1712 Main Street and later added a grill," said Carmella Martin, one of their four children. "After a fire, the family moved to our present location on Blanding Street." The story then fast forwards to the inception of the restaurant. "During World War Two, a great many soldiers of Italian descent found themselves stationed in Columbia," Carmella adds. "They would come to the grill knowing Mama was Italian and missing their mother's cooking. Mama Tronco would cook some of them a pot of pasta and meat balls and the word spread."

The fruit store/grill, which had been known as the Iodine Fruit Store, was transformed into the Iodine Restaurant, later becoming Tony's Spaghetti House before finally settling in as Villa Tronco. Here, Columbians first discovered pizza. "Mama Tronco had to give it away because nobody knew what it was," Carmella said, adding that the crust still is made by hand and the pizza sliced into squares. Sadie ultimately turned over the reins to Carmella and husband Henry. But she ran the register until she died at 87.

Henry Martin graduated from the University of South Carolina in 1949, starring on the basketball team and becoming one of the first players to score 1,000 points during a varsity career. Envisioning a coaching career, he instead stayed at the restaurant for 49 years. The whole Martin family got into the act, with daughter Carmella and husband Joe Roche entering the business in 1972, and eventually taking charge. Son Henry Jr., a Lexington doctor, remembers Villa Tronco as a family endeavor. "I had to clean the restaurant every Sunday before church," Hank said. "I never could clean the floors to my grandmother's satisfaction, no matter how hard I scrubbed."

Carmella Martin's cheesecakes are legendary. Flavors include amaretto, Oreo, chocolate, turtle pie, tiramisu, pistachio ice cream and spumoni.

My family visits Villa Tronco a couple of times a year, usually to celebrate a birthday. Donna orders the Villeto Parmigiana, veal breaded and topped with tomato sauce and mozzarella cheese, baked and served over linguine. Dale opts for the Chicken Cacciatore sautéed in olive oil, and my mother, Miriam, chooses the Eggplant Parmigiana, layered eggplant with tomato sauce and mozzarella over linguine. I usually pick the linguine pasta with the biggest meatballs this side of Roma or the huge Combo Platter of lasagne, cheese ravioli, and fettuccini Tronco. A carry-out plate is the norm because of the large portions.

The Villa Tronco site has been declared a historic landmark. I'm not sure the honor was designated because it's home of the circa 1858 Palmetto Engine Company fire station or because of the revered restaurant operating within its walls. While I'll believe the former; I'll vouch for the latter.

"Our family feels it has done a good job of continuing what my mother started," Carmella said. "She had such a love and enthusiasm for the restaurant. As more people move back to downtown Columbia, we're proud we're still here to serve them."

- Tim Driggers

Zesto's, West Columbia
Lexington County

Zesto's, 504 Twelfth Street, West Columbia; (803) 794-4652. Open Monday-Saturday, 10 a.m.-11 p.m. Closed on Sunday. Credit cards accepted. Don't you wish reservations were accepted when it's 105 degrees, there are 83 people in line, and you just can't wait to get that hand-dipped pineapple ice cream cone in your mouth? No smoking. Inexpensive.

Everybody Knows This Place

When you think of restaurants on the West Columbia side of the Congaree River, chances are the first place that pops to mind is Zesto's, a landmark not only for its history, food, and personality, but because of its huge ice cream cone sign. Almost as incredible are its extremely affordable chicken dinners. Run by Greek cousins Angelo Tsianatis and Gus Manos, Zesto's seems purely American. Located in the middle of Triangle City, there are trucks in the parking lot, a flag waving outside, and a reputation for great chicken, milkshakes, and banana splits.

I doubt there are many folks who grew up in the West Columbia area who haven't made Zesto's a family tradition. In fact, standing in line for an order in the Zesto's lobby usually guarantees meeting friends from school, church, and neighborhood. On a hot summer night, the line can stretch out the door, but a Zesto banana split, sundae, or ice cream cone is always worth the wait.

I tried the "chicken snack" and found it much more than a snack. It's two pieces of chicken, French fries, slaw and two rolls. Follow that with one of Zesto's dipped cones, and you have one happy restaurant writer.

Zesto's is entrenched in West Columbia. Angelo, or "Mr. A.," knows his customers by name, and the restaurant sponsors a little league team. For many of its employees, Zesto's is a second home. Some have been here a quarter century; others put themselves through college working the counter or grill.

Built in 1949, Zesto's started strictly as an ice cream place. As business grew, so did its menu. Eventually, a dining room was added behind the counter.

These days there's another reason to celebrate: Angelo and Gus have been partners for more than three decades. It's a business marriage that's made West Columbia Zesto heaven.

- Aïda Rogers

Sadly, Angelo Tsianatis passed away in March 2006 while awaiting heart bypass surgery. Gus Manos, who's been an institution at Zesto's since 1961, and son Pete, who's been there since 1996, are now the owners. The big ice cream sign is still around and it's as familiar a sight in the midlands as The State House dome. Best sellers are the chocolate dipped ice cream cone, fried chicken, and fabulous Zestoburger. The French fries are among the best you'll ever put in your mouth and the tub of chicken is a popular tailgating item on Gamecock Saturdays. The dining room in the back's been enlarged and folks still jam the lobby to place their orders. The parking spaces along Twelfth Street are always full of Zesto's customers and parking can be at a premium, especially on weekends after a Brookland-Cayce High School pageant or game.

- *Tim Driggers*

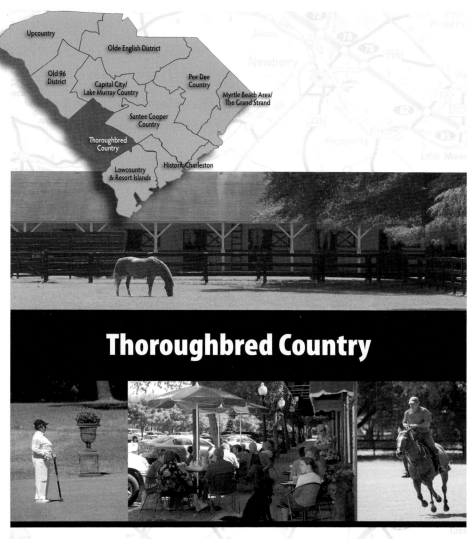

Thoroughbred Country

Aiken, Allendale, Bamberg & Barnwell Counties

Frye's, Bamberg
Bamberg County

Frye's, 1302 Main Highway, Bamberg; (803) 245-4540. Lunch served daily, 11 a.m.-2 p.m. Reservations unnecessary. No credit cards. Smoking allowed in back room. Inexpensive.

Home Cookin' In Bamberg

Seemingly, each small town has a restaurant where everyone from the local doctors and lawyers to the highway department crew go for lunch. And it's not only lunch they go for; it's also for a blue plate special of local gossip, the latest debate on the Clemson-Carolina rivalry, and who saw whom with whom. In Bamberg, that certain restaurant is Frye's, where the home cookin' is renowned.

When Eula and William Frye acquired the restaurant in 1971, it was still a '50s-style drive-in. "I worked the take-out window and waited on cars when I was in high school," their daughter Cheryl Bledsoe recalled. "We had a jukebox outside and served only hot dogs, hamburgers and short-order sandwiches." With the transition of tastes and values from the Eisenhower era to the New Frontier, the familiar drive-in began to fade from the American landscape. Frye's was no different. It closed in 1974 and three years later, with a new addition to the building, the lunch buffet was born.

William Frye died in 1994 and Eula continued the business until her death in 1999. "My mother loved this place," Cheryl said. "She loved to stay busy and she loved to cook for a crowd. She knew just about everyone who walked through the door and she also knew they needed to eat quickly and get back to work. When she died, our customers hoped so much the restaurant would stay open." That's when Cheryl and husband Tony bought the interest of other family members.

Today, Frye's continues as a Bamberg institution, where regulars hover around the buffet for the famous fried chicken and fresh vegetables. "We change the buffet daily, except for the chicken," Tony said, noting that it's fresh and fried in buttermilk batter. "It's not a secret recipe, but there's no way anyone could prepare it like our cooks." The buffet features three meats and 10 side dishes, with the other two meats changing daily. Many of the vegetables are bought locally.

On my visit, the buffet included roast beef, Salisbury steak, rice and gravy, macaroni and cheese, green beans, creamed corn, asparagus, field peas, collards, apple cobbler and pound cake. From the menu you could order hamburger steak with grilled onions, fries, slaw and tea.

Bruce Watson, clerk-treasurer for the City of Bamberg and the Bamberg Board of Public Works, swears by the hamburgers. "They're the best ever," he says, but adds the vegetables are his favorite. Frye's Sunday buffet has more variety, Tony said. "We serve ribs then and a lot of people come just for them."

Bamberg veterinarian John Dalton says Cheryl and Tony's personalities keep people coming back. "Tony never met a stranger in his life." Adds Ed Pruitt: "Tony and Cheryl—they're just down-home."

When you mix down-home cookin' with two owners who are down-home themselves, you've got quite a combination.

- Tim Driggers

Hattie and Fannie's Two, Blackville
Barnwell County

Hattie and Fannie's Two (formerly Hattie's Kitchen), 744 Main Street, Blackville; (803) 284-3756. Open for lunch Monday-Friday, 11 a.m. until 3:30 p.m. Closed Saturday and Sunday. No Smoking. Checks, but no credit cards. No reservations needed. Inexpensive.

Cornbread Heaven With Hattie

Eating a big lunch at Miller's Bread-Basket in Blackville didn't stop me from crossing the railroad tracks to Hattie's Kitchen. I'd heard her cornbread was unsurpassed and decided to see for myself.

Everything I heard was right on target. Hattie Harley cut me a square from a pan right out of the stove, and I learned why people drive all the way from Columbia for a taste. I also learned what many before me have learned: The recipe is unavailable. Even her children don't have it.

"It's not all that famous, but it's mine," she says. Hattie, who once drove a cab in New York, happened upon the formula more than 20 years ago when she substituted one ingredient for another. "It's just as good frozen as it would be if you just got it out of the pan."

You might want to try a square of Hattie's cornbread along with some of her vegetables and meats—ham hocks, chitterlings, and neck bones—as well as the more standard fried chicken, smothered steak and beef stew. Hattie calls her menu "country cooking," but her customers call it "soul food." It really doesn't matter what you call it as long as you know you're welcome. "I want everyone to eat here, not just white collar," she says. "It's not fancy, but I thank God every day for what I got."

"Hattie has the best fried pork chop and the absolute best cornbread I've ever had in my life," said Bobby Frierson, a Lexington resident who finds himself frequently in Blackville. "The cornbread I always save for last because it's better than any cake I've ever had."

Bobby is resolute in his love for Hattie's Kitchen. "I searched long and hard my whole life for Hattie's. I don't care if I go five consecutive days, I get the pork chop. You can get a pork chop breakfast that's out of this world. And if you don't get the pork chop breakfast, she still has real fatback bacon."

I had to ask the obvious: "You don't feel like a salt wad when you walk out?" Bobby smirked. "I feel contented," he said. "Or content. You edit this. I went to Clemson."

- Aïda Rogers

Sandlapper *visited Hattie's Kitchen in January 1990. While updating this book, we learned that Hattie died in 2000. Daughter Fannie and granddaughter Darlene now run the restaurant, renamed Hattie and Fannie's Two. Although Hattie is sorely missed, Fannie and Darlene continue to serve Hattie's brand of down-home country vittles. "We're going strong every day," Darlene said. "And everybody still loves our cornbread." That's certainly welcome news, but there's more. Hattie and Fannie's Two now serves chitlins and stone soup: a combination of pig's ears, hogmaws (pig's stomach for the uninitiated), pig's feet, and pig's tails. Now that's some mighty fine eatin'! Fannie and Darlene also continue to serve Hattie's popular fried chicken and smothered pork chops every day.*

- Tim Driggers

Linda's Bistro, Aiken
Aiken County

Linda's Bistro, 135 York Street, SE, Aiken; (803) 648-4853. Open Tuesday-Saturday, 6-10 p.m. Closed Sunday and Monday. Credit cards accepted. Reservations recommended. Smoking allowed. www.lindasbistro-aiken.com. Expensive to very expensive.

A Little Something Different

Linda's Bistro, formerly A La Carte Gourmet & Café, is a spiffy surprise in Aiken's bevy of restaurants and shops. It's run by Linda Rooney, a former horsewoman ("exercise girl," in horse lingo) who discovered she had a talent in the kitchen as well as in the barn. Lucky for Aiken, because she's serving delicious food—as well as exquisite sweets—to those who enjoy a little something different from standard fare. Thanks to the influx of newcomers to Aiken with the Savannah River Plant and its satellite industries, along with the well-traveled horse crowd, there's a market for Linda's specialties. "This business wouldn't have made it 10 years ago," she said.

Linda's Bistro started as a cart. She laughs now about the freezing cold she tolerated in winter and the worry about melting pastries in the summer. A couple of years of that, and she finally found a space inside. She's been inside 18 years now, baking her own bread and stocking gourmet items hard to find in Aiken—rose water, polenta, teas, spices, oils, relishes, wine biscuits, mustards, and tandoori.

In the late '80s, Linda realized she was getting old to be exercising horses, so she began selling her pastries and shortbreads to gourmet and department stores in New York City. That, along with a three-month stint at the famous Mrs. London's Bake Shop in Saratoga, gave her the confidence to start her own business.

A Montreal native, Linda likes to keep her menu eclectic, restricted only by her imagination. It's not French, not nouvelle, not predictable. It's the result of collecting thoughts from cookbooks and magazines. "I don't take a recipe, but I get an idea, and I'll turn it around to suit my style, whatever that may be."

Linda knows what she's doing and plans to stick by her gourmet guns. And she plans to continue putting oil-cured Greek olives on her Greek salads, although an irate take-out customer was certain they were bad.

"It's pretty hard not to do something that you really don't believe in," she said. "It comes off not right."

- Aïda Rogers

Located between Park and Richland Streets in historic downtown Aiken, Linda's Bistro is open only for dinner in a two-story Victorian manor with hardwood floors, white linen-covered tables, and horse-themed paintings. Owner Linda Rooney has four appetizers on the menu: Scottish smoked salmon, fresh jumbo lump crabmeat, fresh mozzarella with vine ripe tomatoes and basil-infused olive oil and Linda's Bistro's signature organic salad. Main courses include Wild Mushroom Ravioli, Risotto a la Linda, Seared and Roasted Chilean Sea Bass, Grilled Center Cut T-Bone Pork Chop, Grilled Free Range New Zealand Lamb Rib Chops, Grilled 12-ounce Prime Dry Aged New York Strip Steak, and the Shrimp Organic Salad and Chicken Apple Sausage Organic Salad. The menu also offers a soup du jour as well as sides of creamed spinach, frites, and creamy risotto, and a cellar of wine choices. Look for the wine tasting dinners that Linda's Bistro periodically hosts. There's also a private dining room that can accommodate upwards of 300 guests.

- Tim Driggers

Malia's, Aiken
Aiken County

Malia's, 120 Laurens Street, Aiken; (803) 643-3086. Open Tuesday-Friday for lunch, 11:30 a.m.-2 p.m.. Open for dinner Thursday-Friday, 6-9 p.m. and Saturday, 5:30-9 p.m. Credit cards and checks accepted. Reservations not accepted for lunch; reservations recommended for dinner. No smoking. www. maliasrestaurant.com. Moderate to expensive.

Every Plate is Extraordinary

We humans are so weak. Show a group of guys a hot blonde and they get silly. Show some girls Clint Eastwood (I'm thinking of my sister) and they shriek and squeal. Take five college-educated professionals to Malia's and just wait for the war to begin.

"I am sorry, but that strudel is good enough to make you slap your grandmother," said Gerry Lynn Hall, forking into one of the three appetizers we ordered. The Savory Strudel, diced Portobello mushrooms baked with goat cheese in crispy pastry, nearly ignited a battle. Four of us began reaching over to stake Gerry Lynn's claim—except "fungus-free" Fred Robertson, who hung out with the Smoked Salmon Roll. Sliced and rolled in a chipolte tortilla and served with a sesame ginger cream cheese, this appetizer was as interesting and flavorful as the strudel. But then there were the Thai dumplings, served with a spicy hoison dipping sauce. The appetizers went around the table as a chorus of delirious moans rose into the air.

Chef-owner Malia Koelker has been wowing Aikenites since she opened in 1987. A sculptor, Malia's artistic side is evidenced by her food. Every plate is extraordinary.

Here comes the salmon, rubbed with southwestern spices and topped with a tomato-balsamic vinaigrette. The tortilla strips stick out like antennae. Now for the shrimp and scallop linguine. Proving Malia's sculptural skills, it curves up on one side like an ocean wave. Also on the menu: fresh lemon sole stuffed with scallop mousse; crispy duck napped with port wine; and Chicken Portobello, a sautéed breast with grilled Portobello mushrooms and red onions. I may have ordered the most unusual entrée, the Pork Punjabi. Thick pork chops marinated in 10 spices and grilled, this dish is served with Basmati rice, curry sauce and a raisiny chutney.

Malia's is about art and adventure. Stay home if you don't like to experiment.

Portions are generous (most of us brought some home) and salads accompany entreés. You have a choice of two: a traditional house salad and a spinach salad, served with fruit. The dessert list is as imaginative as the entrees: We ordered crème brulee and the house favorite, raspberry pie. Served warm with vanilla ice cream, it almost caused another tabletop war.

The menu changes constantly. One standard is the steak salad at lunch. The favorite is a filet of beef on a bed of greens. Other lunch favorites are shrimp and grits and a souvlaki dinner.

With its old brick walls and exposed beams, Malia's offers an atmosphere that's sophisticated and low-key. "Cozy but not confined" is how Fred described it, to the approval of the four girls he was escorting. As the music moved from Pavarotti to classical guitar, all of us agreed Malia's was a good place to have good food with good friends. We sure did.

- Aïda Rogers

Walk through the dress shop at the front of 120 Laurens Street in Aiken and enter Malia's, a restaurant that has charmed Aiken for two decades. Owner Malia Koelker and husband Robert Shackleton continue to change their menu daily, always offering a new dining adventure to both regulars and the newly initiated. For dinner, there are usually 2-3 appetizers and a choice of 7-8 entrees. The signature dinner selections are Shrimp and Grits and Lake Pontchartrain Shrimp. For lunch, the steak sandwich and spinach salad with raspberry vinaigrette are favorites. Just in time for the 2007 Master's golf tournament, Malia's began offering meals in their 30-seat courtyard.

- *Tim Driggers*

Miller's Bread-Basket, Blackville
Barnwell County

Miller's Bread-Basket, 483 Main Street, Blackville; (803) 475-6912. Open for lunch Monday through Saturday from 11 a.m.-2 p.m. and for dinner Thursday and Friday from 5- 8:30 p.m. Closed on Sunday. Credit cards and checks accepted. No reservations required. No smoking. www.millersbread-basket.com. Inexpensive.

"Pennsylvania Dutch With a Southern Touch"

A few words about shoo-fly pie: There's the wet kind and the dry kind, and Ray Miller can tell you all about both at Miller's Bread-Basket in Blackville. Miller serves the wet kind – wet bottom, to be exact. It's sweeter and easier to eat, he says, and he should know. Born and reared in northern Indiana, this self-described Amish farm boy has opened his "Pennsylvania Dutch with a Southern Touch" restaurant to Barnwell County, and nobody's complaining.

"This is the best restaurant east of the Mississippi, and maybe west of it, too," declares the Rev. Bill Bynum, pastor of Ghents Branch Baptist Church in Denmark.

Bynum often eats a late lunch here and likes being able to get extra slices of Miller's homebaked bread for no extra charge. He also likes the country gospel music Miller plays on the stereo and the assortment of country/quilty art on the walls. He likes it so much he's brought people all the way from Myrtle Beach here to eat.

"They just make you feel so at home," Bynum says. Anybody who walks in for a plate of hot, home-cooked food immediately feels like part of a big, happy family. That's what the Bread-Basket is: a family operation run by Ray and Susie Miller.

"I've always had the inspiration to open a restaurant. The Lord blessed us with six healthy daughters and two sons, and we figured now was the time," Miller says. If he'd known how much work and courage it would take, he's not sure he would have done it. But he did, with the help of his family and other Mennonites in the community. Now, years later, he's got a successful cafeteria-style restaurant for local business people and families with young children. "They can scream and throw food, and Ray won't mind," says Kent Kirkland, who often treats his wife Kelsey and two young sons to Miller's affordable lunch or supper.

Mrs. Kirkland likes Miller's for another reason: vegetables. They're fresh, often straight from Miller's or other local farmers' gardens, and cooked without fat.

Of course, that doesn't help when Miller's famous coconut cream pie is staring you in the face, thick and rich and creamy, topped with toasted, shredded coconut. Even Twila Miller, waitress and daughter of the owners, has a hard time passing it up. "I'm not too fond of coconut," she says, "but I love this pie."

No restaurant is a winner unless it delivers, and Miller's does that and then some. The portions are generous, the variety wide and the food good. Fried chicken and meatloaf always are served; other meats are alternated during the week. Recipes come from Mennonite families. Miller bakes the bread every morning, just in time for 6 a.m. breakfast. Each day begins with prayer.

"There's a basic satisfaction knowing that practicing some of God's principles can be successful even materially," says Miller, creator of the honey oat, cheddar cheese and onion-garlic bread his place is known for. "I give you a baker's dozen. I give you what you pay for and a little bit more."

Bright-eyed and roly-poly, he's as close as you'll get to a non-Irish leprechaun. It's partly his friendly manner that brings customers back. "I remember one rainy day Ray helped some elderly people from their cars into the restaurant under his umbrella," says Margaret Sholar, a Blackville businesswoman. "If more people cared about their customers the way Ray did, everyone would be profitable."

Miller looks pleased and embarrassed. "Oh, I'm going to have to buy her a piece of pie."

- Aïda Rogers

While the children are grown and only occasionally work at the restaurant, Ray and Susie Miller continue Miller's Bread-Basket as one of South Carolina's most unique dining experiences. Over the years, they've added Swedish meatballs and a couple of chicken dishes to their famous buffet, but the rural charm of this Pennsylvania Dutch restaurant along the South Carolina National Heritage Corridor remains the same as when Sandlapper *first visited in 1990.*

- Tim Driggers

The New Moon Café, Aiken
Aiken County

The New Moon Café, 116 Laurens Street, Aiken; (803) 643-7088. Open Monday-Friday, 7 a.m.-5 p.m.; Saturday, 8 a.m. until 5 p.m. Sunday brunch is 9 a.m.-2 p.m. Credit cards accepted, but not checks. Reservations not necessary. No smoking. Inexpensive.

Spacing Out With Blueberry Milkshakes

At the New Moon Café in Aiken, you can disappear into the darkness when the world is too much with you. Get a chair, get a milkshake, get planetary. That *is* the moon on the ceiling above you, beaming down a sense of the celestial. For cosmic eats—or a great big sandwich for not much money—this is the place.

Taking orders at the counter was a young cashierelle with glittery fingernails. I asked what the best-seller was. "The Café Club," she said. "I'll take it," I said back.

But I was sooo hungry, I also ordered a bowl of crab bisque, one of the two soups of the day (the other was black bean). And I was sooo thirsty, I got an iced tea instead of my usual mid-day water. I was celebrating lunch out of town. I could read, eat and watch people. Is there really anything better?

Well, yes, there is, and that's the New Moon blueberry milkshake. I was sooo intrigued, I had to have it. But at least I waited until after my main meal, which proved to be more than I could finish. The bisque was—luckily for me—not very rich, but full of crabbiness. Served with thick black bread, it was a meal by itself.

So was the Café Club, a powerhouse of turkey, ham, bacon, lettuce, tomato, and American Cheese. At The New Moon, where breads are baked fresh daily, you can have your sandwich "built" with sourdough, cracked wheat, pumpernickel, or spring herb. "Built" is right; you need a mighty jaw to neatly encompass that sandwich. Three items accompany sandwich specials: red potato salad, veggie pasta salad, or chips.

The New Moon Café is more than soup and sandwiches. It's a bakery and coffee shop, all within a 10-table space. Try seven different kinds of coffee, or espresso,

Dogs are welcome in the al fresco "dining room" at the New Moon Cafe.

cappuccino, and caffe latte. Bread lovers of all kinds will be hard put to choose between the muffins, croissants, bagels, cinnamon buns, and cookies. Some of the options: chocolate and strawberry cream cheese croissants, blackberry pecan muffins, chocolate chunk cookies, sun-dried tomato bagels. Dieters need not despair; there are lowfat muffins in raspberry graham, blueberry, and apple cinnamon.

"We have a something-for-everyone menu," says employee Michelle Green. "If you can't find something you like, you better to go McDonald's."

Michelle is the sister of owner Christine Tomasetti Allewelt. Originally from Pennsylvania, the Irish-Italian sisters have decided kitchens beat offices. "Michelle was working for a bank in Pennsylvania, and they gave her the option of transferring to Utica, New York, or being laid off," Christine recalls. "I said, 'Come here and make quiche with me.' She's a fantastic cook." Christine herself had realized her chronic college-going was really an excuse to work in restaurants. "I've got almost three degrees but I get up at 4:30 and bake muffins," she jokes.

It's truly a family affair, with the sisters babysitting each other's children when they're not working, and Christine's husband Richard doing the books, greeting customers and managing the rotating art exhibits. An artist who once worked on an Indian reservation, Richard enjoys telling newcomers about Aiken. That's his moon on the ceiling.

Readers of *Aiken County Magazine* voted The New Moon Café "Best New Restaurant in Aiken County" in 1995, the year it opened. The magazine applauded its freshness in food and atmosphere. There are lots of extras: sun-dried tomato cream cheese for the turkey special; Honey Dijon for the chicken salad.

I'm not sure what I liked best about The New Moon Café, but I think it might be the way the two guys at the counter simultaneously pointed me to the tiny restroom behind the kitchen. It's as floaty as the dining room, with clouds and planets painted on the walls. The servers and cooks are appropriately college-looking, in tie-dyed blues and greens. Silver stars and a golden crescent hang from the ceiling; gold stars fleck the navy tablecloths—which aren't as dark as that blueberry milkshake.

It's ingredients are simple: vanilla ice cream, fresh blueberries, whipped cream. "It's a really cool color," Michelle says. "Kids like it because it's Barney purple."

- Aïda Rogers

Owner Christine Tomasetti Alewelt has made a few changes at The New Moon Café since we last visited. The coffee, which so many Aikenites swear by, is now roasted on premises and their bakery has added additional pastries. At lunch, the Honey Dijon chicken sandwich, the Herbed Tuna Salad plate, and Dr. John Panini are big favorites and to wash it all down, the New Moon blueberry milkshake is still popular. Oh, yes, take a gander at the poster of Wonder Woman now adorning the women's bathroom door. And remember, you're in Aiken: While sipping your coffee, you may catch sight of a horse trotting down Laurens Street from one of the town's many stables.

- Tim Driggers

Riley's Whitby Bull, Aiken
Aiken County

Riley's Whitby Bull, 801 E. Pine Log Road, Aiken; (803) 641-6227. Open for dinner Wednesday-Saturday, 5-9 p.m.; breakfast Sunday, 9 a.m.-1 p.m. Reservations required. No smoking. Credit cards accepted. Bring your own magician's wand. www.rileyswhitbybull.com. Expensive.

Have Some Whimsy With Your Meal

There is nothing ordinary about Riley's Whitby Bull in Aiken. When the diminutive co-owner – is she an elf? – greets you at the door in a purplish jester hat waving a magic wand that makes jingly noises, you know the evening won't be blah.

"I've scared people away with it," confesses Lorraine Riley about her wand, recounting how one group of people got up and left after observing her costumed high jinks. But that's all it is. Lorraine believes in having fun. If you get a great meal and some terrific dessert too, then all the better. "It's too serious out there! I can't deal with it. Come here!"

Lorraine says just about anything goes in her fifth restaurant, which she runs with her husband Will. They met at the Culinary Institute of America in Hyde Park, New York, where they graduated in 1981. He's from Ohio, a carver and carpenter as well as chef. She's from New York State; her first love is painting. All their talents can be experienced at their restaurant. An 1880 dwelling with pink trim and mansard roof, Riley's Whitby Bull is surrounded by old trees and thick grass—incongruous on what's become a busy highway. Outside there's a slight air of abandonment, like you've stumbled into *The Ghost and Mrs. Muir*. Walk in and you're engulfed by coziness. Celtic music is playing, orchids are blooming, and tables are waiting by fireplaces decorated with colored lights and lighthouses.

Lighthouses are a major theme here; they represent the seaside English town of Whitby. "That would be as loud as the Whitby Bull," a character said in one of Martha Grimes' murder mysteries, which the Rileys read. Liking the sound of that sentence, Lorraine asked Will if their next restaurant could be named Whitby Bull. Not surprisingly, Will agreed.

Soups and appetizers are appropriately imaginative. There is no soup du jour here; it's "Whim of Will." Tonight's Whim of Will is black bean with red onion marmalade. "Suffused with a subtle spiciness," observes Aleqx Franzgrieg in his best critic's voice. Aleqx teaches Greek and Latin in England and has lived near Whitby at some point in his lifelong European travels. His wife, Nancy Allison (who has written for this magazine and others) works hard not to roll her eyes.

Chicken, seafood, and steaks (aged Black Angus) are available here, but the "Whitby Bull Favorites" are more unusual. Minnesota Elk Steak with mushroom brandy sauce and Riley's Famous Duck Breast with Cherry Port Sauce are on this list. So are New Zealand lamb chops with gingered apple compote. Our quartet ordered the butterflied quail with Cumberland sauce (brown gravy, red currants, oranges, raisins, and almonds), the surf & turf (petite filet and lobster tail), roasted salmon filet (plain or Florentine) and the mixed grill (lobster tail, filet, venison sausage and lamb chop).

Salad, bread, and a choice of French fries, baked stuffed potato, or rice accompany the entrees. You could fill up just on the salad (Bibb lettuce, walnuts, crumbled bleu cheese, and olives) and bread. Will makes brown Irish soda bread every morning. Put plenty of butter on it to confirm what we all know but frequently forget: Bread and butter is one of the best food combinations ever invented. When one of us started coughing, Lorraine rushed over with honey. Butter and honey on Irish soda bread—at least Will's Irish soda bread—is an over-the-moon tableside experience.

The Rileys live upstairs and serve guests below. The thing is, you're not a guest. Waitress Jan Walbring (she spins wool and weaves, too) says, "Everybody who comes in here becomes a friend. That's the neat thing about this place." As Lorraine puts it,

"The people that need us, find us. We're a bunch of aging hippies here; that's all there is to it." Many of their customers from New York and Ohio come to visit and have a meal. They're not disappointed to find their friends in typical creative form.

Maybe that's best seen at the Sunday Breakfast. Besides gingerbread pancakes and vanilla cinnamon French toast, there's a sun-dried tomato garlic and mozzarella omelet. "Special Breakfasts" include the Irish Pub Breakfast (sliced Black-Angus beef, scrambled eggs, cheddar and Port wine sauce served open-faced on French loaf with roasted potatoes) and the Chesapeake Bay Eggs (two poached eggs and Maryland crab cakes on English muffin, Hollandaise, roasted potatoes).

Desserts are available for breakfast and supper. Cheesecakes are Lorraine's domain, and you won't want to miss her lemon poppy seed variety, if she's made any that day. Lemon chess and turtle pies are popular, and egg custard can be served plain or with caramel, raspberry or lemon curd.

The Rileys moved to Aiken in 1994 after visiting a former waitress who'd resettled here. "We just fell in love with this town and said, 'Why not?' " Lorraine explains. Ten years is as long as they've been anywhere, but buying a historic home seems to have given them roots. "We've been gypsies and all of our customers know we move around. They're getting nervous." But they need not worry. " I guess we're sticking here," she concludes. "I'm too happy."

- Aïda Rogers

Exciting news from Riley's Whitby Bull: Lorraine just purchased a new hat to replace her old jester's cap. Imagine that. She and husband Will are also writing a cookbook and they've started an online newsletter telling what's going on at the Bull and who's celebrating a birthday or anniversary in the restaurant's extended family. They're now offering take-out service for Will's renowned Irish Soda Bread, Lemon Chess Pie, Turtle Pie and Cheesecake. Best sellers are Riley's Famous Duck Breast and the Louisiana Shrimp and Rice. You can also add a lobster tail or half dozen shrimp to any entrée. Don't just consider going to Riley's Whitby Bull for Sunday Brunch; make a point to be there when the doors open. There's the Black Angus Steak and Eggs, Mexican Eggs, Eggs Benedict, Chesapeake Bay Eggs with Maryland crab cakes on an English muffin with Hollandaise. What a feast! Enough to make you want to camp on the Rileys' front porch until Sunday morning arrives.

- Tim Driggers

The Track Kitchen, Aiken
Aiken County

The Track Kitchen, 420 Mead Avenue, Aiken; (803) 641-9628. Open daily November-April, 7 a.m. until 1 p.m. No reservations. No credit cards. No smoking. Inexpensive.

Breakfast In Horse Country

With stables in the front and polo fields in the back, The Track Kitchen sits squarely in Aiken's horse country. It's run by the very popular Carol and James "Pockets" Carter, but regulars around here call it simply "Pockets'." Pockets got his name 48 years ago, when as a groom, he was identified as the James (there were two) "with his hands in his pockets." The name stuck, and Pockets still stands with his hands in his pockets. His hands are busy, though, in the kitchen, where he and his wife share cooking duties, and in the yard, where he cooks his famous barbecue on his famous "pig coffins."

Pockets is one of Aiken's most famous citizens. Count on seeing him serving his specialties at the thoroughbred trials, the steeplechase and the harness race, as well as at the polo games. He's a horse lover as well as a natural cook, and he likes to mix the two. "Me without a horse is like cornflakes without milk. I like to be around 'em."

The same could be said about Aiken and The Track Kitchen. It's a favorite with the town and horse set, which comes to Aiken each winter to train thoroughbreds. They quickly find The Track Kitchen, where you can get thick slabs of country bacon or ham with grits or home fries, eggs and coffee. French toast and hotcakes are available too, and you can serve your own coffee behind the counter, if you want. Even though this is Pockets' place, somehow it's everybody else's, too.

"Most horse people know where to eat," Linda Watson points out, tucking into a plate of eggs and bowl of grits. Linda and her fiancé, Jim Friess, are here from Lexington, Kentucky, to see their colt and filly. Jim works at Claiborne Farms in Paris, Kentucky, home of Secretariat, and is patient when translating horse talk to an uninitiated reporter. They know, as do other horse people, that the hours are early. The Track Kitchen opens at 7 a.m. While Carol runs the kitchen solo later in the morning, Pockets takes his van out to the stables to sell breakfast sandwiches, coffee and juice to those who can't break away.

Still, you have to go there to sample certain items—the buttery, spongy hotcakes and the creamy grits.

The Track Kitchen serves breakfast only, although now and then Carol will prepare a country-style lunch. Jockey Laury Nelson of New Hampshire loves the soup. "It's the best," she says. "They use real fresh ingredients with beef or ham."

Because the horse season isn't year-round, neither is The Track Kitchen. It's open November until the end of April, when the horses move on to New York. That's when Pockets devotes himself to his catering business—so well-known he doesn't have to advertise. He's prepared his barbecue in Saratoga, New York, and catered regularly for the late Strom Thurmond and the Medical College of Georgia.

Pockets' pig coffins are his portable cookers, on which he grills chicken, hams, and hogs—up to five at a time. Decorated with painted chickens and pigs, the pig coffins were designed by Pockets and built by a friend. Good smells come from these coffins. He uses a mustard-based sauce.

In operation almost 50 years, The Track Kitchen has been run by the Carters since 1981. It's a simple, cement block place with a pool table, a few tables and ladder-back chairs. Meals come on round green plates; the toast is served with a thick smudge of butter and a fat plop of jelly on the side. Strangers sit together and share salt, pepper, and syrup. This is not a place to show off; it's a place to eat, drink coffee, and talk horses. If you can't talk the language, you can always appreciate the food.

"I think the breakfast is outstanding," says Mickey Burke, a Pittsburgh harness trainer. "He won't eat grits; he's a Yankee," says Mac McMichael, another horse lover.

The Track Kitchen is open until 1 p.m. seven days a week, including race mornings. Go for the food, and go for the surroundings; horses and horse farms are here to be admired from this intersection of two dirt roads. Pockets likes to tell customers to go see the animals in action. "There are some people who've been here a long time and don't know much about it," he says, leaning over a fence.

Over the years, The Track Kitchen has been dressed up a bit, something that chagrins the old timers. There are framed black-and-white photos of Aiken fox hunts and races on the walls, as well as a framed 1993 *New York Times* article about the town and its love for horses. It's a long article, and certainly complete—The Track Kitchen is listed as a place to check out.

- Aïda Rogers

Thankfully, not much has changed at The Track Kitchen since Sandlapper *visited in 1995. Pockets and Carol Carter still run the place, serving the same mouth-watering breakfast meals they have for almost three decades. The hotcakes and French toast remain popular. Carol tells us that during weekdays, the horse folks dominate The Track Kitchen, but on weekends, the locals take over. Of course, at The Track Kitchen, that's purely a human perspective; the horses have always been the real stars.*

- *Tim Driggers*

The Winton Inn, Barnwell
Barnwell County

The Winton Inn, 8273 Marlboro Avenue, Barnwell; (803) 259-7193. Open for lunch Monday-Friday, 11 a.m.-2 p.m. and for dinner Tuesday-Saturday, 6 p.m. until. Sunday lunch is 11 a.m.- 3 p.m. Credit cards and checks accepted. Reservations requested for dinner. No smoking. Moderate.

A Long Winter's Feed

Somebody once said something about politics making strange bedfellows. A friend of mine says the same thing about happy hour. And now let me add that it's true for being single and hungry.

Here's why: I was in Barnwell, hanging out in the Barnwell County Museum, talking to Hildegarde Roberts and Everett Perrin. Miss Hildegarde runs it and Everett—I call him "The Full Colonel"—helps her out some afternoons.

It was getting late, and we all noticed we were hungry. Because none of us had anyone to report to, we were free to hit the buffet at The Winton Inn.

I had heard of the Winton Inn before—its authentic country cooking at lunch, its highly recommended prime rib and crab legs at supper. Lucky for us, it was Thursday, which then meant all-you-can-eat seafood and prime rib. You can't say no to that.

The three of us settled in for a long winter's feed. We ordered white wine and clinked glasses, happy for the spontaneous party. I had to notice how different we were. Miss Hildegarde is a widow in her 80s, a former French and Latin teacher from California. Everett is a divorcee´ in his 50s, a retired Marine officer from Cleveland.

Besides telling me about Barnwell from a nonnative perspective, they made wonderful dining partners. Nobody was shy about the buffet.

Here's what's on it: crab legs, Beaufort stew, deviled crab, fish, shrimp, scallops, clam chowder, and something I love—catfish stew. (Why is it so hard to find?)

I decided to skip the equally loaded salad bar so I could take advantage of all that seafood. But there was a dilemma. It was the prime rib which, as I looked at it, became somehow regal and haughty. It was daring me, taunting me, destroying my quickly waning resolution to lay off the red meat.

I don't know how long I stood there, trying to be strong, when I gave in and got a slice. I had to. It just doesn't come into my life that often.

Miss Hildegarde congratulated me on my decision and admired the thick, red slab that almost covered my whole plate. "Oooh, it's beautiful," she said. I have been feeling somewhat embarrassed by my unfashionable love for beef, but she made me feel better. "Whoever doesn't is crazy," she said, slicing away at her own piece.

Lunch is as southern as you'll find. There was baked ham, fried chicken, and barbeque ribs when I was there, all kinds of vegetables, blueberry cobbler, and probably the best biscuits I've ever had. I asked the waitress what kind they were, and her answer was simple—"homemade."

I suppose one day I'll try the salad bar, but I know I'd rather have a night of crab legs and butter, wine and good company. The only word for Miss Hildegarde is "delightful," and Everett—the voice behind "The Few, The Proud, The Marines"—is truly a character. I like him, even if he said I eat like a horse.

- Aïda Rogers

Over the span of 14 years, a lot can happen at a restaurant. When the Winton Inn was revisited, we found that Peggy Collins, an acquaintance of the late Hildegarde Roberts, had become the owner. The midday buffet still features southern cuisine, highlighted by Winton Inn favorites fried chicken and cucumber salad. The lunch buffet changes daily and there's upscale dining during the evening showcasing a multitude of seafood, pasta, chicken, and steak delights. Also take advantage of the contemporary pub, large banquet rooms and restaurant catering service. The Sunday lunch features turkey and dressing, steamship roast, and fried chicken. Interesting note: Barnwell County was originally known as Winton County. Its name changed in 1785.

- Tim Driggers

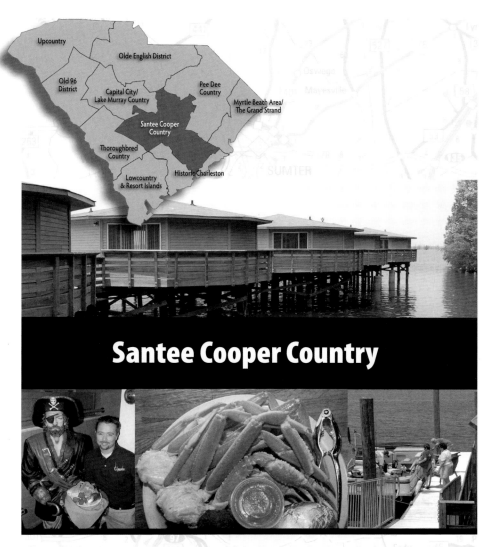

Santee Cooper Country

Berkeley, Calhoun, Clarendon, Orangeburg & Sumter Counties

The Barony House, Moncks Corner
Berkeley County

The Barony House, 401 Altman Street, Moncks Corner; (843) 761-7600. Open Monday-Friday for lunch, 11 a.m.-2:30 p.m. and on Thursday and Friday for dinner, 6-9 p.m. Closed Saturday and Sunday. Reservations not needed, except for large parties at dinner. Credit cards and checks accepted. Smoking in designated areas at dinner. Inexpensive to moderate.

A Good Restaurant in a Small Town

They don't know this, but the only reason my sister and her husband had children was to give me a new dining partner. So one dreary January morning, the adorable Margaret Tompkins and I set off for Moncks Corner. Our destination: The Barony House Restaurant. The verdict? I'll let Margaret handle that: "My name is Margaret and I just went to a very fancy restaurant," my sweet 10-year-old niece told the tape recorder as we were leaving. "It was wonderful. It had the best food and wonderful waitresses. The person who owns it is very nice. I think everyone should go there to eat their food."

And they should. My editor discovered The Barony House a while back and returned with tales of rutabaga and catfish. When we pulled up to see a crowded parking lot and a car that said "sweet tea" on the license plate, I knew a good story was at hand. And what a setting: a spreading live oak on one side, a railroad track on the other, and next door, the Solid Rock of Jesus church. Margaret and I, starving by 1 p.m., couldn't wait to check it out.

"The special Friday night is shrimp and grits. We drive up here for that," said Rev. Bernett Waitt of Summerville. He and wife Jane were waiting for us at a corner table—otherwise, we'd be standing in this popular restaurant. Monday's Shrimp Creole is another reason they'll travel 20-some miles to visit Van "Bubba" High's restaurant.

Server Sharon Johnson vouches for the Shrimp Creole. "Bubba puts a hurtin' on that thing," she said. "He can cook!"

Sharon bustled around our table with a big smile and much friendliness. "My darlings," she called us. Margaret and I were charmed.

Rev. Waitt, who appears to be a shrimp man, ordered Friday's lunch special, the Creek Shrimp Platter. Jane ordered the loaded potato stuffed with turkey, ham, cheese, broccoli, squash, and cucumber. Served with a salad and black bread, Jane had plenty and was sharing it around the table. "Now that's a loaded potato," she said.

I chose another special: fried catfish on grits. Margaret ordered a half sandwich and salad. Though we couldn't finish it all, we couldn't ignore the desserts. The Barony House is famous for them, and they beckon from a case near the door. Among the choices were chocolate raspberry ganache, turtle pie, double chocolate cheesecake, peanut butter pie, and hazelnut cake. We took a long moment to think it over, and

Margaret and I even walked to the case to check them out. "They all look good," she breathed. "Very good."

Finally, we ordered four different ones and rotated them around the table: strawberry banana pie, white chocolate cake with pistachio raspberry filling, Kahula mousse cake, and strawberry banana cake. How can you not be happy doing that?

The Barony House serves a variety of salads and sandwiches at lunch, gyros and hot plate specials. The smoked turkey salad and Arizona turkey melt are favorites. In the evening, white linens are put out to complement the more formal steak, seafood, and chicken entrees.

I love places like The Barony House because they provide such a service to the people around them. A good restaurant in a small town—where customers know each other and stroll from table to table visiting—is not so common anymore. Here, many customers are Bubba's former students at Berkeley High, where he was choral director. Occasionally, Bubba in his apron will sit down at the piano and play for some of those students.

"I reached mountaintop experiences while I taught," Bubba says. "I took students to Europe and we sang all over the United States. I wouldn't trade anything for that."

But after 25 years—and the Order of the Palmetto in 1992—Bubba followed his second calling: cooking. He bought and repaired a 1940s bus station and opened The Barony House. Today, it's a classy place with antiques and oxblood-covered walls, fresh flowers, and prints of sporting scenes. Fittingly, a portrait of Lord Berkeley hangs above a fireplace. Local lawyer and friend Ned Dennis found the portrait at an auction and brought him "home" to his namesake county. Dennis also brought old pine mantels from a Charleston home. Classic Southern comfort is the resulting feel.

"I never wanted it to look institutional," Bubba explains. "I wanted it to look a little eclectic."

Many recipes are from Bubba's family cook, Sarah Motte. "We loved her dearly," he says. "She was with my family 42 years. She's one of the great characters in my life." Other recipes, he admits, are borrowed from elsewhere, or come from loyal cook Alisha Gillians.

Bubba didn't leave music behind when he stopped teaching. He kept playing the organ at church. His Sundays began at 5 a.m., when he ran to the restaurant for prep work. He'd leave three hours later for home, shower and come to the restaurant to print the daily menu. By 10:30 a.m. he was at church with the choir, and at 12:05, after playing the postlude, he drove to the restaurant. "People would almost pull over to the side when they saw my car, because they knew I was making a mad dash to get here."

Since Sunday is the biggest day for Moncks Corner's finest restaurant, it was only polite that they did.

- Aïda Rogers

The menu has changed a bit at The Barony House over the years. Owner Bubba High has daily hot plates for lunch. On Monday it's a Chef's Choice and baked ham, on Tuesday there's Chicken Bog and meatloaf, Wednesday's specials are fried chicken and pork and dressing, on Thursday it's pork backbone and rice and the Chef's Special, and Friday's features are beef stew and turkey and dressing. Everyday items are pot roast of beef, country fried steak, fried shrimp, and fried oysters. There are also plentiful sides and salads. Also available are the Gyro Platter, various wraps, sandwiches, and "The Burger." At night, Bubba has entrée specials – grilled meatloaf, fried grouper, and shrimp and grits. The evening menu includes horseradish soufflé baked salmon, chili seared tuna, pecan encrusted chicken, parmesan artichoke chicken, grilled 12-ounce aged ribeye, and fried pork chops. Or try Bubba's "old favorites" – The Barony Burger and The Barony Melt Club. All entrees (except shrimp and grits) are served with a choice of 3 sides. Bubba still takes an occasional turn at the keyboard.

- Tim Driggers

Chef's Choice Steakhouse, Eutawville
Orangeburg County

Chef's Choice Steakhouse, 12757 Old Number 6 Highway, Eutawville; (803) 492-3410. Open Thursday-Saturday, 5:30-9 p.m. Reservations requested for more than six people. Smoking allowed. Moderate.

Steak at the Lake

The official name of this restaurant is Chef's Choice, but the regulars call it Danny Bell's Chef's Choice. They remember when Danny ran Bell's Marina on Lake Marion, which he did for 28 years before starting a steak place in a large building supply company a mile or so away. He's been running this enterprise 14 years now with wife Maureen and daughter Dareen (Dan and Maureen). He doesn't miss his former establishment.

"That operation is daylight to dark, seven days a week. Here I open at 5 in the afternoon and close about 10, three nights a week. And I'm 72 years old. Does that tell you anything? I was ready to back off a little bit."

Yeah, Danny Bell has simplified his life. His menu has exactly 10 items on it, mostly steak. For the easily confused, Chef's Choice is a blessing.

"Honey, I just had a building way out in the middle of the country and I had to do something with it," he explained. "I went all over the country—to Canton, Ohio, and Memphis, Tennessee, and looked at other restaurants and got ideas about what might work here. So I just built a big grill in the middle of the floor and put a box up here full of steaks and let people come in and pick their own steak—cook it if they want to or let me cook it. It's just a little different concept, that's all."

It's working. Danny and his staff grill 400-500 steaks a weekend for people who drive in from surrounding counties. Fishers and golfers at the Santee Cooper lakes are frequent guests.

Danny's secret is high-quality beef, grain-fed and aged, cooked at the proper heat. His steaks come from a packer in Chicago. "I pay as high as $9 a pound for my meat," he said. "You don't pay that for yours."

You can order filet, rib-eye, strip and T-bone (small or large). Or you can order the "Garbage Steak," a 12-ounce sirloin covered with sautéed onions. "I call it a Garbage Steak to get somebody's attention."

If you're not feeling beefy, your options include shrimp kabobs, steak and shrimp, and grilled chicken breast. Hamburger steak also is available. "Everything I cook I cook on the grill," he pointed out. "I don't have a deep fryer in the house."

Vegetarians can plunder the 30-item salad bar, which contains two favorites from Danny's childhood: pickled okra and watermelon rind preserves. His mother Erma, who died at 96, made them regularly.

The freshness of the salad bar and the focus on grilling has prompted many heart-healthy groups to recommend Chef's Choice. But Danny sounds more interested in taste. "Not responsible for well-done steaks," says a menu disclaimer. What does that mean? "Exactly that," he said. "I hate a well-done steak, and people who want a well-done, cremated steak—honey, that's no good." But he'll cook one if you want it—"and I can still cook one with plenty of flavor in it, but I just don't like it."

Entrees come with baked potato, garlic bread and a trip to the salad bar. Also available are a child's menu and varied desserts, some made in-house, some not. Danny recommends the homemade chocolate walnut pie. Chef's Choice also has a good-sized bar and music—live or deejay—on Friday and Saturday nights.

Businessmen who fish and golf have come from all over the world. Danny remembers one impressed visitor: "This man told me that was the most beautiful steak he'd ever eaten. He said, 'A steak anywhere like that in my restaurant would cost you 65 dollars.' I said, 'My God, where's your restaurant?' And he said, 'In Paris.' "

- Aïda Rogers

We loved Chef's Choice when we visited in 1999, and were saddened to learn Danny Bell had passed away when updating this report. His daughter Dareen is running the restaurant now, and just the way her father did. "Everything is still the same," she says, noting Chef's Choice celebrated its 23rd anniversary in March 2008.

- A. R.

Chestnut Grill, Orangeburg
Orangeburg County

Chestnut Grill, 1455 Chestnut Street, Orangeburg; (803) 531-1747. Lunch: 11 a.m.-4 p.m.; Dinner: Monday-Thursday, 4-9 p.m.; Friday & Saturday, 4-10 p.m. Credit cards accepted. Reservations recommended. Smoking allowed only in bar. www.chestnutgrill.com. Inexpensive to moderate.

Special Occasions in Orangeburg

Once upon a time—and not that long ago—the country club was where you went for a meal on a tablecloth. That's changing. In Orangeburg, there's another option for something a little more "special occasion" than fast food or a meat-and-three. Chestnut Grill to the rescue.

"We found a need and we filled it," said owner Jim Albergotti, a real estate developer who opened the restaurant as part of the Denver-based Mr. Steak franchise 20 years ago. Unhappy with the restaurant in its early years, he eventually went independent, changing the menu and name. Today, Chestnut Grill doesn't reflect any other region but the one it's in. Frozen steaks and frozen, prebreaded seafood are a memory now. "We had to get that stuff out of there," he said. "People in the South, particularly in South Carolina, just aren't prepared to accept frozen, factory-prepared seafood."

Today, the seafood comes from the South Carolina coast, says Jack Albergotti, Jim's son and manager of the restaurant. And seafood sells well, particularly the fried shrimp and seafood casserole, which is Jim's recipe. Flounder, salmon, halibut, oysters, scallops, and soft-shell crabs are also available.

Chestnut Grill includes a choice of vegetable and soup or salad with entrees. "That's an added value to the menu," says Jack, who describes the menu as "upscale country cooking." Besides seafood, there's a variety of steak, chicken, four cuts of prime rib, rack of lamb, pork chops and baby back ribs. The most expensive thing is filet mignon. The Albergottis' Italian heritage appears in the specials: bobolis, spaghetti, fettuccini, and chicken cacciatore.

Our waiter suggested starting with the Not So Awesome Onion, a deep-fried flowered onion served with a Cajun sauce with ranch spices. (The Awesome Onion is bigger and a dollar more.) As we picked and plunged, Dolly Patton, former executive director of Sandlapper Society, and I agonized over the menu. So much to choose from, as illustrated by its three kinds of fries: sweet potato, shoestring, and ranch, which are wedge-cut with ranch flavoring.

We ended up with two kinds of soup, a steak and the Chestnut Sampler. "Hot as blue blazes" is how Dolly described the cheddar soup, thick and bacon-sprinkled. The clam chowder is thick, with red-skinned potatoes and clams. Everything but desserts are made in-house, Jack says, including the banana nut and French-style breads.

The Chestnut Sampler is a beautiful arrangement of teriyaki chicken on rice pilaf, fried or grilled shrimp, baby back ribs and steak kebob, with pineapple slices and a cherry. The iced tea passed Dolly's test—sweet but not too sweet.

Chestnut Grill is simply nice. Ceiling fans, booths, tablecloths, candles, and flowers give it that special touch, but not so special that you can't come in jeans or sweatsuits. It works for families and dates, and Jack says they entertain a lot of white-collar business people at lunch as well as interstate travelers. Ask Jack if there's a dress code, and he just laughs. "Shoes and shirt," he says.

- Aïda Rogers

Jim Albergotti still owns Chestnut Grill, but management has been turned over to son Warren in the evening and to Warren's wife Margie during the daytime. For lunch, Chestnut Grill offers a variety of appetizers, salads, soups, and quiche, together with chicken, steak, and seafood specialties. There are also the sandwiches—a turkey and ham club, Angus beef hamburger, chicken salad croissant, French dip, and grilled chicken. For dinner, Warren rolls out New York strip, peppercorn strip, filet mignon, ribeye, and chopped and topped Angus beef. The Chestnut Grill continues to be noted for its seafood with plates of fried shrimp, flounder, and scallops, along with Maine lobster, grilled salmon, tempura won-ton fried shrimp, low country crab cakes, and seafood combinations and platters.

- *Tim Driggers*

The Compass Family Restaurant, Turbeville
Clarendon County

The Compass Family Restaurant, U.S. Highway 378 and I-95 (Exit 135) near Turbeville; (803) 659-2140. Open seven days a week from 4:30 p.m. until 9 p.m. and open for lunch Thursday-Sunday, 11 a.m.-2 p.m. Credit cards and checks accepted. Reservations not required. Smoking allowed in designated areas. Moderate.

Seafood Surprise in Turbeville

Between 1984 and 1986, when I worked for the *Sun News* in Myrtle Beach, I passed the Compass Family Restaurant about once a month. I always wondered if it was good, and I always wondered if I'd ever find out. But I was always in a hurry either to get home to Lexington or to get back to the beach.

It wasn't until last year that I remembered The Compass. Tommy Leitner, an old

Deviled crabs beckon guests to the Compass buffet.

classmate, told me to check it out. "It's a dang good restaurant. That place is packed all the time."

In March I found out for myself. Columbia artist Anna K. Singley and I were heading down U.S. 378 to Myrtle Beach. We had discussed a light lunch, maybe a salad or sandwich. But there it was, unpretentious in its weather-beaten way, just outside Turbeville on the left. It was lunchtime, we were hungry, and we didn't waste time making a decision.

Deciding what to order wasn't difficult, either. The best deal is the seafood buffet. You get an array of seafood and all the trimmings, plus the salad bar. While some items are what you'd expect – fried fish, shrimp, baked potatoes, fries–there are things you wouldn't. Shrimp Creole, for instance.

The Compass offers other surprises. Bite into a hushpuppy and you're likely to find yourself with something entirely different: a sweet corn fritter, broccoli/cheese fritter or fried apple fritter. Don't underestimate the salad bar. I can get sick of a salad bar in a hurry, but this one is of Mt. Olympus caliber. For this time of year, the fruit was remarkably fresh and there was plenty to choose from. Also known for its steaks, The Compass attracts folks from Sumter, Clarendon and Florence counties.

I'm glad we stopped, if for no other reason than to see how popular it is. The sure-fire way of proving that is to note the number of men who eat there. The fact that more than one had a gun at his side didn't bother us. At The Compass, the food is so good you'd shoot for it.

- Aïda Rogers

Tye Green's Compass Family Restaurant continues to be a popular destination for folks going to and from the beach. With three large dining rooms that can accommodate 250 guests, diners can order from a menu featuring lobster tail, snow crab, stuffed flounder and shrimp, a variety of seafood platters and a smattering of "Land Lover's" entrees, or opt for the extensive buffet. Hint: All-You-Can-Eat Snow Crabs are featured on Monday and Wednesday. Try those crab cakes on the buffet line.

- Tim Driggers

Dukes Bar B Que, Orangeburg
Orangeburg County

Dukes Bar B Que, 1298 Whitman Street, Orangeburg; (803) 534-2916. Open Wednesday, 11 a.m.-8 p.m., Thursday-Saturday, 11 a.m.-9 p.m. and Sunday, 11 a.m.-2 p.m. Reservations not needed. Credit cards not accepted. Smoking allowed in designated area. Inexpensive.

Good Fixin's at the Pepsi-Cola Plant

Eating barbecue is an individual thing. My favorite way is to make sure the barbecue and slaw are on the fork or in the sandwich together. I presented my technique for the staff of Judge Karen Williams at Dukes Bar B Que in Orangeburg, and learned the good judge has her own style. She takes hers with dill pickles.

She also takes it on the road. Williams has carried 20 pounds of Dukes barbecue and hash to meetings in Washington, D.C., and packed a cooler of 160 sandwiches for the boys on her son's football team in Virginia. For her, nothing quite spells contentment like this modest, decades-old establishment in her hometown. "I love it here," she says. "I could eat here every day."

But she can't, because like many barbecue places, Dukes isn't open every day. So every Thursday, Williams brings her staff here for lunch. On Saturdays, she comes back with her family. She's been coming since she was a girl, and brought her children when they were babies. "They'd get rice and pour hash all over it and sit in high chairs and eat that."

Baby David is a big boy now, a football player with a barbecue method of his own. He layers his plate with hash, adds a mound of hushpuppies, then tops with barbecue sauce. His plate makes a simple but mighty statement. "He counts the hash as a vegetable," his mother says dryly.

Meanwhile, Ann Currie Williams, the judge's assistant (no relation), has perfected a different procedure: meat covered with hash and pickles. Like Judge Williams, she's an Orangeburg native and devout believer in Dukes. She also has that special insider knowledge—that you never say you're going to Dukes. You say you're going to what's near the particular operation of Dukes you're visiting. There are three. "Nobody calls it Dukes Bar B Que," Ann Currie says. "You eat at the Pepsi-Cola plant, at the fire station or at the highway department."

We were at the Pepsi-Cola plant, and by the time we got there at 12:45 p.m., it was crowded. Serve yourself to the buffet, and be glad Tupperware pitchers of sweet tea are waiting on every table. You'll be thirsty trying to get down the standard barbecue fare (hash, rice, pulled pork barbecue, pork rinds, and slaw) along with the extras—fried chicken, potato salad, green beans and baked beans.

Going to Dukes is like going to a family reunion in a church fellowship hall. Babies, grandparents, business people and laborers eat together at long tables with folding chairs. Hugs between customers are common. "It's tradition," Judge Williams observes. "It's one of those places you've known all your life. You see people you don't get to see any other time."

While at Dukes, you might also see the board members of Orangeburg's First National Bank. They've come straight from their monthly meeting. Knowing lunch is at Dukes "helps us get out on time," notes Cholly Clark of Santee. Board chairman Bob Horger, an Orangeburg native, says Dukes is a love-at-first-bite kind of place.

"My wife came in one time and she said she wasn't going to eat anything," Horger recalls. "She's from Connecticut. Well, she got a full plate."

- Aïda Rogers

A South Carolina legend since 1955, Earl Dukes continues to cook hickory-smoked pork at one of the most popular barbecue buffets in the state. As for Karen Williams, she's now Chief Judge of the United States Court of Appeals for the Fourth Circuit in Richmond, Virginia, and long rumored to be a possible candidate for appointment to the United States Supreme Court. You don't think this kind of success comes as a result of eating Dukes Bar B Que all your life? Well, of course I do. In a state where downing pork barbecue is akin to a religious experience, Earl Dukes walks on water.

- *Tim Driggers*

Eatery at the Depot, Branchville
Orangeburg County

The Eatery at the Depot (formerly the Edisto Eatery), 7501 Freedom Road, Branchville; (803) 274-8001. Open for dinner Thursday-Saturday, 6-9 p.m. Closed Sunday-Wednesday. No smoking. Credit cards and checks accepted. Reservations not required. Inexpensive to moderate.

Pleasures in Rural River Country

In that vast, fertile land called Orangeburg, the south and north forks of the Edisto River come together about three miles west of Branchville. It was at a regular monthly gathering of a men's river club when a fortuitous introduction occurred. Clifton Ott, hardware store owner, and Norris Jarrett, dry cleaning store manager, discovered their mutual love of cooking. That was in 1997. No telling how many fish fries, venison roasts and chicken bogs later, they gave Branchville—long famous as the oldest railroad junction in the world—something else about which to brag. They gave it a sit-down restaurant, with appetizers and desserts, and art on the walls and cloths on the tables. But mainly they gave people a warm reminder about where they are. This is rural river country, the corner where Bamberg, Dorchester, Colleton and Orangeburg counties come together. People come from these areas and beyond to The Edisto Eatery (now transformed a few doors down at the museum into the Eatery at the Depot), many detouring from I-95. Though highways 21 and 78 are both federal, either will take you at a more refined pace to this town of 1,083.

"It's sort of like Mayberry," reflects Norris, a Charleston boy who grew up in the restaurant business. "I think I surprised a lot of people, including myself, when I moved out here. But it's wonderful. We take a ride to Edisto Beach and don't hit a single red light. Isn't that something?"

It was Norris' wife Kyra who brought him to her hometown. Her children's consignment shop is next to the restaurant; she and Clifton's wife Toni, a teacher from Denmark, work up front while their husbands cook in the back. Meanwhile, Clifton's hardware store is just down the block. Cozy, huh? But that's the appropriate, nostalgic atmosphere here. How fitting that fried yellow squash appears as an appetizer.

Squash wasn't in season when our foursome arrived in December 2002. But sweet potatoes were, and we quickly ordered a basket of them fried and dusted with sugar. We also sampled the fried dolphin chunks, served with cucumber dill tartar sauce. Fried oysters and crab dip complete the appetizer lineup.

"Keep it simple" is the idea here. The solitary beef entree, aside from burgers, is prime rib, with baked potato or buttered new potatoes. It's the Friday and Saturday night special. Lowcountry Shrimp and Grits, sautéed with ham and tomato gravy, is also offered. "Being from Charleston, I thought this thing had its day in the sun, but people like it and it does well," Norris notes.

Evangeline Byrd Hall, a Branchville native now living in Pond Branch, was inspired to order the Combination Plate. Though she could choose two seafood items—shrimp, oysters, catfish, or flounder—it was that accompanying red rice and baby limas that called her name. "Red rice is very Low Country," she informs.

Other favorites are the Grilled Pork Tenderloin (with garlic cheese mashed potatoes and buttered carrots), marinated in Clifton's secret soy and herb sauce; and the fried oysters, a dozen fresh ones with red rice or fries. Deep-fried pork chops; grilled chicken; fried shrimp and catfish; and grilled mahi mahi, salmon and yellow-fin tuna round out the menu. Entrees include a tossed salad and biscuit—on this evening, a garlic-cheese-parsley variety. A children's menu features fried shrimp, chicken strips and corn dog bites.

"Good eats" declares a sign above the dessert case. It's filled with pies Norris makes, and cakes baked by his mother-in-law, Clifton's mother and a church member. The strawberry cream cake, served cold, is the most popular, we're told. It's so popular it's already gone this busy Friday evening. But we're satisfied by the alternatives: a six-layer chocolate cake with caramel icing, and slices of Norris' famous Ritz Cracker and Vinegar pies.

"We pile it on for you," Norris says. "I like for people to get a taste of anything they like."

Though they had no professional cooking experience before opening in August 2000, Norris and Clifton have made a success of their business. Concludes Norris: "Having people talking and smiling here is now such a great thing."

- Aïda Rogers

Norris Jarrett is now sole owner of the Eatery at the Depot, which he relocated and renamed in 2003. These days, the refurbished restaurant is found at the rear of the town museum, itself a testament to the rich history and railroad heritage of Branchville. Norris enjoys relating that Branchville has been visited by three United States Presidents—Taft, Teddy Roosevelt, and McKinley—and its depot was home to the oldest stage coach line and railroad junction in the country. Quite a history and quite a location for a restaurant. Thankfully, the Eatery at the Depot has kept many of the menu selections so popular at its former site. "I still feature the prime rib on Friday and Saturday nights and the grilled marinated pork tenderloin and fried seafood continue to be favorites," Norris said. Weather permitting, diners can enjoy their meal on the outside patio.

- *Tim Driggers*

Lilfred's, Rembert
Sumter County

Lilfred's, 8425 Camden Highway, Rembert; (803) 432-8750. Open Wednesday-Saturday, 5:30-10 p.m. Reservations required. No smoking. MasterCard, Visa, American Express and Discover cards accepted. Expensive.

A Jewel in Sumter County

There are times when you'd like to shoot the person you're eating with, and that time came for me at Lilfred's, a famous dining spot in Rembert. We had made it all the way to dessert, and while he had only vaguely irritated me up to that point, things were pretty dandy—until he tried to take away my raspberry meringue.

He thought he was being cute.

I wanted to kill.

Nobody takes anything off my plate, especially if it was prepared by Chef Mike Jones at Lilfred's. Here, you can count on exquisitely prepared food, from the old faithful rib eye to the exotic New Zealand greenlip mussels. "Green lips?" my dining partner puzzled. "Do mussels have lips? How do they kiss?"

For his protection, my dining partner will not be named. For this story, however, he will be called the OMC, for Official Martini Critic. (He had one while I was visiting in the kitchen.) Cocktails are part of the lore at Lilfred's, where people said it took a drink and a half to get there. Even though you can't have a cocktail in the car anymore, Lilfred's still beckons, a wellspring of cosmopolitan dining in the middle of nowhere.

"It's really like finding a jewel; you would never expect in a tiny little town to find a first-class restaurant, ever," said Reid Buckley, a Camden novelist and frequent customer. Like other regulars, Buckley has acquired an extra enthusiasm for Lilfred's since Jones and his wife Marti (a Boykin of Boykin) bought it in the late '80s. A Camden native who studied cooking in Charleston and France, Jones has taken an old restaurant and spiffed it up. Now there are a few more enterprising additions to the menu along with the old favorites, lobster dainties and seafood platters.

But Lilfred's is still Lilfred's. The novelty items from years past—seasoned baby bees and chocolate ants—are gone, but the ever-famous croutons, onion rings and Cole slaw still abound.

The OMC and I traipsed through a number of appetizers. First came the poached mussels. "Boy, is he good," he said, a sorrowful note in his voice. (The OMC likes to think of himself as a gentleman and a chef.) Next came the softshell crayfish in a shallot and black cracked pepper sauce. "I may lick this place," the OMC announced.

Then came the crab cake. The OMC took a bite and put down his fork. "Should we put our silverware aside and just fistfeed?"

Located halfway between Sumter and Camden, Rembert is a rural community not far from Boykin and Hagood. Because of its obscure location but relative proximity to Columbia, Lilfred's was once a haven for legislators to socialize and do business.

Aside from the food and drink, Buckley thinks the beauty of Lilfred's is the mix of clientele and the comfort of the place. "You get people from all over the state: farmers, timber men, military men, truck drivers, even politicians."

He paused. "Thank God not too many."

- Aïda Rogers

Lilfred's has changed hands a few times since we visited in 1991, but the same knotty pine walls, comfortable furniture and upscale food remain. Trent and Wendy Langston are in charge now, and they're serving pork tenderloin, yellowfin tuna, sea bass and ravioli as well as the famous mussels, rib eye, stuffed potatoes and Cole slaw. Trent is a graduate of Trident Technical College's culinary school, and judging by the "reservations required" rule, is doing his alma mater proud. Established in 1951, Lilfred's is one of those special, not-to-be-missed places in South Carolina.

- Tim Driggers

Lone Star Barbecue and Mercantile, Santee
Orangeburg County

Lone Star Barbecue and Mercantile, 2212 State Park Road, Santee; (803) 854-2000. Open Thursday-Saturday, 11 a.m.-9 p.m. and Sunday, 11 a.m.-4 p.m. Closed Monday-Wednesday. Reservations not required. Credit cards and checks accepted. No smoking. www.nc-sc.com/lonestar. Inexpensive.

The Best Catch in Town

While some folks collect baseball cards, coins, stamps, or art, Pat Williams collects country stores. In 1997, he began gathering four of them, and today they adjoin one another near Santee at the Lone Star Barbecue and Mercantile, a slice of yesterday combining homespun nostalgia with a mouth-watering buffet of popular regional dishes.

You know you're in for a treat when you drive off the main road and into the dirt parking lot. Directly in front are the four circa-1880 buildings, with bluegrass harmonies wafting through the hardwoods and the massed aromas of tomato pie, barbecue, and bread pudding drifting from the kitchen and out into Santee Cooper country.

"I've always had a fondness for farm buildings and old stores," Pat said, pointing out the various structures. Shuler's General Store, built between 1880 and 1890, provides the main dining room. Dantzler's Social Hall is a 1922 farm supply store from nearby Providence. The Zeagler Post Office and family general store dates from the late 1800s. What Pat calls "The Old Green Store" was built in 1896; it got its name from its faded exterior paint and is where you can stroll through the buffet and buy souvenirs. An old smokehouse and outhouse are behind the complex.

Pat's son Chris returned to South Carolina in 2003 to become chief chef. Chris graduated in 1990 from The Citadel and after flirting with the nightclub business, decided on a restaurant career. His first job was as prep cook at Motor Supply Company in Columbia; in 1994 he enrolled at the Culinary Institute of America in New York for what would become a six-year cooking school odyssey.

How does a trained chef adapt to buffet-style cooking? "The creative end of cooking is hard to see in a buffet," he said. "But cooking is all about expression and if you love the taste of food and love to express yourself in your dishes, that's what being a chef is all about." Besides the all-you-can-eat buffet, weekends during spring and summer feature bluegrass entertainment in the Shuler General Store.

Dolores and Charles Gatch of Lexington visit frequently. "We enjoy the rustic atmosphere," Charles said. "These old buildings are a part of my heritage growing up in Orangeburg County." Atmosphere aside, Dolores and Charles love the food. "The tomato pie and bread pudding are wonderful," Dolores said. "It's the only place I've tasted anything like them." Charles recommends the catfish stew—"It's tomato-based without a fishy taste"—and the barbecue "reminds me of Dukes barbecue."

Steve and Jane Hannay of Valdosta, Georgia, make the four-and-a-half-hour drive here twice a month. "The atmosphere is unbelievable and the food couldn't be better," Steve said. "Every time I come here I try something different. The vegetables are so fresh and oh, man, I love the spicy mustard-based barbecue."

Pat and Chris Williams are a successful father-and-son team, Pat providing the country store concept and Chris adding the professional cooking touch. "My dad brings the horses to water," Chris said. "I just get them to drink." In a community noted for its great fishing on the Santee Cooper lakes, the best catch in town might be a meal at Lone Star Barbecue and Mercantile.

- Tim Driggers

The Parish House Tea Room, Eutawville
Orangeburg County

The Parish House Tea Room, 109 Porcher Avenue, Eutawville; (803) 492-7315. Open daily for lunch from 11:30 a.m. until 2 p.m. Reservations highly recommended. Credit cards and checks accepted. Smoking allowed only on back porch. Inexpensive.

A Little History with Your Raspberry Tea

In 1993, Toni Scott was in a quandary. She and husband John had just moved to Eutawville from Alabama, and she hadn't a clue about what she was going to do with herself. John had assumed the pulpit as rector of the historic Church of the Epiphany on Porcher Avenue. The old building across the street not only would prove her salvation but would become a modern landmark in a town where history not only reflects the past but is very much in the present.

Eutawville is hardly a bustling metropolis. No one is in a hurry and everyone seems just fine with that state of being. Rather than being defined by nearby Santee-Cooper, the town relishes its pre-Civil War roots. About three miles out of town is the site of the 1781 Revolutionary War clash of British and Patriot forces at Eutaw Springs, a focal point for travelers on the South Carolina Heritage Corridor. Then there is the Church of the Epiphany, built in 1849 as the parish church of Upper St. John.

Tea rooms trace their origins to the English tradition of afternoon tea—but many were opened by World War II widows who saw them as a means of gaining social respectability and financial independence in a male-dominated business world. With history literally dripping from each timber of its structure, Toni saw potential in the former summer home of Dr. Thomas William Porcher of Walworth Plantation.

"I had a vision of what a tea room should be and kept working toward that ideal," Toni said. That vision became reality in 2000 with the opening of The Parish House Tea Room and Gift Shop.

"I had the concept of a tea room as a place for an elaborate afternoon tea with plates of chicken salad, soups, and little things of dessert," she said. "A tea room should also be an expression of its locale and culture. There was a time when people took time for tea, but then it became the norm for folks to grab a quick lunch and head back to work. I think we've begun to re-examine our values, history and roots. A tea room is that look back in time."

The attractive atmosphere sets the mood for the lunchtime meal. The old pecky cypress paneling is adorned with period pieces and collectibles. "When you have a 200-year-old house and a 200-year-old church, you just enhance the décor already in place," Toni said. The restaurant also houses a gift shop and antique nook operated by Linda Carroll.

I chose the chicken salad plate with lemon dill potato salad and an accompaniment of pineapple and cantaloupe on a bed of lettuce and tomato. Other salad plates available are the shrimp salad and low-carb salad plate. Soups include she-crab and plantation gumbo. Sandwiches and wraps available are chicken salad, ham-Swiss and turkey-Monterey jack. I chose the raspberry tea and it was delicious. Strawberry and peach teas also are on the menu, as are hot tea, lemonade and coffee. For dessert, I couldn't pass up the Hershey Bar Pie.

"It is a privilege to be a part of the rich history of Eutawville and the surrounding area," Toni said. "Being here, it's only natural to share the past by bringing it forward to the present."

There's a certain charm and grace about The Parish House that defines elegance. It's a South Carolina treasure.

- Tim Driggers

The Parish House Tea Room continues to be the ultimate tea room experience. What's not to like? It has a history that spans two centuries, tours of the across-the-street Church of the Epiphany, the proximity of the South Carolina Heritage Corridor and wonderful food. Speaking of that most engaging subject, Toni Scott tells us that best sellers of The Parish House Tea Room now include their signature chicken salad, she-crab soup, BLT soup, lemon dill potato salad, and a dessert of white chocolate macadamia nut cake.

- T. D.

Summerton Diner, Summerton
Clarendon County

Summerton Diner, 32 South Church Street (Exit 108 from Interstate 95 on U.S. Highway 15); (803) 485-6835. Open Monday-Wednesday, 7 a.m.-8:30 p.m. and Friday-Sunday, 6 a.m.-9 p.m. Closed on Thursday. No reservations needed. No smoking. No credit cards. Inexpensive.

"The Aunt Bee of Restaurants"

You've got to love the Summerton Diner, and the reason is simple: The Summerton Diner loves you.

I had good feelings about it just talking to waitress Gwen Edens on the phone. Tammy Faye Baker had just been there last month, she said, and everybody was still talking about it. She wore a denim jump suit, high heels and false eyelashes, Gwen told me. She ordered stuffed bell peppers, butterbeans, okra and tomatoes and mashed potatoes. I asked Gwen if she ate it all. "Sure she did," Gwen said. I asked if I could come tomorrow. "Come on!" was her response.

If I had good feelings the day before, I had better feelings when I slid up to the counter—face to face with a big coconut cake. What is it about a coconut cake on the counter that's such a good sign? And what is it about the Summerton Diner that keeps people coming back?

"After you eat here, you'll know," said Robert Reinhold of Fort Lauderdale, who hauls boats from Maine to Miami. Like many others on the New York to Florida route, Robert makes a point to turn off I-95 for a meal at the Summerton Diner. He discovered it in 1956; today he recommends it to other truckers on his CB. It's the country ham, the iced tea and the southern accents, he said, and the fact that the cooks will take the onions out of his gravy and put his eggs on his toast.

"We have a lot of spoiled people that we do special things for," Gwen said. "We're small and we can cater to people." It's true. The waitresses will call around town if the Canteys aren't there for their lunch every day at 11, and they'll take a check in advance for a week's worth of meals from Clara Richardson, 80, known commonly as "Mammy." Mammy, like other locals, is not shy when it comes to bragging on the diner. "You can put in your article that this place ruins you because you're not satisfied anywhere else."

"Stand right there," Inky Davis told Mammy. "I want to see what a ruined person looks like."

Such is the carefree cheeriness that percolates at the Summerton Diner. People talk across the room, waitresses banter with the customers and Inky Davis lets loose his famous, high-pitched giggle. Inky (he got his name from his first days in an incubator) is a fishing guide on Lake Marion. To him, a fishing trip is not complete without lunch or breakfast at the diner. "We could eat hot dogs or hamburgers at the lake, but I always bring them here and they enjoy it," he said. "There are several things to making a fishing trip successful, and if you can put them onto good food, they're not going to forget that."

The Summerton Diner has worked its spell in other ways. Beth Hinson, broker-in-charge at Century 21 in Santee and a former Miss Striped Bass, said she takes hard-to-sell customers from the North to the diner for lunch. "We bring them to Lynelle and she closes the deal with her food and charm and this atmosphere. We've signed an awful lot of contracts with northern buyers right here at this booth."

Lynelle Blackwell took over the diner from her mother and stepfather when they retired. She had the wisdom to leave well enough alone, from the iron rule that everything will be made from scratch to making sure everyone gets the little calendar that has become the diner's souvenir. "Somebody even sent us a letter and a dollar asking for a calendar because they couldn't get to the diner this year," Lynelle said. "And we get letters from people who forgot to tip and send it to us when they remember."

The price has gone up only once in seven years, and lunch is still affordable. You get a meat, three vegetables, corn muffins, tea or coffee and pudding or cobbler. The fried chicken is famous. (I got mine "Inky-fried," which means it's not dry, the way Inky likes it.) The collard greens, apple salad and mashed potatoes are other popular items, and the coconut cream pie is a wonderful way to finish it all off. The lines are long on Friday nights and Sunday afternoons, but as Gwen said, "People who know us know the wait's not long and the food's worth the wait."

The diner is a citizen of the town, always there with the chicken and cakes at a funeral, always providing a plate to the sick. There is no alcohol; there is no profanity. "This is a family restaurant. We have children here," waitress Betty DuBose said. "We don't run a redneck joint."

No, this is the Aunt Bee of restaurants, chatty and neighborly, sure to remember you when you come in. With the flag waving outside and its aqua and white awnings, it's easy to see why poems have been written in its honor and fan mail is common.

What's the secret? "It's just a real, true, honest-to-goodness diner," Lynelle said. And on a bright, cold day when you're hungry, you can't do any better.

- Aïda Rogers

Since Sandlapper Magazine *visited Summerton Diner in early 1991, very few things have changed. "Miss Kat" has been cooking for 30-plus years and the restaurant is still making the coconut cake, fried chicken, chocolate cream pie, corn muffins, and collard greens. New owners Shannon Allen and Bridgett Wells took over in December 2004. The Summerton Diner continues to distribute the little calendars that are a restaurant tradition. "Someone called me from Florida the other day and asked me if they could stop by and get one," said waitress Jessica Thacker. Jessica reports that regular Robbie Reinhold is still coming in and has now taken a liking to the lemon pepper chicken on the menu. The Summerton Diner continues to feature its meat-and-three-vegetable menu, with drink and dessert each day.*

- *Tim Driggers*

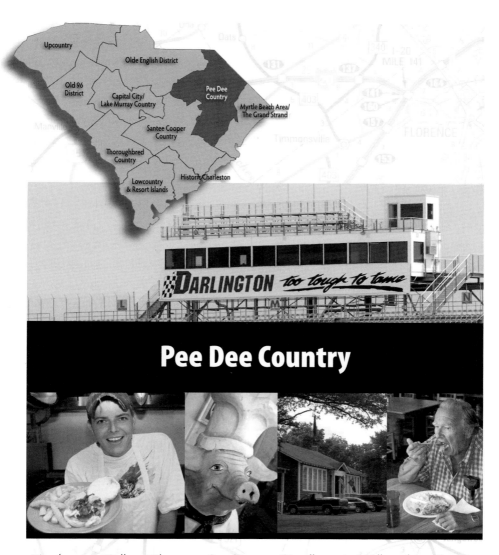

Upcountry

Olde English District

Old 96 District

Capital City/ Lake Murray Country

Pee Dee Country

Myrtle Beach Area/ The Grand Strand

Santee Cooper Country

Thoroughbred Country

Historic Charleston

Lowcountry & Resort Islands

DARLINGTON too tough to tame

Pee Dee Country

Darlington, Dillon, Florence, Lee, Marion, Marlboro & Williamsburg Counties

The Charcoal Grill, Dillon
Dillon County

The Charcoal Grill, 107 North First Avenue, Dillon; (843) 774-0128. Open daily 5 a.m.-2 p.m. No buffet Saturday. Credit cards and local checks accepted. Reservations not required. Smoking allowed, but discouraged. Inexpensive.

Bring the Family

As a child, Allen Grant never paid much attention to cooking. He preferred marching in the Dillon High School band to learning family heirloom recipes from his mother, Ella Mae. All that changed when he went to East Carolina University. "I was living by myself in a little farmhouse and learning to cook was a necessity," he explained. When the food bug bit, it infected Allen for life.

After graduation, he worked with the Hardee's and Cracker Barrel chains. Then he learned a restaurant in his hometown was for sale. The Charcoal Grill had been a garage and in the 1940s had been transformed into Mary's Tea Room. It was small, but Allen saw the possibilities for a family-oriented, home-style restaurant in Dillon. So in 1994, he signed the papers and The Charcoal Grill was his.

As business grew, more space was needed and the restaurant was transformed again. The "back room," as Allen calls it, was added in 1999 and reflects wife Brenda's homey, yet elegant decorating tastes. A modern, stylish dining room with seating for half of downtown Dillon, its attractiveness is the equal of any in the Pee Dee. "We really needed the space," Brenda said. "On Sundays our parking lot is packed with people just out of church and ready to eat."

They find a buffet teeming with many of the same recipes for meats and vegetables Ella Mae Grant cooked for her son. "People in Dillon seem to favor home-cooked meals," Allen said, "and they love to socialize while they eat." A typical buffet features fried chicken (every day), meat loaf, barbecue riblets, fatback (on Sundays) country-fried steak, catfish, and fajita chicken, along with peas and snaps, macaroni and cheese, string beans, okra, rice, and a local favorite, chicken and pastry.

Then there's the cornbread. The Charcoal Grill presents two kinds; flitter cornbread (pancake-shaped fried) and broccoli cornbread. Both are popular.

For a real treat, go early in the morning. The house special breakfast consists of two pancakes, two eggs, bacon, ham, or sausage, with smoked sausage or country ham optional. Of course the food is good, but the conversation coming from "the coffee table" adds, shall we say, a little spice to the morning agenda.

"A bunch of us get together each morning to bat around the latest gossip and catch up on the news," said Johnny Sapp, the jailkeeper at the local lock-up. Dillon native Bobby Lee Thompson eats here twice a day, seven times a week. He describes the banter a little more succinctly. "It's just a lot of foolishness."

Friendliness is a hallmark. "My mother and I always feel welcome here," said Susan McNeil, a primary school teacher in Bennettsville. "Everyone who eats here is family." She's right. At The Charcoal Grill it's all about home-cooking, family, and a certain friendliness that's found in small-town South Carolina.

- Tim Driggers

Owners Allen and Brenda Grant continue to transform The Charcoal Grill. The front dining room has been completely renovated to reflect a more elegant setting with a newly painted interior, stained glass windows, refurbished counter stools, and Charleston-style planters. The old vinyl siding on the front of the building has been removed to expose the original brick. Not to worry about the menu however, The Charcoal Grill continues to specialize in country-style cuisine.

- *T. D.*

Corner Grill, Bishopville
Lee County

Corner Grill, 679 U.S. 15 at the corner of SC 341 (Bethune Highway), Bishopville; (803) 484-5775. Open Monday-Wednesday, 10 a.m. to 3 p.m.; Thursday-Saturday, 10 a.m. to 8 p.m. Closed Sunday. No smoking. No credit cards. No reservations. Inexpensive.

Of Hot Dogs and Cotton Fields

There's something fairly wonderful about walking into an unassuming little restaurant and making friends with unassuming people. Who cares if Victor Newman of *The Young and Restless* is on TV when you've got officer Tony Johnson of Dillon sharing his insights?

"I just kept coming in and eating, 'cause it was good," he explains. "It was good!" It didn't hurt that Mendy Jackson, the girl he later married, was helping her parents out in their business. He'd stopped her twice for a broken headlight—he was a patrolman at the time—and recognized her behind the counter. "Finally I asked her, 'Would you like to go to a rodeo one night?' It just kind of went from there."

Tony lives in Bishopville now, almost across the street from Sheila and Charles Jackson, who have shepherded the Corner Grill from a country grocery to a popular short-order restaurant. They serve customers from the Pee Dee and even the Midlands who've discovered their high-tasting, low-costing burgers, hot dogs, chicken wings and shrimp and oyster baskets.

"It's the most popular place in Bishopville," says Sam Copeland, a former Bishopville restaurateur. Every Thursday night Sam and his wife Shirley hit the Corner Grill. "They've got a good hot dog and cheeseburger," Sam says. "We can go and spend $7 and come back full."

"This place is a big hit, especially during football season and Dixie Youth season," says Robin McCaskill, a substitute teacher from McBee. "Lots of times parents and the players come in here to get something to eat before or after the game. It's a definite plus to the community."

That's gratifying for the Jacksons, who bought the place as a country store in 1974. Charles had worked there in high school and wanted to have his own business. When larger groceries opened and business slowed, they added a hot dog machine to draw new customers. Then came burgers and fried chicken, a long counter and some bar stools. Today, 32 people can sit in the eight booths, and on Thursday and Friday nights, they line up outside. Customers grab their soft drinks from the refrigerator. Two high chairs signal that young children are welcome.

"We just changed with the times," Sheila says, explaining that serving food was more survival technique than dream. But through the years she and working partner Catherine Walton have become expert cooks, and Charles has become a grill wizard. His sauce for chicken wings is highly regarded.

Like others at the booths, Robin and her friend Pam Williams served their tea from a plastic pitcher at their table. At lunch, customers are given pitchers and order from the counter. In the evenings, a waitress takes your order and pours your tea.

Robin and Pam definitely like the price. "We were saying, 'We have four dollars for lunch, where can we go?'"

One celebrity customer is NASCAR driver Sterling Marlin, who once came in for a hot dog.

And that's what's so great about the Corner Grill: It puts you in its place. There's a cotton field behind it and Darlington just down the road. Race cars and hot dogs have been a winning combination for years.

- Aïda Rogers

Charles and Sheila Jackson sold the Corner Grill after Sandlapper *covered it in the Winter 2001-02 issue. But you can still find all-American grill fare here. Terry Cunningham of Bishopville is the owner now, and her menu is much the same, minus the fried chicken. Wonderfully, the restaurant is open on Saturdays.*

- A. R.

Dallis' Café, Marion
Marion County

Dallis' Café, 2305 East U.S. Highway 76 in Marion; (843) 275-0402. Open for breakfast and lunch Monday-Saturday, 7 a.m.-2 p.m. and for dinner Thursday-Saturday, 5-9 p.m. Closed Sunday. Reservations not required. Credit cards, checks and about anything else accepted for payment. Smoking in the private dining room. Inexpensive.

Chef Dallis Brady relaxes with an Ooey Gooey platter.

Letter to Oprah: "Please Try the Ooey Gooey"

"Dear Oprah:

"Girl, I've found someone you should—no, you must—bring on your show. This lady is big time. She is the Picasso of the skillet; the Monet of the spatula...dare I say it: the Da Vinci of the saucepan. I know you've got booking agents who scour the nation for talent, and they do a good job. But this lady I have for you really wants to be on your show. You don't have to pay her union scale or send airfare or anything like that. I'll take her down to the Greyhound station and she should be in Chicago faster than Keith Richards can fall out of a coconut tree.

"Her name is Dallis Brady and she is the best daggone cook in these here United States. Dallis has one dream in her life, and that is to appear on your show and cook her famous Ooey Gooey Sandwich. If you have a few moments, let me tell you about Dallis and her wonderful restaurant in Marion, South Carolina.

"As a little girl, Dallis would perch herself atop a kitchen stool and strain and stretch to cook over the family stove. She would prepare breakfast in bed for her parents, and although the eggs might have been slightly raw and the toast a bit burnt, Dallis persevered and became the chef of the family. 'I loved to cook,' Dallis says. 'Daddy said that half the time he didn't have any idea of what he was eating, but that it was always good.'

"In 2003, Dallis opened her own restaurant, Dallis Downtown, which evolved into Dallis' last year. Located on East U.S. Highway 76 in Marion, the setting is attractive, but not fancy. The real attraction is the food. The legion of loyal diners who make Dallis' a regular dining destination couldn't care less about the decor; just put an Ooey Gooey Sandwich in front of them and get out of the way.

"I guess I should end the suspense and tell you about the Ooey Gooey. 'It's the most gosh-awful messiest sandwich you'll ever eat in your life,' Dallis informs. 'It just oozes and goozes out of the sides of the bread.' Believe it or not, the Ooey Gooey started out as a health-conscious sandwich. 'I grilled some chicken tenderloin and cut it into bite-size pieces,' Dallis says. It wasn't in Dallis' constitution to stop there, however. 'I decided to add sautéed onions and mushrooms and then splash on mozzarella cheese and my homemade honey mustard sauce and stack it onto a Kaiser bun.' It has to be one of the great values of the modern dining world.

"B.J. Hucks of Marion, a four-year veteran of the South Carolina Highway Patrol, eats at Dallis' every Thursday evening and occasionally stops by for lunch. While he's a big fan of the marinated ribeye steak, the Ooey Gooey holds a special fascination for him. 'It's definitely a two-hander with a napkin,' he says. 'I never try to eat it when I'm in uniform. It's great, but it is really messy.'"

"If you decide to pass on the Ooey Gooey Sandwich, you can try Dallis' nine-pound hamburger. 'The morning show on WEGX-FM in Florence challenged Pee Dee restaurants to make a nine-pound burger, and they chose mine as the best,' Dallis reports. 'I sell a lot of them for picnics and tailgate parties.' (I might point out that Dallis' nine-pound hamburger would be the perfect fare, should you invite the Chicago Bears over for a meal.)

"For dinner, the shrimp and grits is very popular. 'Folks from Charleston and travelers through Marion say it's the best they ever had,' Dallis says. 'We use grits flavored with a chicken-based seasoning and add shrimp, bacon, and ham sautéed in bacon drippings, and top the dish with mozzarella, parmesan and cheddar cheeses.' Brian Nolan says it's fantastic. He and wife Patti Donohue now live in Marion after escaping Hurricane Katrina in New Orleans. 'Being from New Orleans, I know a little something about shrimp,' he notes. 'It's not quite New Orleans, but it is real, real close.' At breakfast, Dallis features her 'trash grits' cooked with mozzarella and cheddar cheese, along with a variety of omelets and pancakes.

" 'I love what I do,' Dallis says. 'I couldn't imagine doing anything else. I watch a lot of cooking shows and I know I can do anything they can and I've never been to cooking school.' And that, I attest, is fact and not bragging.

"So Oprah, the choice is clear: Put Dallis and her Ooey Gooey Sandwich on your show or spend the rest of your life wondering just what an Ooey Gooey is and what it tastes like. Dallis can be reached at (843) 275-0402, and from you, she'd probably accept a collect call."

- Tim Driggers

We couldn't resist the opportunity to stop by Marion and see Dallis Brady while putting this book together. While we immensely enjoyed chatting with Marion's answer to Paula Deen, the real reason for the visit was our insatiable hankering for another of Dallis' famous Ooey Gooey sandwiches. So naturally there was really no choice for us other than storming into the kitchen and catching son Dain making one from scratch. We drooled and we fretted as it cooked, waiting most impatiently for Dain to plop it into our plates, along with a side of onion rings. Heaven achieved; Nirvana attained. And that was just our reaction to the absolutely delicious onion rings. Oprah, what you waitin' on to put Dallis on your show?

- T. D.

King's Famous Pizza, Dillon and Latta
Dillon County

King's Famous Pizza, 100 Second Avenue in Dillon; (843) 774-3811 and 241 South Richardson Street, Latta; (843) 752-4370. Open Monday-Saturday, 10:30 a.m.-9 p.m. and Sunday, 11:30 a.m.-9 p.m. Smoking permitted. Credit cards accepted. No reservations needed. Inexpensive.

Oh, Those Hot Oven Subs

Every town has one. You know, that old standby, that always consistent, always friendly, always packed-at-lunch place where you know you'll get a good meal at a good price. In Dillon and Latta, Egyptian-run, Italian-serving King's Famous Pizza meets these criteria.

"The cooks in the back can tell you who's out here by what they order," says Ann Griffin, a regular customer. Ann likes the Khalil family as much as their hot oven subs. "They make such a contribution to Dillon," she says, noting how the Khalils support ball clubs and other groups. Owner Nazmy Khalil treated Griffin's staff—more than 50 people—at the county DSS to lunch.

Then, there are those subs, "I never have been a sub eater," Ann confesses. "That just seemed like dry and uninteresting food." But at a friend's suggestion, she tried one. "It is absolutely to me addictive. I have to be real careful not to put on 40 pounds eating subs."

After that testimony, I had to have one. Nazmy brought out a steak sub. Even the small one is huge, and once fries are added, I had enough for me and Ann to take home. Nazmy's special sauce accompanies the subs, ensuring pleasurable and juicy eating.

A Cairo native, Nazmy came to Dillon via Myrtle Beach in 1981, working for the previous owner of King's Pizza. He bought it three years later. Today, his four brothers and two sisters are in Dillon, too. With children, the Khalil family measures about 25. Dillon County clearly has become home.

Besides subs, King's Pizza offers a variety of salads, pasta, calzones and Greek platters. Pizzas are as popular as subs; anchovies, salami and pastrami are three of the more unusual toppings. "My children in Columbia think this is the only pizza in the world," Ann reports. "They stop on their way to my house and get pizza on Friday night. They just love this place."

Nazmy's brothers Nabil and Nashaat run King's Pizza in Latta, eight miles away. Every afternoon around 5, you can find the town's finest gentlemen drinking iced tea and solving the world's problems. "We call it happy hour," says Ricky Taylor, noting that sometimes they break down and order coffee, sometimes beer.

When Ricky showed me in, I found a group of seven men eating vodka-marinated cherry tomatoes and cream cheese and olive sandwiches from a shower held the day before. That was good—but the iced tea was great.

- Aïda Rogers

People at both locations of King's Famous Pizza tell us that things are pretty much as they always have been since Sandlapper *visited in 1999. The House Special Pizza in Dillon, topped with ham, turkey, roast beef, bacon, and lettuce, is very popular, as is the Super Sub, crammed with ham, turkey, roast beef, and bacon. In Latta, Nabil and Nashaat still welcome the 5 o'clock crowd to their restaurant. No word on whether the group has succeeded in solving any national or international dilemmas.*

- *Tim Driggers*

Magnolia On Main, Bennettsville
Marlboro County

Magnolia on Main, 226 East Main Street, Bennettsville; (843) 479-9495. Open for breakfast Monday-Friday 6:30 a.m.-10 a.m.; Saturday from 7 a.m.-11 a.m. Lunch Monday-Friday 11 a.m.-2 p.m. Closed on Sunday. Credit cards and checks accepted. No reservations. No smoking. Inexpensive.

Layer Cakes and "Bonging" Eyes

Today's trendier desserts—tiramisu, for instance, or crème brulee—would be as out-of-place at this restaurant as a ball gown at a barbecue. At Magnolia on Main, a bustling breakfast and lunch place in Bennettsville's neatly restored downtown, layer cakes are the dessert of choice. They wink at you from clear glass domes on the immaculate counter, where you might see a man in overalls sitting by a man in a tie. Such is the authenticity of the restaurant, where owners Kathy and Bill Sloan took care to pay tribute to a local institution—The Sanitary Café—while adding their own personal touches.

"It's nice to have a place where people can come and see other people they haven't seen in awhile," says Kathy, a native (Bennettsville class of '58) who left after graduation. "At breakfast we have a group that eats every morning, so it brings back a little bit of what it used to be."

The Sanitary Café, an 80-year-old local landmark, had been sold and changed hands in the '90s. It was vacant when Kathy and Bill, then living in Jacksonville, Florida, were visiting Kathy's family at Easter. At her father's suggestion, the Sloans moved back to buy and restore it. Photos of Harry Psihos, who founded and ran The Sanitary Café, line the walls, which also boast framed remnants of the original tin ceiling. "Even though we're not connected by name, it's nice to be a part of that history," Kathy reflects, noting that Mary Elizabeth Psihos, Harry's widow, attended their grand opening in January 2002.

Everything about Magnolia on Main spells old-fashioned small town South. Bread tins and an arrangement of cotton branches adorn the counter area. Fresh flowers top the tables. And two hot-plate specials are available daily: Choose one meat and two vegetables, soup or salad and bread (biscuits or cornbread). On this blustery day, the soups are Tomato Parmesan and chili, and the meats are roast pork and salmon patties. Our foursome sampled each meat and vegetable (sweet potato soufflé, turnips, butterbeans, and pork-favored rice). Two of us also ordered off the salad-and-sandwich menu. Beth Williams, editor of *Pee Dee Magazine* and a Marlboro County native, ordered the hamburger (with fries or pasta salad). "If you're hungry for a real hamburger, this is it," she declares.

Beth was the first person to recommend Magnolia on Main to me, but it was the breakfast she'd tried, not the lunch. The secret behind the famous grits is the water filter system, Bill believes, which is also why the coffee and iced tea are so popular. Omelets and pancakes are the most-ordered items in the mornings.

No southern lunch place is complete without chicken salad, and because I'd been told how wonderful it was, I ordered it. It arrived on a pretty glass plate with pita chips and pasta salad. In the center is what makes this dish extraordinary: the frozen fruit cup. Strawberries and bananas are two ingredients. Our group's best description was this: "It makes your eyes bong out of your head."

Servings are plentiful, and though our entrees were filling, we had to take note of our waitress' comments about the Hershey Bar Cake. "If they let me, I'd eat it every day," Ricka Brummett told us. "It's like it melts in your mouth."

The four of us devoured a slice (whipped cream icing, chocolate shavings, almonds) and today's other cake, pineapple layer with cream cheese icing. One member of our party, the garrulous Tim Driggers, was silenced by baker Katherine Branch's talent. "You want to get on her Christmas card list?" Beth teased. "No, I just want to live with her," he responded. "Just a room on the side."

Each of us at our table is from a small town in South Carolina, so we were comfortable with the table-hopping, hugging, and waving. We weren't surprised to see people flood in at noon and be gone before 1. Country people are up early and they work hard. So do Kathy and Bill Sloan, who recreated a much-loved place in Bennettsville for people to eat and socialize. That's why they chose the name "Magnolia on Main." Explains Kathy: "To me, a magnolia gives a warm southern welcome. We wanted a friendly atmosphere."

That they definitely have.

- Aïda Rogers

So Aïda says I'm garrulous, does she? Good thing for her I'm a country boy and don't have a lot of 'skool lernin' so I don't even know what the word means. I think she meant to say I'm suave, sophisticated, and stimulating. But just in case she meant to say I run my mouth on occasion, well, she's right when it comes to Magnolia on Main. Let me assume my spot on Speakers' Corner and tell you what the latest is down from the Court House in Bennettsville. Doug Jennings is making trillions practicing law, the ghost of Senator John Lindsay is still tramping through Clio looking for votes, and Magnolia On Main continues to be THE place for breakfast and lunch. Kathy and Bill Sloan tell us the Citrus Salad with glazed pecans, and either Granny Smith apples or strawberries, is very popular and that the chicken salad plate continues to be their specialty. Check out the Stanton's BBQ sandwich on the lunch menu and the Farm House Special for breakfast (if you feel like starting the day eating half the Pee Dee). If you're on Main Street in Bennettsville early in the morning or at lunchtime, chances are you're at Magnolia on Main.

- *Tim Driggers*

Mr. B's, Lydia
Darlington County

Mr. B's, 964 West Lydia Highway (U.S.15) in Lydia; (803) 332-5560. Open for lunch Sunday-Friday, 11 a.m.-2 p.m. and for dinner Friday-Saturday, 5-9 p.m. No smoking. Checks and credit cards accepted. Reservations not required. A private room is available at no extra charge. Inexpensive to moderate.

Loosen Your Belt! It's Time for Mr. B's

There comes a time in every woman's life when you have to do what you have to do. For Sara K. Wilds of Hartsville, that time came right after Christmas.

"Come to lunch at Mr. B's" was the edict from her good friend Nancy Nickles, who had heard the same thing from me. Sara K. dropped everything, including her husband's lunch. "I told him he was own his own."

Such is the devotion to Mr. B's, a family-style restaurant in Lydia. Between Bishopville and Hartsville, Lydia is a small community probably best known for its premier restaurant and a beautiful Victorian-style Methodist church. But as Nancy points out, "if you have something good, people will come." And come they do, from all over the Midlands and Pee Dee. Some come every day.

"That's why we always have something different on the buffet," says Bobby Goff, who runs Mr. B's with his wife Reba. The buffet is at lunch only, and you can find a wealth of Carolina cooking on it. All kinds of meats and vegetables are available, and a few constants—rice, vegetable soup, fatback and fried chicken. The vegetable soup is so popular people take it to friends and family in the hospital. The fried chicken is so popular Sara K. didn't tell her husband where she was going because he'd be jealous.

With six sons between them, Sara K. and Nancy can appreciate Mr. B's. Though their boys are grown now, they remember how easy it was to bring them here when they were younger. They could eat all they wanted and not worry about making too much mess. Mr. B's prides itself on its friendliness: No alcohol is served, children younger than 5 eat free and seniors get a discount. Reba and Bobby have twins, and Reba remembers the suppers she missed when they were babies. That's why there's a rocking chair in the back. "I'll rock children so their mothers can eat," Reba says. "I've walked 'em in the yard. We love for families to bring little children."

The Goffs bought Mr. B's from Reba's uncle, Jeryl Best, in 1989. Before that, the restaurant had made a reputation for seafood, which is served in the evenings along with chicken, barbecue and steak. Mr. B's is not named for "Best," however, but for Doug Beckham, his cook. Beckham is dead now, but his recipes still are used, as is the same iron skillet the restaurant opened with in 1969.

At our table, we're having second helpings of fried fish, fried chicken, rice and gravy, green beans, lima beans, mashed potatoes and my favorite: sautéed chicken livers and onions. Peach cobbler, banana pudding and those wonderful, flat, "southren" biscuits bring us to belt-loosening reality: If you're going to Mr. B's, be comfortable. The all-you-can-eat buffet, including drink, dessert and tax is reasonably priced.

Prices are equally reasonable at night. "It's the best seafood around," says Nancy. To her, the clam chowder at Mr. B's is exceptional, and people in Darlington and Lee counties are lucky to have seafood "as good as Murrells Inlet" so close to home.

Count on a crowd every day for lunch, particularly Sunday. The restaurant has become so popular the Goffs have expanded the building and the hours. Since the Sunday staff miss church, Reba leads devotions those mornings.

Railroad engineers like Mr. B's so much they've stopped on the tracks behind for a meal. Law enforcement officers landed a helicopter across the street and came in. Law enforcement people come a lot. "I don't worry about being broken into," Reba says.

David Beasley was a regular before he became governor; Reba's keeping his fried chicken warm.

Meanwhile, Sara K. and Nancy are debating what to tell their husbands they did for lunch. Says Nancy about hers: "He'll be so mad when he finds out."

- Aïda Rogers

The restaurant now seats more than 450 guests and a room has been added since Sandlapper *dined at Mr. B's in 1996. The seafood and country cooking buffet remain constants. "We have so many people that are regulars," Reba Goff said. "A lot of them were babies when they first ate here and now they are bringing their babies."*

- Tim Driggers

Ruth's Drive-In, Hartsville
Darlington County

Ruth's Drive-In, 659 West Carolina Avenue, Hartsville; (843) 332-6771. Open Monday-Friday, 7:30 a.m.-5 p.m.; Saturdays, 7:30 a.m.-3 p.m. No reservations. Credit cards and personal checks accepted. Smoking discouraged. Inexpensive.

Chili Buns and Crowded Parking Lots

I met my buddy Bond Nickles at Ruth's Drive-in in Hartsville, which is the kind of place to meet a buddy. He sauntered up to the counter in a polo shirt and khaki shorts, a cool-looking conservative southern guy who probably looked much different in his

Dixie Youth baseball days. That's when Ruth's Drive-In was a regular thing, especially when the team won.

"When the guys would hit these mammoth homeruns, we'd say, 'Oh, he hit that ball to Ruth's!'"

Ruth's is right down the left center field power alley, Bond told me in his best sportswriter talk. That meant if you knocked a homer, it would come through Ruth's window. "Of course, that never happened," Bond said, laughing. "It was just one of those little boy fantasies."

But now that he's all grown up, Bond realizes Ruth's Drive-In is something of a fantasy itself. Here you can get the famous chili bun, iced tea, and order of old-time crinkle-cut fries for less than $4.

Ruth Lockett started the business as a grocery store and filling station with her husband more than 50 years ago. From hot dogs it grew to burgers and barbecue sandwiches. The homemade chili and iced tea are its calling cards, says Ruth's daughter, Bobbie Jean Hooker, who manages the drive-in now. The chili-cheeseburger is its most popular sandwich.

You can get a hot plate lunch for less than $10 but it's still a simple meal. Nothing fancier is even thought about; Bobbie Jean said she's got all she can handle. (Just try to find a parking place at noon during the week.)

All kinds come here: nurses and working men, office women and business people. So does Bond's father, Bubba Nickles, MD. It's that low-cal double chili-cheeseburger that brings him. "I'm a hamburger freak, and they've got the best," he said, putting one away. "They fix 'em with chili, mustard and onion, and that's the way I like 'em."

Bubba likes the people at Ruth's, too. Bobbie Jean's daughter Angela is a nurse who used to work for him; Ruth was a nurse herself. Old photographs of Angela as homecoming queen, head majorette and Miss Hartsville are on a shelf facing the counter, along with snapshots of her sister Marvene, a former head cheerleader, who still works with her mother at Ruth's. Now Marvene's daughter Maggie works here, too, making Ruth's Drive-In a four-generation Hartsville institution.

Bobbie Jean's husband Doc also helps out, and so have each of their four children at one time. "It's been the whole family's life," Bobbie Jean said simply.

It's meant a lot to Bond and Bubba. No baseball victory was complete without a dad or coach treating the team to a feed at Ruth's, Bond said.

His father can only try to smile when he talks about the two boiled eggs and half a grapefruit wife Nancy gives him for lunch. "That's why I come here," he said. "Sometimes I stop here and get my hamburger and then go home and eat my boiled eggs. She'll never know the difference."

Whoops.

- Aïda Rogers

Bobbie Jean Hooker is now deceased, and Ruth's Drive-In is currently owned by daughter Angela Stokes, who says the restaurant continues to be "the whole family's life." Marvene and Maggie still work here, serving Ruth's what-we're-famous for hot dogs and hamburgers. "We're one of those places that never seems to change," Angela says. We're glad.

- Tim Driggers

Schoolhouse Bar-B-Que, Scranton
Florence County

Schoolhouse Bar-B-Que, 2252 U.S. Highway 52, Scranton; (843) 389-2020. Open Thursday-Saturday, 11 a.m.-9 p.m. and Sunday, 11 a.m.-2 p.m. Closed on Monday-Wednesday. Credit cards not accepted, only cash and checks. Reservations not required. Smoking only in designated area. Inexpensive.

Public School Lunch Didn't Taste Like This

There's a land where blue bottles line window sills, people drink NuGrape, and children wear Red Goose shoes. I'd never been there until I went to Schoolhouse Bar-B-Que in Scranton. It was like entering the world my "daddy's people" knew, where farming was everything, church was almost everything and hog killings were big events. At Schoolhouse Bar-B-Que, you want to say "tablet" instead of notebook, "slate" instead of blackboard.

What you really want to do it hit the buffet. It's a two-table spread of pork barbecue, rice, liver hash, slaw, spiced apples, corn, fruit cocktail, pickled beets, sweet potato soufflé and pickled okra. There's also barbeque chicken, fried chicken, chicken and dumplings, potato salad, and a very cheesy macaroni. Desserts are just as *southren*, banana pudding being the most poplar. The buttermilk biscuits are another favorite; they're flat, round, and "melt-in-your-mouth" divine, says Mary S. Gibson, a regular take-out customer from Evergreen.

Sunday's buffet often includes pot roast and shrimp Creole. "It's good quality food," says owner Howell Myers, who left a railroad career to open the restaurant, "not a bunch of cheap junk."

"I like the way the food tastes," says Matthew Burgess, having supper with his son before going to the circus in Florence. "A lot of food in restaurants is not cooked with salt. This is seasoned. My mom raised me and she seasoned things real good."

The variety of buffet items can only be matched by the size of the building and the amount of memorabilia on the walls. Built as a school for children in 1930 by the WPA, it was restored in 1982. And what a stunner: Ceilings are 12 feet high; floors, walls and tables are oak. Jim Harrison prints and vintage signs of obscure soft drinks add to the rural South feel.

Howell, a Scranton native, opened Schoolhouse Bar-B-Que in 1994. He's doing his part to promote the town: A mural in the back dining room shows local storefronts (including Maxie and Greta's fresh-air market) and the Atlantic Coastline train.

"Once again, these rooms are filled with laughter, talking and even learning," reads a chalkboard in one dining room. I just want to know what a Quiky tastes like.

- Aïda Rogers

Martha Sowers checks the chicken at Schoolhouse Bar-B-Que.

Sandlapper *hadn't stopped by Schoolhouse Bar-B-Que in a number of years, so when we called owner Howell Myers to find out what was new at his popular restaurant, he said "the only thing that's changed is that the food has gone from good to better." If Howell is right—and we're betting he is—then he's cooking some mighty fine barbecue in Scranton these days. The buffet still features whole hog barbecue slow-roasted over hickory coals, and the traditional sides of hash and rice, slaw, and barbecue chicken. They've still got those melt-in-your-mouth biscuits too. In South Carolina, barbecue sauces are usually regional, tomato-based in the upstate, mustard-based in the midlands, and vinegar-based in the low country. Howell has his own recipe for a vinegar-and-pepper sauce. "That's the only thing the people down here will eat," he said. "They aren't going to put that mustard or tomato sauce on their barbecue." Some say Howell's fried chicken is as good as his barbecue or, as singer Jimmy Hall once said, "so good it'd make the Colonel run and hide."*

- Tim Driggers

Shug's Smokehouse Grill and Tavern, Hartsville
Darlington County

Shug's Smokehouse Grill and Tavern, 2404 Kelleytown Road, Hartsvillle; (843) 383-3747. Open Tuesday-Thursday, 11 a.m.-9 p.m.; Friday, 11 a.m.-10 p.m. Saturday, 5-10 p.m. Closed Sunday and Monday. No reservations. Credit cards and checks accepted. Smoking only in bar and The Pole Barn. Inexpensive to moderate.

American Food in a Pee Dee Hideout

Leave it to a writer to find the romance in a place. Mark Shaffer, a writer for this magazine and others, had been telling me about Shug's Smokehouse near Hartsville for months before I finally made it out there. When I did, I saw what he meant. "It feels like you're in a real country hideout," he said. "All you need is some Spanish moss and oak trees."

"We've got cotton fields," his girlfriend Susan Kelley offered helpfully. Susan is from nearby Turkey Creek, not Kelleytown where Shug's is located. Owners Jay and Julie Mahn took a gas station/convenience store and turned it into an Old West saloon. The walls are knotty pine, the roof is partially tin, and your only choice for seating is oversized booths with high backs for privacy. Roasted peanuts arrive in tin pails. And the Bloody Marys are marvelous.

"Jay's got a secret Bloody Mary mix that he makes on his own," Mark informed. An accomplished cook himself, Mark has been watching the Mahns as they've brought good eats to Darlington County. Before opening Shug's in 2001, Jay and Julie established the popular Culinary Company in downtown Hartsville about 10 years before. With Shug's—named after Jay's favorite "southern term of endearment"—he's moved from gourmet lunch fare to Real Man Food. "The hamburgers are to die for and I love their home fries," Anne Sanderlin said. Anne, another Hartsville writer, has been fast to recommend good restaurants. She advises the parking lot is always full here.

Fortunately, there are pleasant places to wait. Long church pews line the front porch; in the back is a cozy bar. Outside is a covered patio, "The Pole Barn," with a wood-burning fireplace and tables. Live music is played Friday and Saturday nights, and occasional Thursdays.

As befits a place with vintage photos of the 1907 Harvard–Yale football game and Judge Roy Bean, the appetizers are Americana: fried cheese, cheese fries, wings, calamari, nachos. We took our server's advice and ordered the Onion Blossom. While dipping and eating, we agonized over the menu. Shug's serves seafood, salads, sandwiches, beef, chicken, and ribs, some prepared over hickory chips for that smoked flavor. I took Mark's suggestion and ordered the BBQ Beef Brisket. "Slow cooked to melt in your mouth," the menu said. The menu was right. Mark opted for the special:

the Bleu Cheese-encrusted 12-ounce sirloin.

Susan ordered a platter of catfish and deviled crab. The dinners are immense, with a side or Caesar salad and a choice of rice pilaf, baked potato, sweet potato, seasoned fries, or home fries. "I never have room for dessert," she confessed later, noting the sweet flavor of the crab.

Shug's gives you a lot for your money. The priciest things on the menu are the porterhouse steak and platter of baby back ribs and they're both less than $20. The remaining Smokehouse beef, BBQ, seafood and pasta specialties are also reasonable, as are the large variety of sandwiches and burgers.

A graduate of USC's hotel/restaurant/tourism program, Jay's worked in restaurants since he was 14. "Working and cooking with my parents and grandparents are where I honed my skills," he said, adding that many of the recipes at Shug's are family favorites. The southern-pulled barbecue sandwich has a vinegar-based sauce created by his grandfather, E. L. Mitchum of Manning. His mother-in-law, Louise Jones of Hartsville, is responsible for the Mile High Mud Pie, a brownie with vanilla bean ice cream, hot fudge, and toasted pecans.

"I think we've taken the best of a lot of restaurants that probably would not locate in Hartsville because of the demographic," Jay said, explaining that there aren't enough people here to support an Outback Steakhouse. But Hartsville has plenty of visitors, to Sonoco, Coker College, and the Governor's School for Math and Science. It needed a place that's neither fast food nor elitist, the Mahns thought. They've succeeded in creating a way to fill the need. "We might have the president of Sonoco Products in one booth and someone on the assembly line making $10 an hour sitting right behind him."

- Aïda Rogers

The menu has changed a bit since Stop Where the Parking Lot's Full *visited in 2003. Shug's now has live music on occasion. The Pole Barn remains, as do all the original trappings that make Shug's Smokehouse Grill and Tavern a favorite Pee Dee destination. Why not start with an order of Garlic Marinated Fried Mushrooms, Firecracker Shrimp or Nacho Nacho Man? For the main course, there is a choice of seven steaks, each available with toppings including jumbo lump crab with cheese, Shug's pimiento cheese, or horseradish. Barbecue specialties include a Beef Brisket Platter, E.L.'s Pulled Pork Platter (it's splashed with vinegar sauce and based on Jay's grandfather's recipe) and St. Louis Style Ribs. On the seafood menu are Select Shrimp or Oysters, Fresh Flounder, Scallops and Catfish Filets. Don't forget Uncle Bubba's Seafood Pot Pie or the Buffalo Chicken Pasta. A popular new item is the Beach Grits and Shrimp (or quail and gravy). If you want just a bite, the burger with homemade pimiento cheese is a favorite.*

- Tim Driggers

Shuler's BBQ, Latta
Dillon County

Shuler's BBQ, 419 Highway 38, Latta; (843) 752-4700. Open Thursday-Saturday, 4:30-9 p.m. Only cash and checks ("that's the way old barbeque places are supposed to be" per Norton). No reservations needed. No smoking. Inexpensive.

"Some of the Eatingest People God Put on This Earth"

You know it's the real thing when the cornbread is made with homemade lard. And when there's crackling in it, too–Granny Clampett can't do better than this.

Step in to Shuler's Barbecue, just outside the Dillon County town of Latta. With a high-pitched ceiling of Arkansas white pine and a pond full of ducks and geese out back, it's clean, unpretentious and family-style. Its buffet is all-you-can-eat.

"I've seen some of the eatingest people God has put on this earth," says Norton Shuler Hughes, who owns the restaurant with his wife Lynn. "I don't know where they put it or what they do with it. Women are not excused from that comment, either."

But a thorough job requires more than one trip down the line. One plate can't hold the ribs, chicken, pulled barbecue, slaw, pickles, lima beans, sweet potato soufflé, green beans, rice and liver hash, rutabaga, and "little biscuits" Lynn's mother makes. Then there's the dessert table (banana pudding, bread pudding, peach cobbler).

"We come once a month," says Beth Rogers Williams of Blenheim. She's perfected her buffet routine: It's once up for green beans, rutabaga, barbecue, and sweet potato soufflé. The second trip is reserved for fried chicken.

Shuler's barbecue is vinegar-based, but it does have a bit of mustard added. People come from all over the Pee Dee to try it. Even folks from Lexington, N.C., are fans; some say Shuler's barbecue is better than theirs.

The secret may lie in the sauce. It was concocted 40 years ago by Shuler Hughes, Norton's father. A butcher who owned several grocery stores, Shuler Hughes began selling barbecue from his store in Sellers. "He always had a hankering to start a steak-house and barbecue place," Norton says. "He would have had a ball."

Shuler died in 1986. Years later, his son–armed with the secret recipe–opened the restaurant in his name. "I think I inherited his love of people and the love of cooking. I used to love to cook. When we got married, I just hated to clean up."

"Still does," Lynn says. A schoolteacher and church pianist, Lynn handles the register and other duties while Norton manages the cooking. Lynn's mother Lorraine Hamilton makes many of the side dishes. Hamilton's career has come full circle: She was a wedding caterer before she went to college in mid-life. After retiring as an English teacher at Dillon High, she's back in the kitchen.

Business was good from the beginning. Norton left the Century 21 office he opened in Dillon in the late '70s and with it, the stresses of an unpredictable market. "Somebody asked me if I missed the real estate business in front of Lynn, and she said she'd only seen me buy one pack of Rolaids in the last four years. I always had a pack in my pocket at the office."

At Shuler's, he works a 65-hour week cooking Boston butts over pecan, oak, or charcoal. But it's fun. "You may be eating out here and all of a sudden hear raucous laughter coming out of the kitchen. It sounds like four women laughing at one time."

Shuler's is open only in the evenings, but customers are pressing for lunch. That probably will happen, along with some expansion and perhaps another Shuler's in a different location.

"The way we look at it, we have a Christian-based business," Norton says. "I think the Lord led me into doing this, and because of that, we all get along."

- Aïda Rogers

Norton maintains his barbecue restaurant really never changes, although "it does improve with age." Lynn serves her "little biscuits" because, as Norton says, "we'd go out of business without them." Shuler's BBQ once hired a lot of Junior Miss beauty pageant contestants and was known for having the "best-looking waitresses around. Still have a lot of nice lookin' ones," he says. As a certified judge with the South Carolina Barbeque Association, I often hear it said that Shuler's BBQ is "about as good as it gets" in the Pee Dee and South Carolina...and that's without the "little biscuits." Dixie-Dining.com has given Shuler's gold fork status, emblematic of its highest rating.

- Tim Driggers

Skeets Barbecue, Mechanicsville
Darlington County

Skeets Barbecue, 116 North Charleston Road, Darlington (Mechanicsville); (843) 393-7339. Open for buffet lunch Sunday-Friday from 11 a.m.-2 p.m. and for dinner Thursday-Saturday, 4:30-9:30 p.m. Smoking allowed. No credit cards, but checks allowed. No reservations needed. Inexpensive to moderate.

For *True* Barbecue in Darlington County ...

Got some advice from Dr. Wayne King, history professor of the "Old South, New South and Odd South" at Francis Marion College (now University). He has penned the following:

What Westminster Abbey is to England,
What the Eiffel Tower is to France,
What the Brandenburg Gate is to Germany,
What the Kremlin is to Russia,
What the Roman Coliseum is to Italy,
What the Parthenon is to Greece,
What St. Sophia is to Turkey,
What the Temple of Luxor is to Egypt,
What the Taj Mahal is to India,
What the Angkor Wat is to Cambodia,
What the Great Wall is to China,
What Mt. Fuji is to Japan,
Skeets Barbecue is to the Pee Dee.

I don't let a letter like that go by without a phone call. Wayne, a native of "Flo Town," recounted the day he discovered Skeets Barbecue. It was 1969, and he had just come home to teach.

"I was going into the back areas to get a feel for the countryside and I smelled barbecue and followed the smell, as any good southerner would," he recalled. He found himself in Mechanicsville, a crossroads in Darlington County. Skeets Barbecue was brand new, but as Wayne said, "you don't need age to reflect the ethos of the area."

In fact, it's the peculiar authenticity of the atmosphere as much as the food that keeps Wayne going back. "One of the things that disturbs me about the new barbecue places is they're becoming too gentrified. They have carpet on the floor. You're not supposed to have carpet on the floor in a barbecue place."

The fact that carpet is a no-no but "stuff on the walls" is suitable sounds inconsistent, he admitted, but "there's just certain ways that things are supposed to be. A true southerner knows what fits in. Skeets doesn't have to strain to be a southern barbecue place. It just is, and that's what makes it so entrancing."

Serving vinegar-based barbecue chicken, pork, ribs, hash, even chicken bog, Skeets is run by Eugene Austin "Skeets" Gardner.

Skeets is 12 miles from Florence, eight from Darlington. As for an exact address, this is the best I could do: If you're coming from Florence, take Mechanicsville Highway and "come straight all the way. At the crossroads, go straight. Skeets Barbecue is right behind Skeen's Grocery.

Good luck and good eats.

- Aïda Rogers

Sandlapper first wrote about Skeets Barbecue in the winter of 1991 and when the magazine revisited, "Skeets" told us "we still treat our guests as company and cook the old school way." The barbecue is cooked on premises and continues to be the major part of the restaurant's business, although a buffet has been added Sunday through Friday featuring steak, seafood, and barbecue. The steak is cut by hand and to the weight specified by the customer. Two barbecue sauces are provided, a "Sandlapper" catsup-based sauce, and a "Tarheel" vinegar-based sauce. The handmade-from-scratch biscuits are not to be missed and Skeets wants everyone to know everything on the menu continues to be "homemade."

- Tim Driggers

Webster Manor, Mullins
Marion County

Webster Manor, 115 East James St., Mullins; (843) 464-9632. Open for lunch buffet only Monday-Friday, 10:30 a.m.-2 p.m., closed on Saturday and Sunday. Reservations not required. Smoking allowed only on patio. Credit cards accepted. Inexpensive.

The Buffet of Buffets

Webster Manor is a restaurant that begs for visits again and again.

Located in downtown Mullins, Webster Manor has a storied history. Built as a private residence in 1903, it was converted into a boarding house in the 1920s, primarily for school teachers. In those days unmarried women teachers often lived in boarding houses during the nine-month school year. For the remaining three months, Webster Manor was filled with tobacconists selling their crop at one of the 21 warehouses that flourished in town. At the time, Mullins was the largest tobacco market in South Carolina, with daily auctions attracting growers and buyers from throughout area. In the 1940s a restaurant was added and the property was purchased by Ann and Kenneth McDonald in 1986, as an investment.

Kenneth was in the grocery business and had started buying real estate on the side. He also started dabbling in politics. He was elected to town council that year and served 19 years until elected mayor in 2004. Keeping the rooms upstairs as a bed and breakfast, the downstairs was converted into multiple dining spaces, with a buffet serving area, dessert cranny, and large kitchen. There are four restored fireplaces in the dining area, each featuring ornate iron plating. There also are attractive Blue Willow plates and antiques throughout.

The house is beautifully appointed, but let's get down to what really draws the crowds—the Webster Manor buffet. Nan and Ralph Ford of Columbia come frequently. "It's a place you want to get back to every chance you get," says Ralph, whose family is from the nearby Nichols community. He's big on the vegetable dishes. "The vegetables taste just like my grandma Lurline Fogle made and she was a great cook," he said. Kenneth says there's good reason why the vegetables are so tasty. "We don't cook with fatback or pork fat," he said. "We season our vegetable dishes with de-fatted chicken broth." The broth also makes its way into the restaurant's seasoned rice and chicken bog.

The fried chicken is popular too. "It's perfect," Ralph said. "Not too crispy or heavily breaded, not too anything, it's just right." Nan agrees. "I'm a fried chicken junkie and it's the best." She also recommends the chicken and dumplings. "They're what I grew up with," she explained. "The dumplings are really noodles, just like the ones my mom made." I thought the chicken was the most delicious I had ever tried. Paul McCravy, my assistant culinary expert, must have thought the same; he returned to the buffet four times. "I went back and scraped the bottom of the crock pot for the last dregs of sweet Pee Dee barbecue, which taught me a valuable lesson," he noted. "Next time, I'll come early." Paul didn't forget the desserts. "They serve some of the best coconut cake, banana pudding, apple-cherry cobbler, and pound cake with strawberries in these parts, and their buttermilk pie is out of this world."

Jean and Grady Funderburke of Lake City have been regulars for 17 years. "Eating at Webster's is like eating with family," Jean said. "It's operated by family for family. We always see people that we know and the staff is very friendly. Even the first time you go there, they don't treat you like a stranger. It has such a homey feel."

Drawing crowds from the Grand Strand, Columbia, Raleigh, and the I-95 corridor from Florence to the low country, Webster Manor is not to be missed. As Jean Funderburke puts it, "it's just great food, period."

- Tim Driggers

Myrtle Beach Area/The Grand Strand

Georgetown & Horry Counties

Big E's Seafood, Longs
Horry County

Big E's Seafood, SC Highway 9 on the Waccamaw River, Longs; (843) 399-3399. Open Mondays 11 a.m.-2:30 p.m.; Tuesday-Thursday, 11 a.m.-9 p.m.; Friday-Saturday, 11 a.m. to 10 p.m.; Sunday, 11 a.m.-9 p.m. Reservations not required. Both smoking and non-smoking areas. Checks, cash, debit cards, Master Card, and Visa accepted. Inexpensive.

"Great Seafood with Southern Hospitality"

Randy Davis and I had just plopped down in a booth at Big E's Seafood in Longs when a waitress bounced over to our table and asked whether we needed a menu to place our order. Being somewhat of a smart you-know-what, I informed the young lady that since I neither possessed ESP nor the ability to read her mind, a menu might just come in handy. Randy, being the perceptive lawyer that he is, had a different take. "Big E's is a restaurant where the locals come to eat and if you're a local and eat here all the time, then you don't need a menu." That made sense.

Located midway between Loris and Little River in the Horry County community of Longs, Big E's Seafood is nestled alongside the Aberdeen golf community and the creeping expansion of North Myrtle Beach. What once was farmland is now urban sprawl, with Big E's a dining oasis for local folks who crave fresh seafood served by one of their own. The dining is casual, with emphasis on the food rather than the fancy. "You don't have to put on your church go-to-meetin' clothes," Randy observed. We sat in the popular closed-in porch overlooking the countryside, punctuated by ever-present cars streaming beachward.

Loris native Betty Hughes never dreamed she would work at or own a restaurant, at least not until she met Everett Hughes in 1977. In the late '80s, Everett bought some land on S.C. 9 in Longs and Big E's Seafood was born. "He built the restaurant just for me," Betty said. "I did the work and he provided the backing. Everett was heavyset, and Big E's seemed a natural name for the restaurant."

Pam Hodges, a state constable with the Horry County police, recalls Everett, who passed away in 2000. "He certainly livened up the place. He was quite flamboyant and you could hear him laugh from one side of the restaurant to the other."

Betty is a virtual whirlwind. Look up and she's at the cash register, look again and she's running back to the kitchen, then moments later she's sauntering between tables visiting with customers. "I think it's important to recognize your customers," she said. "I love to talk; never have met a stranger." Those are qualities her regulars appreciate. "Miss Betty has a way with people that you don't often see," Constable Hodges said. "It's important to her that when you leave Big E's you take a little of her home."

The specialty is seafood and the plates are enormous. Randy ordered a seafood platter with generous helpings of fried shrimp, flounder, oysters, scallops, and deviled crab. He was impressed. "I'd rate my meal an A," he said, describing its light batter and "not heavy-tasting" flavor. The creamy Cole slaw was the best either of us had ever tasted. "I liked that the waitress brought a big pitcher of tea to the table with equally big glasses," Randy said. "When you eat fried seafood, you always want tea and a lot of it."

Besides seafood, Big E's offers a daily lunch buffet. Usually it includes chicken bog, roast beef, fried chicken, spaghetti and meatballs and several vegetables.

As if rising to give a final summation to the jury, Randy offered this last appraisal. "Big E's serves great seafood with a large order of southern hospitality," he said. "The prices are right, the food is ample and fresh, and the service is quick."

What more could you ask? Unanimous verdict for Big E's Seafood.

- Tim Driggers

When Sandlapper *called Betty Hughes to check on Big E's Seafood, she gave us the assurance we wanted to hear. "Everything's the same as it always has been," she said. "If it isn't broke, don't fix it." Thanks, Betty, for keeping your seafood platters that way. We'll take Big E's Seafood "like it is" any time.*

- T. D.

Collector's Café Gallery and Coffee House, Myrtle Beach
Horry County

Collector's Café, Gallery, and Coffee House, 7726 North Kings Highway, Myrtle Beach; (843) 449-9370. Café open Monday-Saturday, 5:30-10 p.m. Gallery and Coffee House open noon-midnight. Closed Sunday. Credit cards and checks accepted. Reservations preferred. Smoking only in designated areas. Expensive.

A Little Art With Your Meal?

Owners Thomas Davis and Mike Smith were clueless about the restaurant business when they opened Collector's Café, Gallery & Coffee House in 1997. Mike grew up in The Netherlands and moved to Myrtle Beach in the mid '80s to pursue an engineering career. Thomas is a third-generation Myrtle Beach native who worked in graphics and design. Both shared a love of art and desire to create something unique on the Carolina coast. Finding the perfect location in an abandoned vision center, they set out to transform it into an art gallery, night club, and coffee house. Or so they thought.

"When we started, neither of us had any idea of what we would build," Mike said. "We were both artists and needed a place to display our artwork and at the time, coffee houses were the hot thing." About five months into the project, the night club was scuttled because of zoning problems, prompting Mike and Thomas to ask Mike's sister Rhonda for help. She had some restaurant experience, so only two months before the grand opening, a restaurant was born. It didn't hurt that Carlos McGrigor, a Cuban chef looking for work, happened by one day. He's been executive chef since.

The Collector's is an evolving restaurant. Its six rooms might have a different look and feel upon each visit. "In business, you have to bob, weave, and adjust," Thomas observed, adding that the restaurant closes two weeks in January. "We come in and take the place apart. Up go new ceilings, new walls and new artwork" (for sale on-premises). The cuisine also changes. "Carlos travels extensively in Europe," Thomas said. "He's a self-taught chef who prefers the old European style of cooking. In the winter his menu will have a more hearty flavor, while in the spring he employs lighter foods emphasizing spices, herbs, and salads. During the summer months, he specializes in nonfried less fattening selections."

Each area of the restaurant has a distinctive feel with its own style of artwork. "Our art gallery of 6,000 square feet is the largest in South Carolina and we encourage our guests to walk around and digest the works on display," Thomas said. The main dining room has white tablecloths scattered amidst classical Greek columns. The Gallery has a distinctive sculpture hanging from the ceiling. The Lion's Den is for intimate dining, while The Grill Room features ceramic tables and bar. In the cozy Lounge diners can luxuriate in velvety chairs and sofas with an old English appeal. I dined in The Coffee House, a relaxed room with painted tables—themselves works of art.

I began with Filet of Beef Carpaccio. Named for Renaissance painter Victore Carpaccio, this appetizer featured razor-thin slices of raw beef in extra virgin olive oil, balsamic vinegar, and spicy mustard. I took the advice of several diners and ordered the signature Pan Sauteéd Scallop Cakes as my entree. It had to have been prepared by the gods. Each of the two cakes contained four sea scallops blended with tomato, scallion, and garlic in a butter sauce.

Determined to stuff myself to the fullest, I chose a dessert of tiramisu—espresso-dipped lady fingers and Italian Kahlua custard topped with dark chocolate shavings.

Other menu favorites include grilled somoran yellowfin tuna with Cuban black bean sauce, mango salsa, saffron rice, and chipotle pepper, roasted prawn over creamy basil pesto-artichoke fettuccine, Collector marinara sauce topped with roasted sweet peppers and crispy pancetta and grilled wild Pacific salmon over grilled asparagus, topped with grilled tomato basil sauce, shitake and Portabello mushroom beurre blanc. The restaurant's extensive quality wine collection has garnered the Award for Excellence from *Wine Spectator* magazine.

Collector's Café offers an alternative to the seafood buffets along U.S. 17 from

Murrells Inlet to Calabash. Quality food prepared by a quality chef amid quality art-work all blended by quality owners—that's a prescription for a rare and decidedly different experience that should not be missed.

- Tim Driggers

Emi's Fusion Bistro, Pawleys Island
Georgetown County

Emi's Fusion Bistro, 47-A Da Gullah Way, Pawleys Island; (843) 235-2313. Open Monday-Saturday, 5-10 p.m. Closed Sunday. Reservations recommended on the weekends. Credit cards and checks accepted. Smoking only on patio. www.emibistro.com. Moderate to expensive.

A Country Boy Grooves on Sushi

Chopsticks are something I've never been able to master. I've practiced ad nauseum, but I've never been able to eat with them. I may as well try to put two fence posts between my fingers and pick up a cumquat. Chopsticks are as incomprehensible to me as the Vienna Boys Choir opening a concert with "Wooly Bully."

So there I was at Emi's Fusion Bistro in Pawleys Island staring at a plate of sushi with a couple of chopsticks dangling from my fingers. Then a strange logic swept over me: If I couldn't use chopsticks, then I couldn't eat the sushi, and I was safe. You see, I had tried sushi once before and could not stand it. Eating raw fish was appalling to this ole country boy.

I decided to close my eyes and take a small nibble on the tuna with asparagus and sesame sauce. I swallowed, expecting the worst and hoping, like a prisoner awaiting execution, that the end would come swiftly. But that's not how my taste buds responded. I was flabbergasted. The tuna was absolutely delicious. I suddenly found myself ravenously attacking smoked salmon, spring roll, and duck breast potsticker like a man who hadn't eaten in years. There I was, furiously dipping sushi in soy, ginger, and wasabi sauces and clamoring for more.

According to Ben Cachila, my reaction is a common one. Ben moved from Chicago to help in-laws Keiko and Shozo Sakata open Emi's in 2004. "The first time you try sushi, you're indifferent to it," he said. "The second time, you begin to like it and the third time, you start craving it like an addict."

Located on U.S. 17 in the sprawl of Pawleys Island, Emi's combines not only exceptional sushi but a fusion of Japanese and southern flavors and cooking styles. "Fusion" has become a trendy word in culinary jargon, chicly describing the melding of local tastes and ingredients with a decided ethnic bent.

Natives of Beppu and Tokyo, Japan, respectively, Keiko and Shozo Sakata opened their first restaurant in Chicago in 1979. "We wanted to own our business and since we loved to eat, we opened a small storefront restaurant," Keiko said. Six years later they moved to a larger location in nearby Evanston and in 1995 moved south. "We wanted to open a restaurant in Myrtle Beach emphasizing quality over quantity, serving fresh and seasonal meals infused with the Japanese way of life," she explained.

That dream reached fruition with the opening of Emi's in 2004. Named after their first grandchild, Emi Madeleine Cachila, the restaurant followed Keiko's game plan. "Shozo, Ben and I wanted a sushi bar; but also wanted to serve a fusion of contemporary Asian, French and southern dishes," Keiko said.

"It's all very logical," Ben added. "We're not only selling food, but also a culture. We combine what we are good at and the things around us, like fresh local products, together in a creative mix."

At the modern sushi bar, Shozo runs the show. Displayed are sashimi (thinly sliced raw seafood), nigiri (sashimi atop sushi rice) and maki (rolled sushi). Fifty-four varieties of sushi are available. A well-stocked bar with an extensive wine list lies straight ahead, and to the right is an attractive dining room where customers can order entrees including Chilean Sea Bass with rice wine miso marinade, roasted eggplant, steamed rice, and asparagus salad; Moo Shu Crepes made of duck confit with wok-tossed julienned vegetables and hoisin plum sauce; and Asian Bouillabaisse of coconut curry broth, king crab, shrimp, mussels, and scallops. Diners split their allegiances between the sushi bar and restaurant wing.

Emi's Fusion Bistro is a coastal treasure. Fabulous sushi and a cuisine merging French and southern cooking traditions with Japanese culture make it truly unique.

- Tim Driggers

The Fish House, Litchfield Beach
Georgetown County

The Fish House, 13060 Ocean Highway, Litchfield; (843) 237-3949. Open Tuesday-Saturday for lunch, 11:30 a.m.-3 p.m. and for dinner, 5-9 p.m. Credit cards accepted. Reservations recommended for dinner. Smoking in designated areas. www.lbfishhouse.com. Inexpensive to moderate.

Lick Your Fingers and Smile

Here's a place that illustrates what a small state we live in. One May evening we looked over our shoulders—and plates of crabcakes—and saw relatives from Lexington. It seems we see more people from home when we're out of town.

That happens a lot at The Fish House, a casual seafood spot that locals love and tourists have found. People come for the large quantities of food, lower prices, and pure simplicity of the setting. No need to dress up here. There's beer, there's noise, there's the best onion rings I've ever had.

"Not fancy. Just fresh" is the motto, and locals agree. "It's just a little hole in the wall, but it's got the freshest seafood in town," said Christy O'Rear Lubert, who grew up in Pawleys Island. "The parking lot's always full," added her sister-in-law Cheryl O'Rear.

I piled in a car with Christy, Cheryl, and some other girls one drizzly day during a week-long vacation at Pawleys. It was a day for shopping and eating. We left the boys behind. We had more important things to do, like have the Crabcake Supreme Sandwich for lunch.

"All I can remember is it was heaven," Marcia Purday said, ordering one and then raving about the crab balls and sesame scallops she'd had before. Naturally, that inspired me to order both those appetizers, a cup of fish stew and a side of onion rings. Here, a side is a platter, and I could have made my meal on those. Hot, sweet, big and lightly battered, the Fish House onion rings are delectable and addictive. Even Sally Diaz, a BBC researcher and onion stay-awayer, had to agree. "I'll have to say, these are nice onion rings," she understated.

Maybe we overdid the appetizers, because when the sandwiches came—and they're big ones—we were licking our fingers and smiling. The crab balls are hot, rich, and spicy, and the sesame scallops are worth fighting over.

Sandwiches are served in baskets, with a choice of French fries or coleslaw. Besides fish, oyster and other seafood sandwiches, the Fish House serves burgers and steak and chicken sandwiches. Several salads and seafood entrees are available, too.

The Fish House is known by the shark that reaches head-first from the roof. At Christmas, owner Bob Mimms puts a Santa in its mouth. At Halloween, he loans it to the haunted house at Waccamaw Elementary School. We like a restaurant with a sense of humor.

- Aïda Rogers

For 20 years, owner Bob Mimms has warmed the hearts and stomachs of locals and vacationers on the Grand Strand. He's still got that daunting shark on the roof and a terrific seafood dinner menu. For landlubbers, there's the Pawleys Island Steak House Rib Eye. The Fish House also features a Children's Menu, with an optional fresh fruit side instead of the standard fries.

- *Tim Driggers*

Inlet Crab House and Raw Bar, Murrells Inlet
Georgetown County

Inlet Crab House and Raw Bar, 3572 Business Highway 17, Murrells Inlet; (843) 651-8452. Open daily 11:30 a.m.-10 p.m. No reservations needed. Credit cards accepted. Smoking allowed. www.inletcrabhouseandrawbar.com. Inexpensive to moderate.

Eating with the Locals in the Inlet

I first discovered the Inlet Crab House several years ago while visiting friends Hamp and Beverly Davis at their condominium in Myrtle Beach. Hamp and Beverly have traveled extensively and know good restaurants in every hemisphere. So when they suggested a "locals" restaurant in Murrells Inlet, my ears perked.

"Locals restaurant" has a decided appeal along the Grand Strand. With seafood buffets anchoring real estate from Calabash to Pawleys Island, a lot of hungry folk are on the lookout for an unassuming roadside diner the natives haunt. The Inlet Crab House and Raw Bar fits that description.

It would be easy to drive past it and assume it's just another rustic cabin alongside Business 17 in Murrells Inlet. That not only would be a huge mistake, but the gastronomic equivalent of the Hindenburg disaster. The pink roof hints this isn't your ordinary seafood joint. Open the door and you'll find the funky interior inviting; taste the food and you'll be convinced this is the real deal.

Jimmy and Kim Mayes opened the Inlet Crab House in 1992. Jimmy's great-grandfather had built a summer retreat in Murrells Inlet during World War I and Jimmy spent his summers working at Captain Alex's Marina. After a stint at Spartanburg Junior College, Jimmy returned to the seafaring life, operating private sport fishing boats along the east coast and down to the Exuma Islands in the Bahamas. He's been a sea captain for 30-plus years, continuing even after opening the Inlet Crab House.

"We wanted a small place to sell steamed crabs and shrimp," Jimmy explained. "Nothing big, just a place that would be friendly and comfortable; a place customers would want to come back to time after time. Good food was an extra." He found the inspiration for the restaurant's folksy, lively interior on his "islanding" through the Caribbean. "A lot of places on the islands were colorful and laid back, and that's the kind of unpretentious restaurant we aimed for."

They hit the target. "The Inlet Crab House reminds Beverly and me of a Key West kind of place the locals would frequent," Hamp said. With strands of Christmas lights hanging from the walls, its pink ceiling and open rafters, rustic wooden tables and Murrells Inlet artifacts, The Inlet Crab House has all the feeling of a cozy, seaside shack. "The only thing missing is a little Jimmy B on the jukebox," Paul McCravy said, just before Jimmy Buffet's "Margaritaville" hit the speakers.

That made him happy, but not as much as his she-crab soup ("outstanding," he said) and fried grouper sandwich. I also had the she-crab soup, but opted for the lightly fried oyster basket. The basket was generous and more than enough for a full meal. "We don't believe in heavy crust and batter on our seafood," Jimmy said. The formula works, allowing the natural taste of the oysters and grouper to come through.

Best sellers are the she-crab soup and the fried shrimp, fish, and oyster platters, with a scallop platter available at market price. "Our she-crab soup is so popular, we ship it all over the country," Jimmy said. "We keep it basic and simple, without adding a lot of extras. Our customers love it." The raw bar features select oyster or clam roasts, peel-and-eat shrimp, and snow crab legs. For landlubbers, there are 12 and 16 ounce rib eye steaks, chicken breasts, and a baby back rib dinner.

Beverly and Hamp like the selection of po boy sandwiches. "We usually get different ones and share," Hamp said. "The portions are just the right size for us. The quality is good, the price is right, and the service is prompt and efficient."

"Murrells Inlet is not like it used to be and never will be again," Jimmy noted. "I just want The Inlet Crab House to keep what has made us successful—fresh seafood in a laid back atmosphere the people I grew up with enjoy and that they enjoy telling others about." That's as good a definition of and recommendation for a "locals restaurant" that I know.

- Tim Driggers

Landolfi's, Pawleys Island
Georgetown County

Landolfi's, 9305 Highway 17 South, Pawleys Island; (843) 237-7900. Open Tuesday and Wednesday, 10 a.m.-5 p.m. and Thursday-Saturday, 10 a.m.-9 p.m. Closed Sunday and Monday. No reservations. Credit cards and local checks accepted. No smoking. Inexpensive.

"Where the Fruit Tarts Gleam Like Jewels"

Looking for Wonderland? Then park yourself in front of the dessert case at Landolfi's, an Italian café and bakery where the cream puffs and fruit tarts gleam like jewels in Aladdin's cave. The magician who conjures them uses hundred-year-old recipes from an old black book, brought to New Jersey from Naples by Pasquale Landolfi. Uncle Pasquale is gone now, but he left those recipes to his nephews, one of whom begat Gary Bencivengo. Happily for those who appreciate Italian pastry, Gary rejected college for the family business. He's a baker of the first order—don't call him a pastry chef—and the fourth generation to produce profiteroles, cannoli, and zuppa Inglese. That's a rum cake with custard, almonds and whipped cream.

I strolled into Landolfi's with Rosie O'Rear, a food snob of the first order. Rosie writes for this magazine, cooks gourmet meals, and has traveled frequently in Europe. Landolfi's, she says, is worth her time and taste buds. "We eat here a lot, and I'm picky," she told me. Rarely does she try the desserts, so impressed she is with the soups, salads, and breads, all homemade. So is the pizza, prepared in a wood-fired brick oven from Tuscany. Tuscan clay cooks fast, explains Suzanne Bencivengo, Gary's wife and business partner, allowing Landolfi's thin-crust pizza to be extra crispy and flavorful.

"In the summer, people have waited an hour to get a pizza," Suzanne said. "That boggles my mind."

Landolfi's serves eight different 10-inch gourmet pizzas. Pizza Bianco uses mozzarella and ricotta with sautéed spinach, black olives and garlic. Pizza ala Romana has anchovies, kalamata olives and capers. Roasted garlic, gorgonzola, mozzarella, and pine nuts top the Tuscan-Style Pizza. We ordered the Pizza Rustica—roasted red peppers, sweet Italian sausage, fresh tomatoes, mozzarella, and black olives. Until it arrived, we took advantage of the specials board.

Rosie eyed the soups. Today's is a potato cheddar ale which, on this blustery March afternoon, can't be ignored. Brothy more than creamy, it's full of potatoes and carrots, with cheese on top. "I think that soup is fabulous," Rosie pronounced as we spooned it out with the Italian bread (she often buys the bread to serve at home or freeze).

Homemade bread makes the paninis popular, too. Grilled sandwiches on Italian bread, the five paninis on the menu sound sufficiently Mediterranean, save for the Panini Reuben. The Genovese has wood-roasted chicken; the Greco has sautéed spinach, black olives, feta, and marinated tomatoes; the del Campagnoli has roasted eggplant, prosciutto, and gorgonzola. The Panini Porker is a favorite: wood-roasted pork loin with roasted red peppers, melted provolone and balsamic vinaigrette. The key, Suzanne says, is the wood-roasting. Oak is used, which Gary buys and splits himself.

The Bencivengos decided to close their much-loved, 110-year-old family bakery in Trenton, New Jersey, when its Italian neighborhood began changing. The old families moved to the suburbs. Gary's father had retired to Myrtle Beach, and Gary and Suzanne loved Pawleys Island. So they too came south, knowing they'd have to offer more than Italian pastries to make it in a less ethnic area. Gary quit baking wedding cakes and began making key lime pies and red velvet and carrot cakes. He created bread and pizza dough, while Suzanne perfected her soups and salads. They offer something besides fried seafood, in an old Montessori school they gutted and rebuilt into a Mediterranean-style bistro. Stucco, wrought iron, lavish window boxes, and a patio create a sense of relaxed festivity.

The Bencivengos plan to expand their restaurant, adding a bar and fireplace where people can wait for tables. Beer and wine are served now, and liquor is in the offing.

But maybe it's really a cappuccino or latte you want, or perhaps an espresso or mochaccino. Especially with one (or more) of those desserts. Gaze upon them in awe, and consider that a human wrought them.

- Aïda Rogers

Mrs. Fish Seafood Grill, Myrtle Beach
Horry County

Mrs. Fish Seafood Grill (formerly Mr. Fish), 919 Broadway, Myrtle Beach; (843) 946-6869. Open Monday-Saturday, 11 a.m.-10 p.m. Closed Sunday. Smoking allowed. Credit cards accepted. Reservations accepted. Inexpensive to moderate.

A Fresh Fish Sandwich at the Counter

Contrary to common impressions, there is a downtown in Myrtle Beach. In the middle of it is a place where locals go to read the paper, talk among themselves and get a fresh fish sandwich cheap. It's Mrs. Fish Seafood Grill (when we visited in the spring of 1997, it was Mr. Fish Seafood Grill, Raw Bar, and Market), a tucked-away place in Myrtle Beach's confusing downtown district. Don't look for any pink flamingos here.

"There's no pretension," said then-owner Ted Hammerman, or "Mr. Fish." He looked at my plate—a blackened triggerfish sandwich with slaw and roasted potatoes, for which I paid $5.98. "Restaurants in Myrtle Beach would charge $18 for that." Those were prices from a decade ago, but the value remains today.

Ted, son of a chicken farmer, opened Mr. Fish in January 1996 as an extension of his wholesale fish market. Triple A named it one of the 15 best new Strand restaurants. Beside sushi, fish stew, and grouper "jawdaddys," it has interesting soups: black bean and crab, crab and cauliflower. "This is not an ordinary squat-and-gobble or chat-and-chew," Ted said.

Not hardly. Though casual in décor—everybody sits at a counter and eats on Styrofoam plates—Mrs. Fish offers a wonderment of seafood in a number of ways. Depending on the season, you can get grouper, tuna, flounder, mahi mahi, triggerfish, and salmon, and you can get it fried, grilled, sautéed, jerked, blackened, barbecued or broiled. As former cook Jay Madden put it, "For $5, anything you want, any way you want it."

So it's no surprise locals have found it and made it theirs. "Yep, 12:15. Here they come," said Charles Moody, watching the first of the lunch crowd come in. "We get strictly locals: print shop owners, doctors, lawyers—lots of lawyers. The mayor pops in sometimes. We probably don't do 10 percent tourist business, at the most."

When we visited, Mr. Fish's menu changed every day. That kept the cooks from getting bored, Moody said. He trained at Johnson & Wales before working at Kiawah Island and country clubs, and said his present job is much harder. He and Ted create the recipes, among them a fiery "Turbo Tartar" and "Tuna Lisa." Named after his wife, Tuna Lisa includes of sauce of Dijon, soy, garlic, black pepper, lime, cilantro and "a little bit of Chardonnay," Ted said. Also on the menu: "Mahi Mahi Yo Mama" when available and varieties of shellfish all the time.

With its black-and-white checkerboard floor and bright green-and-orange walls, Mrs. Fish seems like an old-time grocery and frat bar put together. At one counter, you can watch the cooks—all guys—prepare fish. Behind swinging doors in the back is the fish market, where Ted sells to 60 percent of area restaurants wholesale. If the cooks aren't too busy, they'll fix your own catch.

"They're really providing a service," said Rosanne Howard, who covered food and restaurants for *The Sun News* at the time. "You can get fresh fish here that you'd pay $22 for somewhere else."

Classy food in casual surroundings is always a winner—particularly when it's affordable. "People get a glass of wine and grouper and not worry about dressing up," Charles said. Ted added, "Two people under $20? That's pretty strong."

- Aïda Rogers

Andrew Chu acquired Mr. Fish 10 years ago and changed its gender. "We're still a locals' favorite," he said. "Today, our best sellers include the grilled grouper with a spicy Asian sauce, sea tuna, mussels, and our crab and shrimp dishes." Ted Hammerman is still around town as a consultant to fishing businesses, providing services ranging from employee education to product development (website: www.mrfish.com).

- *Tim Driggers*

Nibils, Surfside Beach
Horry County

Nibils, 11 South Ocean Boulevard on the Pier, Surfside Beach; (843) 238-5080. Open daily for breakfast, 6:30-11:15 a.m., for lunch, 11:15 a.m.-4 p.m. and for dinner, 4:30-8:45 p.m. Closed at 2 p.m. Sunday. Nibils closes the weekend of Thanksgiving through Valentine's Day. Credit cards accepted. Reservations recommended for dinner. No smoking. www.mrnibils.com. Moderate.

Pier Pleasures in Surfside

For a real old-style beachy feeling, you can't beat Nibils, a cozy, comfy spot on the pier in Surfside Beach. Not only does it have the kind of view only a pier can provide; it has the food most tourists want.

"This is strictly the beach. People want fried seafood or broiled seafood," says Jack Cahill, owner. "They don't want sautéed items. I used to sauté when I came down here, but it didn't work."

What they seem to want Nibils offers in spades: friendly, bustling atmosphere; fresh, affordable seafood; and the idea that here, you're experiencing something that's hard to find.

Jack Cahill presents specialties of the house.

"I think it's refreshing that places still exist like this, with all the slick chains coming in here," said Rosanne Howard, my dining partner. Rosanne writes about food and restaurants for *The Sun News* and has seen her share of "slick." For the record, Nibils is not that— particularly with Eula Mae Windly, bubbling with cheer, seating and serving you. Eula Mae was at the restaurant almost 20 years before Jack and his wife Margaret bought it 20-plus years ago. She was too much of an asset not to keep.

"All the people I've met in the past 28 years I learned to love like family," Eula Mae said. "I've seem 'em grow up. They've gotten married and they're bringing their babies back."

There were more older folks than babies the Thursday morning I ate breakfast there with Rosanne. Over a western omelet and French toast, we watched the conviviality. Coffee cups were clinking, waitresses hustling and every table was packed. Nibils seats 90; usually it's filled to capacity. "I love places that bustle like this," Rosanne observed. "I hate going places where there are only two couples. Here, you feel like you're part of the energy of the place."

No doubt that energy begins with Jack, father of six and first-generation Irishman.

He gave up his very successful restaurant in the Bronx to bring his children to a safer environment. Not one regret has he.

"I love this. It's labor-intensive but there's not much stress, because the audience is wonderful," he said, explaining that it's easy to please people on vacation. "All their problems are back home and they're here to have a good time and relax."

Because of its casual décor—cypress walls, blue cloths and curtains—many newcomers expect food that's just okay, Jack added. But when they try the creamy shrimp and seafood salads, Angus beef, center-cut country ham and fresh-squeezed orange juice, they decide otherwise. "We do the little things that make things better."

True to his roots, Jack has designated every Thursday "Irish Night." Corned beef and cabbage with Irish soda bread is the special, and Dr. Orin Anderson, an Irish tenor and professor at Horry-Georgetown TEC, entertains. The special Monday through Wednesday is a 10-ounce Black Angus Prime Rib. Fresh Sea Scallops are the special Friday and Saturday. A variety of sandwiches and chicken dishes are available for those who aren't in the mood for seafood.

Before I left, Jack loaded me up with containers of shrimp salad, chicken salad, and neptune salad, each served with fresh fruit. I enjoyed them later on the beach with Dolly Patton, former executive director of Sandlapper Society, Inc. We didn't have forks, so we used our fingers and Captain's Wafers. Small price to pay when eating delicious food on a bright breezy day at the beach.

- Aïda Rogers

While Surfside Beach continues to grow and restyle itself, Nibils remains a constant. There have been few changes. Irish Night is no more, but Irish fare is still served on Thursday. Dinnertime bestsellers include fresh Atlantic grouper and flounder. For breakfast, the seafood omelet with fresh shrimp and crabmeat is a daybreak favorite. If you like the familiar when you walk in a restaurant, Nibils is the place for you. All the cooks and waitresses have been here for the past 12 years.

- Tim Driggers

Oliver's Lodge, Murrells Inlet
Georgetown County

Oliver's Lodge, 4204 Highway 17 Business, Murrells Inlet; (843) 651-9523. Open daily, 4:30-9 p.m. Sunday brunch, 11 a.m.-2 p.m. Reservations accepted. Credit cards and checks accepted. Smoking allowed in bar. www.oliverslodgerestaurant.com. Moderate to expensive.

A Coastal Tradition

Dining at Oliver's Lodge has always been a treat. I first visited here more than 30 years ago, drawn by curiosity to the history of a century-old house amid the marinas of Murrells Inlet. The inlet in those days was off the Grand Strand's beaten path, a quiet fishing village where an occasional restaurant interrupted the view of the waterway and charter boats chugging out for the Atlantic Ocean fishing grounds. All that has changed—but Oliver's Lodge is a steadying constant, a reminder of Murrells Inlet's past, updated by new ownership into the 21st Century. Although it looks a bit different and the menu is more diverse, the charm of the historic seafaring lodge is intact.

"My husband and I never envisioned owning a restaurant," Tracy Fisher said. "We had eaten at Oliver's Lodge and had many fond memories." Those memories led them to purchase it in 2004. As her husband Powell put it, "I just wanted to bring Oliver's Lodge back to life. It used to be the place to eat. It was just so pretty at night with the house lit up along the inlet."

The original Oliver's Lodge was built in 1860 at Laurel Hill Plantation, now part of Brookgreen Gardens. Owned by Lt. Gov. Plowden C.J. Weston, it was moved to its present site as a summer home to escape the mosquitoes and malaria that menaced riverbank plantations. Capt. Bill Oliver purchased the property in 1885. "He was a steamship captain who ran a passenger route between Georgetown and Conway," Powell said. "After retiring, he opened the home in 1910 as a restaurant serving three meals a day and a lodge for hunters and fishers. Capt. Mack Oliver, Bill's son, discontinued the lodge in 1947 and started menu-oriented meals. He continued the family fishing charter business. Maxine Oliver was the last member of the family to operate the restaurant and adorned the restaurant with many of her artworks."

The Fishers have renovated the house extensively while remaining true to the legacy of the Oliver family and the history of Murrells Inlet. I visited Oliver's Lodge for Sunday brunch and was escorted to my table in the redesigned porch overlooking the inlet. The buffet sits near the bar and featured quiche, waffles, link sausage and bacon, creamy grits, garlic mashed potatoes, green beans, buttermilk biscuits, scallops (lightly dusted but without seafood breading), a carving station serving great beef tenderloin, and chicken.

Let me talk about the chicken for a second. This chicken was good—really, really good. "We butcher and cut the chicken ourselves," Tracy said. "Then we soak it in salt water for 24 to 36 hours to draw out the blood and finally fry it in a black skillet just like your grandmother's."

The signature dish is Flounder Roosevelt, named for custodian Roosevelt "Rooster" Pickett, who has worked and lived on the property since the 1940s. "Rooster loves flounder and our chef, Mike Vaitsas, created the dish," Powell said. "It's fresh flounder stuffed with crabmeat and topped with a lobster cream sauce."

Weddings often are held on the lawn adjacent to the inlet. The late author Mickey Spillane, a local resident and frequent customer, was married here in 1983 and reputedly ended his vows with the immortal line, "I do; let's eat."

June and Bill Miller of Pawleys Island have dined at Oliver's Lodge for 35 years. "When June and I first started coming here, Murrells Inlet was quite rural and there weren't nearly as many restaurants," Bill said. "Oliver's Lodge has always been good. We've never been disappointed in our meals. The food is honest and tasty."

Oliver's Lodge bills itself as the oldest restaurant on the Grand Strand. That's no accident. "They've been here a long time because people enjoy it," Bill said. Our bet is that people will continue to enjoy it for a long, long time.

- Tim Driggers

In her memoir Heaven is a Beautiful Place, *Genevieve Peterkin captures Murrells Inlet as it grew from a quaint fishing village with a couple of dozen homes and two restaurants at the turn of the 20th Century to a booming bedroom community of Myrtle Beach. One of her friends during that era was Maxine Oliver, of Oliver's Lodge renown. The renovated restaurant continues to exude Maxine's southern charm and graciousness on Murrells Inlet's revamped restaurant row under the ownership of Tracy and Bill Fisher. Jeremy Borsh is now Executive Chef, while Ashley Wright fills the manager's position. Oliver's Lodge offers scenic waterfront views from every table and continues a menu featuring its signature Flounder Roosevelt and new favorite Seafood Fra Diablo (mussels, clams, and shrimp with spicy marinara sauce over linguini). Tracy says to give her steaks a try. "They're cut to order and are simply phenomenal."*

- T. D.

The Parson's Table, Little River
Horry County

The Parson's Table, U.S. 17 North (4305 McCorsley Avenue), Little River; (843) 249-3702. Open Monday-Wednesday, 4:30-9 p.m.; Thursday-Saturday, 4:30-9:30 p.m. Closed on Sunday. Reservations needed. Credit cards and local checks accepted. No smoking. www.parsonstable.com. Moderate to expensive.

Adventurous Cuisine in Oceangoing Surroundings

For many, a visit to the beach would be incomplete without dining at The Parson's Table in Little River. The food alone is a magnet for repeat diners, but that's just one of the reasons for its popularity. Entering through the ancient cypress doors begins a journey to the Carolina coast of the late 19th Century. In 1885, long separated from its past as a haven for marauding pirates, Little River was a popular destination for oceangoing steamships linking the town with Georgetown and Wilmington. The original Little River Methodist Church held its first service that year. A century later, the church, and its heart of pine flooring, is the main dining room of The Parson's Table. Ed and Nancy Murray purchased the restaurant in 1991, augmenting the interior with antique stained glass, a large chandelier from a Baptist church in Mullins, a Tiffany lamp and an array of crystal patterns. By the time they turned operations over to son Ed Jr. in 2001, The Parson's Table had earned a reputation as one of the most captivating restaurants along the Grand Strand.

A quick glance at the extensive menu revealed entrées as intriguing as the decor. I selected escargot baked in a rich garlic Madeira white cheese sauce. The escargots were tender, plump and tasty. I congratulated each snail for the supreme sacrifice of escaping their shells in favor of my digestive system. Honors concluded, Teresa, my attentive waitress, returned to my table hand-tossing a huge salad accompanied by a homemade olive oil-based house dressing.

"To clean the palate" was Teresa's expression as she next served a small cup of beef consommé. For the main course, I opted for one of the specialties, the Carpetbagger, a tenderloin filet cooked with an embedded oyster and served with Bordelaise sauce and heaping mound of garlic mashed potatoes. Bursting with flavor, the steak was incredibly tender and easily cut without a sharp knife.

Each entrée is paired with a suggested wine selection. That's a big plus for those of us not wine connoisseurs.

Owner-chef Ed Murray Jr.'s style of cooking evolved from his fusion background in Boston and the Low Country style here. "While working on Daufuskie Island near Hilton Head, I developed a love for the regional flair of Gullah cooking," he explained. "Using just the fresh vegetables available on the island, I became a believer in cooking with what's pulled up from the land." Murray's signature dishes of shrimp and grits and veal and shrimp Bombay embody that spirit of resourcefulness.

Howard Sullivan of Chesterland, Ohio has made visits to The Parson's Table a family tradition spanning three-and-a-half decades. "The quality is always the same," he said. "You always know the food is going to be good."

It's a tradition Ed Murray Jr. values and appreciates. "I love that adrenaline rush when the restaurant fills up," he said. It shows. The Parson's Table offers a unique dining adventure that begs to be experienced over and over again. That's nothing less than tradition requires.

- Tim Driggers

In 2007, The Parson's Table received five prestigious awards: The Golden Fork Award from the Gourmet Diners Club of America, Three-Diamond Award from the AAA Travel Guide, International Restaurant Hospitality Rating Bureau International Award of Excellence and Gold Wine Award, Wine Enthusiast Magazine *Award of Unique Distinction, and* Wine Spectator *Award of Excellence.*

- *T. D.*

The Rice Paddy, Georgetown
Georgetown County

The Rice Paddy, 732 Front Street, Georgetown; (843) 546-2021. Open Monday through Saturday for lunch, 11:30 a.m.-2:30 p.m. and for dinner, 6 p.m.-10 p.m. Closed on Sunday. Credit cards and checks accepted. Reservations requested during the summer months and on all weekends throughout the year. Smoking allowed only at the bar. www.ricepaddyrestaurant.com. Lunch: inexpensive. Dinner: expensive.

It's Got the Mood and the Food

As the town square is the heart of many South Carolina communities, so is Front Street the pulse of Georgetown. That's where a historical harborwalk lines the Sampit River, and where several restaurants await those who like to eat overlooking the water. But for those who look for the less obvious, there's The Rice Paddy, located in an old bank building that nonetheless attracts locals and tourists.

"I go a certain period of time when I can't go without the shrimp salad," said Janice Shoemaker, who was enjoying lunch with her husband. "They put fruit or avocado with it. It's the best I've tried."

Full of light and bright colors, The Rice Paddy is owned and run by "the two Susans" (Hibbs of Bardstown, Kentucky, and Felder of Columbia). What they seem to do that other Georgetown restaurants don't is offer the exotic: smoked tenderloin with mustard sauce, Bahamian grouper, smoked quail with angel hair pasta. The fact that they serve lamb is reason enough for lawyers Tom and Nancy Rubillo to make it a regular dining spot.

But The Rice Paddy's more ordinary items are worth celebrating, too, as I discovered when the Rubillos told me they were treating one of their employees, Sharon Herriott, for her birthday. I asked Harriott why she chose The Rice Paddy. In four words: "chicken salad on croissant!"

While it offers no view of the river or marsh, The Rice Paddy almost can take you to the tropics just with a walk inside. Maybe it's the bamboo décor, plants and colorful paintings. Or maybe it's the South Pacific soundtrack playing on the stereo.

Whatever the reason, The Rice Paddy's reputation is sterling in a town where food is important. Hibbs said once people find it, they come back. "Seventy percent of our business is repeat," she said. "People come from Pawleys and Charleston every week, so that's saying something."

- Aïda Rogers

Since we last visited The Rice Paddy, "the two Susans" have added an outdoor dining area. The Bahamian Grouper remains their signature dish, with the Seafarer's Platter running just behind. There are different lunch and dinner menus.

- *Tim Driggers*

Rivertown Bistro, Conway
Horry County

Rivertown Bistro, 1111 Third Avenue, Conway; (843) 248-3733. Open for lunch Monday-Saturday, 11:30 a.m.-2 p.m. and for dinner Tuesday-Saturday, 5-9:30 p.m. Reservations recommended for dinner. Credit cards accepted. Smoking allowed on upstairs terrace. www.rivertownbistro.net. Lunch: inexpensive to moderate. Dinner: Moderate.

Innovative Fare on the Waccamaw

"My problem is I love everything," said Charlene Heaton, my "bored housewife" waitress at Rivertown Bistro in Conway. She didn't seem bored. She seemed thrilled to be working the lunch shift at this bright place with interesting food. For one thing, there are so many things to recommend.

"Today's quesadilla is crawfish and black bean with Monterey Jack and sautéed onions and peppers," she said. "It is to die for. I took two home. All the salad dressings are homemade every day; so are all our soups and sauces. The Greek salad has four different kinds of olives. Our garnish is different too; it's pickled okra, cherry tomatoes and baby corn."

I took Charlene's advice and started with Rivertown Bistro's signature appetizer, the Low Country Spring Rolls. Stuffed with chicken, spinach and spicy ham, they come two to a plate and are crispy, hot and good. One order is enough for a small or medium appetite.

The lunch menu presents a number of delectable-sounding salads and sandwiches. Favorites include the fried oyster spinach salad with blackened green tomatoes, boiled egg and hot bacon vinaigrette (available only during "R" months), and the fire-roasted pimiento cheese BLT club sandwich. Pasta, soup and yam chips also are available.

I ordered the shrimp and sausage in tasso gravy over jalapeno grit cake. "You won't be sorry," Charlene said, and she was right. It was spicy and filling, and enough (especially after those spring rolls) to take some home.

Rivertown Bistro is a mom-and-pop—in this case, Cyndi and Darren Smith. They met while working at a Charleston restaurant and decided to set up their own in Conway, Cyndi's hometown, in 1994. Since then, they've been wowing the locals with innovative fare. That means Conwayites don't have to drive to Myrtle Beach to experience the latest in food.

The core menu, which changes every three months, includes seafood, chicken, fish, beef, duck, veal, quail and pork. Evening appetizers include crawfish au gratin over fried zucchini with roasted red pepper cream, and a lobster crab cake with lemon butter sauce and tarragon corn sauté. Darren's crabmeat-topped grouper with a two-potato artichoke hash is especially popular.

Rivertown Bistro takes its name from Conway's place on the Waccamaw. The Smiths are happy to make their customers happy. And, Darren adds, to have "made it in a fickle business."

- Aïda Rogers

After suffering a fire in early 2008, Rivertown Bistro will reopen in late 2008. The "new" restaurant will include a second story with an outdoor terrace. "I've been working in some high-end restaurants in Charleston, researching and developing different cooking techniques to bring back home," Darren Smith said. Fresh produce from local farmers and seafood from local fishermen dominate the menu. Rivertown Bistro is "very wine-friendly," Darren added, noting its full bar and extensive wine list that includes boutique wineries.

- A.R.

Sea Captain's House, Myrtle Beach
Horry County

Sea Captain's House, 3002 North Ocean Boulevard, Myrtle Beach; (843) 448-8082. Open daily for breakfast, 6-10 a.m.; for lunch, 11:30-2:30 p.m, and for dinner, 5-10 p.m. Credit cards accepted. No checks. No reservations. No smoking. www.seacaptains.com. Breakfast: inexpensive. Lunch: inexpensive to moderate. Dinner: moderate, a few items expensive.

"Simply a Grand Strand Legend"

The only constant is change, and nowhere is that more true than in Myrtle Beach. The exception here is at 30th Avenue North and Ocean Boulevard, where the Sea Captain's House is still serving its famous crab casserole, shrimp salad, and grasshopper pie to tourists so regular they've become family.

"I see a group of golfers who've been coming here longer than I've worked here," said Joye Nesbitt, a dining room manager who's worked at the restaurant 23 years. "They come every year. And that's what most people do. They come back year after year and they eat at least one meal here. Some people will have all their meals here."

That's devotion. But the Brittain family, who own the restaurant, earned and maintained its reputation by keeping old favorites on the menu and offering new specials at night. Its architecture and atmosphere don't hurt, either. Dwarfed by the high rises around it, the Sea Captain's House sticks to its New England-style simplicity. People wait in line outside in the summer or inside by one of two fireplaces. What it has that some Grand Strand places don't is age.

"We're all really loyal to the place, and I think it's because the Brittains are traditional and always strive for the best," Joye said. "I appreciate the fact that they've kept this building. They could sell it and put their feet up the rest of their lives, but they continue to run it."

Open since 1962, the Sea Captain's House has pecky cypress walls, a fine view of the Atlantic, and the best she-crab soup around. "That's our Number One bestseller," said Tom Mullally, executive chef. "I've tried it at six other restaurants and haven't found one that compares to us yet."

Mullally is Boston-bred, with training from Johnson & Wales, University of Providence, RI, Florida, and Switzerland. While the unusual specials are his domain, he can't take credit for the she-crab soup. "That had nothing to do with me at all. They've been running that same soup for the past 20 years. The soup, crab casserole, and grasshopper pie will never come off the menu."

For those with more daring tastes, Mullally offers a few different appetizers and specials each night. Lobster lasagna and shrimp ravioli are two of his favorites; grilled salmon with a roasted garlic, sherry and shrimp sauce and grouper with a sun-dried tomato basil crust are two more. Mullally's not one to accept the average.

"When I put myself in the guest position, I don't want that grilled salmon with a dill cream sauce. You can get that at any restaurant on the beach. But how about a roasted Bermuda onion crabmeat dill sauce, something crazy like that?"

Mullally, who is writing a book about sauces, keeps a notepad by his bed at night. "People laugh at me, but some of my best ideas come when I'm sleeping." It must be working, because Mullally's been the overall grand winner at the Taste of the Tidelands competition and has won the Taste of the Town event on two occasions.

The accolades don't stop there. Readers of *The Sun News* have chosen The Sea Captain's House top restaurant on the Grand Strand numerous times. It's also won the "Best Breakfast on the Beach" category. That breakfast is something to behold. Besides omelets, waffles, French toast, eggs benedict, and pancakes, the Sea Captain's House offers Brie and Bacon Omelet and Crab Cakes Benedict. The Seafarer's omelet is a three-egg omelet with shrimp, lump crabmeat, mushrooms, and Monterey Jack Cheese. Breakfast is offered seven days a week, as are lunch and supper.

So popular the employees eat there on their days off, the Sea Captain's House even attracts the gulls. Every October, about the 15th, swarms of seagulls flock to the restaurant at night. They seem suspended over the water, birds of bright white against midnight blue. It's a dramatic show, one that plays every night until mid-April. "I never get tired of looking at that," Joye said.

Who could? Pull up a chair, enjoy the view, and don't forget to try a dessert by Charlene LaMarre, the ultra-talented pastry chef. We suggest the White Chocolate Macadamia Nut Pie, served cold with cream. For this, there simply are no words.

- Aïda Rogers

The Sea Captain's House is simply a Grand Strand legend. Originally constructed as an oceanfront beach cottage in 1930, the building was home to Howard's Manor, a guest home for tourists, during the war years, and continued as a stopover for beach visitors until the early '60s. That's when the Brittain family scrapped plans to build a multi-story hotel and opted to open the Sea Captain's House. And the rest is history. Since we visited, Mary Heyde has taken the reigns as dining room manager and Andrew Fortner now fills the position of Executive Chef. The food, well, it's still great, and the she crab-soup, crab casserole, shrimp salad, and grasshopper pie remain their "what we're famous for." There are three or four nightly specials and as Mary Heyde says, "everything's good." She's right, you know.

- *Tim Driggers*

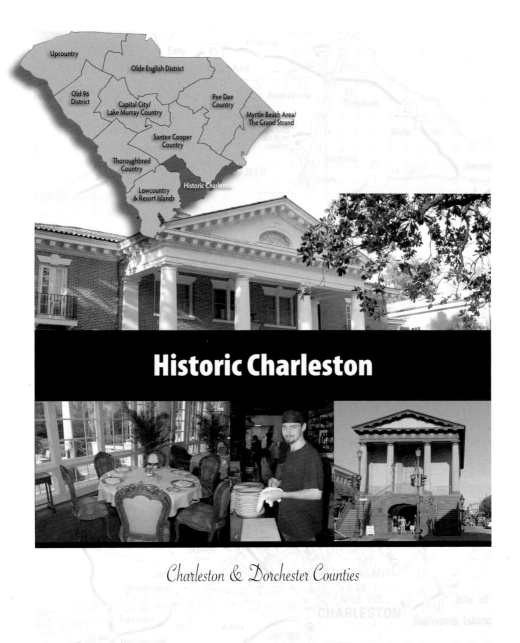

Upcountry

Olde English District

Old 96
District

Capital City/
Lake Murray Country

Pee Dee
Country

Myrtle Beach Area/
The Grand Strand

Santee Cooper
Country

Thoroughbred
Country

Lowcountry
& Resort Islands

Historic Charleston

Historic Charleston

Charleston & Dorchester Counties

Circa 1886 at Wentworth Mansion, Charleston
Charleston County

Circa 1886 at Wentworth Mansion, 149 Wentworth Street, Charleston; (843) 853-7828. Open Monday-Saturday, 5:30-9:30 p.m. Closed Sunday. Credit cards accepted. Reservations recommended. No smoking. www.circa1886.com. Expensive to very expensive.

This Place is Special All the Way Around

Situated in the garden of Wentworth Mansion Inn at the corner of Wentworth and Smith, Circa 1886 is housed in the restored carriage house on the grounds of the then Rodgers' Mansion. It was built by Francis Silas Rodgers, a cotton merchant, in 1886, just before the famous Charleston earthquake. A private residence and later a corporate headquarters, Wentworth Mansion was restored in 1998 by Richard Widman into a 21-room luxury hotel of uncommon Southern splendor. The carriage house was converted into the present restaurant in 2000.

Entrance is via a pathway winding through lush gardens and attending tree grove. Guests may indulge in a drink at the bar dominated by a large fireplace that once was a kiln for the carriage house blacksmith. The original stable doors remain. The restaurant is elegantly intimate with a posh, softly-lit khaki decor providing seating in recessed paneled booths and chandelier-sheltered tables for 50 diners.

Jesse Smith, a graduate student at MUSC, is a waiter extraordinaire. He suggested I try the Carolina crab cake soufflé, a signature item, for my first course. "Our menu changes every four to six months," said executive chef Marc Collins, "but we always serve the crab cake soufflé and our spicy grilled shrimp." The crab cake was surrounded by a sunburst of roasted red peppers, topped with a garnish of mango purée and sweet potato frills.

I opted for the soup course rather than a salad and enjoyed a sampler of creamy bean soup before delving into the cheese course. Circa 1886's cheeses are produced at Sweet Grass Dairy Farm in Thomasville, Georgia. With Jesse's guidance, I selected the botana, a raw, aged goat's milk cheese served with red pepper coulis, caramelized Vidalia onion purée, and micro fennel. Jesse was ever-attentive; courses arrived at my table with flawless timing.

For my entree, I chose the antelope. Jesse described the taste perfectly: the appearance and taste of beef with a slight hint of gaminess. Rolled in peanuts, the antelope, like its living embodiment, was mounted on a slope of potato purée surrounded by artichoke barigoule with accents of cilantro and ginger sabayon.

Jesse insisted I try the patisserie course and suggested the banana trio. The first offering was a peanut butter banana parfait—simply heaven. Close behind was banana cream tart with Italian meringue and banana shortcake and strawberry gastrique.

Throughout the year, Circa 1886 hosts themed meals for its guests. There's a Colonial Dinner, a Gullah Dinner, and a Halloween Ghost Tales Dinner. Often featured is the storytelling of Tim Lowery, who spent years with Charleston's basket-weavers, learning Gullah stories and dialect. During the weeks before Christmas, Lowery portrays Dickens characters. In progressive dinners, diners are driven from restaurant to restaurant in horse-drawn carriages.

In a city famous for extraordinary restaurants, Circa 1886 offers all the ingredients for a wonderful dining experience. If you aren't celebrating something, you will most certainly celebrate a memorable evening here.

- Tim Driggers

Continental Corner, Summerville
Dorchester County

Continental Corner, 123 Richardson Avenue, Summerville; (843) 871-1160. Open Monday-Thursday 11 a.m.-8:30 p.m.; Friday and Saturday 11 a.m.-9 p.m., and on Sunday 11:30 a.m-2:30 p.m. (Sunday following Labor Day through the first Sunday in June). Reservations recommended for parties of 8 or more. Credit cards accepted. Smoking in designated area. Inexpensive to moderate.

What a Beautiful Friendship Hath Wrought

When a partnership works, good things happen, and not just for the parties involved. The people of Summerville have known this since 1973, when one of their own, Ernie Yatrelis, opened The Continental Corner with his good friend Thomas Mavrikes of Cleveland. Greek restaurants were rare then, and Summerville wasn't the metro place it is now. But for more than 30 years, locals have come to The Continental Corner to satisfy their need for all things Greek. People have been sampling lamb with lemon and oregano, salads with Feta and Kalamata olives, and Rizogolo, a cinnamony rice pudding with whipped cream. "Even the Greek ladies say our grape leaves are excellent," Ernie observes, adding that he believes they may be one of the first, if not the first, to sell gyros in South Carolina.

"Mr. E. met "Mr. T" in Massachusetts, where they were students at Holy Cross Greek Orthodox Seminary. A few years later, disenchanted with their jobs in South Carolina's upstate, they came to Summerville to open a deli. Ernie had been a high school assistant principal; Tom was working with the vocational rehab system. A sandwich shop, selling the New York-style fare they'd loved in Massachusetts, sounded more appealing.

Ernie says their lack of business skills was their only handicap. But they learned as they went, added to their menu and their restaurant, and eventually created a place that's become a mainstay of their town.

At Continental Corner, a gyro is served with a choice of chips, potato salad, Cole slaw, pasta salad, or fruit. It's one of the most popular items on the menu. Add Feta and it becomes the Royal Gyro Sandwich. Spanakopita, a spinach-filled phyllo pastry, is on the appetizer list. Stuffed Grape Leaves also are popular; this appetizer is an herbed meat and rice-filled grape leaf topped with Avgolemono sauce, served with pita bread and lemon wedges. With 10 per plate, it's enough for a meal.

The menu is so broad it's hard to decide what to order. When our server described the Chicken Mavrodaphne (breast sautéed with fresh mushrooms, onions, and Mavrodaphne, a sweet Greek wine used for church communion), I knew we should try it. This is Ernie's juicy creation, served with rice and a Greek salad. After much struggle, we also ordered a combo plate of grilled salmon (olive oil, lemon, parsley) and sliced lamb (baked with lemon and oregano). When salads, seasoned potatoes, and vegetables were added, there was more than enough.

This might be the best Greek salad I've ever had—and beautiful, too. Kalamata olives, Salonika peppers and Feta cheese are part of the deal, and marvelously, anchovies are available if you want them. Tom created the dressing, and frequently gets requests to bottle and sell it.

Servings are generous. Had there been more than two of us, it would have made sense to order one of the Greek Grills. The Village Mixed Grill includes baked lamb, grape leaves, chicken breast, and Greek sausage. Shrimp, scallops, and salmon compose the Seafood Mixed Grill and marinated steak strips, chicken breast, gyro, and Greek sausage are in the Greek Mixed Grill. The sausage, sliced in rounds, is imported from Boston, and has orange rind in it.

Kebabs (lamb, chicken, beef, and chicken-and-sausage) are on the menu, along with pasta and specials. Family recipes and Greek cookbooks are used. Ernie roasts the lamb and concocts specials while Tom makes the soups, Spanakopita, and grape leaves. Their partnership continues into the church behind the restaurant. They helped organized St. Cyril and Methodius Orthodox Christian church. Ernie, ordained in 1995, leads the services; Tom is the warden. You'll see "Welcome" and "Bon appetite" on the menu, with the same message in Greek, Russian, and Italian.

That welcoming spirit pervades the restaurant, with its casual atmosphere, al fresco dining, and flamingo-colored walls. Built in a former dress shop, The Continental Corner draws all kinds of people—families, couples, old, and young. That suits Ernie, who notes that restaurants in Greece are friendly places where families and friends talk across tables. That happens here, too.

- Aïda Rogers

Mr. E" and "Mr. T" are still serving their special brand of authentic Greek favorites. At lunch, try one of the Meze'thes; not exactly an appetizer, but more of a small meal, served alone or in combinations. Featured are the Stuffed Grape Leaves, The Alexia (grilled shrimp and chicken tenders), The Tanya (gyro with Greek sausage, tiropita, Spanakopita and Kalamata olives) or The Steven (grilled Greek sausage with Feta cheese and Kalamata olives). Dinner favorites include charbroiled chicken Riganato, Sliced Lamb, Sliced Gyro, Grill Shrimp and/or Scallops, Grilled Salmon, Grilled Tilapia, Charbroiled Rib Eye and Charbroiled Angus Filet Mignon.

- Tim Driggers

Cru Café, Charleston
Charleston County

Cru Café, 18 Pinckney Street, Charleston; (843) 534-2434. Open for lunch Tuesday-Saturday, 11 a.m.-3 p.m. and for dinner Tuesday-Thursday, 5-10 p.m. and on Friday-Saturday, 5-11 p.m. Reservations recommended. Credit cards accepted. No smoking. Cru Café is also available for catering. www.crucafe.com. Moderate.

Mama's Favorites and Gourmet Creations

Sandlapper Magazine first heard about Cru Café from Tom Vitale, producer of *Anthony Bourdain: No Reservations* on the Travel Channel. Seems that Tom, Tony, and crew raved about the restaurant during a visit to Charleston to film an episode of the series in March 2007. Naturally, we had to head down to the Holy City to see just what the hubbub was all about.

It was pouring rain when we bolted from our car and dashed to the front porch of the 18th Century Charleston single house on Pinckney Street between Meeting and East Bay streets. The rain ruined our chances for dining on the porch, but the deluge provided the impetus for the discovery of the charm and conviviality of Cru Café.

Owner/chef John Zucker opened Cru Café in February 2002 after extensive renovations to the former Pinckney Café. Using raised tables, Charleston prints, and homey nuances, Zucker has fashioned a cozy-chic atmosphere where dining with strangers becomes dining with friends over an ecumenical menu rife with mama's favorites and gourmet creations.

Paul McCravy and I scrambled into the two remaining chairs lining a long table at the restaurant's entrance. It wasn't long before we were hobnobbing with table mates, asking the obligatory "where you from?" and "what brings you to Charleston?", and comparing menu notes.

"Cru Café is one of those great little dining spots in Charleston's historic district whose allure lies not only in its great food, but its close quarters," Paul said. "You might wonder just what's so great about close quarters. Well, it's the interesting people that you meet."

Dr. Steve Gooding from Fayetteville was munching on a bib lettuce salad and sipping gazpacho next to Paul and me. Down the table were speech pathologist Diane Reynolds and daughter Betty from Charlotte. Diane was eating a butter lettuce salad of candied pears, walnuts, gorgonzola cheese and honey sherry dressing, while Betty was enjoying a small plate of mozzarella, tomatoes, and sweet peppers. You'd have thought we were lifelong friends reunited over comfort food with a twist of pizzazz.

They were quite willing to share their Cru Café critiques. "I loved the combination of flavors in my meal," Betty said. "The sweetness of the peppers and zesty balsamic vinegar blend together for a salad that's both light and tasty." Diane, who makes Cru Café a "must stop" on family visits to Charleston, was equally impressed. "My butter lettuce salad had an interesting blend of flavors," she said. "It was hearty and quite filling." Dr. Gooding was succinct: "Everything was fresh, with an excellent flavor."

Paul and I could not resist trying the Chinese Chicken Salad, an amalgamation of julienned Napa cabbage, carrots, peppers, daikon, and ginger dressing, served with accompanying tiny fried onion straws. "This stuff is great," Paul said. "Boy, am I glad I followed my waitress' advice." It was crunchy and delicious and the onion straws added a flavorful zing.

According to manager Sarah Rohl, the signature dishes at Cru Café are the mac and cheese ("Number 1 in Charleston," she said), the Pablano and Mozzarella Fried Chicken, aforementioned Chinese Chicken Salad, and the Grilled Basil Marinated Shrimp with Kielbasa, Peas, and Orecchiette Pasta. Other intriguing menu selections were the Thai Seafood Risotto, Seared Duck Breast, Braised Pork a la Napoli, Pan Roasted Black Grouper, Ginger Seared Salmon and Lemon Risotto and Grilled Scallops and Angel Hair Pasta.

"We loved Cru Café," Tom Vitale told me while shooting a future No Reservations *chapter with Tony Bourdain in India. After dining all over the world, that's a heady endorsement. But then again, as we discovered, what's there not to love about Cru Café?*

- Tim Driggers

The Dining Room at Woodlands, Summerville
Dorchester County

The Dining Room at Woodlands, 125 Parsons Road, Summerville; (843) 875-2600 (toll free: (800) 774-9999). Open for breakfast daily, 7-10 a.m.; for lunch daily, 11 a.m.-2 p.m. and for dinner Monday-Saturday, 6-9 p.m. No dinner served on Sunday. Credit cards accepted. No smoking. Gentlemen requested to wear jackets at dinner. www.woodlandsinn.com. Expensive to very expensive.

One of South Carolina's most revered dining establishments is in Summerville.

Five-Diamond Perfection

Within 12 hours I had two meals at The Dining Room at Woodlands. Am I a well-fed chick or what?

There I was, all alone with my fresh-squeezed orange juice, house-made wheat toast and one of the most unusual things on the breakfast menu: lump crab hash with roasted peppers and poached eggs with herb Hollandaise. Now, all I had to do was listen to the classical music and watch the flames dance in the lanterns on the terrace, where the wind was bending the magnolias and palmettos. This isn't a five-diamond restaurant for nothing.

"When you sit down, we don't need your table for anything else," reassured Steve Williams, my able server. "You want to come when you're ready to live it up a bit, and take your time while you're doing it."

Yes, it would be an ungodly waste to barrel through any meal at this "country estate" inn and resort in Summerville. The Dining Room at Woodlands, South Carolina's only Triple A-five diamond restaurant and resort, is big on perfection and short on anything less.

"We're control freaks," admitted Cathy Schefstad, director of sales and marketing. "We're all about details. We want to appeal to all your senses."

Here are some of the ways they do that:

The signature yellow roses have no fragrance, the better for diners to enjoy their food. Before having dessert, you're served a small predessert to prepare your palate. In our case, it was a tiny ramekin of crème brulee. My dessert choice: warm spiced crepes with roasted winter fruits and pomegranate-maple ice cream. (It was the pomegranate that got me.)

Management installed an elaborate water filtration system which, as Cathy explained, "guarantees that cooking is not compromised by essences in the water that might change the flavor." The water is so pure, she adds, that their coffee machine had difficulty reading their specially selected coffee beans.

Hundred-year-old balsamic vinegar is used. Salad tomatoes are never chilled, but served garden fresh.

Of course, that's not everything. There's the way the servers "detail" the tables between meals and cooks tear rosemary leaf by leaf in the kitchen. The butter for the buttermilk cheddar biscuits is a three-layer affair—regular, garlic herb and honey pecan—and the experts in the bar make chocolate martinis with espresso.

Between the vanilla beans from Tahiti, the Turbot fish from Chile and the 800 wines from around the world, TDRAW offers the simple diner a spectacular experience. If my mouth hadn't been so full, it would have fallen open in astonishment.

"The difference between four diamonds and five diamonds is that day after day, you will get exceptional service, food and surroundings," Cathy said. "Four diamonds is exceptional. But five diamonds is wow."

The wow-maker in the kitchen is Chef Ken Vedrinsky, lured here by Woodlands proprietor and CEO Joe Whitmore. An Ohio native and former sous chef at Chicago's Four Seasons Hotel and executive chef at Atlanta's Swissotel, Ken has been lauded by *Esquire, Gourmet* and has cooked on the "Today Show." His style is "New American," and his menus offer imaginative takes on beef, fish, fowl, and game. Ken's entrees are enhanced by wines chosen by sommelier Stephane Peltier and desserts by pastry chef Keith Chinn.

Evening diners can choose between a regular menu and a "Tasting Menu." We opted for the latter, which would include five courses of what's best in the house, with a different wine for each. The Tasting Menu is $89 per person (a vegetarian version is $56) and must be ordered by everyone at your table because of its synchronized serving style.

We had—and this is a long sentence—carpaccio of buffalo, black truffle oil, baby arugula and Parmesan Tuile (with a 1998 Pinot Grigio from Valdadige, Italy); butter-poached Maine lobster, artichokes, pancetta (with a 1996 Chardonnay from New York); filet of Turbot, wild oyster mushrooms, 100-year-old Balsamic (with a 1998 Pinto Noir from France); roasted breast of quail, foie gras ravioli, sour cherry au jus (with a 1998 syrah from California); and warm persimmon pudding, roasted pears, candied kumquat compote (with a 1996 Muscat Canelli from Washington).

"We're into matching the right wine with food," Cathy said, adding that winemakers visit from across the globe for special wine dinners at TDRAW. Nationally known guest chefs also bring their talents here to introduce diners to special cooking styles.

That's the key here: Everything is special, from the Angus beef hamburgers at lunch to the raisin oatmeal at breakfast. When I asked Cathy my number one restaurant question—"What are you famous for?"—she had to say, oh-so-truthfully: "We are famous for our food."

- Aïda Rogers

In 2001, Conde Nast Traveler's Reader's Poll named The Dining Room at Woodlands one of the top three restaurants in North America. Our question: How could any restaurant be better? Now owned by Sheila C. Johnson, chief executive officer of Salamander Hospitality, The Dining Room at Woodlands continues to rack up awards at a dizzying pace. For starters, it's the only South Carolina restaurant to receive the AAA Five Diamond Culinary Award for Excellence. Then there's the 2007 Mobil Five Star Award for dining and lodging excellence (one of only three hotels in America to earn this joint recognition) and the highest Relais and Chateau designation for dining excellence. Get the picture? The Dining Room at Woodlands continues to live up to its reputation as one of the great restaurants in America. There's a new Executive Chef on board, Tarver King, whose lists of credits would fill an encyclopedia. The Dining Room at Woodlands now has "Summerville Nights" every Thursday during the summer where locals receive a 25 percent discount; the Wines of the World Series is the third Tuesday of each month. The a la carte menu changes daily, there's a new tasting menu every month, and check the presses for the popular wine tasting events.

- *Tim Driggers*

Fulton Five, Charleston
Charleston County

Fulton Five, 5 Fulton Street, Charleston; (843) 853-5555. Open for dinner Monday through Thursday, 5:30-10 p.m. and Friday-Saturday, 5:30-11 p.m. Closed on Sunday. Also closed for 2 weeks in late August before Labor Day. Credit cards accepted. Reservations recommended because the restaurant seats approximately 40 guests. No smoking. Moderate to expensive.

Red Wine and Olive Oil

Bill Hall is a red wine man, which means he's my kind of man. We shared a bottle at one of his favorite places, Fulton Five in Charleston. Bill likes Fulton Five for many reasons: the food, atmosphere, and the fact that it's "off the beaten track." Charleston has plenty of "see and be seen" restaurants and he wanted something different.

That suited me. One look around and I could tell Fulton Five would be fun. It was small and lively and cityish, with white tablecloths, dim lights, and lots of people laughing. For a hot Wednesday night in July, the place was packed. Bill and I snagged a table for two at the window, a great spot for watching people stroll down this side street off King. Fulton Five has been discovered by the locals; and Bill, co-owner of the Charleston Tea Plantation, is one of its most appreciative customers. A Canadian who once lived in Buenos Aires, he knows how to find good Italian food. Fulton Five hasn't let him down yet.

Here, the food is northern Italian, and proprietor Silvia Meier goes for the best. She's introduced Charlestonians to carpaccio on arugula with shaved parmesan. That's thinly sliced meat served on a kind of mustard green. Carpaccio can be salmon, tuna, or beef; Fulton Five serves beef. Arugula, which has a slightly bitter taste, looks like an oak leaf. A Munich native, Silvia has found such exotic produce on Johns Island.

The fare may be unusual, but it's simple. That's how Silvia likes it. "I always like to emphasize the simpleness—simple and true ingredients. You know, not too much frou-frou, like the French do, not too much crème de la crème. That's what the next decade is going to be about, and I think the same thing will happen in food."

Her philosophy is if you have good ingredients, you'll have good food. Only fresh herbs and extra virgin olive oil are used. Canned tomatoes are something to be shunned. Carpaccio might sound complicated, but it's not. "To pasta, you can add anything, as long as it is fresh," she said. "It doesn't take much, really."

The menu at Fulton Five changes seasonally, although its signature dishes—minestrone, salads, and Antipasto Assortiti—remain constant. A tiny piazza upstairs is available to those who'd like a dolci or cappuccino after a concert or play.

Silvia's restaurant in Munich served "inside things"—sweetbreads, kidneys, and brains. She doesn't think a similar restaurant would work here, although those items are delicacies in Europe. Italian food is her favorite, and she predicts it will become the cuisine of choice in the South. "It's light, and it's made for hot weather."

Fulton Five takes its name from its address. It's located in a restored fire station in a former German neighborhood. Aside from that and Silvia's Bavarian background, the restaurant is purely Italian, right down to the color of its walls. Most are olive green, the same shade as the oil served on the side. There's also a wall the color of eggplant.

Black Sambuca, a licorice-flavored drink, is a great way to finish a meal. Not surprisingly, Fulton Five was the first restaurant to bring it to town.

Bill and I had a glass to celebrate our good time and then headed to Charleston's Waterfront Park. This is a great job. If it wasn't mine, I'd be pretty sick about it.

- Aïda Rogers

While Silvia Meier has relinquished ownership of the restaurant, Fulton Five wisely continues to use her extensive recipes and classic cooking style. Recognized as one of Charleston's leading Italian restaurants, Fulton Five is noted for its authentic non-tomato based Northern Italian cuisine. The upstairs piazza remains a popular haunt for lighter fare.

- *Tim Driggers*

Hominy Grill, Cannonborough Neighborhood, Charleston
Charleston County

Hominy Grill, 207 Rutledge Avenue (corner of Rutledge Avenue and Cannon Street), Charleston; (843) 937-0930. Open for breakfast Monday-Friday 7:30-11:30 a.m. Lunch and dinner served Monday-Friday 11:30 a.m.- 8 p.m. Brunch served Saturday and Sunday 9 a.m.-3 p.m. Reservations accepted for dinner only. Credit cards and checks accepted. Smoking only on patio. www.hominygrill.com. Inexpensive to moderate.

Shrimp and Grits for Breakfast; Desserts to Make You Swoon

Chef/owner Robert Stehling is wearing a green, John Deere bandana, appropriate for this unassuming but much-lauded Old South café. You can get a shrimp-and-grits breakfast here—*Cooking Light* called it the best in town—and eat it while listening to old-time country music. This three-story, 1897 shotgun building was a barbershop once. Scraped-up red and white poles guard the inside door, inviting you to look up at the lacy, pressed-tin ceiling and down at the unvarnished wood floors. Bright, Depression-era advertisements provide artwork. My impression: Nostalgic without overkill.

"We open very few cans," Robert says, a statement that, like his bandana, reflects his respect for shortcut-free, true South cooking. "I'm not interested in anything frozen. That's not why I got into this."

Robert grew up near Kernersville, North Carolina, and cut his cooking teeth in Chapel Hill, where he rose from dishwasher to head chef at Crook's Corner. There he studied under its founding partner and chef Bill Neal, author of well-known southern cookbooks. After more work in Durham and New York City, Robert came to Charleston with his wife Nunally Kersh, a Spoleto producer he'd met working at Crook's Corner. Hominy Grill is indicative of their desire to give locals and tourists regional cooking. Interestingly, you can't find much of that downtown anymore.

"We're trying to reflect the traditions of Charleston," Robert says, describing his vision of a neighborhood restaurant for people of the coming-back Cannonborough section. Students at the Medical University of South Carolina are regulars; so are employees at the nearby hospitals. Business is good enough to have built a $75,000 kitchen a block away; the kitchen here is too small. Hominy Grill also offers a lunch delivery service loaded with old southern favorites—sandwiches of pimento cheese, pan-fried catfish, barbecue chicken, and meatloaf with green tomato ketchup. Those with taste buds for something more unusual can order sliced lamb with eggplant relish, curried chicken salad with apples and toasted almonds, a turkey club BLT, and grilled Cajun pork chops with caramelized onions. Salads range from basic chef to avocado and Wehani rice salad with grilled vegetables.

It was the shrimp-and-grits breakfast I'd heard about, so I came in the a.m. to try it. Served with mushrooms, green onions, and bacon, it's a spicy way to start the day. Sweeten it with a serving of the equally famous banana bread—thick, buttered, hot, and fragrant. Buy a loaf or, if your tastes run to the salty side, a wheel of cornbread.

Hominy Grill offers specials. This morning it's sliced cornbread with sausage gravy, and two eggs cooked your way. Others are strawberry pancakes and an asparagus and cheddar omelet. But breakfast is mostly simple: eggs, biscuits, sausage, bacon, and hominy. Brunch, served on weekends, is more elaborate. On the menu are Huevos Rancheros, smothered eggs, a grilled vegetable omelet, salmon potato cake with poached egg, and cinnamon French toast with apple-maple syrup and pecan butter. Many of the national publications to cover Hominy Grill—*The New York Times, Esquire* and the *London Financial Times*—have remarked on its reasonable prices.

Robert believes in black-eyed peas, collards, okra, and chicken livers. Here, you can find them dressed up for dinner. Chicken livers are sautéed with shitake mushrooms and red peppers and served over angel hair pasta. Catfish is crusted with sesame and accompanied by fried okra, baked cheese grits, and "Geechee peanut sauce." Grilled duck breast comes with fried eggplant and sautéed greens; fried chicken emerges with mashed potatoes, collards, and spiced peach sauce. Shrimp, ribeye, and pork chops also are imaginatively presented. Vegetarians can try the black-eyed pea croquettes with avocado relish, jasmine rice, and fresh roasted tomato sauce.

Hominy Grill has a full bar, extensive wine list, and swoony-sounding desserts. Two of the cakes are caramel with toasted pecan icing and lemon cornmeal pound. Pies are pecan, buttermilk, chocolate, and peanut butter. Cookies, brownies, and cupcakes can be bought singly or by the dozen.

Shaped something like a shoebox, Hominy Grill opened in 1996. Its later renovation won a Caropolis Award from the Board of Architectural Review. It's not big, so you should make reservations for evenings and weekends. In pretty weather, a patio seats 30 for an overflow.

Music is much of the appeal. For breakfast, it's bluegrass and old-time country. At lunch, you'll hear soul and New Orleans-style R&B. Jazz plays at night. Hominy Grill will definitely put you in the American South. And doesn't it have a great name?

- Aïda Rogers

In Charleston, look for David Boatwright's painting of the Grits Lady on the side of a Cannonborough building and you've found Hominy Grill. In December 2006, owner and Chef Robert Stehling combined his lunch and dinner menus, which now result in the restaurant being open all day. He recently released his latest cookbook, Recipes from Hominy Grill.

- *Tim Driggers*

Il Cortile del Re, Charleston
Charleston County

Il Cortile del Re, 193 King Street in Charleston; (843) 853-1888. Open Monday-Saturday with bar service beginning at 5 p.m. and dinner 6-10 p.m. Reservations recommended. Credit cards and checks accepted (no separate checks). Smoking in courtyard only. Moderate to expensive.

Eclectic Energy, Splendid Italian Cuisine

Located on King Street in the heart of Charleston is Il Cortile del Re. Maybe I should say tucked away on King Street because of the restaurant's unassuming entranceway. The small door and narrow hallway herald a charming, warm atmosphere. Whether you opt for the outside courtyard or the cozy, European feel of the interior dining rooms, Il Cortile del Re is the definition of "romantic restaurant."

Romantic dining is often a catchphrase rather than an experience–romance invented rather than complemented. For myself, I've always thought one brings the mood

Chef Billy Pope shows off the fish he's rolled and tied with string.

and the restaurant accentuates the moment. Il Cortile del Re, with its dark red walls, ancient wooden floors, fireplace, and view of the passing scene on King, enhances rather than creates an ambience. Single women at the end of the bar eating olives and sipping red wine; out on the town, stylishly dressed. Old men drinking martinis alongside, wistfully wishing to join, but left on their own. My dining companion and I watching and taking it all in; dipping our bread in olive oil and chatting about the framed pig wearing glasses and Mardi Gras beads pictured on the wall. Servers in black, plates white; kerosene lamps of amber, and an atmosphere decidedly warm red. An appetizer of Formaggi Misti—telligio, truffle, black peppercorn, ubrico and broduro—imported artisanal Italian cheeses served on a wooden tray with grapes; some mild and some hot, all delicious. Drinking gaja promis, a super Tuscan wine (55 percent Merlot, 35 percent Syrah and 10 percent Sangiovese); savoring the elegant taste and buoyant surroundings. Then my entrée of Filetto Di Manzo Al Gorgonzola—beef tenderloin with gorgonzola sauce and roasted rosemary potatoes. Next, her entrée of Penne Alla Cetosina, replete with the requisite olives she fancies. Nibbling on the pasta, ever observing the passing scene, she's totally immersed in the energy of Il Cortile del Re.

Kim Green opened Il Cortile del Re in 1997 after a three-year residence in Italy's Tuscany region. "I wanted to bring the great food and culture of Italy to someplace beautiful and warm—like Charleston," she said. "It's very cosmopolitan here, with people from different walks of life and diverse homelands."

Kim found a small building on King Street that was a horse stable in the 17th Century. The middle dining room was a kitchen in the 1700s, and the 1800s section, adjoining King Street, emerged from a renovated antique store. A small courtyard was added and later enlarged. "It's a perfect place for al fresco dining," she said.

"Il Cortile del Re" translates into "Courtyard of the King," a natural considering the courtyard and King Street location. Co-owner Alfredo Tamelini, a Milan native, came on board in early 2007 after years managing the Peninsula Grill in Charleston.

Signature dishes are the Ravioli Al Funghi Porcini, ravioli stuffed and topped with wild mushrooms in a light cream sauce and Romano cheese; Cinghiale Con Fagiole E Polento, a traditional Tuscan favorite, slowly stewed wild boar with cannelloni beans and polenta in tomato sauce, and Alfredo Funghi Fritti, fried mushrooms.

Biscotti (crisp Italian cookies), a gift from the kitchen, ends our meal. From our standpoint, the real gift was the comfortable atmosphere, eclectic energy, and splendid Italian cuisine.

- Tim Driggers

Jack's Cosmic Dogs, Mt. Pleasant
Charleston County

Jack's Cosmic Dogs, 2805 Highway 17 North, Mt. Pleasant; (843) 884-7677. Open 7days a week, 11 a.m.-8 p.m. No smoking. No reservations. MasterCard and Visa accepted. www.jackscosmicdogs.com. Inexpensive.

"A Fun Shack Where Great Hot Dogs Rule Supreme"

On our Palmetto Cheeseburger Tour, my comrade-in-cholesterol Paul McCravy and I found ourselves at Jack's Cosmic Dogs in Mt. Pleasant. Although Jack's doesn't serve cheeseburgers, we'd heard the hot dogs were top-notch. We weren't disappointed.

"This is soooo good," said Shaun Gillies of Mt. Pleasant, biting into an Omega Dog. That's right, an Omega Dog. Think that's weird? Then what about the other Boars Head hot dogs on the menu? Here are the Astro Dog, Atomic Dog, Cosmic Dog, Earth Dog, Galactic Dog, Johnny Dog, Krypto Kraut Dog, Morph Slaw Dog, Blue Galactic Dog, and Vegeroid Dog.

Someone's got a sense of humor around here. With its funky interior colors, Flash Gordon rocket ship, and 1950s décor, Jack's Cosmic Dogs is a fun shack where great hot dogs rule supreme. They're the creation of owner John "Jack" Hurley, who opened the hot dog parlor in the late 1990s. "John had owned several restaurants, but decided a hot dog stand would be less stressful," explained manager David Jackson. "He made up names for the hot dogs that were crazy enough to be funny. It was a way for customers to get an additional kick out of the place."

But back to Shaun Gillies and his Omega Dog. A native New Yorker, Shaun landed in Mt. Pleasant with wife Adrienne by way of Florida. "The hot dogs here are different from the ones in New York," he said. "You don't get the snap you do with a New York hot dog. But that's a good difference." The Omega Dog comes with blue cheese slaw and Jack's sweet potato mustard. They're both Jack Hurley original recipes and, as Shaun says, "guaranteed to be a different experience."

Adrienne's Johnny Dog has onions, pickles, and spicy mustard. "It's delicious," she said, praising the soft, spicy buns. She likes the atmosphere too. "It's lots of fun. I'd compare it to some of the places I used to go on Staten Island. When we have friends visiting from out of town, we always bring them here."

In an adjacent booth, Dan Wolf of Awendaw was hunkered down over a Cosmic Dog. "I like the blue cheese Cole slaw on the hot dog," the USC student said. "It's unique." Dan appreciates Jack's "multi-generational" ambience. "It's not unusual to see friends from Bishop England High School eating at booths and their mothers and fathers sitting at tables across the room."

I started with a root beer float, then moved to a Blue Galactic Dog, replete with chili, blue cheese Cole slaw, and spicy mustard. A chocolate and vanilla swirl of soft-serve ice cream finished me off.

Paul happily attacked a Cosmic Dog and fresh-cut fries. "If you loved old sci-fi comic books as a kid, you'll feel right at home," Paul said. "Jack's Cosmic Dogs is where Flash Gordon meets the Oscar Meyer Wiener Mobile. Now, if Jack could only get Robby the Robot to wait tables."

- Tim Driggers

Jestine's Kitchen, Charleston
Charleston County

Jestine's Kitchen, 251 Meeting Street, Charleston; (843) 722-7224. Open Tuesday-Thursday, 11 a.m.- 9:30 p.m.; Friday-Saturday, 11 a.m.-10 p.m.. Open Sunday, 11: a.m.-9 p.m. Closed on Monday. Credit cards accepted. No reservations. No smoking. Inexpensive to moderate.

There's Nothing a Little Coconut Cream Pie Can't Cure

If I were feeling low—way, way low—I'd beeline to Jestine's Kitchen in Charleston. There's nothing a little coconut cream pie can't cure.

"At night with the lights on, it's so cozy and homey," says Susie Molony, a devoted customer and Mt. Pleasant businesswoman. She looked at her dinner plate, devoid completely of the meatloaf she ordered. "I didn't leave enough for manners."

We knew good things were coming when the waiter greeted us with a bowl of cucumbers in vinegar. Jestine's Kitchen is nothing if not authentic southern, and you'll see it in the extra touches. Baskets of cornbread come with pats of butter covered with honey; skins are left in the mashed potatoes. Fried green tomatoes are an appetizer here; so are big, sweet corn fritters served with relish. At Jestine's Kitchen, you can get fried chicken and pork chops, red rice and collards. "No pasta here," declares Dana Berlin. "Only macaroni and cheese."

Dana opened Jestine's Kitchen to honor one of her family's most cherished members, Jestine Matthews. Now 112, Jestine looked after Dana's mother, Shera Lee Ellison, from infancy to marriage, and then after Shera Lee's four children. Born to a Native American mother and the son of a freed slave, Jestine grew up on Rosebank Plantation on Wadmalaw Island. During her 70 years working for the Berlin family, she adapted her recipes to a Jewish household. That means there's no meat in the gumbo or red rice, but there is in the collards and green beans. Still, Jestine's personal recipes are served, along with items created by kitchen staff.

"The specials have to be Dana-approved," Dana jokes.

Specials this Sunday evening are pan-seared catfish, baked trout with sweet and sour sauce, pan-fried crab cakes with sweet pepper relish, and pot roast. Shrimp and grits with gravy is the special every Sunday. Insurance agent Charlie Karesh was reading a newspaper and putting away the pot roast, red rice, and potato salad. The home cooking and proximity to his office bring him to Jestine's Kitchen about three times a week. "I like vegetables and not plastic vegetables, but ones with seasonings. My biggest decision is not whether to get vegetables, but which ones to get."

The atmosphere comforts as much as the food. The walls are a warm pumpkin color, the floors black-and-white checkerboard. A Gibson refrigerator, crates of bottled soft drinks, and mismatched crockery make you feel you're in a country store.

Besides caring for the Berlin children, Jestine cared for her own daughter and six grandchildren. There's a picture of her surrounded by family on the back wall, and another of her on Shera Lee's wedding day in 1954, holding a hand mirror up to the bride. It's a formal photograph; the pots and pans hanging on the wall around it are somehow appropriate.

"She's an incredible lady and a sophisticated woman," Dana says, explaining that when Jestine got sick two years ago, she felt compelled to do something. "I thought how terrible if she was gone and nobody knew about her."

While Jestine's "table wine" is sweet iced tea, you also can order a variety of wine, beer and sodas. For the true southerner, YooHoo and a peanut butter and banana sandwich are available. Serious eaters will appreciate the towel-like napkins.

"Southern food with lots of soul" is the slogan here, and the desserts fit that description. Three-layer "true" banana pudding means it has meringue; Coca-Cola Cake is made with Coke syrup and walnuts. Black Magic Cake, a chocolate angel food cake,

___

pecan pie, and coconut cream pie also are available. Our waiter made no bones that the coconut cream pie is the best, so three of our foursome respectfully ordered it and were glad. It's hard to beat thick custard topped with toasted coconut. Still, Susie's verdict on the banana pudding– "It's just like my mother's and grandmother's"– sums up the whole spirit of Jestine's Kitchen.

- Aïda Rogers

Jestine Matthews died shortly after this story appeared in the winter 1997 Sandlapper. While Mrs. Matthews is gone, her influence still infuses her namesake restaurant. Charleston is a city of quality restaurants and Jestine's Kitchen, still run by Dana Berlin, ranks with the best.

P.S. If there's a line outside the Meeting Street entrance, don't panic. It's definitely worth the short wait.

- Tim Driggers

Joseph's Restaurant, Charleston
Charleston County

Joseph's Restaurant, 129 Meeting Street, Charleston; (843) 958-8500. Open Monday-Saturday, 8-11 a.m. for breakfast and from 11:30 a.m.-3 p.m. for lunch. Open Sunday, 9 a.m.-2 p.m. for breakfast only. Reservations recommended. Checks and major credit cards accepted. No smoking. www.josephsofcharleston.com. Inexpensive.

Holy City Nirvana

"Oh my goodness," Paul McCravy said, biting into his Cranberry Bog sandwich at Joseph's Restaurant in Charleston. "*This* may be the best sandwich I've ever had." It's sad to see a grown man cry, but I swear there was a tear welling in Paul's eye. For a brief moment, I thought Paul had been caught up in the Rapture. Seems he had achieved Nirvana with the help of a sun-dried tomato tortilla, filled with grilled chicken, warm spinach, feta cheese, toasted pecans, dried cranberries, and balsamic vinaigrette.

I thought this behavior a bit odd, that is until I chomped down on my oyster po boy sandwich. The only thing I could say was "oh my." I've eaten po boys at Central Grocery and Acme Oyster in New Orleans and long believed they were the ultimate shellfish on a roll. I was wrong. This thing was huge and the relish aioli provided a delicious complement to all those fried oysters packed into the French loaf.

Joseph's has made an art form of serving high quality food in an unassuming atmosphere at prices amazingly modest. "Upscale dining on a lunch budget," Paul observed. It's a formula that has catapulted Joseph's from obscurity eight years ago to rave reviews in *The New York Times*, *Boston Globe*, and on The Food Network.

"Everyone said we wouldn't make it," said Donna Belli, who owns Joseph's with her son and restaurant namesake Joseph Passarini. "It seemed there was a pecking order for Charleston restaurants and new people had a difficult time being accepted." But accepted they were and in a big way. Charleston has embraced Joseph's as a crown jewel in a city where dining is perhaps the favorite pastime.

"We never wanted to be a typical southern restaurant," Donna said. "I had one little old lady tell me that if we didn't serve grits, then we weren't going to make it in Charleston. I said OK, but I'll make grits my way with heavy cream and butter."

Joseph's way means plentiful helpings, consistently good food, and great service. The restaurant is small, with wait staff buzzing hurriedly from kitchen to table. "Not pretentious, but honest and open with its approach to food," culinary expert McCravy said. "Sorta reminds me of my favorite khakis."

The lunchtime menu features the aforesaid Cranberry Bog and the 129 Meeting Street, which is Boar's Head roast beef stacked on a croissant with mozzarella cheese, roasted red peppers, and balsamic syrup. "Everything is made from scratch," said Joseph, who studied at Johnson and Wales culinary school and with Michael Rousell, executive chef for 40 years at Brennan's in New Orleans. "I like to cook the things I like to eat. We make our portions a little larger than normal and our customers seem happy we do. They return over and over again."

Says his mother: "We had a lady who came here for breakfast and lunch seven days a week. If she didn't come, we'd call and make sure she wasn't in the hospital."

Paul and I tried the fried green tomatoes prepared lightly in "frying dust," and found them a tasty treat. Then there was dessert. The beignets were delicious, but then came the Bananas Foster. Oh my. Oh my. For breakfast, the sweet potato pancakes and French toast are favorites, along with six varieties of omelets and three styles of Eggs Benedict.

While dining, ask Donna about the ghost of Mr. White, a lawyer who once practiced in the building and still makes an occasional visit. It seems even ghosts like a great meal.

- Tim Driggers

Juanita Greenberg's Nacho Royale, Charleston
Charleston County

Juanita Greenberg's Nacho Royale, 439 King Street, Charleston, (843) 723-6224. Open daily at 11 a.m., closes at 11 p.m. on Monday-Thursday and remains open until 1 a.m. on Friday and Saturday. The bar stays open until 1:45 a.m. on weekends. Reservations suggested for large parties. Credit cards accepted, but no checks. No smoking. www.juanitagreenbergs.com. Inexpensive.

World Famous Margaritas and Proper Quesadillas

Port cities always have been melting pots. So it shouldn't be unusual that Michael Rabin, a New Yorker of Russian Jewish descent, is serving Mexican food in Charleston. "I know what good food is, that's for sure."

That *is* for sure. Rabin and his wife Edie run Andolini's Pizza as well as the popular Juanita Greenberg's Nacho Royale. It's here where business people, students, tourists, families, and seniors find an affordable, filling Mexican meal and "World Famous" margaritas. Rabin knows good business, too: When he arrived in 1990, he saw no burritos. He proceeded to change that.

"We were in a hole in the wall and we were killing it," he says of his first Mexican restaurant, Juanita Greenberg's Burrito Palace. He opened it on Wentworth Street in 1994, introducing Charleston to its first burrito shop. Then came Juanita Greenberg's Nacho Royale on King Street in 1998. Though Rabin closed the Palace in 2000, customers find the same– but expanded–fare at the Royale. It's a narrow, shoebox-shaped building that leads to a patio in the back. Corona banners hang on exposed brick walls; colored lights decorate the bar. It'd be hard to be uncomfortable here, where brown paper towels are your napkins and meals come on round, aluminum pizza pans. The very name "Juanita Greenberg"–Rabin's stepfather's last name is Greenberg; there is no Juanita–clues you in to Rabin's humor.

Not that he doesn't take cooking seriously. The spicy guacamole and cilantro-rich salsa are homemade. "We don't buy anything packaged," he says. The burritos are packaged, though, in foil with directions on how to eat them. "They're great, but they're sloppy. People don't realize they need to leave it in the wrapper and fold it down." There are four kinds: bean, chicken, sausage and steak. More than one pound each and wrapped in a flour tortilla, the burritos are filled with black beans, Monterey Jack cheese, sour cream and lettuce. Pico, that lively mix of tomatoes, cilantro and red onion, adds an exclamation point to the flavor.

The menu is simple. Besides burritos, Juanita Greenberg's serves quesadillas, taco salads, nachos and Royale nachos. They're either vegetarian–cheese or bean–or meaty, with a choice of chicken, sausage, or steak. Royale nachos include black beans, pico, black olives, jalapenos, lettuce and Monterey Jack cheese, with salsa and sour cream on the side. Juanita Greenberg's nachos are baked, not fried, attracting the health-conscious.

"Coming here means I can sample Mexico without having to go south of the border," observes Joy Simpson, a friend who raises money for The Citadel Foundation. Juanita Greenberg's, she says, knows how to make a quesadilla: "It has your basic food groups—cheese and meat. All the ones that count."

"This is not fast food," advises the menu. "This is real food prepared fresh & fast!" Rabin says his restaurant isn't like some burrito places, where customers watch their meals being prepared and delivered immediately, like a submarine sandwich shop. While you can watch your order being put together, that's where the similarity ends. "We cook it. To make a proper quesadilla, it's gotta cook!"

Rabin has been cooking since high school in Queens. "I know what I say very often to my help and it sums it all up: Anybody can overcook something and anybody can undercook something. But try to cook it just right. When someone tells me they can't cook, it tells me they don't have patience. That's what it's all about."

- Aïda Rogers

Things are really poppin' at Juanita Greenberg's Nacho Royale. Operating partner Amy Olsen tells us a new 50-foot deck opened in February 2007 and, besides offering expanded seating, it's allowed the restaurant to book live music at least once a week. Amy says the margaritas remain "world famous" and their signature quesadillas are still the most popular item on the menu. Amy advises all Juanita Greenberg fans to be on the lookout for the tacos they'll soon be adding to the lineup and to check out the full service bar that's now open. It continues to be a popular hangout for College of Charleston students ("They're our bread and butter," Amy says). Owners Edie and Michael Rabin have added to their flagship Andolini's Pizza chain, with restaurants now on Wentworth Street downtown, James Island, West Ashley, Mount Pleasant, and North Charleston.

- Tim Driggers

Magnolias, Charleston
Charleston County

Magnolias, 185 East Bay Street, Charleston; (843) 577-7771. Open Monday-Thursday, 11:30 a.m.-10 p.m.; Friday-Saturday, 11:30 a.m.-11 p.m., Sunday, 11 a.m.-10 p.m. Reservations encouraged and frequently necessary. Complimentary parking available. Credit cards accepted. No smoking. www.magnolias-blossom-cypress.com. Moderate to expensive.

Where Collards are Classy

It's not easy eating clumpy fried rice from a plastic bowl and writing about Magnolias at the same time. But I've got my notes, my memories and a menu for inspiration, which only further emphasizes the difference between an ordinary egg roll and the marvel created by Donald Barickman, Magnolias' executive chef. At Magnolias the egg roll is "down south," testament to Barickman's belief in serving food of the region. It has collard greens in it.

"This is a very competitive business and you have to be ever-changing," he said. "We're really making an effort of become more southern."

For proof, look at the menu. Pan-fried chicken livers are on the appetizer list, as is barbecue pork with mustard slaw. Tobacco onions come with the veal meatloaf sandwich, and yellow corn relish accompanies the yellow grits cake appetizer. With the smoked strip steak comes a "hash of sweet potatoes," and a succotash of shrimp, butterbeans, yellow corn, and spinach is part of the grilled dolphin entrée.

Collards are everywhere. They come with the smoked pork loin chop, the pan-fried catfish, the salmon filet, and the garlic marinated lamb loin. They're also stuffed in the "Down South Eggroll," which contains chicken and tasso ham. Served with a spicy mustard sauce, red pepper purée and peach chutney, the "Down South Eggroll" is nothing less than a work of art.

But Magnolias itself is a giant work of art, with many pieces of art working within it. It takes your pleasure seriously and functions like a highly efficient machine. It has to; Barickman supervises 25 chefs and 170 employees, some of whom work at Blossom Café, Magnolias' sister restaurant next door. Magnolias serves lunch and dinner every day, seating 170 in three different dining rooms.

"They knew exactly what they wanted to do," said server Jules Olsen about Hospitality Management Group, which owns and operates both restaurants. One look around and you can see she's right; Magnolias is polished and in place. It's impeccable but not intimidating.

"I'd like dinner, but am I underdressed?" a woman in jeans wants to know. "Of course not," she's assured before being seated at a window table. Magnolias caters to tourists and locals and considers itself "dressy casual," Olsen said. Tourists have learned from locals—as well as national and international travel magazines—that Magnolias is *the* place to try. "We try to stay on the cutting edge," Olsen said.

Check out one of Magnolias' most popular entrees, the shrimp and grits. "That's an old tradition but we've added sausage and tasso ham and flavor and gravy," Barickman said. This recipe and 89 others appear in the cookbook *Magnolias: Authentic Southern Cuisine*, first published in July 1995. It also includes suggestions about cookware, ingredients, and ingredient sources.

Magnolias combines Southeast and Southwest. Bright, bold paintings of magnolia leaves and blossoms are a departure from the pastel live oaks and Spanish moss you often see in the Low Country. There are southwestern dishes on the menu, which Barickman is filtering out in his quest to become more Deep South. A new menu will include chicken and dumplings and catfish and chips, along with cornbread loaves and buttermilk biscuits and honey.

Simplicity is why Magnolias has done so well, Barickman says. Plans to duplicate Magnolias or Blossom Café are in the works; he and Thomas Parsell, president of Hospitality Management Group, just have to figure out where, when, and which one.

Heart pine floors were imported from a North Carolina tobacco warehouse for "The Alley" dining room; a custom-built horseshoe bar of antique heart pine and black granite is in the "Veranda Bar." Iron magnolia leaves and blossoms by Dick Averett, a Charleston artist, decorate the handles of the front door, the wall as you walk in, and the hostess table. In the "Gallery," the most formal dining room in the back, "Mama Magnolia" presides. This oil painting has become the restaurant's symbol; you can see her on the restaurants' T-shirts and sweatshirts.

The desserts are as artistic and skillfully rendered as everything else. And as southern: pecan pie with bourbon sauce, berry cobblers with vanilla ice cream, chocolate cake with a benne seed basket and baked butterscotch custard with chocolate sauce and toasted pecans. I caught up with two snowbirds, Diane DeSalvo and Ruth Butterfield of Maine. They skipped the collards earlier, but went full south with desserts. Diane ordered creamy sweet potato pie "because Oprah had it on her show," and Ruth tried the sweet biscuit with strawberries and orange custard sauce. Like many tourists, they asked a local which restaurant to try, and Magnolias was the answer.

At our table, Dolly Patton and I opted for Magnolias' Warm Cream Cheese Brownie with White Chocolate Ice Cream and Chocolate Sauce. Waitress Keri Kirkley put it before us on the table, and we stared—silent, awestruck, transfixed. "It's beautiful," Dolly breathed, and we realized we probably looked like brand new parents.

Barickman's parents were worried about him in his younger days. Apparently he played more than studied in college; it wasn't "hands-on" enough for him. But in his early 20s he left his home in West Virginia for the Culinary Institute of America in

Hyde Park. Soon afterward he made a name for himself as sous chef at the Wine Cellar and executive chef of Carolina's, both in Charleston. Today at Magnolias, Barickman is the father of twins and in his element. I don't think his parents need to worry now.

- Aïda Rogers

Donald Barickman is revolutionary. No, he isn't marching up and down East Bay Street waving the little red book of quotes from Chairman Mao, but he's kindled a revolution nonetheless. His is a culinary upheaval along the lines of Bourdain, Bertolli, and Boulud. Barickman was, and is, an innovator, a chef who inspired the imaginative southern low country cuisines that swept the restaurants of coastal South Carolina in the early 1990s. That style continues front row and center at Magnolias, which calls itself "Charleston's Pioneer for Low-Country Cuisine." Barickman is now Executive Chef at the Magnolias, Blossom, and Cypress restaurant empire of Hospitality Management Group and Donald Drake is the Chef at Magnolias. The Down South Eggroll remains a staple of the lunch menu, while the Carolina Carpetbagger Filet, with fried oysters, green beans, and Madeira and Béarnaise sauces is the bestseller at dinner. Magnolias also features an expansive wine list.

- Tim Driggers

Marina Variety Store & Restaurant, Charleston
Charleston County

Marina Variety Store and Restaurant, 17 Lockwood Drive, Charleston in the Charleston City Marina; (843) 723-6326. Open daily from 6 a.m. until 10 p.m. for breakfast, lunch, and dinner. Reservations accepted for large parties. Credit cards and checks accepted. No smoking. www.varietystorerestaurant.com. Inexpensive to moderate.

Comfort Food In Charleston

Whoever said that a hot bath could cure anything never ate lunch—or supper or breakfast—at the Marina Variety Store in Charleston. Here is a menu with red rice, sweet and hot with sausage; onion rings two inches thick; okra soup with corn, lima beans, and ham hocks. You can hunch over a bowl of she-crab soup and then gaze out at the marsh, where stalky birds will be picking and preening and boats will be rattling at their docks. To my mind, hot food and a good view can make any problem less worrisome.

"You can come here for comfort food, but it's unexpected comfort food," observes my friend and comforter Joy Simpson. Joy knows well how a meal here can prepare you for a satisfying morning church service or a trying afternoon at the office. "They ran a special where you could get a lobster omelet that was just to die for. They have fried gator tails. It's just a little twist on the Mom and Pop hamburgers."

Joy and I slid into a varnished wood booth in the rear, where the iced tea came fast and the Folly River Crab Dip came soon after. It's an Altine family recipe and a local favorite. The Altines, of Greek heritage, have run the Marina Variety Store since 1947, moving to its present location in 1960. It may be one of—if not the—oldest restaurants run by the same family in Charleston.

While spreading crab dip on crackers, we shamelessly ordered two appetizer specials: bacon-wrapped scallops in apricot-mango chutney and oyster pie. Like the rest of the menu, the appetizers represent the restaurant's adherence to progress and tradition. The fried green tomatoes are coated in pecans and served with honey mustard; the Bear Island Shrimp and Grits include grilled sausage with peasant gravy. Meanwhile there's a wealth of old favorites: country fried steak, roast beef, club and BLT sandwiches and a hamburger platter. Today's blue plate special is a smothered chopped sirloin with two sides; the sandwich is turkey melt with smoked Gouda. Catfish, flounder, and a blackened mahi-mahi spinach salad also are available.

Because I live in the middle of the state, there was no question that I'd order seafood. It comes in combinations and platters—fried (in peanut oil), grilled, blackened, and sautéed. The regular Carolina seafoods are here, including softshell crab, when available. Entrées include hushpuppies and a choice of two sides: onion rings, red rice, veggie of the day, fries or fried chips. The fried chips are popular and exceptional.

Comfort food must be served in a comforting environment. The Marina Variety Store is appropriately casual and seafaring, with cafeteria-style plates, ship lanterns hanging overhead, and paper placemats with seashells on them. Come dressed up or not; come alone or on a big date. It's hard to go wrong here.

The Marina Variety Store is located at the Charleston City Marina, and parking is easy. You can stroll to the docks after a filling lunch or breakfast. That might be nice, especially if you've been looking at the sun make sparkles on the water, and gotten sufficiently hypnotized.

- Aïda Rogers

Marina Variety Store and Restaurant continues to be one of Charleston's favorite breakfast spots. With a picturesque waterside view of the Ashley River, diners have the option of arriving by boat to lounge about with coffee cup in one hand and morning newspaper in the other, all while sampling the restaurant's famous crab omelets and shrimp and grits. Mike Altine, Jr. has owned the Marina Variety Store and Restaurant since 1973.

- Tim Driggers

Med Bistro, Charleston
Charleston County

Med Bistro, 90 Folly Road in the South Windermere Shopping Center, West of the Ashley River, Charleston; (843) 766-0323. Open Monday-Friday 11 a.m.-midnight; Saturday, 10:30 a.m.-midnight. Closed Sunday. Reservations requested for large parties. Credit cards accepted. No smoking. www.themedbistro.com. Inexpensive to expensive.

Noisy Conviviality, Atypical Menu

One of the joys of eating alone is sitting at the bar and getting to know the people around you. At Med Bistro, in the South Windermere Shopping Center, the bar is big and stainless steel—the better to sprawl and enjoy the noisy conviviality. "Olive oil for the whole bar!" came a man's voice from three seats down. Oooh, I like this place.

So does Angie Easterby. She's been coming since sixth grade, and made a special point to have lunch here on visits home from Newberry College. Now that she's graduated and back home, and keeping company with bartender Jon Smith, she's even more regular than before. "The food's pretty," she says. She and two girlfriends come every Saturday night, sit at the bar and order pasta. "I like to watch the specials go by. Nothing comes out of that kitchen that doesn't look like it's been prepared." She marvels at a grouper special with garlic mashed potatoes and criss-crossed zucchini sticks. Angie is a potter and painter, so artistic food catches her eye.

Med Bistro isn't only about presentation. It's mainly about good food and drink. Servers wear black T-shirts that say "Got Wine?" and "Got beer?"—testimony to the restaurant's 200-plus wines and 100-plus beers. Walk in the door and you're greeted by shelves of wine. Across from the bar is a refrigerator case of beer. It feels like a lively grocery where the owners decided they might as well prepare food as well as sell it.

"No other restaurant has such an extensive retail selection," general manager Lee Kistler says. "And our ambience—people come here for that."

Though it started selling kosher and Mediterranean-style food when it opened in the late '70s, Med Bistro's menu today is more "American Eclectic," Lee says. Don't look for Low Country cooking here. The closest they got last week was a proscuitto-wrapped filet mignon, served with pan-fried cheese grits, goat cheese-stuffed artichoke hearts, and mushrooms.

I started supper with a soup special—sweet potato chipotle with roasted red pepper. "It's spicy," Jon warned, but what's better on a cold night? A basket of bread comes fast, ready for dipping in your soup. Jon helped me choose the wine, a red Lurton Malbec from Argentina. "Our wines are so inexpensive. We don't mark up but a slim margin," he told me.

Because my lunch had been so monumental, I figured a salad was in my best interest. I ordered the evening's special, a spinach Greek salad with proscuitto-wrapped scallops. Eating it was like plundering a magic forest; I kept poking into olives and chunks of feta, red onions, tomatoes, peppers, and fat scallops. Dressing is a fresh lemon dill vinaigrette.

Med Bistro serves soups, sandwiches, salads, and grill items at lunch. Pastas (in "regular" and "small" portions) are offered in the evening. So are more elaborate specials. Crab cakes are popular; they're pan-seared with basmati rice and sautéed baby spinach in a citrus buerre Blanc. Fresh fish is the emphasis, though: Salmon, flounder, tuna, and grouper are offered, along with a grilled filet mignon and New York Strip. Other popular dishes are the sesame-seared salmon wrap with cucumber salad and soup and bacon-wrapped grilled filet mignon topped with roasted red pepper cheese gratinee, with cheese grits and sautéed spinach.

Angie kept me pleasant company at the bar. We agreed Med Bistro is one of those foolproof destinations where anyone should feel at home. "It has that romantic feel," Angie says. "It's the perfect place to bring your wife or husband for an anniversary, but at the next table, there's a young family with crayons and white paper."

- Aïda Rogers

In the restaurant business, things can change quickly. When Sandlapper *visited in summer 2002, Med Bistro was known as Med-Deli; later it re-invented itself as Med Deli Café. Judy Anagnos sold the restaurant in late July 2007 to Piggly Wiggly supermarket board chairman Joseph T. "Buzzy" Newton and wife Rebecca. Longtime customers of Med Bistro, the Newtons are making their first foray into the restaurant business. No major changes are planned, although it's certain the menu will be beefed up and a wood-burning pizza oven installed. The décor of the 50-plus year restaurant building will also be enhanced. The appetizer menu features the popular crab cakes served with sweet corn compote and herb butter sauce, clams, calamari, hummus, seared scallops, and Portobello fries. There are also four different salads, two soup choices and four sandwich offerings. Entrees include seared tuna, roasted chicken, Rex and Sherry (shrimp and scallops in a Cajun cream sauce), grilled flank steak, salmon, roast pork tenderloin, crab cakes, sautéed shrimp, penne or fettuccine pasta, Catch of the Day, and Chef's Vegetable Plate. These days the servers' black T-shirts say "Great Food," "Great Wine," and "Great Art."*

- *Tim Driggers*

Ms. Jackie's Big Ollie's, St. George
Dorchester County

Ms. Jackie's Big Ollie's, 5530 Memorial Boulevard, St. George; (843) 563-9655. Open Monday-Wednesday, 11 a.m.-4 p.m.; Thursday-Saturday, 11 a.m.-7 p.m. Closed Sunday. No credit cards. Inexpensive.

"Double-Wide Dining At Its Best"

Normally I refer to my friend Paul McCravy as my "Assistant Culinary Expert." But truthfully, he's my own personal J. Wellington Wimpy, a man obsessed and possessed by cheeseburgers. He convinced me to travel the state searching for the best cheeseburger joints, many of which are covered in this book. Paul took the wheel, driving, drooling, completely cheeseburger-mad. One favorite discovery was Ms. Jackie's Big Ollie's in St. George.

We'd read about it on the web site www.hollyeats.com. It rated Big Ollie's cheeseburger with Four Grease Stains. That's Holly Eats lingo for "excellent."

Big Ollie's is in an old, white vinyl mobile home. When we arrived, we found Alexia Garvin placing an order at the window. She lives five miles down the road and has been coming here for breakfast and lunch for 10 years. She often orders the salmon patties and grits for breakfast. "I love them," she said. "They cook real salmon that's nice and brown." Alexia also likes the whiting and grits. "The fish is covered in cornmeal and has a mild taste. The grits are lightly buttered and served with homemade gravy and biscuits."

At lunch, she alternates between cheeseburgers and fish sandwiches. "A bite of the cheeseburger takes me to heaven," she said. "Big Ollie's always has good food and the restaurant is nice and clean."

Observed Paul after some reflection: "Big Ollie's is double-wide dining at its best. It serves the biggest pork chop sandwich in the land. When we tried to photograph this leaning tower on a bun, it fell over twice. If you don't have unhinged jaws, it might be best to eat this monster disassembled."

Big Ollie's also serves fish and chips and deep-fried chicken. "Our food is not greasy and is always well-cooked and fresh," maintains Tori Riley, cook/chef. Specials are served daily. Ours were country ham, Buffalo wings and shrimp, pork chops, shrimp and fish combination, and chicken tenders. Paul ordered the cheeseburger while I opted for the pork chop sandwich. We sat outside on one of the two cement picnic tables. Served on plain white bread, the pork chop sandwich was very good and too huge for one sitting. Paul was ecstatic about the cheeseburger. "It was as good as a cheeseburger could be."

- Tim Driggers

The Mustard Seed, Mt. Pleasant
Charleston County

The Mustard Seed, 1220 Ben Sawyer Boulevard, Mt. Pleasant; (843) 849-0050. Open for lunch Monday-Saturday, 11 a.m.-2:30 p.m.; dinner Monday-Thursday, 5-9:30 p.m. and Friday, 5-10 p.m. Closed Sunday. No reservations. No smoking, but there are benches outside. Credit cards and local personal checks accepted. Inexpensive to moderate.

The Mt. Pleasant Alternative

"That was a terrible movie," Margot is complaining. She doesn't like spending full price for what she considered TV-movie-of-the-week material, and we had just tolerated two hours of blonde silliness in a flick I won't name. Irritated, she plopped across the booth from me at The Mustard Seed, a restaurant as good as the movie was bad.

The basil rosemary bread—served fresh, fast, and hot—was an instant antidote to our sour moods and empty stomachs. On this Friday at 9:30 p.m., the place was hopping and we were starving. We looked around and noted the lively atmosphere. I asked Margot for some adjectives and she complied with "cozy, unique, and alternative." We like those things, and yeah, the sign of alternativeness presented itself in the stack of *Skirt!* magazines on a chair near the door. Don't look for anything mainstream here. From the mustard-colored walls filled with local art (for sale) and lights on the greenery at the windows, The Mustard Seed presents an experience that's funky, educated and fun.

And lucky for us, it won't drain our savings.

"Our most expensive bottle of wine is $25," informed our server, Zachary Dennis. "We *are* in Mt. Pleasant."

Zachary popped the menu board on a chair in front of us and—at this late hour—wiped off some of the specials that had already run out. The remaining ones looked tempting: pan-roasted salmon with asparagus, spinach, tomato and lemon over garlic mashed potatoes, and eggplant lasagna with artichokes, spinach and parmesan topped with tomato-basil sauce. I took Zachary's advice and ordered the linguini with Prince Edward Island mussels with tomatoes, garlic and spinach. Margot decided to order the Fresh Stir Fry vegetables from the menu. This dish is served with black beans and ginger soy sauce on brown rice.

"There's nothing higher than $15 here," says Tom Ford, chef de cuisine and 1991 grad of Johnson & Wales, Rhode Island campus. "That's the most challenging thing, keeping good food at lower prices."

He studied my plate, quickly emptied of its linguini with mussels. "That would be $15 downtown and fish would be $18 or up."

Open since 1996, The Mustard Seed has gained something of a false reputation as a vegetarian place. While it offers several vegetarian dishes, there are much more seafood, pasta, and chicken entrees. The Pecan-Crusted Chicken with honey mustard sauce, fresh vegetables and garlic mashed potatoes is one of the most popular items. Ford says The Mustard Seed serves Mexican, Italian and health food, and nothing is fried. Very little red meat and butter are served.

It's a menu to delight in. The Caesar salad comes with gorgonzola cheese and grilled Portobello mushrooms; the spinach salad is topped with artichoke fritters. The most expensive salad is the pan-roasted asparagus with red onion and walnuts over spinach with gorgonzola cheese and lemon. Soups include chilled gazpacho with herb croutons and roasted onion and garlic with parmesan croutons.

The lunch menu is a bit simpler, though still innovative. Try the Grilled Zucchini Roll with spinach feta, tomato, and guacamole in a grilled flour tortilla; or the Artichoke Gyro, herb-marinated with tomatoes and garlic-lemon mayo on grilled pita.

Owner Sal Parco came to the area from Boston. Since starting The Mustard Seed in Mt. Pleasant—it's in the Sea Island Shopping Center, the oldest in town—he's opened another on James Island. Recently he opened The Blue Mango, also in Mt. Pleasant, which serves southwestern and Asian foods.

Parco obviously has the magic touch. The word is out—with very little advertising—that his restaurants serve good, affordable food in interesting surroundings. Not hurting that reputation at all is pastry chef Jim Smeal. Smeal prepares desserts for Friday and Saturday nights only; regulars know to come early to get the specials, desserts, and wines before they run out.

Tarts are his thing. A mango-raspberry tart was available when Margot and I were there; but typically, they already had run out. Still, a wedge of lemon pie was in the case, and we were given a sample of its not-too-sweet, not-too-sour yumminess. The Mustard Seed's signature dessert is white chocolate banana cream tart. Another favorite dessert is coconut cream pie.

Now, what was that movie about?

- Aïda Rogers

True to its reputation, The Mustard Seed remains a largely vegetarian hangout. A new chef, Drew Taylor, creates a menu that stays constantly fresh and vibrant. Popular items continue to be the fresh fish and crab cakes and a lot of folks are ordering the Fettuccini Carbonara. Owner Sal Parco redecorated the place here and there and continues to add to his restaurant empire. There are now three Mustard Seeds in the area, including Summerville, and he also owns both Italian (Sette) and Mexican (Uno Mas) restaurants, The Long Point Grille, The Village Bakery, and The Boulevard Diner.

- Tim Driggers

Old Firehouse Restaurant, Hollywood
Charleston County

The Old Firehouse Restaurant, 6350 Highway 162, Hollywood; (843) 889-9512. Open Tuesday-Saturday, 5-9 p.m. Closed Sunday and Monday. Reservations not accepted. Credit cards accepted. No smoking. Moderate.

Fine Food in an Old Firehouse

"You absolutely must visit the Old Firehouse," Ellen White gushed. Now, while I value Ellen's sage counsel, there were a few things I had on my list of priorities before traipsing off to the Hollywood community near Charleston and grabbing a bite at the Old Firehouse Restaurant. After all, I still hadn't had the opportunity to sit down with the Pope and discuss that Da Vinci Code thing, play rhythm guitar with The Hives, take the stage of La Scala as Rodolfo in *La Boheme*, or debate String Theory with Stephen Hawking. But after dining at the Old Firehouse, I find those ambitions simply misplaced priorities. Ellen is right; the Old Firehouse is a restaurant not to be missed.

Hollywood is a short 20-mile jaunt from Charleston via U.S. 17. About 15 miles from the city, veer left onto S.C. 162 and in a few minutes you're at the Old Firehouse. The restaurant is located in—yes—an old fire station that was abandoned in the mid 1980s, became an Italian restaurant for a spell, was abandoned again, left for dead, and brought back to life in 2002, by owner/chef Bill Twaler and wife Lia Sanders. Bill, an Iowa native who graduated from Johnson and Wales in Charleston, cooked at the Old Post Office restaurant on Edisto Island. Lia, a low country girl, had worked there with Bill as a waitress. When Bill and Lia married in 2002, they pursued their dream of owning a restaurant to a dilapidated building smack dab in the middle of the town of Hollywood

"The building was a complete mess when we started renovations," Lia said. "In fact, it was plain filthy." Despite the daunting challenges of restoration, the couple persevered, deciding to utilize the structure's firehouse history as the theme for their restaurant. Adding firehouse memorabilia to the red brick interior, the decor has been constantly augmented by customers bringing Lia and Bill firehouse items to enhance the motif. Although the Old Firehouse is anything but a pizzeria, the leftover brick oven is smartly incorporated for both practical and decorative touches.

While the firehouse theme provides an arresting dining backdrop, it's the food that's the real draw. "Our menu is all Bill," Lia said. "It's what he was familiar with cooking in Charleston and on Edisto Island for both locals and tourists. We have a big variety of servings; you can find just about anything here." Indeed you can. My assistant culinary expert, Paul McCravy, ordered the Whole Crispy Flounder ("our biggest seller" Lia says), and to say he enjoyed his entree is a vast understatement. I don't think the man stopped smiling during his entire meal. "We use only fresh flounder, never frozen or farm-raised," Bill said. "It's scored so you don't get a bone with each bite and topped with a peach-jalapeno sauce and served with grits." While Paul was stuffing himself, I casually mentioned to Bill my on-going quest to find the best cheese-burger in South Carolina. He took this as a personal challenge. Bill dashed to the open kitchen and prepared an awesome cheeseburger, his 10-ounce certified Angus beef St. John's Burger, served on a homemade roll. It was fantastic, the best I have tasted in the low country. Both Paul and I were convinced Bill is a cooking genius, a chef with an imagination to match his incredible talent.

Another menu favorite is the Hollywood Scallops. "Combining sautéed scallops with country ham and grits is so down-home and southern," Bill said. "We add some garlic and toss in some parmesan cheese and finish it with parmesan grits, a mix of yellow and white grits that aren't finely ground." The Meggett Chicken, seasoned chicken sautéed with pepper and onion, then topped with country ham and provolone cheese and served with Bill's made-from-scratch mashed potatoes, is another popular choice, as are the Edisto Shrimp and Grits, Crab Artichoke Cakes, and Black and Blue Flank Steak. Ellen, who owns a vacation condominium on nearby Edisto Island, rec-ommends the Edisto Shrimp Scampi and the Arugula Salad.

As Paul and I were finishing our meal, waitress Tammy Smith rushed over and said, "ask about dessert." That turned out to be a great piece of advice. "My Coconut-Pecan Cream Cake and Chocolate Surprise Cake are always on the menu," Lia said. "My customers would be really upset if we didn't have them." I tried the coconut cake and Paul opted for the chocolate. They were absolutely delicious, a perfect topping to a wonderful dining experience.

Ellen tells this story about her first visit to the Old Firehouse. "I had brought my Connecticut friends with me and they were indeed shocked that we could find a place like this in the middle of the low country," she said. "The prices are fair and the owner/chef is a master to watch in action. The atmosphere is like you have stepped into some-one's casual kitchen and are watching them cook. He is meticulous about every detail of his work. It was the most delightful evening I had spent in a long time." Ellen, you won't get any argument from me. I can't wait to go back.

- Tim Driggers

Old Towne Restaurant, Charleston
Charleston County

Old Towne Restaurant, 229 King Street, Charleston; (843)723-8170. Open Monday through Thursday, 11 a.m.-10 p.m. and Fridays and Saturdays, 11 a.m.-11 p.m. Sunday brunch is 10 a.m.-2 p.m. Credit cards and checks are accepted. Reservations requested. No smoking. www.oldtownerestaurant.com. Inexpensive to moderate.

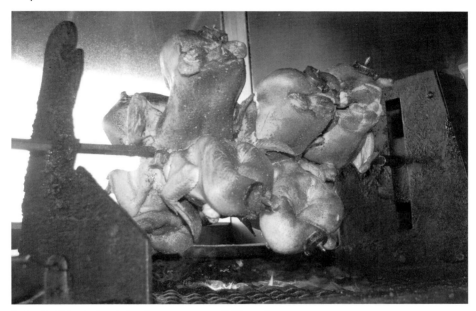

Rotisserie chicken in the window draws customers to Old Towne Restaurant.

But Did He Find a Greek Girl to Marry?

There are so many outstanding restaurants in Charleston and another success story awaits at 229 King Street, where Old Towne Restaurant has been thrilling the taste-buds since 1972. Athan Fokas was a child then, a bus boy who grew up working at the restaurant run by his father Spiros and his uncle, Steve Ferderigos. Now 40, he's part-ners with his uncle and managing the restaurant. He's also opened a Greek restaurant of his own in North Charleston called North Towne, a bit spiffier in looks and with a more expansive seafood menu, and Zeus Grill and Seafood in Mt. Pleasant. But we met him where it all began, in a booth just feet away from the famous window where that mesmerizing chicken turns over and over in its spit. That's the Greek chicken, the most popular item on the menu.

The secret, Athan says, is the restaurant's special spices and the three hours spent for roasting. The Greek willingness to devote that much time to cooking is what makes their food so good, he believes. "Most authentic" are the words he hears the most.

Old Towne is famous across South Carolina, Athan said. "When people from the upper part of the state want to know where the Omni is, people tell them, 'Well, do you know where Old Towne is?' And they do."

Despite the popularity of the Greek Chicken, the restaurant often is recognized as having the best hamburger in Charleston. Chef Louis Osteen of Pawleys Island can attest to that. He was leaving as we were coming in. Later we nabbed him for a few comments. "It's good and it's cheap," he said of Old Towne and its hamburger plate. "You get a bowl of soup and a Greek salad with plenty of Greek spices on it. And then you get the hamburger with French fries or what they call Greek potatoes, which is kinda hash browns."

We didn't get the hamburger. Kathy Britzius, director of the Charleston Restaurant Association, got her usual, the Greek chicken, which comes with Greek potatoes and a Greek salad. I was treated to Steve's Special. This is the Pu Pu platter of the Greek nation, the pride of Old Towne. Simply put, it's a pile of food and ideal for a family. If you're alone, you can have the Super for 1. It includes a gyro, shishkabob, shrimp, pork, chicken, potatoes, a Greek salad and pita bread on the side. This dinner should be approached with caution and joy; make sure you're wearing loose-fitting clothes, and don't ruin it with guilt. This is food to celebrate.

Finish the festivities with one of three desserts. Try the Galaktobouriko, an egg custard square topped with filo, dripping syrup. Baklava, of course, is also available.

Other Mediterranean wonders are here: mousaka, pasticio, stuffed cabbage and pork and lamb kabobs with Greek shrimp. But there are chicken liver plates, spaghetti and chef salads, too. Lunch and supper are served seven days a week.

Greek was Athan's first language, and he plans to follow Old World tradition his parents set before him. One day he'll marry a girl from Greece, and he hopes his son will carry on the business. Despite its popularity with tourists, Old Towne has always enjoyed a loyal local clientele. "That's something almost all successful restaurants have," Osteen said. "LLC, it's called in the trade." He laughed. "I just made that up."

- Aïda Rogers

Since we last caught up with Athan Fokus, he'd added a grocery store to the Old Towne Restaurant, where you can take home a jar of his renowned Greek spices, Greek salad dressing, Old Towne Calamata Olives, and Old Towne Pepperoccini. He's also offering curbside takeout of any item from the grocery or menu. One last note: Athan married a Greek girl. They have three sons.

- *Tim Driggers*

Peninsula Grill, Charleston
Charleston County

The Peninsula Grill, 112 North Market Street, Charleston; (843) 723-0700. Open Sunday-Thursday, 5:30-10 p.m.and on Friday and Saturday, 5:30-11 p.m. Credit cards accepted. Reservations recommended. No cell phones. Business attire and jackets recommended. No smoking. www.peninsulagrill.com. Expensive to very expensive.

Dessert Time with the Chicks

There are two things professional women talk about when they're out for drinks and dinner. One is their jobs. The other is their mothers. And so it was that warm January night in Charleston, when two buddies and I gathered at Peninsula Grill to feast and fret. "My mother likes the idea of me more than the reality of me,"stated "Jo," a former classmate who, in the fifth grade, briefly changed her name to match her favorite *Little Women* heroine.

"So does mine," agreed "Sally," who is fraught with career frustrations.

Just as I was trying to boost morale with my remedy for fun—having a beer in the shower—eight hands swooped down bearing plates of glory. On one: The Ultimate Coconut Cake, a snowy vision in six layers. On another: Chocolate Extravaganza, multiple levels of cheesecake, mousse, fudge cake, and mocha butter cream, topped with a chocolate crescent and served with a shot of cold milk. (That shut Sally up.) The Banana Panna Cotta Pudding was a mound of caramel lusciousness, and the White Chocolate Espresso Parfait was so cute with its spun sugar-wrapped chocolate straw that the three of us stared at it stupefied.

Now, what were we complaining about?

"Coming to Peninsula Grill and not getting dessert is like going to Disney World without seeing Mickey Mouse," said our server, Steve Palmer, who is almost as good-looking as the desserts. But Steve only got a glance from us, because this is the truth: Men, moms, and work don't mean much when it's dessert time with the chicks.

"Sin on a stick," Jo declared. "Heaven," breathed Sally. But when I asked Jo for details on the banana pudding, she got stuck. (And this from a woman who raises millions for higher education.) Finally, this stumbling observation emerged:

"Well," she said, tasting and pausing, "it's an excellent dish for people who love," and she paused again, "bananas."

Bless her. She gave me the key to describing the desserts. They're full of themselves. The coconut cake is coconutty. The Chocolate Extravaganza is chocolatey and I'm sure the plate of lemon treats is lemony. When we come back, we'll sample that and the Vanilla Bean-Ginger Brulee, sorbet assortment and cheese plate. Why visit an art museum when you can gaze and graze so happily?

"Fun" is chef Robert Carter's word for the desserts. "I want them to put a smile on people's faces. So many people skip the dessert portion, so I end up buying a lot of desserts for people."

Besides being gorgeous, they taste good. Carter's desire for great flavor combined with his pastry chef's European sensibilities are why the desserts score so well.

Not that you'd want to skip the appetizers and entrees, or the wines. Peninsula Grill has about 300, enough and of such quality to win *Wine Spectator's* "Award of Excellence." But that's just one of the many accolades Carter and his restaurant has acquired in its history. Assurances that the food is great have come from *Esquire, Playboy, The Los Angeles Times,* and *The Atlanta Journal-Constitution.*

Located in Planters Inn at the Market, Peninsula Grill serves upscale American food in a muted, interesting environment. The designer juxtaposed Charleston's historic formality with its coastal casualness. On the velvet walls are portraits of pale, unsmiling people from centuries ago. On the floor is sea grass carpeting. Carter likes the painting of the horse with a mule's head.

Sally, Jo, and I started with signature appetizers of wild mushroom grits with Low Country Oyster Stew (with plump oysters in a brown, seasoned broth), lobster tempura with cucumber spaghetti and sesame aioli (light and yummy) and the jumbo lump crab, tomato and spinach salad with fried green tomatoes (sweet and tangy). As soon as Ed McMahon calls, we'll try the Osetra Caviar, Southern Service, which comes with fried green tomatoes.

That was a hit with former president George Bush, Carter recalls. "He liked it so much he came three rooms over to ask me what was under the caviar."

Bush was at a private party Carter was catering. Celebrities aren't rare at Peninsula Grill. On the evening we visited, a Wednesday night so lively you'd think it was Saturday, Vanna White was in attendance. We tried to be discreet in our search operations, visiting the restroom for a decent peek.

Entrees include fish, fowl, game, pork, and seafood. Our threesome selected the benne seed-crusted rack of New Zealand lamb, pan-roasted Muscovy duck and bourbon-grilled jumbo shrimp. Less expensive items include seared mountain trout, salmon and grilled chicken.

"I'd put my food up against anybody's for flavor," asserts Carter, a Johnson and Wales graduate who has cooked all over the Southeast. "I'm certainly not trying to do Charlie Trotter-type food here; it's not going to be as perfectly presented and all that. But if you close your eyes and eat, it will be bursting with flavor."

It looked good to us. Asparagus fanned out from the wild mushroom potatoes that accompanied the lamb. Shrimp came with hopping john, creamed corn and lobster basil hushpuppies. Spinach and smoked bacon potato gratin accompanied the duck.

But more important to us, it tasted good. Between the food, conversation, cold medication, and yes, the wine, Sally, Jo, and I had a wonderful time. And for that, Peninsula Grill, we thank you.

- Aïda Rogers

The New York Times *said the Peninsula Grill "may be Charleston's most sophisticated restaurant with wines to match." One of this book's benefactors, Beegie Truesdale, flew to Charleston from the West Coast to dine after reading a smash review in* The Los Angeles Times. *The Peninsula Grill is that good. Let's pretend we have a reservation. After a glass of Veuve Cliquie Ponsardin Brut, we try the signature Wild Mushroom Grits and Low Country Okra and Tomato Soup. Then what for an entree? Shall it be the Bourbon Grilled Jumbo Shrimp, Crispy "Craklin" Pork Osso Bucco, the Grilled Boneless "Berkshire" Pork Chop, Pan Seared and Sliced Muscovy Duck Breast, Sautéed Jumbo Sea Scallops, Benne Crusted Rack of New Zealand Lamb, or one of their steak and seafood selections? Heck, I'll order them all! If you forget dessert, Chef Carter will ship his grandmother's recipe for Ultimate Chocolate Cake or Ultimate Coconut Cake for a couple of C-Notes. Might sound a tad high, but not after you've eaten at the Peninsula Grill.*

- Tim Driggers

The Sea Biscuit Café, Isle of Palms
Charleston County

The Sea Biscuit Café, 21 J.C. Long Boulevard on the Isle of Palms; (843) 886-4079. Open for breakfast Tuesday-Friday, 6-11 a.m. and for lunch Tuesday-Friday, 11:30 a.m.-2:30 p.m. Open for breakfast Saturday and Sunday, 7:30 a.m.-1 p.m. Closed on Monday. No credit cards. No reservations. No smoking. Inexpensive.

Breakfast on the Beach

It'd be hard to maintain a bad mood at The Sea Biscuit Café, particularly at breakfast. Here you can drink coffee and read the paper, listen to the clink of china, watch the breeze riffle through the hair of adorable young children.

In this instance, the adorable young children are my nieces Charlotte and Paige. They've wisely ordered (well, their mother ordered) pancakes. The Sea Biscuit is kid-friendly, as proven by those pancakes. They've been turned into smiley faces with strawberry noses, banana eyes and other fruit features. It's a fun touch, indicative of why so many people love this place.

"We come all the time," says Tyler Small Harris, an Augusta resident who spends summers and holidays at Isle of Palms. "The atmosphere is nice and the food is excellent." Right now, Tyler is on the porch holding 10-month-old Tatum, another pancake eater. Tyler usually orders Eggs Benedict or blueberry pancakes if they're available. "I like the way they garnish. They don't just dump on the plate."

So true. I've ordered a house special, Crabcake Benedict. It's crabby and wonderful, and the fruit assortment is bright and glorious. Likewise, a thick slice of ripe tomato adorns a breakfast of eggs and smoked sausage, bacon, country ham, salmon patties, and corned beef hash. The Sea Biscuit is special without being frou-frou, no doubt a reflection of its down-to-earth, slightly bohemian owner.

"It's plain, simple food," Brenda Smith says. "We don't have a lot of coffees and espresso. I call it 'country yuppy.'"

Brenda started the restaurant in 1986 when she noticed there were no breakfast places on Isle of Palms or Sullivan's Island. Business was good from the beginning. After closing six months after Hurricane Hugo, she rebuilt it exactly the way it was.

These days, people wait a half-hour or more for breakfast on weekends; some come after church. "We did 360 people two Sundays ago," Brenda reports. For a 48-seater, that's pretty good.

At our table, breakfast is leisurely and noisy. We're on the screened porch where two fans keep things breezy and comfortable. A chalkboard menu lists the specials: banana nut and raisin bread French toast, veggie quiche and bacon/mushroom and ham/mushroom omelettes. The most expensive items are shrimp and gravy, corned beef hash (homemade and boiled from scratch), country ham and Crabcake Benedict. A variety of omelettes and biscuits are available.

The Sea Biscuit also serves lunch. Crab soup, salads, sandwiches and burgers are on the menu, along with a handful of entrees. Big sellers are the Greek salad and crabcake sandwich.

The Sea Biscuit has been patronized by Jimmy Buffet and Kyle Petty. But Brenda doesn't care much about celebrities. "People who come here are all special, and I try to treat everybody the same." Her finest moment came in 1994, when *The New York Times* included The Sea Biscuit on its list of "off the beaten path" places to eat. "I was so proud. It was like, finally, a coming of age." Customers from Florida, Atlanta, and Chicago clipped that article and brought it to her when they visited. "That means more to me than someone famous coming in."

A flowing-haired mermaid is The Sea Biscuit's logo. Artist Suzanne Schmidt created her from steel as a wall sculpture. Now she decorates the porch wall and menu.

What's her name? "She's supposed to be me," Brenda said, and laughed. "The face part, anyway. The tail part is much larger than that."

- Aïda Rogers

What's the old saying, something like "breakfast is the most important meal of the day"? Let me amend that adage somewhat: "Breakfast at The Sea Biscuit Café is the best thing that can happen to your day." We wrote about The Sea Biscuit in the fall of 1998, but always visit when staying overnight on the Isle of Palms. Everything is the same as it always has been and that's just fine with us.

– Tim Driggers

Skoogie's, Mt. Pleasant
Charleston County

Skoogie's, 840-C Coleman Boulevard, Mt. Pleasant; (843) 884-0172. Open Monday-Saturday, 10:30 a.m.-4 p.m. Closed on Sunday. No reservations. No credit cards; cash and check only. No smoking, but picnic tables outside for smokers. Inexpensive.

Milkshake Days in Mt. Pleasant

After a fun vacation in Mt. Pleasant, Sunday arrived and it was time for my sister Margot and me to return home. Naturally, all the leave-the-beach-and-go-home days are beautiful. It was what I call a "Convertible Day" or a "Milkshake Day," just right for joyrides in a ragtop, listening to upbeat pop music and slurping a thick one. Breezy, sunny, perfect.

Well, we didn't have a convertible or the kind of music I like. But we did have a sunroof and a CD of *Into the Woods* (Margot's a theater person). And best of all, we had Skoogie's, that informal bastion of hot dogs, shakes and fries.

"Jiggs told us about it," Margot said when I mentioned I'd like to hit a few restaurants for this column while we were in town. "We'll have to get a milkshake."

Jiggs is our brother-in-law, and we still haven't figured out how he knows about these places. He's the one who guided me to Mac's Drive-In in Pendleton, where I was introduced to his concept of Thousand Island salad dressing on cheeseburgers. Here, where the hot dogs are 100-percent beef Vienna franks from Chicago, the Skoogie Dog seemingly comes with everything except that. Feeling patriotic, Margot and I both ordered one.

A Skoogie Dog comes with mustard, relish, onions, sauerkraut, hot pepper, kosher dill, provolone cheese, tomato and celery salt on a steamed poppy seed bun. You also can get chili dogs, footlongs, Italian sausage dogs, German Bratwurst dogs, Polish dogs and the "Homewrecker," which is the same as a Skoogie Dog but with a quarter pound of "dynamite dog."

We also ordered chili cheese fries and root beer ("Root Beer Days" often coincide with "Milkshake Days"). We agreed that we got a lot of food for a little money.

At Skoogie's, you order at the counter and take a number. While Margot and I waited, we took a look around. Located in a renovated McDonald's, the restaurant is casual-plus. A surfboard hangs from the ceiling, a beach scene adorns one wall and arcade games await anyone who wants to play. Skoogie's slogan is "The Best Serving The Best Since 1979."

A bar area on the side invites those who like beer with their food. Besides hot dogs, Skoogie's serves chicken wings and deli and sub sandwiches.

On this early Sunday afternoon, Skoogie's was crowded with all kinds of people—a father and son after church, students eating pizza, a couple in shorts with a baby.

By the time our order was called, we were too hungry to pick up the plastic utensils. That means we ate those chili cheese fries with our fingers. Skoogie's specializes in roll-up-your-sleeves food, where the gratification comes fast and messy. It wasn't long before we were wearing part of what we ordered.

But we didn't care; we were going to be in the car the next few hours. We stared at the menu above the counter, eyes focused on the milkshake section. Would it be vanilla, chocolate, strawberry, or cappuccino? Margot was resolute. "Chocolate," she said. "Make it a malt."

I wiggled and squirmed and finally chose strawberry. We grabbed our shakes and got in the car, Columbia-bound.

And somehow, leaving the beach on a beautiful day didn't seem so bad.

- Aïda Rogers

Owner Jeff Argenio still cooks those great Vienna Beef hot dogs, which the menu proclaims "for which we are frankly famous." His weenie menu includes the all-the-way Skoogie Dog, the Skoogie Chili Dog, the jumbo "Homewrecker," Chili Wrecker, basic Naked Dog (mustard and ketchup only), the Polish Sausage Dog and the Skoogie Polish with chili. Jeff serves a variety of deli and hot sandwiches. Try the Skoogie Reuben or Hot Pastrami and add an order of chili cheese fries. Then you'll see why Skoogie's calls itself the "Best Little Deli South of Chicago."

- *Tim Driggers*

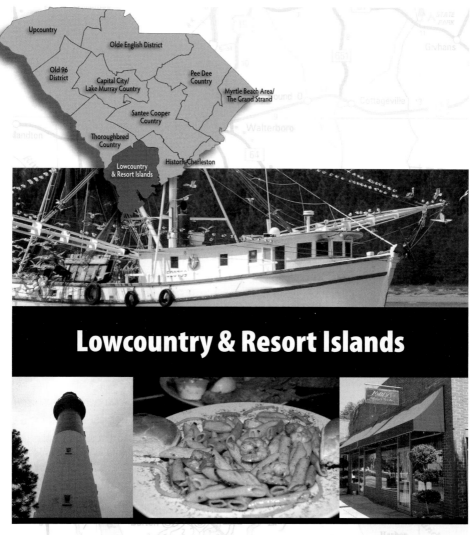

Upcountry

Olde English District

Old 96 District

Capital City/ Lake Murray Country

Pee Dee Country

Myrtle Beach Area/ The Grand Strand

Santee Cooper Country

Thoroughbred Country

Lowcountry & Resort Islands

Historic Charleston

Lowcountry & Resort Islands

Beaufort, Colleton, Hampton & Jasper Counties

Charley's Crab, Hilton Head Island
Beaufort County

Charley's Crab, 2 Hudson Road, Hilton Head Island; (843) 342-9066. Open Monday-Saturday, 11:30 a.m.-9 p.m. Reservations recommended. Credit cards accepted, but no checks. No smoking. www.muer.com and www.landryrestaurants.com. Moderate to expensive.

Digging for Gold - Er, Seafood

Ain't it great to be on vacation? Schedules disappear and fun beckons. Why not sleep late? Why not dawdle until your stomach says howdy?

Two good friends and I wandered into Charley's Crab one breezy May afternoon, ready for lunch. It was after 2 and the place had almost cleared out, but the friendly staff ushered us to a patio table. From here we could gaze across Skull Creek to Pinckney Island, watch the pelicans, and discuss which shrimp boat we wanted. While calypso music played, we languished over the menu and quizzed our server about the favorites. We quickly learned the crabcake appetizer was voted best on the island and that it's made with 99-percent lump crabmeat and 1-percent filler. How could we not order that?

Firm and spicy, the crabcakes are served with a mayonnaise-based sauce of Creole mustard, lemon juice, scallions, and parsley. Other recommended appetizers are the fried green tomatoes, served with warm rock shrimp and crawfish salsa, pepperjack cheese and chipotle cream; and the buttermilk fried calamari, tossed with calamata olives and banana peppers.

Seafood is definitely the main attraction at Charley's Crab, with a variety of fresh fish: mahi mahi, halibut, swordfish, salmon, and even mountain trout and catfish. But there is Lamb Osso Bucco, a burger, club sandwich, and Thai chicken wrap for those who need something different. Our threesome have no problem with seafood, so plundering this menu was like digging for gold. We emerged with an order for she-crab soup, catfish fingers, and a softshell crab sandwich, served on a Kaiser roll with lemon remoulade sauce.

The she-crab soup was unforgettably presented. Our server brought a cup of the crabmeat and put it in the bowl, then poured the pink, herbed broth over it. It was enough to shut up our chattering trio for at least one minute.

Charley's Crab is one of about 20 restaurants in the Chuck Muer "collection" of dining establishments. An avid commercial fisherman and brilliant businessman, Muer left his job at IBM in 1964 at age 26. He started a series of seafood restaurants in his home state of Michigan. Today there are Chuck Muer restaurants in six states. Charley's Crab Hilton Head is the only one in the Carolinas, and it's different from the rest. Only a few items on the menu are the same: gazpacho, garlic bread, chowder, crabcakes, and key lime pie. The Hilton Head restaurant is more casual. Some customers come by boat and jet ski; shorts and tennis shoes are allowed.

Charley's Crab is big. With three dining rooms, the open-air deck and two screened-in porches, it can accommodate families and large parties. A good-sized bar is available, and so is a large wine list. But size doesn't preclude quality. This is a place of special touches—ketchup comes in stainless steel cups, mint chocolate chip cookies come with your bill. The breadbasket comes fast, filled with biscuits and cornbread. Desserts are gorgeous; the macadamia nut coconut cream pie is a thriller.

The restaurant has a mystery: Founder Muer, his wife and crew disappeared in a storm in the Bermuda Triangle. They later were declared dead.

He's sure to approve of this newest addition: Charley's Crab Hilton Head is stunning: amber-colored, globe-like lights from Israel, mosaic tile walls made of Italian glass, railings created from ship refuse. Large canvas murals of crabs adorn the walls; lobsters prowl in a large tank. A copper crab sculpture and fountain greet you as you cross the boardwalk into the front door. Gardeners will enjoy the massive pots of flowers and trees outside.

While my pals ordered the key lime pie—a smooth, yellow creation with whipped cream on a graham cracker crust—I found my own personal heaven dipping the garlic bread into the she-crab soup. It was now 3:20 p.m. The ceiling fans whirred and Jimmy Buffet songs played. Soon we'd stroll down the dock to look at the boats. That'd be our daily exercise.

- Aïda Rogers

Chef Patrick Marker has fashioned a menu featuring Carmelized Catfish, Carolina Rainbow Trout, Q'ued Tuna, Dynamite Mahi Mahi, Macadamia Encrusted Mahi Mahi, Salmon in Puff Pastry, Shrimp Fresca, Alaskan King Crab Legs, Australian Coldwater Lobster Tail, Live Main Lobster, and Coconut Macadamia Encrusted Shrimp. Then there's the Low County She-Crab Soup, selections from the raw bar, and appetizers like Corn Dusted Fried Oysters, Buttermilk Fried Calamari, and Maryland Style Crab Cakes. Landlubbers can try the Carpetbagger filet mignon with fried oysters, the Filet Mignon with Cabernet demi-glace, New York Strip Steak, Tomato Basil Chicken, Cajun Chicken Tortellini, and Chicken Marsala. Charley's Crab is now part of the Landry's Restaurants empire.

- *Tim Driggers*

Charlie's L'Etoile Verte, Hilton Head Island
Beaufort County

Charlie's L'Etoile Verte, 8 New Orleans Road, Hilton Head Island; (843) 785-9277. Open Monday, 5:30-9 p.m. for dinner and Tuesday-Saturday for lunch, 11:30 a.m.-2 p.m., and dinner, 5:30-9 p.m. Closed on Sunday. Reservations recommended for dinner. www.charliesofhiltonhead.com. Moderate to expensive.

Food, Fun, and a Great Cobb Salad

More likely than not, people love a restaurant because they love the people in it. People love Charlie's L'Etoile Verte on Hilton Head Island for three reasons: Charlie, Charlie's wife Nancy, and Leah, who is not just a waitress but a heroine.

The food, of course, is wonderful. But the people...We pause now in a moment of French-like rapture, lips in a kiss," La Vie en Rose" in our ears...*exquizeeeeet*! Charlie Golson is straight-faced and humorous, good-looking and good-cooking. Adulation, awards, and owning his own restaurant after years of cheffing in hotels haven't puffed him up a bit. "It's not a dream," he said. "It's just high blood pressure."

Nancy is ebullient and divine, laughing and talking and eating and passing around food and gossip. Nancy believes in French bread and rich desserts, and she believes food and fun should always go together. That happens at Charlie's.

Leah—well, I didn't meet Leah. Sanin is her last name; people don't seem to use last names here. But I heard about her. Heard about how she babysits the children on the island, sews for people, and drives senior citizens where they need to go. If she doesn't have a table for two, she'll put two couples—strangers to each other—at a table for four, knowing they'll make friends. When she cut two tendons in her hand, customers overwhelmed her with cards, flowers, and candy. Leah is definitely well-loved on Hilton Head.

Maybe it's just as well I didn't meet her, because there was so much talk at the table I couldn't keep up with it. Nor could I keep up with the enormous Cobb Salad, which is so popular people come to Charlie's just for that. "If we're out of it, they'll walk out the door," waitress Erica Phipps told us. "They're adamant. I've come in and just pouted because they were out."

I tasted why. The Cobb Salad is a winning combination of tomatoes, avocado, turkey, bacon, boiled eggs, and romaine, iceberg, and leaf lettuce. The dressing is tomato vinaigrette—homemade, of course. It also has a cheese from Wales called Caerphily, something Charlie introduced to the island. It's become such a hit that local cheese stores stock it now. A veritable mountain, the Cobb Salad is so big most people take half home for supper. At the price Charlie charges, it's a good deal.

A bit pricier on the evening menu are domestic rack of lamb, fish entrees, the filet mignon with jalapeno butter, and veal prime rib with wild mushroom sauce. The menu is handwritten daily and reflects what's fresh on the market.

This is a French bistro, one that prides itself not on trendy food but on solid, hearty food prepared well. At lunchtime, you'll see plenty of men. "Their wives are so skinny and they know they're going to have carrots at night, so they come here and eat fried flounder," Nancy said. That would be Flounder Meuniere, sautéed and finished with a white wine and lemon juice sauce. Charlie does the same with grouper.

"No cheeseburgers" is something of a motto at Charlie's, which bears a sign saying such in its window. Nor will you get sandwiches. But for lunch, you'll find a variety of salads, omelettes, appetizers and desserts, as well as daily specials. Chicken crepes and fish cakes are favorites; lamb chili with black beans is Nancy's preference. The salsas include pineapple, tomato and avocado, corn and ginger, and black bean.

Nancy doesn't believe in stuffiness. Artwork constantly changes. Nancy and Leah make new tablecloths, and a huge spray of gladiolus is always on the bar. Gladiolus is common in France, and the Golsons aim for that French conviviality.

"If you've traveled to France, you really feel you've got a holiday for a few hours when you come in and eat," said Dotti Trivison, food editor at *The Island Packet*. Dotti and her husband retired to Hilton Head from Cleveland and have made Charlie's a regular haunt. They love the wine, they love the food, and like everybody else, they love the people.

Open 20-plus years, Charlie's has played an important part in the lives of its patrons. Susan and John Treadway got engaged here—her ring came in a chocolate torte—and later they brought their children. Now it's their daughter's favorite place. It's clearly a place for locals, and some of them, John told me, don't like the idea of magazine reporters writing it up.

But Charlie's has been exposed before, recently winning an award from *Wine Spectator* magazine. And good news, like bad, somehow finds a way of spreading.

We were spreading Charlie's Pâté Maison on French bread and passing around spicy conch fritters when I was there. There was a lot of food and talk and laughing all around, but I managed to pick up a few facts: The restaurant is named after one Charlie loved in Paris, where he lived for a year; and former President Clinton and his family had dinner there during a Renaissance Weekend.

Nancy is still laughing at how daughter Margaret kept taking coffee and fresh whole grain bread to the Secret Servicemen outside. "On the way home, Margaret was in awe and kept saying, 'I can't believe the president hugged me,' " Nancy said.

As for me, I couldn't believe I had eaten all I did (well, I do), especially when we tried all the desserts: blueberry cobbler, bread pudding, crème caramel, and sailor's trifle. Chocolate desserts are a specialty; three are available each night.

Turns out the Golsons are as good as their food. It's not unusual for Charlie to make special meals for sick patrons; Dotti said she almost cried when he came to the hospital with a tray of all the things she likes. When Hurricane Hugo struck, the staff made a huge chicken and pork perlo and carried it to the devastated communities in the Francis Marion National Forest.

Still, my favorite thing about Charlie's L'Etoile Verte is Nancy's attitude about bread. To her, bread is something that should be fast and freely given; at Charlie's everyone gets a basket as soon as possible. Not so at a well-known North Carolina inn, where the Golsons had an expensive birthday dinner. Management was stingy with bread, and Nancy still talks about it. "That drives us crazy," she said. "I think I should eat all the bread I want."

- Aïda Rogers

Since we visited in the spring of 1994, the affable Charlie Golson has moved his restaurant two miles down the road towards Sea Pines Plantation, where wife Nancy owns a business. It now sits beneath two large oaks and there's a garden outside. The dining room is divided into three sections and there's a homey bar with an attractive green granite décor. Best sellers are the rack of lamb, which Charlie points out is grown in America rather than New Zealand, fish cakes, his famous Cobb Salad, tilapia, and grilled fish. The menu is still hand-written daily and the flowers adorning the tables change every morning. The wine list has expanded to an impressive 450 selections emphasizing American cabernets, wines from the Rhone Valley, and Oregon pinot noir. Although Charlie doesn't think of his restaurant as being particularly French, to countless scores of diners, Charlie's L'Etoile Verte is the French bistro of Hilton Head.

- Tim Driggers

Emily's Restaurant and Tapas Bar, Beaufort
Beaufort County

Emily's Restaurant and Tapas Bar, 906 Port Republic Street, Beaufort; (843) 522-1866. Open Monday-Saturday. Closed Sunday. Tapas Bar open 4:30-10 p.m. Dinner 5-10 p.m. Bar opens at 4 p.m. and closes "whenever." Reservations recommended. Smoking only in bar. Credit cards accepted. www. emilysrestaurant.com. Moderate to expensive.

Taking the Road Less Traveled

As an occasional visitor to Beaufort, I naturally gravitate to Bay Street. That's too bad. I've discovered the historic district encompasses a great deal more than the trendy restaurants and shops along this avenue. Not that there aren't really good restaurants along this path, but all you have to do is turn the corner and head down Port Republic

Street to find a place the locals treasure. That would be Emily's.

A good recommendation often leads to an enjoyable dining experience and that's what I found here, courtesy of Mark Shaffer and John Shurr.

"My wife Susan and I had just relocated from Seattle and we were looking for a restaurant with a relaxed Southern atmosphere," explained Mark, a writer whose articles have appeared in *Sandlapper*. "We found the people at Emily's spoke our language. We were treated like regulars and, after a few visits, everyone knew our names. We felt like we had become part of an extended family."

That's the type of atmosphere Tommy Windburn hoped for when he acquired Emily's some 10 years ago. "Because of our location one block off Bay Street, we're not as touristy as downtown," he said. "As a result 60-70 percent of our guests are locals. Emily's is not a destination, like places on the waterfront. We're recommended by locals and shop owners."

Emily's is what I would call comfortably elegant. The restaurant features a 30-foot mahogany, antique bar fronted by black-and-white tiles depicting the 88 keys of a piano. "I found the bar on E-Bay in Appleton, Wisconsin, and had it shipped here and reassembled," Tommy said. The bar area is Prohibition-era picturesque and accented by an Art Deco ceiling.

I chose a seafood platter of fried scallops, oysters, and flounder. The seafood was lightly battered, with not a hint of grease. I also ordered a bowl of the she-crab soup. "It's delicious," Tommy said. "We've used the same recipe since we opened. It's thick and creamy with real crab meat and sherry." It was exceptional, resulting in my patented scrape-the-bowl-empty technique.

Tommy also recommends the Steak Au Poivre. "It's Emily's signature meat dish," he said. "It's really good." Mark Shaffer agrees. "It's one of the best pieces of meat I've ever had, always tender and flavorful and done to perfection." On the 45-item tapas menu, local favorites are the broiled Escargot Bourguignon, Morgan, Rockefeller, and Casino Oysters, and Tuna Tatar.

John Shurr, retired bureau chief for Associated Press in Columbia, recommends the Bronzed Tuna. "The sauce is the secret," he said. "It's terrific. I want the recipe." Wife Debbie is a fan of the pork chop entree and both the Oyster Rockefeller and Tuna Tapas. "We keep eating at Emily's not only for the wonderful tapas menu, but it's first class and relaxed atmosphere," he said.

Mark Shaffer echoes those thoughts. "Susan and I love Emily's," he said. "It's an unpretentious place where real people meet, greet, and eat. Emily's is Beaufort's informal living room."

- Tim Driggers

The Gullah Grub, St. Helena Island
Beaufort County

The Gullah Grub, 877 Sea Island Parkway, St. Helena Island; (843) 838-3841. Open Monday-Thursday, noon-5:30 p.m. and Friday-Saturday, noon-6 p.m. No reservations. Credit cards and checks accepted. No smoking. Inexpensive.

Expect a real lowcountry culinary experience at The Gullah Grub.

A Lesson In Discovery

Dining at The Gullah Grub restaurant on St. Helena Island is much more than a meal; it is an exploration of the Gullah culture and heritage of the Sea Islands. It's a history that chronicles the subjugation of tribes from West Africa and their relocation to southern plantations. It's an oral tradition passed from generation to generation in a rich dialect extolling the virtues of spirituality rooted in nature and family. The food of the Gullah people is expressed with clarity and passion at The Gullah Grub.

Sitting at a crossroads on U.S. 21 across the street from the Penn School (the first school for freed slaves in South Carolina), the one-room restaurant is filled with Gullah artifacts and the spirit of a community constantly buffering itself from the onslaught of coastal development. The restaurant represents not only a food tradition but a people's hope for economic betterment and survival of their culture.

"About 90 percent of our customers are from out of town," said William "Bubba" Green III, who with father Bill—one of the last Gullah deer drivers—operates the restaurant. "On St. Helena Island, we have a connection with the things around us. We are rooted in the ground and environment and our food is a reflection of those values."

Nancy McFarland from Cape Town, South Africa, and her boyfriend David Campbell from Palo Alto, California, were at The Gullah Grub. "I've always been fascinated by history and cultural identities," David said over a plate of red rice and shrimp gumbo. "It's intriguing to fathom the depth and soul of the Gullahs and their African ancestry." "I love the indigenous food of the Gullahs and the cultural expression of this restaurant," Nancy said, sipping she-crab soup and "swamp water," a blend of lemonade and sweet tea. I dined on catfish chowder, collard greens, and red rice, choosing from a menu of fried shark strips, barbecue ribs, and chicken, shrimp, fried fish, and shrimp gumbo.

Bubba and his family are from James Island but lived for years on Middleton Plantation, where they learned from some of the great Low Country cooks. "In 1989 my father began marketing his freshwater catfish chowder under the Oshi's Finest label," Bubba said. (Oshi is Bill's daughter.) "Over the next 10 years, Oshi's Finest expanded to include crab soup, Bill's BBQ sauce, and gumbo. In 1999, it seemed Gullah became something to be proud to be a part of. Our forefathers were people of their environment—the sea and the land—people of deep spirituality and happiness who loved God and His creation." With help from the South Carolina Coastal Community Development Corporation, The Gullah Grub was born.

"Gullah is a diverse and rich tradition," Bubba said. "You have the salt-water Gullahs known as Geechies in Charleston and the freshwater Gullahs of the Beaufort area. They were two major African tribes that came to the United States as slaves. Now they are intertwined. After the Civil War, a lot of Gullahs left the South, but after 30 or 40 years they came back to be a part of their families and the land. Today's young people say they are trying to find themselves. All they have to do is look to their Gullah heritage to discover who they are and how they got here."

In a real sense, a trip to The Gullah Grub restaurant is a lesson in discovery. The food of the Gullahs and their history tell a story of relationships with a people from whom we can learn much. Thanks to Bill and Bubba Green, The Gullah Grub continues to provide a primer in culture and tradition—virtues we can all cherish and absorb into our own personal history.

- Tim Driggers

When Tom Vitale, producer of the Travel Channel's Anthony Bourdain: No Reservations *show, contacted* Sandlapper *about places of interest in the South Carolina Low Country, The Gullah Grub was recommended. We thought the restaurant's combination of traditional Gullah cuisine, accompanied by a heaping helping of Gullah cul-*

ture, would be the perfect stop for Tony's first visit to our state. Bill Green and daughter Oshi cooked Tony a dinner featuring Frogmore Stew and she-crab soup, washed down with a mason jar of swamp water. Bill later led Tony on a fox-hunting expedition on Middleton Plantation. The episode aired in September 2007.

- T. D.

Hampton Restaurant, Hampton
Hampton County

Hampton Restaurant, 704 Elm Street West, Hampton; (803) 943-3002. Open Monday-Saturday, 6 a.m. -10 p.m. for breakfast, lunch, and dinner. Breakfast buffet on Saturday only, 6-10 a.m. Open Sunday, 8 a.m.-9 p.m. No reservations needed, except for back meeting room. Smoking allowed. Credit cards and local checks accepted. Inexpensive.

Down-Home Dixie Dining

I was clueless. Looking at the single-level, red brick building on Elm Street in Hampton, I hadn't the foggiest notion of what the Hampton Restaurant was all about. Roaming restaurant authorities John Coles and Mark Tiedje had recommended the place and they're reliable sources, yet I wasn't quite sure. The restaurant was jammed and everyone seemed happy, but I really didn't know what to expect. One trip through the buffet provided the answer: Plenty!!!

Hampton Restaurant is equal part finger-lickin', down-home Dixie dining and equal part family reunion. Here, "how's the family?" is heard as much as "pass the ketchup." It seems eating at the Hampton Restaurant is as much a way of life as the annual Watermelon Festival.

Local pharmacist Rhonda Hardison has been a regular for 30 years. When she first landed in Hampton, the restaurant was known as the Hampton House. In the mid-1980s it morphed into Ernie's Restaurant, and in 2006, was purchased by Carnell Rivers and became the Hampton Restaurant. "Eating there is like going to grandmother's instead of a restaurant," Rhonda said. "At one table you'll have the Jarells, at another are the Reynolds, then the Hardisons and Parkers. You see them every morning for breakfast and each evening for dinner." From the booth behind Rhonda, a voice chimed in. "She's right," Mary Ann Jarell said. "You see everyone in Hampton here."

Rhonda points out a unique feature: "Since most everyone in town is at Hampton Restaurant for their morning coffee, you can make a dentist appointment, order a prescription, line up yard work, set a time for a car wish, even get the sewer serviced."

Carnell Rivers and Cindy Heape ate daily at Ernie's Restaurant for a decade before Carnell bought the place as an investment. Cindy became the manager. "I always wanted to be an airline stewardess," Cindy confessed. "I never dreamed of being in the restaurant business." Cindy, however, made two great moves when she and Carnell took over. She continued the buffet and she kept the employees. "I didn't know anything and the employees were an enormous help in telling me how things worked. We've become a family team."

This "we are family" theme is all well and good, but let's talk about the food. "We rotate our buffet, but always have at least three or four vegetables, three different kinds of meats, and some starches," Cindy said. "On Monday and Saturday we have pot luck featuring whatever our cook feels like that day, on Tuesday there's beef liver, Wednesday specials include spaghetti, lasagna, and pork steak with gravy and onions, on Friday, we have fried whiting, grits, and rutabagas, and Sunday we serve barbecue beef ribs, chicken, wings, and ham."

On the Tuesday night I visited, the buffet was stocked with mashed potatoes, rice, gravy, fried okra, black-eyed peas, sweet potatoes, collard greens, barbecue pork chops, country steak, and fried chicken. Spread before me, the buffet looked ordinary; the taste was anything but. The vegetables were seasoned—or as my grandmother Beatrice Kaminer would have said, "doctored up,"—to perfection. The barbecue pork ribs were simply fantastic. Only "how my mama and daddy raised me" prevented me from going to the buffet, taking the entire pan of pork chops back to the table, and devouring the entire helping.

Try the popular pig tails and rice or the butter beans, prepared with a dab of fatback and a tad of ham drippings, and you've tasted southern soul cooking Peg Powell and Wilhelmina Wiley-style. They've cooked here for a combined 39 years and that translates into some mighty good eating. "Our pig tails and rice are a local favorite," Cindy said. "I never thought I'd eat anything like it, but they are wonderful; seasoned perfectly, not greasy at all, and served in a special seasoning."

Grilled chicken and shrimp and grilled vegetables over rice are new items here. "We're all trying to be a little more health-conscious these days and this is the perfect meal for watching calories," Rhonda said. Her favorite, though, is Saturday's breakfast buffet, with liver pudding, fried bologna, grits, gravy, eggs, omelettes, and pancakes. "It's down-home cooking served with love."

Hampton Restaurant serves up to 700 folks a day—not bad for a town with a population of 2,800. I can only wonder where in blazes is everyone else. Maybe Cindy could send Peg and Wilhelmina with a scouting party to round up the rest. They don't know what they're missing.

- Tim Driggers

Jasper's Porch, Ridgeland
Jasper County

Jasper's Porch, 100 James F. Taylor Drive, Ridgeland (I-95 Exit 21); (843) 717-2699. Open Monday-Saturday, 7 a.m.-9 p.m. Sunday buffet, 11 a.m.-2 p.m. Reservations suggested. Credit cards and local checks accepted. Smoking allowed on porch. Moderate.

"Honey, Let's Pull Off the Interstate!"

How many times have we all traveled that giant conveyor belt running north and south along the Atlantic seaboard known as Interstate Highway 95 and longed for something more than a quick bite at a fast food joint at the next convenient exit? We know nearby a great restaurant lurks where all the locals eat, but it's a mystery worthy of Hercule Poirot where it's hidden. So we down a chili/bacon cheeseburger with supersized potato facsimiles, knowing that somewhere was a really good place with a heaping helping of local color.

There is such a place in Ridgeland, near Savannah, just before I-95 crosses into Georgia. Set on picturesque Lake Blue Heron, Jasper's Porch offers the friendly atmosphere of a family-owned restaurant with Low Country cuisine equal to any on nearby Hilton Head Island or Savannah.

I was seated at a red-and-white-checkered table on the attractive porch overlooking the lake and nature trail. The view was scenic and the food outstanding. I started with a cup of she-crab soup and found myself scraping at the enamel with my spoon, trying to capture every drop. The soup is the creation of master chef James Bush, a self-taught genius who came to Jasper's Porch four years ago after a long run on Hilton Head. "My cooking is a touch of this and that with a Low Country flair," he said. "The Bentzes just let me create."

Former Gov. Carroll Campbell thought so much of the she-crab soup that he once shipped 200 gallons to a governors meeting in New Mexico. I thought so much of the she-crab soup that I wouldn't leave until James packaged a couple of quarts for the road back home.

Next came the appetizer of Buffalo oysters. The generous order of bite-sized fried oysters was served with a hot Buffalo sauce and a tangy blue cheese dip. For my entree I selected the baked grouper, lightly coated with herbs and prepared in a red pepper cream sauce. Coconut cream pie concluded the evening. I like a thick crust; this selection did not disappoint.

Other menu favorites include Angel of the Sea, sautéed shrimp and scallops tossed with linguine in a white wine sauce; baked flounder stuffed with crab meat; Captain Nick's combination seafood platter; grilled, blackened, or sautéed mahi mahi; and Charlie's Crab Pot, a bucket of snow crab legs, smoked sausage, corn on the cob, and baked potato.

Norman and Nancy Lajoie of Concord, New Hampshire, happened onto Jasper's Porch four years ago returning home from Florida. "We heard about the restaurant at the visitor's center at the South Carolina border on I-95," Norman said. "Jasper's Porch sounded unique and it turned into quite a pleasant surprise. It's an unexpected find along the interstate—something we never would have thought existed. We tell all our friends to stop there when they travel south."

- Tim Driggers

For 10 years, Wanda Davis was both a waitress and manager at Jasper's Porch. Today, she owns the place. She and Chef Anthony Parlor have retained the same menu and decor and for that, travelers along the busy I-95 corridor and Ridgeland locals collectively say "thank you."
- T. D.

Marshside Mama's, Daufuskie Island
Beaufort County

Marshside Mama's, 10 Old Haig Point Road at the County Landing, Daufuskie Island; (843) 785-4755. If coming by boat, it's Marker 39 in the New River on the Intracoastal Waterway. Open for dinner Wednesday-Saturday, 6-10 p.m. and for lunch Saturday, 12:10-2:50 p.m. Closed Sunday-Tuesday. Credit cards accepted. Smoking allowed. Reservations available. Inexpensive to moderate.

Get Your Gumbo Groove Here

At deadline crunch time, when nerves are all a-skitter, a fantasy arises like a genie from a bottle. It involves food, drink, friends, and water. Restaurants by the water provide the relaxation quotient, and lucky for us, South Carolina offers a boatload. To experience that "get away from it all" feeling, I headed down I-95 towards the Georgia border and Marshside Mama's.

"Don't Whine, Just Dance" is the motto here, and it's a goody. Come when you just can't take it anymore. There's food, wine, a jukebox with a big blue and green crab on it and, out the window, the New River. In the distance you can see the port of Savannah and the Talmadge Bridge, but for now, you're on Daufuskie Island, an outpost, coastal-style *Northern Exposure* for The Palmetto State.

"It's like Madison Avenue meets the Third World," observed resident Bo Bryan, author of the book *Shag*. But the island's old-timers and new resorters groove together well at Marshside Mama's. "At times, it's sort of a transcendent rock-and-roll experience to have the jukebox on and your shoes off and start dancing. We have millionaires and paupers dancing together."

That's just what we saw one hot Friday night. Precisely at 9:05 p.m., somebody punched in "Oh Suzy Q" on the jukebox and the party began. A preview occurred about 15 minutes earlier, when a father and his young daughter boogied together to a fast Santana. By 10, Whitney Houston was singing "I Will Always Love You" and people of all ages, colors and dress codes were dancing together.

"We're going to sell our business and come down here and live," declares Louise Wood Royal, an Oconee County native now living in New Jersey. "My husband's going to bring in the ice and I'm going to sit by the jukebox and welcome everybody."

No doubt she would recommend the gumbo. It's famous for two things: It's always spicy (my lips actually sizzled) and it's never the same. Chef/owner Beth Shipman had mixed up golden sea bass, chicken, sausage, crab, clams, and shrimp—"kitchen sink gumbo," she quips. Maybe most noticeable is the unmushy, bright-green okra, always added last. "I've eaten gumbo from Apalachicola to the Mexican border, and I've never had any as good as this," says writer Roger Pinckney XI, who has chronicled the lifeways of Daufuskie in books and articles.

Beth keeps her menu simple and relies on local fishermen and divers to bring her their best catch. Cobia and tuna sometimes appear; shrimp and ribs are a constant. Nothing is fried, except pan-fried catfish (on this evening, served with grits, white beans, and andouille sausage). Appetizers included gazpacho with shrimp, Caribbean-style jerk barbecue wings, and Ethel Mae's "Devil" Crab. Among the entrees: barbecue babyback ribs, grilled tuna with mango salsa, and grilled center-cut pork chops. Daufuskie Seafood Boil includes snow crab, shrimp, sausage and corn. Our foursome ordered Beth's famous shrimp and grits, family-style. Like the gumbo, it's never the same. This time, scallops and artichoke hearts were added, all served with salad. The combination also was available over pasta.

"Tastefully tacky" is how someone described the décor. Pink flamingos, little colored lights and plastic picnic furniture help guests relieve any feelings of starchiness. Have a Heineken or, as Bo puts it, "red wine of some description" in a plastic cup, and let it out. Everybody else is.

"We just like to hoot and holler and have a fun time," says Tom Beavor, a former Atlantan now living at Daufuskie Island Inn and Resort (still called "Melrose" by the islanders). Like Bo, he compares Marshside Mama's to restaurants in the Caribbean. "This is as close as I can get to that part of the world."

A note of warning: Good food takes time to prepare, and sometimes longer when there's only one person in the kitchen. "It's just me, and I don't say no to anybody," Beth says. But she guarantees you won't go hungry while you wait, because there's always fresh bread on the table, whether it's homemade biscuits or corn muffins.

Located at the county landing adjacent to Daufuskie's post office and general store (Beth's husband Brian runs the post office and is a ferryboat captain for the Daufuskie Island Club and Resort), Marshside Mama's is a meeting place for islanders. It's also home to an assorted lot of moonlighters—a FedEx delivery woman, a schoolteacher, an accountant, and a prosthetics maker. "They're here because they want to be here," Brian points out. "It's *fun* to be here."

Ain't that the truth?

- Aïda Rogers

It is with great sadness that we report the untimely passing of Ned the Pig at age 18. Ned and Marshside Mama's were synonymous. Ned arrived on the scene just as Beth Shipman opened her restaurant in 1997 and became the restaurant's pot-bellied mascot, freely roaming the dining area and living up to his reputation as quite the beer swiller. Ned lived beneath the restaurant, but in reality, Marshside Mama's was his home. As the nightly party unfolded, Ned was a familiar site sash-shaying about the dance floor, bumming a swig of Corona from the nearest table, and then being chased and shooed away by Beth.

Since Sandlapper *visited a few years ago, there have been a few changes. "Our wonderful jukebox has been replaced, mostly because it broke," Beth said. "We now have live music Thursday through Saturday night. We alternate local bands from Bluffton and Hilton Head, with bands from anywhere between Miami and Detroit. It's mostly blues music or classic rock. No matter the tunes, at some time during the night, the tables get moved and the dancing begins." The menu at Marshside Mama's changes a bit every week, sometimes every night. "Our shrimp is bought locally, as is most of our fresh fish," Beth reports. "I'm lucky to have many friends whose occupations require boats, fishing poles, and crab nets." The Shrimp-N-Grits is a popular choice, as is the Spicy Creole with Shrimp and Andouille. Try the homemade crab and shrimp tamales or the Carolina Boil with fresh shrimp, sausage, corn on the cob, and blue crab. Nothing on the menu is fried.*

- Tim Driggers

24

Old Fort Pub, Hilton Head Island
Beaufort County

Old Fort Pub, 65 Skull Creek Dr., Hilton Head Island; (843) 681-2386. Open for dinner March-November, seven days a week, 5-10 p.m. Open for dinner December-February each day, 5-9:30 p.m. Sunday brunch is 11 a.m.-2 p.m. Reservations recommended. Credit cards accepted. No smoking. www.oldfortpub.com. Moderate to expensive.

Happily Lost at This Romantic Hideaway

There is one eternal truth, one sure-fire certainty, one thing that is absolutely and totally inevitable when I visit Hilton Head Island .....I'll get lost. It's a lead-pipe cinch: Can't find nothin' down there.

So when Bonnie Hinnant suggested the Old Fort Pub, I figured I'd need to enlist 10 Comanche scouts, an array of NASA satellites, and the Amazing Kreskin to find the place. Of course, I was right. Got lost. Wandered hopelessly for a couple of hours—doing the man thing, never stooping to stop and ask for directions.

Then, like Brigadoon in the mist, it appeared. Nestled on the banks of Skull Creek amidst the live oaks on the Intra-Coastal waterway was the Old Fort Pub. Built in 1973 in the heart of Hilton Head Plantation, the restaurant has an eco-friendly appeal, blending in with the environment and remaining faithful to its roots. In this beautiful, almost tropical landscape, it was difficult to picture the site as encampment to 13,000 invading Northern soldiers during the "Recent Unpleasantness." During the early days of the Civil War, the North seized the strategic waterfront midway between Charleston and Savannah and constructed a series of protective batteries. One, Fort Michel, was built adjacent to the Old Fort Pub grounds and its earthen works can still be found.

The dining area shows off its surroundings. Panoramic windows allow an unfettered view of the watercourse outside and, although the sun had long set when I arrived, I could imagine how beautiful sunset would appear against the marshes. Instead, I had to "settle" for a waxing crescent moon, hanging motionless amongst the glitter of a thousand stars, speckling each wave with a silver glow. Bonnie hadn't led me astray. This was a special place and I hadn't even tasted the food yet.

There are waiters and then there is Fili Herrera. He is the consummate professional. Even gave me his business card. Courteous, knowledgeable, Fili provided the kickstart to a great meal, recommending one of the evening's specials. The swordfish with pomegranate and fennel arrived in a Callaway cream sauce, was served with mashed potatoes and, surprise, a passel of roasted chestnuts. Earlier, Fili brought a bowl of creamy, what-we're-famous-for she-crab soup. It was the stuff of legends.

Bonnie recommends the Bouillabaisse. "That's our signature dish," said restaurant general manager David Nadeau. "Everyone loves it. Instead of a tomato broth, we use a saffron roux, which is richer and creamier." The lamb and filet mignon are "scrumptious," Bonnie said, adding that she "craves" the paté.

"The Old Fort Pub is the first place I think of when I need a special occasion restaurant for birthdays and other celebrations," she said. "There are several over-the-top restaurants on the island and the Old Fort Pub is definitely one of them. I've seen restaurants come and go, but the Old Fort Pub continues to be consistent in quality of food and service. It also has such a romantic feel."

Keith Josefiak is Executive Chef. "He serves an American-Continental cuisine, influenced by southern tastes," Nadeau said. "He changes the menu each season to reflect local favorites, often adding grits, collard greens, black-eyed peas, and tasso ham to his plates. If I ever took his Carolina trout off the menu, my customers would come looking for me."

Thanks to Bonnie for telling me about the Old Fort Pub. Now that I know how to get there, you can bet I'll be making a return trip.

- Tim Driggers

Old House Smoke House, Near Ridgeland
Jasper County

Old House Smoke House, corner of SC 336 and SC 462 near Ridgeland; (843) 258-4444. Open Monday-Thursday, 5-9 p.m. and Friday-Saturday, 5-10 p.m. Smoking allowed in designated areas. Credit cards accepted. Reservations accepted. Moderate to expensive.

"Upscale Redneck" Near Palm Key

South Carolinians owe a great debt to Frank Crutchfield. Owner/chef of Old House Smoke House in Ridgeland, he's the man who brought crispy whole flounder to the Palmetto State.

Many of us have had it—that big, flat fish covering an entire plate, flavored with apricot, raspberry or orange sauce. Crispy flounder has made its way to Columbia to Lexington to Newberry, but its origins are in New Orleans, where Crutchfield honed his skills under Paul Prudhomme.

"It's easy," Crutchfield says. "The hardest part is getting the fish." While Crutchfield lays claim to introducing the dish to these parts during his days as executive chef for Garibaldi's in Savannah and Charleston, he's fast to say he stole it from another restaurant in New Orleans. "It's a Thai or Asian thing. There was a place called Genghis Khan's that served a crispy whole fried redfish." So enamored was he that he reinvented it with flounder. I for one am glad.

You can have Crutchfield's flounder—his is with a sweet, tangy orange sauce—at his "upscale redneck" restaurant in the Old House community of Jasper County. Mindful of local history (Old House was the popular name for Thomas Heyward's plantation after his son built his own "new house" nearby), Crutchfield is trying to get "Old House" on the map. He may do that with his smoked baby-back ribs, smoked New York strip, half-smoked chicken and blackened smoked pork chops. But if you don't like smoked food, there are plenty of other items to try. Besides grilled Andouille sausage with Creole Mustard and jambalaya with Sauce Piquant, there are crab cakes with Creole Mustard. Specials one chilly Saturday night included sautéed veal with crawfish Creole sauce, crawfish ettoufee over rice and jambalaya with Sauce Piquant. "Piquant," the menu explains, means "hot" in south Louisiana. That's where Crutchfield grew up, "on the banks of the Tchefuncte River."

Though he's five states north of home, the landscape is similar. Spanish moss and centuries-old churches create a setting for his blend of Carolina/Louisiana fare. Located in a former produce market, Old House Smoke House breathes rusticity. On the walls are saddles and horseshoes, animal skulls and a deer head. Tables are covered with brown-and-white, spotted cow cloths, and beverages come in plastic cups.

Crutchfield's goal was to serve barbecue, but his customers—many from the resort islands in Beaufort County—began asking for beef tenderloin and fish. So Crutchfield complied. Today, residents of Dataw, Fripp and Callawassie Islands and the inland towns of Estill and Bluffton drive 50 or 60 miles for Crutchfield's cooking. "It's crazy," he says. But he's not complaining.

The good people at Palm Key send their guests here. Martha Gregory is a believer in the grilled Greek chicken. I took our server's advice and ordered the pan-fried grouper with oyster tasso cream. Other specialties included the Chicken Voo-Doo Vindaloo, Eggplant Pirogue with Seafood Dianne and Shrimp Puttanesca with Penne Pasta.

Crutchfield's talents are more than culinary. He has an MFA in photography from Louisiana Technical University. His photos of churches in north Louisiana line the walls in a separate banquet area. You can look at them while waiting for desserts, which generally include German chocolate cake, crème brulee, and a couple of pies.

Old House Smoke House is at the head of the oak alley that once led to Thomas Heyward's plantation, and the statesman is buried in a cemetery not far behind. It appears Crutchfield has taken to South Carolina. "I learned to cook in Louisiana," he observes, "but the fish and crab are much better here than there."

-Aïda Rogers

Saltus River Grill, Beaufort
Beaufort County

Saltus River Grill, 802 Bay Street in Beaufort; (843) 379-3474. Open seven days a week at 4 p.m. for drinks and 5 p.m. to whenever for dinner. Reservations requested. Credit cards accepted. Smoking only at bar. www.saltusrivergrill.com. Moderate to expensive.

Dreamy Dining On the Beaufort River

At Saltus River Grill in Beaufort, you can dine indoors in an ambiance reflecting the stylish decor of its big-city kin or enjoy a meal on the outdoor patio where the soft evening breeze from the Beaufort River provides a relaxing accompaniment to Low Country cuisine.

Located off a lane from Bay Street to Waterfront Park, Saltus River Grill has quite a storied past. The restaurant is built at the site of one of the earliest tabby buildings—a mix of lime, sand, and oyster shells solidified into clay—constructed in colonial America. The location was acquired in the late 1700s by noted shipbuilder John Francis Saltus. The Saltus and Talbird Shipyard produced gunboats here until the 19th Century. It eventually became a Belk-Simpson department store in the 1950s, but after the store closed, the building was vacant for many years. In 2003, owner Lantz Price, chef Jim Spratling, and Tennessee designer Whitney Rietz began the renovation process that would transform the crumbling site into Saltus River Grill.

"I had the concept of opening a place serving great contemporary seafood with an equally impressive wine list," Price explained. "The Beaufort community enjoys a diverse demographic mix of residents, and I didn't want to pigeon-hole myself with a menu of unfamiliar items. It was important that our dishes be comprised of the freshest local products and that the food be of a certain consistent quality—but elemental and not that sophisticated."

Price has succeeded. The spacious, indoor dining area seats 130 amid modernistic furnishings, stained wood trappings, and a relaxed atmosphere harmoniously augmented by a sleek bar serving an extensive array of wines and drink selections. "Familiar, affordable, and adaptive to the menu" is how he describes the wine list.

Price points to his shrimp and grits entrée—a local favorite. "It's important that our diners select from menu items they know. Familiar sells, especially if the food is delicious and consistent at each dining experience."

I chose the atmospheric, lamppost-lighted patio, which seats approximately 50 guests. With the moonlight reflecting off the waters of the panoramic Intracoastal Waterway and the autumn breeze wafting through the trees, the surroundings complemented my meal. I began with an appetizer of oyster tempura with ponzi dipping sauce that provided a tasty alternative to their fried cousins. The crab bisque was absolutely delicious—so much so that I asked for an order to take home. My entree was the grilled black grouper, attractively presented with smashed fingerling potatoes, crab gratin, and ragout of asparagus, bacon, and fennel, accompanied by a sauce of chive beurre blanc. The wine choice was a Louis Latour Pouilly-Fuisse chardonnay, whose fruity aroma and taste perfectly suited my meal. Other entree items include fried fillet of flounder, Low Country flounder stuffed with shrimp and crab, grilled barrel-cut fillet of beef, fried Maine lobster tails, seared organic salmon, and black pepper-crusted strip steak. Saltus also offers an extensive selection of oysters and sushi.

Saltus is great for food and conversation. I happened upon local attorneys Lauren Caraway, Carson Twombley, and Kimberly Smith, who were enjoying the evening with Ivey McClam of the Beaufort Chamber of Commerce. "The atmosphere at Saltus is unlike anything in Beaufort," Kimberly said. Ivey added another salient observation. "It's a place to see and be seen."

Clearly, Saltus River Grill is a winning choice for a delectable meal in Low Country Beaufort.

- Tim Driggers

Squat 'n' Gobble, Bluffton
Beaufort County

The Squat 'n' Gobble, 1231 May River Road, Bluffton; (843) 757-4242. Monday-Friday, 7 a.m.-9 p.m. and on Saturday and Sunday, 7 a.m.-3 p.m. No reservations. Credit cards accepted.Both smoking and non-smoking sections available. Inexpensive.

"Our Menu is What People Like to Eat"

Before heading to most restaurants, it's typical to inquire if reservations are required, whether a check or credit card is accepted—and just what pray tell, are the specials of the day? At The Squat 'n' Gobble, the folks in Bluffton take a slightly different approach. Here you need to find out whether owner Paul Raganas is on the premises.

Dining here is a unique experience, but the pleasure is doubled when the garrulous elf of an owner is holding court. He's in the kitchen, he's at your table, he's greeting guests at the door; he's everywhere. When you dine at the Squat 'n' Gobble, you're the special guest of Paul and wife Star and there is nothing they or their staff won't do to make your visit pleasant. It isn't that the Squat 'n' Gobble is huge and opulent. It's not. The restaurant is located alongside a chain grocery and down the street from Paul's other dining establishment, the popular Pepper's Porch. The Squat 'n' Gobble is bright and cheery and decidedly friendly, but don't confuse it with its big-city brethren on nearby Hilton Head. It's not meant to compete; it's meant to provide an enjoyable meal at a modest price amidst locals who appreciate the friendly service and incredibly large menu of both short order items and dinner specials.

Born in South America and reared in Greece, Paul began his restaurant career on Long Island. "Eventually, Paul and I decided to move South and figured we'd wind up in Florida," Star explained. "A friend asked if we had ever been to Hilton Head, so we stopped by and fell in love with the area. The climate and sea reminded Paul of Greece, and the people were so friendly and nice."

On December 1, 2001, Paul bought the Squat 'n' Gobble as a birthday gift for Star. "I thought about changing the name," Paul said, "but it was such a conversation piece that my customers were totally against it." And just how did the Squat 'n' Gobble get its name? "The previous owners said there was a place in Columbia called the "Stand 'n' Snack" and they wanted something sounding similar."

Though they kept the name, the Raganases immediately took steps to instill their own brand of ownership. "Our menu is what the people like to eat," Paul said. "There is no use having a menu with dinners no one wants." Personal service also makes a difference. Star manages the business while Paul visits with guests. "Oh, he's very popular," Star said. "If Paul is not here, everyone wants to know where he is."

The menu is an amalgamation of both Greek and American favorites. "Our Big Fat Greek Cheeseburger" is very popular," Paul said, describing a juicy half-pounder with Greek olives, spinach, and feta cheese. "It's a lot like a spanakopita hamburger." Another big seller is the Greek salad. "Some people come here for it every day," Paul noted, adding that its cousin, the Greek Chicken Salad, is popular too. That's Darlene Epperson's favorite. "I just love the homemade Greek dressing," the Bluffton librarian said. "The salad is made of pita bread cut up in triangles topped with lettuce and chicken. As you dig in, all these flavors combine with Greek olives and real feta cheese."

Like many of their regulars, Star and Paul consider The S&G their second home. Star describes a typical morning: "We have coffee with our customers and get all the news about town. You don't have to buy a newspaper, just come here and listen to everyone's stories."

Paul added a final bit of his restaurant philosophy. "People aren't stupid," he said. "We're honest with our customers and don't try to steal from their pockets."

It is quite a bargain. Good food, reasonable prices, great service, and owners and staff who genuinely care for their customers. Not a bad combination.

- Tim Driggers

Star and Paul Raganas are becoming quite the celebrity couple. Dolly Parton features The Squat 'n' Gobble *in her book,* Dolly's Dixie Fixin's, *and the Presidential wannabes have also taken notice. Republican candidate Rudy Giuliani made* The S&G *a 2007 campaign stop; no word on whether Paul and Star will cater an Obama or McCain inaugural with their Big Fat Greek cheeseburger or homemade pizza.*

- T. D.

Steamer Oyster & Steakhouse, Beaufort (Lady's Island)
Beaufort County

Steamer Oyster & Steakhouse, 168 Island Parkway, Beaufort (Lady's Island); (843) 522-0210. Open Monday-Thursday, 11 a.m.-10 p.m.; Friday and Saturday, 11 a.m.-11 p.m. Closed on Sunday. Credit cards accepted, but no personal checks. No smoking. Moderate.

Oyster Etiquette On Lady's Island

I was sitting in the seat where Charlie Sheen once sat at Steamer Oyster & Steakhouse on Lady's Island when I learned something significant, something that will carry me far in South Carolina's finest social circles, something bound to impress everyone I meet in the future. It was something I'd never heard before: *what is, and how to eat, a Low Country Hors D'oeuvre.* Tom Garrett was my friendly instructor.

"You put the cocktail sauce on the Captain's Wafer," he told me, watching me squirt and eat. And that's it. It's fast, free, and "goes real good with beer," said JoAnn Dilsaver, manager of Steamer and one of the many Sullivan family members who run the place. JoAnn will tell you there's a certain etiquette to abide by when preparing and eating a Low Country Hors D'oeuvre: Only use Captain's Wafers; never use Saltines. But if you're eating an oyster, please use a Saltine. "Don't ask me why," she said.

Those are probably the only rules you have to follow at Steamer, known and loved across the country for its casual seafaring atmosphere and unswerving unpretentiousness. Built in an old feed-and-seed store, Steamer attracts tourists and business people from New York and Canada who've heard its reputation and make special trips to check it out. People in Columbia and Charlotte fly down just for supper; the restaurant crew will pick them up from the airport and take them back. They do the same with those who dock at the marina.

"People will stand in line in the summer for two-and-a-half to three hours and it amazes me," JoAnn said. "And they'll sit here and fuss at me because they don't have a table yet, but they'll just stand there. I just tell them to shut up; the one that fusses the

Steamed shellfish is the specialty at Steamer Oyster & Steakhouse.

most goes to the back of the line."

Apparently, JoAnn's cheery, no-nonsense manner works. Steamer is a restaurant founded on democracy; when Barbra Streisand wanted to rent the whole place one day when filming *The Prince of Tides*, she was turned down. "We don't do that for nobody," JoAnn said.

And still, the people come. Tom believes Steamer succeeds because it appeals to people of every income and background. "They created an environment for everybody from the striker on the shrimp boat to the general out at Parris Island," he said. "And the food is wonderful"

Tom and his wife Marguerite and I took JoAnn's advice and ordered Steamer's most popular dishes: Frogmore Stew, cups of gumbo, Oysters Eleanora and a ribeye dinner (Steamer serves Black Angus). You get plenty for your money. And we didn't come close to finishing. Maybe it was because of the gumbo we'd had first—thick, not too spicy—and the Oysters Eleanora, a dozen oysters on the half shell with bacon, onions, mushrooms and cheddar.

Steamer is also famous for its huge Steamer burger and shellfish platter, which is large enough for two people to share. A variety of sandwiches, salads, even barbecue and country cooking specials are available. Serious eating is encouraged; each table bears a roll of paper towels and a bucket lodged in the center for shells.

The restaurant has had to grow to keep up with business and the Beaufort area.

Since it opened in 1981, Steamer has expanded three times. JoAnn said she has more applications for jobs than she'll ever get to. Turnover is so slow and tips so good that the restaurant has become a beacon to those looking for steady work.

It's also a beacon to the many actors who've filmed many movies in Beaufort. The cast of *The Big Chill* ate here; it's where Tom Berenger met his wife, who was a Steamer waitress. Robert Urich has dined here; so have Charlie Sheen and Steve Yeager when they worked on *Major League*. Tom Hanks and his family were in while he shot *Forrest Gump*.

Serving stars isn't easy because the staff has to curb its natural friendliness, JoAnn said. The actors don't want to be gushed over or annoyed, so employees adopt a more diffident manner. "I'll go by and check how things are, but I would be much friendlier to you than I would be to a star. It's really kind of tacky; I feel guilty sometimes. But I think they're in here to eat and spend time with their families and they don't want to be bothered."

A quartet of retired men didn't seem bothered when I asked them why they like Steamer. They have lunch here every Monday when their wives are playing bridge. "We have to do something, so rather than go to a bar, we come here and pig out," said Tom Costen, a Seattle native. There's nothing like Steamer in Seattle, nor in Long Island or Menlo Park, where the other men are from. Bill Nelson has been eating a Steamburger every Monday for 10 years, Costen pointed out, "and look how healthy he is."

Another Monday men's group meets at a swankier place in Beaufort, but this crowd plans to stick with the more informal Steamer. If they move, they might have to become—heaven forbid—respectable. "We don't do one worthy thing," Costen said.

"We talk worthily," Mario Fog pointed out.

Back at the Garrett table, Tom and Marguerite were filling to-go containers with the food we couldn't finish. Marguerite won't have to cook tonight. "For 20 years of my life I proved that I could cook; for the next 20 years I don't have to."

I like that kind of thinking.

- Aïda Rogers

Since we visited Steamer Oyster & Steakhouse in 1993, a few things have changed, but this low country-themed restaurant remains a popular choice for locals, tourists, and the occasional film celebrity on location along the South Carolina coast. Adam Rosica is now the owner, having acquired the restaurant in 2002, and there's a new manager on board. Frogmore Stew continues as a popular menu selection, as well as steaks and fresh seafood. Rosica tells us one traditon also continues that is downright refreshing: They'll still pick up a diner from the airport and take them back after the meal. That's low country hospitality.

- Tim Driggers

Truffles Market and Café, Hilton Head Island
Beaufort County

Truffles Café, 71 Lighthouse Road in Sea Pines Center on Hilton Head Island; (843) 671-6136. Open daily, 11 a.m.-10 p.m. Credit cards accepted. No reservations. No smoking. www.trufflescafe.com. Inexpensive to expensive.

Bread and Boursin On the Island

Truffles Market & Café at Sea Pines Center on Hilton Head Island is a haven of fresh bread, good smells, and good vibes. I was a regular at its Savannah branch before it closed and I moved from there years ago. So I was happy to see it thriving on Hilton Head, and even happier to dive into a basket of Truffles' bread and boursin.

Fresh fish of all types is the specialty here, but I went with a vegetable pizza with three Italian cheese and veggies tossed in pesto. It looked like Christmas when it arrived—bright red and green. As a TV commercial once put it, "I can't believe I ate the whole thang."

Truffles serves a variety of soups, salads, sandwiches and light meals—and a whole lot of wine. Owners Price and Karen Beall have put together a jazzy, uptown place.

- Aïda Rogers

Has it been 24 years since owners Price and Karen Beall opened Truffles Market and Café? They've added a second Truffles Café in Bluffton and a third, Truffles Grill, on Hilton Head. Besides the fresh local seafood, black angus steaks, entrée salads, sandwiches upon sandwiches, and desserts upon desserts, Truffles is famous for their baby back ribs, New Orleans pasta, pork tenderloin, and chicken pot pie.

- Tim Driggers

Index

Photos

Note to Readers Page:
South Carolinians can sample down-home, upscale, and sweet eats at (from left) Schoolhouse Bar-B-Que in Scranton, Steven W's Downtown Bistro in Newberry, and The Cyclone Restaurant in Chester.

For Starters Page:
The authors with Azmi Jebali at The Mediterranean Cafe in Lexington.

Title Page:
Customers anticipate innovative cuisine at Steven W's Downtown Bistro in Newberry. The famous tiramisu at Garibaldi Cafe in Columbia; fish preparation at Il Cortile del Re in Charleston.

Upcountry Section Page:
South Carolina's Upcountry is marked by hilly terrain, including this view of Table Rock from Caesar's Head. Cook Mike Harris at Stax's Omega Diner in Greenville; Eggs Benedict and hash browns at Stax's; Senior Chef Marshall Watkins at the Lake Lanier Tea Room in Landrum; Barbara and Richard Vallely at Stax's.

Olde English District Section Page:
Winthrop University draws students to its picturesque campus in Rock Hill. A horse show in Camden; breakfast customer Robert Ecford at The Cyclone Restaurant in Chester; Milton and Mary Petrou at The Cyclone.

Old 96 District Section Page:
Peaches, "The Queen of Fruits," have brightened roadside orchards for decades. Pastoral pleasures at The Red Barn restaurant in Gray Court; stately elegance at Old Edgefield Grill in Edgefield.

Capital City/Lake Murray Country Section Page:
South Carolina's seat of government is found at Main and Gervais streets in Columbia. Lake Murray's iconic

towers; Chef Steve Foulis at Steven W's Downtown Bistro in Newberry; celebrating good times at Steven W's.

Thoroughbred Country Section Page:
Horse stables are popular residences in Aiken. Playing croquet on a sunny morning; sidewalk Saturdays at the New Moon Café in Aiken; Pascual Salatino practicing on an Aiken polo field.

Santee Cooper Country Section Page:
Ten rondette cabins rest on piers at Santee State Park in Orangeburg County. Manager Ty Green at The Compass Family Restaurant in Turbeville; crab legs at The Compass; Lake Marion at Santee State Park.

Pee Dee Country Section Page:
Built in 1950, the Darlington Raceway is "too tough to tame." Chef Blake Perritt shows off the Ooey Gooey Sandwich at Dallis' Cafe in Marion; scenes from Schoolhouse Bar-B-Que in Scranton include happy customer Tom Perry of Moncks Corner.

Myrtle Beach Area/The Grand Strand Section Page:
Ocean Boulevard is the place to cruise in Myrtle Beach. Myrtle Beach lifeguard; fresh fruit salad at Nibils in Surfside Beach; Charles and Ellen Head of Central at Nibils.

Historic Charleston Section Page:
Woodlands Resort and Inn has brought Five Star, Five Diamond glamour to Summerville. The Dining Room at Woodlands in Summerville; cook Shaun Rutledge preparing food at Old Towne Restaurant in Charleston; The Market in Charleston.

Lowcountry & Resort Islands Section Page:
Lowcountry suppers often arrive by trawler. Hunting Island Lighthouse; seafood pasta at Steamer Oyster & Steakhouse on Lady's Island; Emily's in downtown Beaufort.

Acknowledgements

Stop Where the Parking Lot's Full would never have gotten out of the garage without help from several important people. We thank benefactors Beegie Truesdale, Hugh and Maro Rogers, Tim Driggers and Rose Wilkins. Our thank-you list also includes Lauren Stewart, our game College of Charleston student who helped us update our information, and Lou Linn, our valiant proofreader. Sandy Fox and Rose Wilkins typed years-old copy into a database. We're grateful to the South Carolina Department of Transportation, which provided maps for illustration, and to Zesto's in West Columbia, where the parking lot is always full except on Sundays, when our photo shoot occurred. Eternal thanks to the staff at *Sandlapper Magazine* (Dan Harmon, Dianne Lance, Tom Linn, Bob Wilkins, Rose Wilkins) for their support. And finally, a big thank-you to Patty and Pete Korn, who let us borrow their 1962 Chevrolet Impala for photos for this book. We're ready to ride when you are.

Behind the Wheel

Aïda Rogers is the product of a champion cook from Baghdad and a Clean-Your-Plate "Depression Baby" from Lexington. A University of South Carolina journalism graduate, Rogers spent 15 years covering the state's favorite restaurants for *Sandlapper, The Magazine of South Carolina*. Though now the magazine's editor, she remains a kitchen disaster.

Lexington native **Tim Driggers** graduated from Newberry College where he majored in Dopey's cheeseburgers and minored in the Grateful Dead. A humor columnist and music writer, Driggers has practiced law in Lexington since 1973. He took over "Stop Where the Parking Lot's Full" in 2005. His favorite food? Potted meat.

Designer/Illustrator/Photographer **Becky Hyatt Rickenbaker** grew up in Summerville and studied in Atlanta but found more dining treasures in the Palmetto State. When she's not balancing giant ice cream cones, she's working from her Lexington office.

My Tasty Adventures

A few notes and photos of my personal culinary discoveries in
South Carolina ...